# Relations Between Africans and African Americans: Misconceptions, Myths and Realities

## Godfrey Mwakikagile

Relations Between Africans and African Americans

Third Edition

ISBN-10: 0-9802534-5-4
ISBN-13: 978-0-9802534-5-0

New Africa Press
Dar es Salaam, Tanzania
Pretoria, South Africa

American spelling is used in this edition to maintain the integrity of the original work first published in the United States.

**Dedication:**

**To the youth of Africa
in whose hands lies
the future of our continent**

# New Africa Press

Our books focus on the African world. They are intended for members of the general public and the academic community.

We cover a wide of range of subjects, reflected by the diversity of our titles, with  primary emphasis on trade books. Academic works published by New Africa Press are also intended for the general public. Few titles, if any, are published exclusively for members of the academic community.

All our works are non-fiction addressing contemporary issues, history, politics, economics, international affairs relating to Africa, and many other subjects. People of African descent in the diaspora are an integral part of the African world and the focus of some of our works.

Because of the wide range of subjects we cover, some of our titles may not seem to be relevant to Africa and the African diaspora.. But many of our readers will find them to be useful if for no other reason than that their experience is human experience and the diversity reflected by our works derives its legitimacy from our identity as an integral part of humanity.

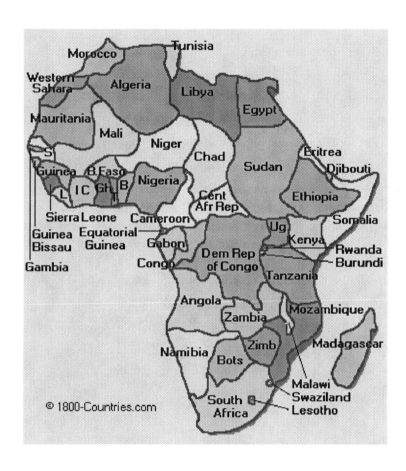

"All peoples of African descent whether they live in North or South America, the Caribbean or in other parts of the world, are Africans and belong to the African nation." - Kwame Nkrumah.

# Contents

# Acknowledgments

AFRICANS on both sides of the Atlantic, that is Africans in Africa and African Americans who as a people of African descent are also Africans, equally inspired this study. So did African immigrants and students in the United States. I myself went to school in the United States and have lived and interacted with African Americans for more than 30 years.

Although African Americans are also Africans in the genealogical sense, I have used the term Africans in the book almost exclusively to mean those born in the motherland for identification purposes to distinguish them from African Americans in my study of relations between the two. Professor Ali Mazrui, a Kenyan who has taught at universities in the United States since the early seventies, has coined a term to identify African immigrants in America and calls them American Africans as opposed to African Americans.

The idea for this book has been in my mind for quite some time, although I cannot say for sure exactly when I first thought about writing it. It probably goes back to the eighties when I was in my thirties, although my interest in the subject goes back further than that, at least to the early seventies when I was a student in Detroit, Michigan, and wrote an article in a student newspaper about relations between Africans and African Americans.

I wrote the article in 1973 and it was published in *Open Door*, a student newspaper of Wayne County Community College which I briefly attended before transferring to Wayne State University in the same city where I graduated in 1975. Part of my article was reproduced in *The Michigan Chronicle*, a black weekly newspaper published in Detroit, and the state's largest black newspaper and one of the most influential black papers in the country for years.

I remember the editor of the school newspaper asked me to write an article on the subject.

One factor that played a role in his decision to ask me to write the article was my background. He knew that I once was a news reporter in Tanzania.

He was a black student from Detroit, a city with a long history of black activism, also known as the birthplace of black nationalist organizations such as the Nation of Islam founded in the early thirties; the Shrine of Black Madonna (Black Christian Nationalism), in 1967 by Reverend Albert Cleage; the Republic of New Afrika in 1968; and the Pan-African Congress-USA, founded in 1970, and which sponsored me as a student. It is also a city to which Malcolm X had strong ties, personal and family. Many people who knew him or about him or followed his political career also remember him by his nickname, "Detroit Red."

When I wrote the article in the student newspaper, *Open Door*, I was free to address the subject the way I wanted to.

But the focus of my article was undoubtedly influenced and dictated by my interest in attempting to answer one perennial question Africans from Africa are often asked by black people in the United States: "Is it true that they don't want us over there?" Or something along those lines.

And later on, towards the end of 2004 when I started writing this book, I stumbled upon an article by a Nigerian student at the University of North Carolina in the student newspaper addressing the same subject, although from a perspective different from mine in this inquiry.

There were, however, no fundamental differences, if any, between what he said in his article and what I say in this book in terms of the nature of relations between Africans and African Americans, and on why there are some misunderstandings between the two groups. The difference may have been on the focus.

And I am sure others have tackled the same subject from different angles and perspectives, agreeing and disagreeing on a number of issues critical to an understanding of what is at the heart of some of this misunderstanding between Africans and African Americans, and what binds us together.

Therefore, in a very direct way, it is African Americans who have had a profound impact on my decision to write this book probably more than Africans from the motherland have. And I am grateful to them for being the source of such inspiration.

It is African Americans, at least from my experience and I am sure of many others, who have shown great interest in the relations between the two groups probably more than Africans have. It is they who ask questions about Africa, whether or not it is true that they are not welcome over there.

And it is they who see all of us, black people in Africa and in the United States, as one people, although there are also many among them who don't want to have anything to do with Africa because they are ashamed of their African heritage rooted in a "backward, primitive" continent.

But even they, the hostile ones, helped to inspire this study, focusing my attention on some of the myths propagated in the United States and elsewhere about Africa, the so-called Dark Continent.

Many of our white conquerors believe that because we have a dark skin, our continent is also dark, living in darkness, and we also have a dark mind. And some of our people are ashamed of their African roots, and of themselves, because of this. It is a myth that has inspired me to write this book as much as positive attributes of Africa have.

Therefore, in acknowledging the interest of African Americans in Africa as an inspiration in my pursuit of this study, I must also admit that our detractors have been an equally powerful motivation in my decision to undertake the project even if such motivation has sometimes been out of anger because of the way many people look at us as the most backward, and most primitive human beings, in the world.

Fellow Africans born and raised in Africa like I was, also inspired me in a very special way to write this book. I am a part of them as much as  they are a part of me in terms of common experience as a people born and brought up in Africa. Therefore we share common perspectives on a number of issues.

They are also the focus of this study as much as African Americans are. Many of them are also genuinely interested in the subject and in the well-being of our brethren, African Americans.

And probably just as many are equally interested in the improvement of relations between the two, a subject that continues to be of paramount importance to both groups, especially to those individuals who sincerely believe that we all have one destiny as children of Africa.

# Introduction

THIS work looks at relations between Africans and African Americans from the perspective of an African, and of shared perceptions on both sides of the Atlantic.

Incorporated into the analysis are stories of individuals who have interacted, worked and lived with members of both groups in Africa and in the United States, including myself.

Stereotypes and misunderstandings of each other constitute an integral part of this study, explained from both perspectives, African and African-American.

As a former journalist in Tanzania, I have drawn upon my experience as a news reporter to write this book, with fairness and a passion for truth even if some of the things I say may offend some people. But my interest is not please anyone.

I am interested in only one thing: to tell the truth as I know it. And having lived in the United States, mostly in the black community, for more than 30 years, I have first-hand knowledge of African Americans I have used to complement my analysis.

I also articulate my position from the vantage point of someone who has lived on both sides of the Atlantic, focusing on a subject that has generated a lot of interest among Africans and African Americans through the years. And it continues to be one of great misunderstanding between the two sides, in spite of increased contacts and communication between Africa and Black America, and between individual Africans and African Americans in the United States and in Africa.

Although some people such as Professor Harold Cruse of the University of Michigan in contemporary times, and others such as Professor E. Franklin Frazier of Howard University in the past, contend that after more than 300 years of physical separation since the slave trade, virtually all cultural ties between Africa and black America have been severed, I believe that there are still some elements in African-American culture which can be traced back to Africa.

You find that in music, foods, and life styles; and may be even in linguistic patterns of African Americans as Professor Geneva Smitherman at Michigan State University – formerly  Wayne State University when I was a student there - and others argue. Therefore, it was more than just hair braids that survived the middle passage across the Atlantic.

Other people have made the same arguments in the past. One of them was Kwame Nkrumah when he was a student in the United States.

He once debated Professor Frazier at Howard University on this subject, contending that there were still vestiges of African culture among African Americans, proving that slavery and centuries of physical separation had not erased all cultural ties to Africa.

Nkrumah won the debate, partly because of his oratorical skills which served him well years later when he became a leader of the African independence movement and president of Ghana, but mainly because of his factual presentation. However, Frazier maintained his position and the two agreed to disagree.

Many Africans and African Americans may also disagree with me and others who contend that some elements of African culture survived slavery. And probably just as many will agree with this position. But whatever the case, it is one of the subjects I address in this book but in a much wider context with an emphasis on the ties that have existed between Africa and black America for centuries.

I have also included in the book some information about African immigrants in the United States because, together with foreign students from Africa, they constitute the largest number of continental Africans who interact with African Americans on daily basis.

A number of other subjects are also covered in this book. The image of Africa among Americans of all races, the attitude of Africans and African Americans towards each other, misunderstandings, myths and realities which characterize their relationship, and the role African Americans played  in the liberation struggle in Africa are some of those  subjects.

And their role in this struggle cannot be underestimated, especially by some Africans who may be inclined to minimize the contribution of our brethren in the United States.

Because of their strategic position within the United States as American citizens, African Americans kept the struggle in the spotlight with marches, demonstrations and contributions, with the support of other Americans and remained a constant reminder to the American government and racist forces supporting the apartheid regime in South Africa and other white racist governments on the African continent that nothing was going to stop them from supporting the independence struggle in Africa until the white minority regimes were swept out of power.

Black people in the United States also pushed economic sanctions against the apartheid regime and exposed the hypocritical nature of the American leaders who supported white minority regimes in Africa while professing democracy at home and abroad.

There is no question that African Americans played a bigger role in supporting the liberation struggle in Africa than Africans did in supporting the civil rights movement. But it was also for understandable reasons. African countries were still under colonial rule or had just won independence and could not have supported the civil rights struggle in the United States through international forums as much as they would have liked to.

Other subjects I have covered in the book include the treatment of African Americans by Africans in Africa, especially those who have returned to the motherland after centuries of separation, seeing Africa for the first time.

Have they been well-received? Do they have any regrets? Do they wish they had never gone back to Africa? These are some of the questions I try to answer, citing disgruntled and satisfied African Americans who have lived in Africa as the primary source of information.

Some of them lived in my home country, Tanzania. There were those who stayed, and there were those who left. Some of those who stayed include a well-known Black Panther leader, Pete

O'Neal, who has lived in Tanzania since the early seventies and whose life became the subject of a documentary film shown in the United States, Tanzania and other countries. His life in Tanzania and as a former Black Panther leader is one of the subjects I also address in this book.

He was later joined in Tanzania by Geronimo Pratt, former deputy defense minister of the Black Panther Party under Huey P. Newton. Pratt served 27 years in prison, on death row, after he was falsely accused and convicted of killing a white woman hundreds of miles away from where he actually was.

A former FBI agent later admitted Pratt was framed. He won his freedom with the help of Johnnie Cochran, the famous African American lawyer, and later went to live in Tanzania where he and his wife built a house next to Pete O'Neal's, as we will learn more about that later on in the book.

I have also addressed the treatment of African Americans by the white majority in the United States, and how Africans see the United States especially in terms of her relations with Africa and as a predominantly white nation in whose bosom are millions of people of African descent who ended up where they are by "accident."

It was this "accident" of history that has also been a subject of utmost importance in trying to understand what the United States is all about, as nation that portrayed itself to the whole world as the embodiment of the ideals of liberty and equality while at the same time upholding the institution of slavery.

Even today, the subject of slavery inflames passions across the racial divide. And the demand for reparations by African Americans, which I also discuss in the book, has only fueled intense debate on the legacy and relevance of slavery in contemporary America.

Coincidentally, it is a subject on which many Africans and African Americans agree, even if they disagree on other things, because people in Africa are also demanding reparations from the European powers who played the biggest role in the enslavement of Africans. They also also colonized us, which is another case for reparations. As Ed Vaughn, one of the leaders of the Detroit-based Pan-African Congress-USA who later served as assistant to Detroit Mayor Coleman Young and as a state representative in the

Michigan state legislature, said about reparations: they have paid everybody else except us.

And as Wole Soyinka, the Nigerian writer, also said, others have been paid reparations. So why not African Americans? He also supports the claim for reparations by African countries but has made it clear that if we are going to demand that from Europeans, we should also claim reparations from the Arabs who also enslaved us.

But that is a subject that is beyond the scope of this work in terms of comprehensive analysis. I have restricted myself to the case for reparations presented by African Americans in the American context. And even here I may not have done justice to the subject, although I have tried my best to do so.

I have concluded my study on an optimistic note in the quest for greater cooperation and understanding between our two peoples who have always been one in spite of centuries of physical separation resulting from slavery whose devastating impact is still felt across Africa and Black America today

It is also encouraging to note that in acknowledgment of our common ties, the African diaspora which includes Black America is represented in the African Union (AU) as an integral part of Africa and the African world.

# Chapter One:

# Enduring Ties Between Africa and the Diaspora

AFRICA has always been in the consciousness of black Americans as their ancestral homeland even if some of them have not positively identified with it. And there are those who still don't. But even when they became Americans after they ended up in the United States in chains, they never ceased to be African whether some of them like it or not.

Even those who have a negative attitude towards Africa know where they came from. They know Africa is their motherland. They also know they were taken away in chains to a country that claims to have been founded on the twin ideals of liberty and equality while denying Africans freedom on its soil. Instead, it kept them in chains as slaves for centuries, a factor that helps to keep alive memories of Africa among millions of black Americans, and sustain a longing for their motherland.

Black people in the United States have ties to Africa that can never be broken even if those ties are just historical and psychological because of the physical separation from the motherland. But they have bonds that are even deeper than that. They are biological ties.

All blacks in the United States, including those who are racially mixed and have some European and other blood, have blood ties to Africa. In fact, every black person in the United States has relatives in Africa. All of them were not enslaved and shipped to America; all of them did not die during slave raids or perish in the Atlantic, thrown overboard. Most of the relatives remained in the motherland.

Even people with very little African blood have relatives in Africa. This can go on and on, of course, in terms of biological and genealogical roots. But it is a fact that, however little it may be, you could not have been born without that blood. You cannot flush it out of your veins or change your genes. If there is some African blood in you, even just one drop, you have ties to Africa, and have relatives in Africa still living today as you read this book.

In fact, it is estimated that between 70 million and 100 million whites in the United States have some African blood. And I wouldn't be surprised if it's more than that. This does not mean that they are Africans, like African Americans are, any more than black people who have some European blood are European. But it means that denying this biological fact does not change your roots, or at least a part of what you are. You were born that way, and you will die that way, with all your genes intact.

But besides the genetic link to Africa, and the cultural and historical ties that have maintained the identity of black Americans as an African people, the oppression and discrimination they have suffered in the United States through the centuries at the hands of the white majority has also been a powerful motive in their strong identification with Africa. However, it is also important to remember that even after blacks won the civil rights struggle, at least in the courts and in the legislative chambers, a very large number of them have always identified with Africa and have shown great interest in their African heritage.

Therefore, it is not only during hard times that black Americans have shown great interest in Africa, and a longing for their motherland from which they were forcibly removed. They have also shown great interest in the continent and in things African even when they are prosperous. And that includes a large number of middle- and upper-class blacks who have strongly identified with Africa and African causes as an African people themselves. But even those who identify themselves as Americans only, also have shown great interest in Africa.

We should, however, not forget that there is also a significant number of blacks of all classes who don't want to identify themselves with Africa even if they don't say so publicly but instead profess their love for Africa and pride in their African roots. Privately, they resent that or feel ashamed.

Yet, from the slave songs on the plantations and the establishment of the African Methodist Church (AME) and other African-oriented institutions and organizations by blacks throughout their history in the United States, to the founding of Liberia, there is strong evidence that interest in Africa among blacks Americans has always been there, even if it has not been one of enduring obsession of the nationalist kind in all cases.

Sometimes, there have been conflicting responses to African events from the black American community, showing that not only as a people blacks in the United States are not a monolithic whole but also that there are those who are not concerned about Africa as might be expected. For example, during the Italian invasion of Ethiopia in 1935, some leading black Americans said Ethiopians should not expect help from blacks in the United States because black people in America had never been given any help by Africans during their struggle against racial oppression; and that they had their own problems to contend with. Africans should therefore do the same over there: help themselves.

However, this attitude cannot be said to have been typical of the majority of black Americans during that time, or of even a large number of them, although there was no way to accurately or even approximately gauge such sentiment. Still, the mere fact that there were some influential blacks, as well as others, who felt this way shows that relations between Africa and black America have had some serious problems through the years.

It is also worth remembering that it was during the same time that a number of black American pilots and soldiers volunteered to go to Ethiopia to help the Ethiopians fight Mussolini and his forces, even when it was felt that Ethiopians in general did not want to identify themselves with black Africa, as black people, as Rupert Emerson and Martin Kilson, professors at Harvard University, stated in an essay they wrote in the sixties. The essay was entitled "The American Dilemma in a Changing World: The Rise of Africa and the Negro American," published in a volume of essays on black America, *The Negro American*:

The Italian attack on Ethiopia in 1935, it has been said, had the effect of giving large numbers of Negroes a sense of involvement in world events for the first time, even though the Ethiopians were then by no means sure that they wanted to counted among the black Africans. - (*The Negro American*, p. 642).

Others made the same observation which has some credibility even today, as it does in the case of Somalis, as well, who also in general don't want to identify themselves with black Africans and think they are better than other Africans, clearly shown by the brutal mistreatment of members of Bantu tribes from Tanzania and Mozambique who were taken to Somalia by the Arabs as slaves more than 300 years ago. Their descendants are still mistreated in Somalia today.

Some of them, for example, members of the Zigua tribe from Tanga region in northeastern Tanzania, returned to their ancestral homeland in the late 1990s with the help of the Tanzanian government and were given some land and some help to settle in Tanzania permanently.

They told of the persecution they suffered in Somalia at the hands of the Somalis who considered them to be inferior and fit only for slave labor. And more than ten thousand other Bantus from Somalia were allowed to emigrate to the United States with the help of the American government and the United Nations in the late nineties and beyond, fleeing persecution.

And during the civil war when American troops were sent to Somalia in the early nineties to help capture one of the warlords and restore order, black American soldiers complained about insults by Somalis when they tried to identify with them. They made fun of their "Negro" features - kinky hair, thick lips, black skin, and wide noses - and made it clear that they had nothing to do with them.

However, one cannot generalize and argue that all Somalis and Ethiopians feel that they are better than other Africans and don't even consider themselves to be black. There are those who do and those who don't.

But even from my own experience, I have noticed that quite a few of them don't want to mingle with other Africans the way members of different African tribes do, identifying themselves as one people: black Africans. I have roots of northeast African

23

origin myself, on my mother's side, and a number of my family members and relatives are easily identified by those features, including my mother. And I know Ethiopians and Somalis who don't have a problem identifying themselves with other Africans. But there is a problem with some of them.

And it is a problem other Africans have noticed, including some Nigerians and Liberians as well as Kenyans I knew when I was a student in the United States, as Rupert Emerson and Martin Kilson did back in the sixties when they wrote an article about black America and the newly independent states of Africa and how blacks in the United States identified with them. That is how Ethiopia and the Italian invasion of Ethiopia came into the picture. Ethiopia was seen as symbol of African dignity, being the oldest independent country in Africa that was never colonized until it was briefly occupied by Mussolini.

Ethiopia's long history of independence, unprecedented anywhere else in Africa, was one of the main factors in the decision by African leaders in 1963 when they chose Addis Ababa, Ethiopia's capital, to be the headquarters of the Organization of African Unity (OAU), now of the African Union (AU). The choice also was in deference to Emperor Haile Selassie, the Lion of Judah, King of Kings, and descendant of King Solomon, although some dispute his lineage as Solomon's descendant.

But whatever the case, a number of black Americans paid attention to all that, especially the humiliation of Ethiopia and Emperor Haile Selassie by the Italian invaders. Some of them were deeply offended by the invasion, prompting them to volunteer as soldiers and as pilots to go to Ethiopia and fight the Italians, not only as brothers in the struggle for justice which they themselves were waging in the United States, but mainly as fellow Africans or members of the same black "race."

Unfortunately, their feelings were probably not reciprocated, to the extent that they should have been, by the Ethiopians who were expected to fully embrace black Americans as their kith-and-kin, although there were those who appreciated the help.

And in terms of race, Ethiopians in general are not "Negro" like black Americans or the majority of black Africans are. They also have their own physical features of Semitic - or some other

24

"non-Negro" - origin just like the Somalis do. Even some of their languages, for example Amharic which is the main and official language, and Tigrinya, have Semitic roots.

Those are some of the examples, Ethiopia and Somalia, that help to demonstrate the complex nature of the relations between Africans and African Americans, and between Africans themselves, but which also should be viewed in their proper context instead of making sweeping generalizations that don't have validity in all cases.

Compounding the problem is the way some black Americans have treated Africans in Africa through the years. There were a number of American blacks who went to Africa as missionaries in the nineteenth century, and others even in the twentieth century after the continent had already been "saturated" with missionaries from Europe. While their migration to Africa demonstrated an enduring interest in the continent among them and other black Americans, there was also a paternalistic attitude towards the "natives" in Africa as a "primitive," "backward" people who needed to be "civilized."

So, they went to Africa not only to propagate the gospel among these "heathens"; they returned to the motherland to "civilize" them, whatever the term entails in terms of Western civilization in the African context.

There may have been some black American missionaries who saw African "natives" as their equal, especially as members of the same black race. But a higher percentage of them obviously saw Africans as inferior to them, in terms of education and civilization, along the same lines Albert Schweitzer did; that great humanitarian and missionary doctor who, while working  in Gabon in French Equatorial Africa, bluntly proclaimed to whole world: "The Negro is a child, and with children nothing can be done without authority. We must, therefore, so arrange the circumstances of daily life that my natural authority can find expression. With regard to the Negroes, then, I have coined the formula: 'I am your brother, it is true, but your elder brother.'"

Then came the founding of Liberia around the same time some black American missionaries were thinking about spreading the gospel in Africa. And their kinship with Africans was a critical factor in their decision to embark on this mission. Even some

American whites who wanted to spread the gospel in Africa felt that black American missionaries were better equipped to do that than they were.

Although the black American missionaries knew that as Christians they were supposed to spread Christianity to all peoples regardless of race, they felt they had a special obligation to do so first in Africa for a number of reasons. They believed that they would be more welcome than their white counterparts because of their biological ties to their ancestral homeland as blacks themselves.

They also, together with whites, believed that they were better equipped, physically, to survive in tropical Africa than white missionaries would because of their genetic adaptation to this environment; that is why American blacks die from sickle cell anemia. They can no longer fight malaria in their new environment in a totally different climate in North America. What was a weapon in their system in the African tropical climate to fight malaria has now been turned against them in the alien environment of America.

Racism also was a critical factor. Very often, whites directed their attention to other parts of the world to spread the gospel, ignoring Africa. And when they did go to Africa and other parts such as the Caribbean, inhabited by blacks, their racist attitude and practices alienated many would-be converts and even those who had already been converted.

That was also the case with white missionaries from Europe. For example, in Nyasaland, now Malawi, just across the border from my home district on the Tanzania-Malawi border, Scottish missionaries did not even allow blacks to wear shoes and refused to share the same quarters with black missionary workers. And it happened in other parts of Africa, including my country Tanzania even in contemporary times.

I remember Professor Henry Louis Gates, chairman of the African American studies center at Harvard University, explaining what he experienced when he worked in Tanzania as a young student. He said in one of his books, *Great Zimbabwe to Kilimatinde* published in 1996, that when he was a student at Yale University, he went to Tanzania and stayed there for one year from 1970 to 1971, the entire academic year, working at a hospital in Kilimatinde in the central region.

He lived in an *ujamaa* village and was trained to deliver general anesthesia at an Anglican Missionary Hospital. He said the hospital was run by white Australian missionaries, and their racism towards black patients and other Africans working there was clearly evident.

This is one of the main reasons why many Africans did not trust white missionaries working on the continent. We also remember very well that missionaries helped pave the way for the colonization of Africa. As Jomo Kenyatta said, "When the white man came, he said 'Shut your eyes, let us pray.' When we opened our eyes it was too late. Our land was gone!"

Chinua Achebe, in his classic work *Things Fall Apart*, articulates the same sentiment when, towards the end of his book, Obierika, in a conversation with Okonkwo, laments: "The white man is very clever. He came  quietly and peaceably with his religion and...put a knife on the things that held us together and we have fallen apart."

This kind of sentiment was obviously still strong among many Africans in the nineteenth century when American missionaries, especially of the Baptist church, were making plans to spread Christianity in Africa. The slave trade was still fresh in the minds of Africans, having ended only recently, and it would have been hard for many of them to trust the people, whites, who not too long ago had been busy shipping their kith-and-kin across the Atlantic into slavery in America. The only people who could have been well-received, also as brothers and sisters returning home after being freed as slaves, were black American missionaries.

Black Baptists were among the first Christians to launch missionary campaigns in Africa and elsewhere. For example, David George and other American blacks went to Sierra Leone in 1792 and established the first Baptist church on the continent. They also settled there permanently.

In 1815, Lott Carey and Hilary Teague together with a white deacon, William Crane, of Richmond, Virginia, formed the Richmond African Baptist Foreign Missionary Society to spread Christianity in Africa. In 1821, Carey and his wife went to Sierra Leone and established a mission among members of the Mandingo tribe. He was killed in 1828 in a battle with some of the indigenous people in Liberia and is acclaimed as the first American missionary to Africa.

Together with the Southern Baptist Convention and the American Colonization Society, the Richmond African Baptist Foreign Missionary Society, founded by Lott Carey who was the pastor of the African Baptist Church in Richmond, sent missionary workers to West Africa from 1845 and continued its activities on the continent in the following years. Liberia was one of the main targets. Even before then, Lott Carey and Hilary Teague were, in the early 1820s, among the first missionaries to work in an area that later became the Republic of Liberia. They settled there permanently, spreading the gospel among the indigenous tribes in the region.

After the Civil War, other black Christian groups also sent missionaries to Africa. They included the Virginia Baptists who continued to send missionaries overseas well into the twentieth century; the Baptist Foreign Mission Convention organized in 1880; the National Baptist Convention established in 1895; the Lott Carey Baptist Convention launched in 1897, and other Baptist and non-Baptist missionary groups.

Other black missionaries who spread the gospel in Africa included Robert Hill who was sent to Liberia by the Southern Baptist Convention; Alexander Crummell who settled in Liberia and encouraged other African Americans to move to Africa; John Bryant Small who established a mission station in the Gold Coast, what is Ghana today; William Colley who was sent to Nigeria; William Henry Shepherd who went to Congo; Mary Tearing, and Joseph Phipps, also to Congo. And other black American missionaries went to other parts of Africa including South Africa.

Especially since the mid- and late 1800s, black American missionaries continued, together with other Christians including Presbyterians, to spread the gospel well into the twentieth century and beyond, especially in West Africa, the ancestral homeland of the majority of black Americans, although not all; a significant number of them came from East Africa, especially from what is Mozambique and Tanzania today, mainly after the slave trade was officially abolished and the slave traders turned their attention to East Africa as anti-slavery patrols intensified on the West African coast. For example, I remember reading an article in *The New York Times* in 1998 which contained excerpts of old slave records showing that some of the slaves who arrived and were sold in Louisiana were members of the Makua tribe who had been captured in what is southern Tanzania today.

One of the West African regions which attracted the largest number of black missionaries from the United States was, of course, Liberia. Founded by freed black American slaves in 1822, at the behest of the American Colonization Society some of whose members wanted all blacks kicked out of the United States and sent back to Africa or to some other place including Venezuela, Liberia became a haven of peace for these former slaves, away from the persecution and lynchings in the United States. Yet, for the "natives" it became, in a very tragic way, living hell.

Black Americans who settled in the area expropriated land owned by the "natives," launched wars against them to forcibly acquire more land, and established a country in which the indigenous people were denied equal rights and virtually became slaves in their own native land; ironically, at the hands of former slaves and fellow blacks. As late as the 1930s, native Liberians were also being sold as slaves to work in Panama, ostensibly sent there on labor contracts negotiated on their behalf by the Liberian government dominated by descendants of the freed American slaves who came to be known as Americo-Liberians as they still are today.

Even within Liberia itself, members of the local tribes were treated as second-class citizens and had no political rights comparable to those enjoyed by Americo-Liberians. House servants and others working for Americo-Liberian families were treated as virtual slaves. Native Liberian leaders such as Didwho Tweh tried to fight for their rights as equal citizens, to no avail. Their plea for help from the League of Nations in the 1930s fell on deaf ears.

It was not until 1980 when members of the indigenous tribes in the army launched a military coup against the government that domination by Americo-Liberians came to an end after 150 years of hegemonic control of the territory and the indigenous population. It had been a long time since the country was founded in 1822 and became a republic in 1847, but with the total exclusion of the indigenous people from power.

The plight of the native Liberians, at the hands of the settler community known as Americo-Liberians, was unique in one fundamental respect: They were the only blacks on the continent who were colonized by fellow blacks. And the people who colonized them were fellow citizens who, ironically, proclaimed to the whole world when they first arrived there to found the colony: "The love of liberty brought us here." To which the indigenous people could have responded: "We have known nothing but misery and oppression since you came here." And it was a sentiment that was expressed in various ways by members of the native tribes some of whom attended school in the United States during the same time I did.

When I was a student in Detroit, Michigan, in the early and mid-seventies, I remember some of them confronting their fellow countrymen, Americo-Liberians who were also students, with ominous warnings such as: "You Americo-Liberians are going to pay for this one day." Their prediction was fulfilled in one of the bloodiest military coups in African post-colonial history when 17 members of the Liberian army led by a 28-year sergeant, Samuel Doe, a member of the Krahn tribe, stormed the Executive Mansion, the president's official residence, in April 1980 and killed President William Tolbert. They also disemboweled him, and his body was displayed in public.

He was the last Americo-Liberian president in the dynasty of the True Whig Party that had ruled Liberia for 150 years. Like his predecessor, William Tubman, his family members had emigrated from South Carolina and became some of the most prominent members of the Americo-Liberian settler community which dominated politics and the economy. And like Tubman, Tolbert was also born in Liberia.

But although the mistreatment of the indigenous tribes by Americo-Liberians had some negative impact on relations between Africans and African-Americans, it was only in a limited way. The wrath was directed against the oppressive Americo-Liberian settler community, and not against African Americans in the United States, although Americo-Liberians were descended from freed American slaves.

And most of this wrath and anger came from members of the indigenous tribes within Liberia itself, and not from other African countries, although there were people in other African countries who sympathized with them.

There was not much response from the people in other African countries to the plight of the members of the native tribes in Liberia at the hands of Americo-Liberians partly because many of them did not know what was going on in that country, and partly because they had their own problems to contend with in their own countries.

But even if many of them had known what was going on in Liberia, they may not have responded as forcefully as they did against racial oppression in South Africa under apartheid because they would not have seen Americo-Liberians as outsiders, like whites in South Africa. They were fellow blacks, and racial solidarity was paramount in the struggle against the apartheid regime and other white minority regimes on the continent. The Americo-Liberian dynasty in Liberia certainly did not fit that category as a foreign institution created by and belonging to whites. It was black. Apartheid was white. The difference was clear as day and night. And it was obvious who the real enemy was.

It should also be remembered that Liberia was only one of two independent countries in black Africa. The other one was Ethiopia. And both, in international forums, spoke on behalf of the rest of the African countries that were still under colonial and white minority rule. And when Ethiopia was invaded by Mussolini, Liberia was the only independent African country during that time that spoke out against the invasion.

Therefore, in spite of the oppressive rule imposed by the Americo-Liberian community on the indigenous people of Liberia, the Americo-Liberian rulers still had some credibility among other Africans as champions of African rights and independence in the international arena, especially at a time when African colonial subjects across the continent had no spokesmen to speak for them in international forums. Only Liberia and Ethiopia did.

And while Liberia has served as a bridge between Africa and black America, it has also facilitated dialogue in a wider context internationally. As the oldest republic in black Africa, it was seen as a beacon of hope for the rest of the continent south of the Sahara during the struggle for independence and inspired those still under colonial rule to fight for their freedom. Liberia also was a source of inspiration to African Americans in their struggle for racial equality which gained momentum in the fifties and sixties.

Together with Liberia were other black African countries which were among the first to win independence: Ghana in 1957, Guinea in 1958, and many others in 1960 which came to be known as Africa's Year and was declared as such by the United Nations because of what happened that year. It was the year in which the largest number of African countries, 17 of them, won independence. And the feat was not duplicated in any of the following years; by 1968, most African countries had won independence.

Coincidentally, it was also during this period that the civil rights movement in the United States gained full momentum. By 1964 when the Civil Rights Bill was passed, more than 30 black African countries had won independence in less than 10 years, beginning with Ghana in 1957. Thus, where some American blacks had been ashamed of Africa, there was now pride, by the same people, of their African heritage. They, and many other blacks, looked to Africa for vindication. If blacks in Africa could prove their worth and rise to towering heights to be equal to the best among the best in governance and other achievements including education, black people in the United States could do no less. That was the rationale.

Even before independence, Africans in Africa had profound influence on black America in terms of inspiration in the struggle for racial equality. The civil rights movement, which simply came to be known as the Movement, started to gain momentum in the 1950s, especially after Dr. Martin Luther King was thrust into the international spotlight by the Montgomery bus boycott in Alabama in December 1955 when Rosa Parks refused to give up her seat on the city bus to a white man. She came to be known as the "Mother of the Civil Rights Movement," although she had been preceded by Claudette Colvin, a 15-year old black girl, who refused to give up her seat on the city bus to a white man many months earlier in March the same year.

But black civil rights leaders in Montgomery decided not to use her as a test case and rallying point because she was very dark, a liability even among blacks in those days, unlike Rosa Parks who was light-complexioned. Claudette was also pregnant and not married, while Rosa Parks was married. And she was already active in the struggle for racial equality as a member of the NAACP and did some work for the organization.

The bus boycott would probably have taken place, anyway, even if nothing had taken place in Africa in terms of struggle for racial equality. But a precedent had been set earlier, in South Africa, when black people and a few whites and Indians as well as Coloureds launched the Defiance Campaign in 1952 led by the African National Congress (ANC) which was multiracial but predominantly black.

They employed non-violent tactics to protest against racial injustice, the same tactics Dr. Martin Luther King and others used in their struggle for racial equality during the civil rights movement. There is no question that the spirit of this campaign in South Africa inspired blacks in the United States during the Montgomery bus boycott and in their struggle for justice. Defiance against injustice was one of the main characteristics of both campaigns. As Rosa Parks said in an interview with *Scholastic* years later when she was asked, "What made you decide on December 1, 1955, not to get up from your seat?":

"That particular day that I decided was not the first time I had trouble with that particular driver. He evicted me before, because I would not go around to the back door after I was already onto the bus.

The evening that I boarded the bus, and noticed that he was the same driver, I decided to get on anyway. I did not sit at the very front of the bus; I took a seat with a man who was next to the window - the first seat that was allowed for 'colored' people to sit in. We were not disturbed until we reached the third stop after I boarded the bus.

At this point, a few white people boarded the bus, and one white man was left standing. When the driver noticed him standing, he spoke to us (the man and two women across the aisle) and told us to let the man have the seat. The other three all stood up. But the driver saw me still sitting there. He said would I stand up, and I said, 'No, I will not.' Then he said, 'I'll have you arrested.' And I told him he could do that. So he didn't move the bus any farther. Several black people left the bus.

Two policemen got on the bus in a couple of minutes. The driver told the police that I would not stand up. The policeman walked down and asked me why I didn't stand up, and I said I didn't think I should stand up. 'Why do you push us around?' I asked him. And he said, 'I don't know. But the law is the law and you are under arrest.' As soon as he said that, I stood up, and the rest of us left the bus together.

One of them picked up my purse, the other picked up my shopping bag. And we left the bus together. It was the first time I'd had that particular thing happen. I was determined that I let it be known that I did not want to be treated in this manner. The policemen had their squad car waiting, they gave me my purse and bag, and they opened the back door of the police car for me to enter."

It was defiance against injustice at its best. And as the campaigns for freedom and equality went on around the same time in Africa and in the United States, they also reinforced each other and strengthened ties that had always existed between blacks on both sides of the Atlantic.

Apart from the non-violent struggle for freedom that went on in Africa against the colonial authorities and which encouraged the civil rights campaign among blacks in the United States, was the more militant struggle waged by Mau Mau in Kenya. Coincidentally, the launching of the Defiance Campaign in South Africa in 1952 coincided with the arrest of Jomo Kenyatta who was accused of leading Mau Mau. He was arrested in the same year, 1952, together with 182 other African leaders. In 1953, he was sentenced to seven years in prison, with hard labor, and was sent to the barren region of northwestern Kenya to serve his sentence. He was released in 1961.

His release in 1961 was another important milestone in the struggle for freedom and justice for black people on both sides of the Atlantic. It took place only about three years before passage of the Civil Rights Bill in the United States in 1964, and there is no doubt that Kenyatta's release from prison further inspired blacks in America in their struggle for racial justice. If blacks in Kenya could win, there was also some hope that blacks in the United States would win one day. As the civil rights movement anthem went: "Oh, deep in my heart, I do believe, we shall overcome someday."

The militancy of Mau Mau in Kenya, involving armed struggle by the Kikuyu against the British, also inspired pride among many blacks in the United States including those who may not have used violence themselves to win freedom. But they saw in the Kikuyu the same burning desire to be free they saw among themselves in the United States. Black militants even endorsed Mau Mau tactics. And the father of the black militant movement in the United States, Malcolm X, spoke proudly of Mau Mau, as much as he did about the liberation war in Algeria which drove the French out after seven years of bitter conflict in which about one million Algerians were killed. And as he said about the Mau Mau in one of his speeches: "It was Mau Mau that brought independence to Kenya."

Malcolm X also worked diligently to forge new and strengthen existing ties between Africa and black America. In 1964, he went to Africa and visited a number of countries where he met with different leaders. He also addressed the OAU summit of the African heads of state and government in Cairo, Egypt, in July 1964 where he almost died when his food was poisoned in a hotel. He was followed by CIA agents throughout his African trip and the American intelligence agency may have been behind the attempt on his life. As he stated in his speech at the OAU summit in Cairo:

"The Organization of Afro-American Unity has sent me to attend this historic African Summit Conference as an observer to represent the interests of 22 million African-Americans whose human rights are being violated daily by the racism of American imperialists.

The Organization of Afro-American Unity has been formed by a cross section of America's African-American community, and is patterned after the letter and spirit of the Organization of African Unity.

35

Just as the Organization of African Unity has called upon all African leaders to submerge their differences and unite on common objectives for the common good of all Africans, in America the Organization of Afro-American Unity has called upon Afro-American leaders to submerge their differences and find areas of agreement wherein we can work in unity for the good of the entire 22 million African Americans.

Since the 22 million of us were originally Africans, who are now in America, not by choice but only by a cruel accident in our history, we strongly believe that African problems are our problems and our problems are African problems.

We also believe that as heads of the independent African states you are the shepherds of all African peoples everywhere, whether they are still at home here on the mother continent or have been scattered abroad.

Some African leaders at this conference have implied that they have enough problems here on the mother continent without adding the Afro-American problem.

With all due respect to your esteemed positions, I must remind all of you that the Good Shepherd will leave ninety-nine sheep who are safe at home to go to the aid of the one who is lost and has fallen into the clutches of the imperialist wolf.

We in America are your long-lost brothers and sisters, and I am here only to remind you that our problems are your problems. As the African-Americans 'awaken' today, we find ourselves in a strange land that has rejected us, and, like the prodigal son, we are turning to our elder brothers for help. We pray our pleas will not fall upon deaf ears.

We were taken forcibly in chains from this mother continent and have now spent over three hundred years in America, suffering the most inhuman forms of physical and psychological tortures imaginable.

During the past ten years the entire world has witnessed our men, women, and children being attacked and bitten by vicious police dogs, brutally beaten by police clubs, and washed down the sewers by high-pressure water hoses that would rip the clothes from our bodies and the flesh from our limbs.

And all of these inhuman atrocities have been inflicted upon us by the American governmental authorities, the police themselves, for no reason other than that we seek the recognition and respect granted other human beings in America.

The American Government is either unable or unwilling to protect the lives and property of your 22 million African-American brothers and sisters.

We stand defenseless, at the mercy of American racists who murder us at will for no reason other than we are black and of African descent.

Last week an unarmed African-American educator was murdered in cold blood in Georgia; a few days before that three civil rights workers disappeared completely, perhaps murdered also, only because they were teaching our people in Mississippi how to vote and how to secure their political rights.

Our problems are your problems. We have lived for over three hundred years in that American den of racist wolves in constant fear of losing life and limb. Recently, three students from Kenya were mistaken for American Negroes and were brutally beaten by the New York police. Shortly after that two diplomats from Uganda were also beaten by the New York City police, who mistook them for American Negroes.

If Africans are brutally beaten while only visiting in America, imagine the physical and psychological suffering received by your brothers and sisters who have lived there for over three hundred years.

Our problem is your problem. No matter how much independence Africans get here on the mother continent, unless you wear your national dress at all time when you visit America, you may be mistaken for one of us and suffer the same psychological and physical mutilation that is an everyday occurrence in our lives.

Your problems will never be fully solved until and unless ours are solved. You will never be fully respected until and unless we are also respected. You will never be recognized as free human beings until and unless we are also recognized and treated as human beings.

Our problem is your problem. It is not a Negro problem, nor an American problem. This is a world problem, a problem for humanity. It is not a problem of civil rights, it is a problem of human rights.

We pray that our African brothers have not freed themselves of European colonialism only to be overcome and held in check now by American dollarism. Don't let American racism be 'legalized' by American dollarism.

America is worse than South Africa, because not only is America racist, but she is also deceitful and hypocritical. South Africa preaches segregation and practices segregation. She, at least, practices what she preaches. America preaches integration and practices segregation. She preaches one thing while deceitfully practicing another.

South Africa is like a vicious wolf, openly hostile toward black humanity. But America is cunning like a fox, friendly and smiling, but even more vicious and deadly than the wolf.

The wolf and the fox are both enemies of humanity, both are canine, both humiliate and mutilate their victims. Both have the same objectives, but differ only in methods.

If South Africa is guilty of violating the human rights of Africans here on the mother continent, then America is guilty of worse violations of the 22 million Africans on the American continent. And if South African racism is not a domestic issue, then American racism also is not a domestic issue.

We beseech independent African states to help us bring our problem before the United Nations, on the grounds that the United States Government is morally incapable of protecting the lives and the property of 22 million African-Americans. And on the grounds that our deteriorating plight is definitely becoming a threat to world peace.

Out of frustration and hopelessness our young people have reached the point of no return. We no longer endorse patience and turning the other cheek. We assert the right of self-defense by whatever means necessary, and reserve the right of maximum retaliation against our racist oppressors, no matter what the odds against us are.

We are well aware that our future efforts to defend ourselves by retaliating- by meeting violence with violence, eye for eye and tooth for tooth-could create the type of racial conflict in America that could easily escalate into a violent, worldwide, bloody race war.

In the interests of world peace and security, we beseech the heads of the independent African states to recommend an immediate investigation into our problem by the United Nations Commission on Human Rights.

One last word, my beloved brothers at this African Summit: 'No one knows the master better than his servant.' We have been servants in America for over three hundred years. We have a thorough inside knowledge of this man who calls himself 'Uncle Sam.' Therefore, you must heed our warning. Don't escape from European colonialism only to become even more enslaved by deceitful,'friendly' American dollarism.

May Allah's blessings of good health and wisdom be upon you all".

His speech to the Organization of African Unity (OAU) conference of African leaders was a plea for help. He believed African countries would be able to help African Americans in their struggle for racial equality in the United States by bringing up their case before the United Nations. And a number of African countries agreed to do so. Among the leaders he talked to about the plight of African Americans were Emperor Haile Selassie of Ethiopia, Presidents Jomo Kenyatta of Kenya, Julius Nyerere of Tanzania, Nnamdi Azikiwe of Nigeria, and Kwame Nkrumah of Ghana. And he was well-received wherever he went in Africa. Tanzania was one of the countries he visited, and he mentions this trip in one of his speeches.

When I was working on the second edition of my book, *Nyerere and Africa: End of an Era*, in 2004, I was in regular contact with Andrew Nyerere, President Nyerere's eldest son who was my high schoolmate in Tanzania, and who said he remembered when Malcolm X visited them at their house in Dar es Salaam in July 1964. As he said in a letter to me: "When he came to Msasani (on the outskirts of Dar es Salaam where President Nyerere and his family lived in a simple house instead of living in the official residence, the State House), he gave Mwalimu the record of 'Message to the Grassroots,' a speech by Malcolm X."

President Nyerere, popularly known as Mwalimu which means teacher in Kiswahili since he was once a teacher, understood the plight of African Americans even before he talked to Malcolm X

39

and was one of the African leaders, together with others such as Nkrumah, who strongly identified with the struggle for racial equality in the United States. And he believed there was an imperative need to strengthen ties between the nations of Africa and black America which black American sociologist E. Franklin Frazier defined as a nation, even if a captive one. In his book, *Black Bourgeoisie* published in 1957, Professor Frazier argued that black people in the United States constituted "a nation within a nation." And it is a thesis that has some validity and credibility beyond black nationalist circles. Their isolation, because of segregation, helped to solidify this identity. And they looked to Africa for inspiration and spiritual sustenance in their struggle for racial equality in a country that was supposed to be the citadel of democracy.

Therefore, the success of the independence struggles in different African countries in the fifties and sixties served as a great source of inspiration to African Americans during the civil rights movement as much as the civil rights struggle in the United States was a source of great encouragement to many Africans still groaning under white minority rule, especially in South Africa. The situation of black people under apartheid was similar to that of black Americans. And both were being oppressed by a power that was an integral of their country. It was a colonial power within, not a foreign power like in the rest of the African countries ruled by the British, the French and the Portuguese. They were fighting for freedom from fellow citizens who were going nowhere, unlike the British, the French and the Portuguse who left their African colonies and returned to Europe after the colonies won independence. Black Americans were also "colonized" within.

It is also critical to remember that even during the darkest hour in the history of our continent when we were under colonial rule and did not even have political parties fighting for independence, Africans in the diaspora played a major role in championing the cause of African freedom going as back as the early 1900s. Sylvester Williams from Trinidad, and W.E.B. DuBois from the United States, were the most prominent, followed later by George Padmore and CLR James also from Trinidad. They were joined by Kwame Nkrumah, Jomo Kenyatta, Nnamdi Azikiwe and other

African leaders in the 1940s, carrying on a tradition that went back to the early years of the twentieth century when the first Pan-African Congress was held in London in 1900.

The second Pan-African Congress was held in Paris in 1919. It coincided with the Paris Peace Conference by the Allied Powers ending World War I and demanded the right to self-determination in the African colonies. It was also in the same year that there were widespread protests against the exclusion of racial equality from the Covenant of the League of Nations, and delegates from the Pan-African Congress presented resolutions to the League of Nations demanding freedom and independence for Africans. A few years earlier, the African National Congress (ANC) was founded in January 1912 in Bloemfontein, South Africa, and more than 80 years later won the struggle against apartheid.

Dr. DuBois played a critical role in organizing these conferences. It was he, together with Blaise Diagne, a Senegalese and highest-ranking African in French politics and deputy to the French parliament, who organized the Pan-African Congress in Paris in 1919. It was attended by at least 57 delegates representing 15 countries and colonies, including Liberia, Haiti, the British West Indies, West African British and French colonies, and the United States. At least 19 delegates came from Africa.

The 1919 conference is often referred to as the First Pan-African Congress. But it was actually patterned after the Pan-African Conference, which was really the first Pan-African Congress, convened by Henry Sylvester Williams in London in 1919. DuBois also attended this conference as a delegate. The London conference petitioned the Allied Nations to take specific steps to end oppressive political and economic conditions in predominantly black colonies in Africa and the West Indies.

The Second (or third) Pan-African Congress was held in 1921 in the three main colonial centers - London, Paris, and Brussels - and was attended by 113 delegates. Again, Africans in the diaspora, with DuBois being the most prominent among them, played a major role in organizing this conference. The NAACP was also represented at the conference and provided financial support. The Third Pan-African Congress was held in 1923 in London, and in Lisbon, Portugal, pursuing the same goals as those pursued at the previous conferences. The main goal was independence for black countries in Africa and in the Caribbean.

The Fourth Pan-African Congress was held in Harlem, New York, in 1927 and was funded by an organization of black women, the Circle of Peace and Foreign Relations, long interested in improving the lives of black people in Africa and in the diaspora, including attainment of independence for the African colonies. The conference was chaired by Dr. W.E.B. DuBois and attended by 208 delegates. And about 5000 people participated in the conference. Several sessions were also held in black churches in Harlem. African countries represented included Sierra Leone, the Gold Coast (later renamed Ghana), Nigeria, and Liberia. There were also representatives from the United States and the West Indies.

Dr. DuBois tried to make arrangements for the Fifth Pan-African Congress to be held on African soil, in Tunis, Tunisia. He chose Tunis because it was accessible by shipping lines and was somewhat centrally located to enable many delegates from Africa and Europe to attend the conference. But the French government feared that such a conference held on African soil would lead to unrest in the colonies on the continent, and denied the organizers permission to hold the conference in its colony of Tunisia.

The French told DuBois and other organizers that they could hold the conference in Paris, but the Depression, which came in 1929, the same year the conference was planned, precluded any possibility that the conference would be held anytime soon. Financial problems were one of the main reasons why other conferences could not be held sooner. There were also ideological divisions among the organizers.

There were those who supported the ideology of Marcus Garvey which was strictly racial and excluded anybody who was not black or considered black enough including racially mixed people such as Dr. DuBois himself. And there were those who supported Dr. DuBois and his colleagues whose philosophy was inclusive.

It was not until 16 years later, in 1945, that the Fifth Pan-African Congress was held. It was held in Manchester, England, and was attended by Dr. DuBois, George Padmore, CLR James, Kwame Nkrumah, Jomo Kenyatta, Nnamdi Azikiwe, Ras Makonnen, and others. Nkrumah and Kenyatta served as secretaries and played a critical role in organizing the conference.

It was also in the same year that Nkrumah left the United States for Britain after attending school in America for 10 years. When he was still a student in the United States, he met CLR James. CLR James said Nkrumah used to talk a lot and "he talked a lot of nonsense in those days," as he said in an article he wrote. But he said he was very much impressed by him because of his determination to achieve his goals. Other people who met Nkrumah were also very much impressed by his personality. He was charismatic. He was dynamic. I remember Professor Ali Mazrui, a Kenyan, saying when he first met Nkrumah, he was impressed by his charisma right away.

CLR James went on to say that when Nkrumah was getting ready to go to Britain to study at the London School of Economics, he wrote George Padmore introducing Nkrumah to him. Padmore lived in London. CLR James said he told Padmore to help Nkrumah, and went on to say: "He's not very bright. But he's determined to throw the white man out of Africa."

Nkrumah also read Karl Marx when he was a student in the United States. CLR James, who was a Marxist, didn't think that Nkrumah understood Marxism well. But he gave him credit saying that he studied further, and when Nkrumah gave a speech at the Fifth Pan-African Congress in Manchester, CLR James said "it was an absolute masterpiece."

Nkrumah never looked back. He returned to the Gold Coast in 1947 and, ten years later, led his country to independence, earning it distinction as the first black African country to emerge from colonial rule.

When the Gold Coast won independence as Ghana on March 6, 1957, representatives from the African diaspora were invited to Accra, Ghana's capital, to celebrate. Nkrumah also invited people of African descent to go to Ghana and other parts of Africa to help build the continent.

The people invited by Nkrumah to celebrate Ghana's attainment of independence included Dr. Martin Luther King, Ralph Bunche, A. Philip Randolph, Adam Clayton Powell, Andrew Young, Ralph Abernathy, and Richard Wright. There were also common citizens from the diaspora, such as Lucille Davis, an African American who was working in Los Angeles when the Gold Coast won independence and became Ghana. She wrote Nkrumah directly asking him to intervene on her behalf when the British embassy in Washington tried to stop her from going to Ghana to attend the independence celebrations. As Mary Ellen Ray who has lived in Ghana for almost 20 years stated in her article, "Ghana: 'Home' For African Americans":

"Kwame Nkrumah, Ghana's first president, sent out a call to skilled and talented African Americans to come to Ghana to help with the building of a new independent African nation. Many came; some left and some stayed. Today, it's estimated there are between 1,500 and 2,000 residing permanently in the country. This count isn't entirely accurate because many settled outside the larger towns and cities preferring to stay in villages and/or not registering with the U.S. Embassy.

African Americans residing in Ghana represent almost every state in the U.S., even Hawaii. A large number came as the wives of Ghanaians they met in the States. And each year more retirees arrive. Though inflation has hit Ghana and the "bargain" prices are not as much of a bargain anymore, water and electricity and telephone services continue to 'come and go' without notice, and cultural differences can get sticky at times, many of us African Americans 'hang in thar'.

Several have been here for fifty years. Dr. Robert Lee, a classmate of Kwame Nkrumah at Lincoln University, and his wife, Dr. Sara Lee (now deceased) were among Ghana's pioneering dentists. Sara Lee started the nation's first school dental clinic. After five decades of dental practice, Dr. Lee retired in 2002.

When Lucille Davis heard about the upcoming independence of Ghana in 1957 she was working in Los Angeles, an Upper State New Yorker, and decided she wanted to attend this historic event. The British Consulate discouraged her from making the trip. Undeterred, she went home, sat down and wrote a letter directly to Kwame Nkrumah, the president-to-be, explaining her desire and her plight. Within two weeks the British Consulate called Mrs. Davis saying Kwame Nkrumah was inviting her to the independence celebration as an honored guest. She now owns and operates the Beachcomber Guest House facing the Guinea Sea in

Teshie Nunga, a suburb of Accra."

Dr. DuBois was one of the African Americans who moved to Ghana and renounced his American citizenship. In 1961, Nkrumah invited Dr. DuBois to spend his last days in Ghana. DuBois was then in conflict with the American government for his opposition to America's Cold War and imperial policies. He left the United States and became a citizen of Ghana and died on August 27, 1963, in Accra, the day before the March on Washington when Dr. Martin Luther King gave his famous "I Have A Dream" speech on August 28. He was 95 and died shortly after becoming a Ghanaian citizen.

The involvement of Dr. DuBois and others in the African independence struggle, and the participation in Pan-African conferences by Africans from Africa together with those from the United States, the Caribbean and Europe, demonstrates the indissoluble bonds that have always existed between Africa and the diaspora. Black people in the Americas and elsewhere have always known that the well-being of Africa is inextricably linked with their destiny because whatever affects one, affects the other. No black person is free until all blacks are free.

And until Africa is free and united, there is no hope for the black race. If there is dignity in numbers, there is also humiliation in numbers. If more than 600 million black people in Africa - more than 200 million Africans in Africa are not black - cannot do anything to uplift the black race, 35 million blacks in the United States, or others elsewhere in the diaspora, cannot do it alone. Therefore the destiny of the black race lies with Africa. That is where the numbers and the resources are. And the bonds that have always existed between Africa and the diaspora should be strengthened to help Africans, at home and abroad, achieve their goals to be among the best among men.

When the Sixth Pan-African Congress was held in Dar es Salaam, Tanzania, in 1974, under the stewardship of President Julius Nyerere almost 35 years after the Fifth Pan-African Congress was held in Manchester in England in 1945, it was the first of its kind to be held on African soil. It was held in Nkrumah Hall at the University of Dar es Salaam. The hall was named after Nkrumah in memory of his dedication and achievements as a Pan-

Africanist and Pan-African leader, one of the greatest leaders Africa has ever produced. In a survey of Africans in 2000, as reported by the BBC, the majority of the people voted for Nkrumah as the most influential African leader.

And in a Pan-African context, he probably had the strongest links to black America among all African leaders. And the years he spent as a student in the United States helped to strengthen those ties. But it was the depth of his Pan-African commitment, his ability to fully embrace the people in the diaspora as fellow Africans, as well as his colorful style as a leader, which was the biggest attraction to him among African Americans.

When he was a student, he was also attracted to Marcus Garvey and said in his autobiography that it was the teachings of Garvey which had the biggest influence on him. As he stated: "Of all the literature that I studied, the book that did more than any other to fire my enthusiasm was *Philosophy and Opinions of Marcus Garvey*. Garvey, with his philosophy of 'Africa for Africans' and his 'Back to Africa' movement, did much to inspire the Negroes of America in the 1920's."

Garvey founded the Universal Negro Improvement Association (UNIA) in Kingston, Jamaica, in 1914 at the age of 28. After he moved to Harlem in 1916, New York became the new headquarters of the movement. It was the largest black movement in American history, attracting millions of followers and admirers with its mission to uplift the black race.

Marcus Garvey wanted to unite blacks worldwide and build a strong empire in Africa. Thus, the UNIA also became a back-to-Africa movement. As Garvey stated when he developed his vision for the Universal Negro Improvement Association: "Where is the black man's government? Where is his King and his kingdom? Where is his President, his ambassador, his country, his men of big affairs? I could not find them, and then I declared, 'I will help to make them.'" And the place where he was going to achieve his goal was Africa.

Garvey's vision undoubtedly had a profound impact on Nkrumah when he was a student in the United States and after he became president of Ghana as he sought to unite Africa. He became the most forceful exponent of immediate continental unification with his slogan, "Africa Must Unite." It was also the title of his book published to coincide with the founding of the Organization of African Unity (OAU) in Addis Ababa, Ethiopia, in May 1963.

Nyerere had the same kind of Pan-African commitment like Nkrumah. He embraced the African diaspora as much as Nkrumah did but did not have a flamboyant style like Nkrumah's. His style was simple, deceptively simple. Underneath lay a deep commitment to Pan-African causes transcending continental boundaries, without parallel among his contemporaries since Nkrumah whose political career was abruptly cut short by a military coup engineered by the CIA in February 1966.

And while Nkrumah, together with Jomo Kenyatta, played a key role in organizing the Fifth Pan-African Congress which was attended by a number of future African leaders including future presidents such as Nnamdi Azikiwe, Dr. Hastings Kamuzu Banda, and Nkrumah and Kenyatta themselves; Nyerere presided over the Sixth Pan-African Congress during a period when the liberation struggle in southern Africa was most intense.

It was also during this critical phase that African Americans launched a sustained campaign to influence American policy towards Africa, especially southern Africa. Leaders such as Reverend Leo Sullivan who drew up the Sullivan principles with which American companies doing business in apartheid South Africa were required to comply to advance the cause of racial justice in that country; black members of the United States Congress who formed the Congressional Black Caucus (CBC); and groups such as TransAfrica led by Randall Robinson, played a critical role in this campaign and in helping to advance the cause of liberation in southern Africa. It was Pan-African unity at its best.

In Africa, Nyerere was, among all African leaders since Nkrumah, the most relentless supporter of the African liberation movements and their most articulate exponent in international forums. And he believed, until his last days, that the destiny of Africans in Africa was inextricably linked with the destiny of black people in the diaspora whom he considered to be Africans like Nkrumah and other African leaders did. As he said in one of his last interviews with the *New Internationalist* in December 1998 almost one year before he died in October 1999:

47

"After independence, the wider African community became clear to me. I was concerned about education; the work of Booker T. Washington resonated with me. There were skills we needed and black people outside Africa had them. I gave our US ambassador the specific job of recruiting skilled Africans from the US Diaspora. A few came, like you (the interviewer, Ikaweba Bunting). Some stayed; others left.

We should try to revive it (Pan-Africanism). We should look to our brothers and sisters in the West. We should build a broader Pan-Africansim. There is still room - and the need."

# Chapter Two:

# My Life with African Americans

MY INTEREST in black America goes back to my teens when I was in secondary school in Tanzania in the sixties. In fact, the first American school I applied to when I was in secondary school was Lincoln University, a black academic institution in Pennsylvania. I decided to apply to this school after I read Kwame Nkrumah's autobiography in 1966. Nkrumah himself attended Lincoln University, and that is how I first came to know about the school.

But I never went to Lincoln University. Instead, I ended up elsewhere in the United States. But that is another story, as I explain in this chapter.

My first contact, or encounter, with an African American was in 1965. I was 15 years old attending Songea Secondary School in Ruvuma Region on the Tanzanian-Mozambican border; the other Tanzanian administrative region bordering Mozambique is Mtwara, east of Ruvuma. And River Ruvuma is the boundary between the two countries.

I also remember the bombings by the Portuguese in these two regions, especially Mtwara Region, during the Mozambican struggle for independence in the sixties and early seventies. Our country provided sanctuary to the Mozambican freedom fighters (FRELIMO) and refugees, and thus incurred the wrath of the Portuguese. Fortunately, our school and many other parts of southern Tanzania escaped the bombings mainly because of the defense provided by our armed forces.

I was in standard 9, what Americans call grade 9, in 1965

when I first "met" a black American for the first time. It was not a direct personal meeting but a group encounter, together with other students. But I had met other Americans before. They were my teachers and all were white.

Earlier, when I was a student at Mpuguso Middle School (from standard 5 to standard 8) from 1961 to 1964 in my home district, Rungwe, in the Southern Highlands of southwestern Tanzania close to the border with Malawi, I had been taught by two American Peace Corp teachers in my last year, 1964, the only American teachers we had. One of them, Leonard Levitt, wrote a book, *African Season*, about his experiences at our school and in Tanzania in general, and later ended up as a news reporter at *Newsday*, Long Island, New York, where he was still working when I was writing this book.

I vividly remember what he said when he first introduced himself to our class one morning: "My name is Leonard Levitt. I am a Jew from New York City." He taught English and math. The other teacher was named Wayne. But I don't remember his other name, if we ever knew it; we simply called him Mr. Wayne. I think he came from Colorado.

But I had never met an African American, or black American, back then until I went to Songea Secondary School in 1965. He came to our school with other Peace Corps teachers who taught at other schools in Tanzania. They came to visit their counterparts at our school. We had a number of Peace Corp teachers but none of them was black. We also had quite a few teachers from Britain. Others came from India, and the rest were Tanzanians, all black. But the majority of the teachers were white, mostly from Britain, a colonial legacy since Tanzania was once a British colony.

The American Peace Corp teachers who came to visit their counterparts at our school were all white except one, the black American. And that's what we called him: black American. Black Americans back then hardly called themselves African Americans as many of them do nowadays.

There are, of course, those who don't like the term "African American." For example, I remember reading a letter to the editor of the black conservative journal *National Minority Politics*, renamed *Headway*, published in Houston, Texas, in which the writer said "whenever I see the term 'African American' used in a newspaper or magazine, I drop it right there." That was in 1997.

*Headway* was not a very popular publication among blacks, anyway, because of its conservative philosophy and went out of business in less than five years. Black conservative radio talk show host Larry Elder also doesn't like term "African American." He calls it "silly terminology," as he said in the late 1990s in an interview with *The Washington Times*, a conservative newspaper, and blames Jesse Jackson for imposing this "new" identity on black Americans.

Anyway, the black American, or African American, Peace Corp teacher who came to our school became the focus of our attention because he was black, like us, and American. We identified with him and sympathized with blacks in the United States because of the racial discrimination they were going through in the land of their birth and the only country they knew as home. As John Alfred Williams, a black writer from Mississippi, said, "This is my country too," which is also the title of his non-fiction book published in 1965, the same year I saw a black American for the first time in my life.

Williams' passion for racial justice and identification with Africa is clearly evident in his works. And he never downplayed racism. As he put it in some of his writings, it takes a lot of courage for a black person to drive out there on a highway, let alone across the United States. A victim of blatant racism himself, he was once awarded a grant to the American Academy in Rome in 1961 because of his excellent novel, *Night Song*, but the grant was rescinded because he was black; also because of rumors that he was getting ready to marry a white woman, which he did.

Many of his works revolve around one theme: what it means to be black in America. He taught, into the 1990s, at a number of colleges and universities including Boston University, the University of California-Santa Barbara, the University of Hawaii, the City University of New York, and Rutgers University from where he retired in 1994 as professor of English. But he was never accorded full recognition as a writer, let alone as one of the finest black novelists of his generation, because of racism, until years later. The author of 21 fiction and non-fiction books, he won the American Book Award in 1998 for *Safari West*, an outstanding collection of his poems.

His book, *This is My Country Too*, was definitely one of those works that did not win him endearment among many whites who believe black people are not entitled to equal rights and should "go back to Africa," a common expression among them.

Williams' identification with Africa was, among other things, demonstrated by his non-fiction book, *Africa: Her History, Lands, and People*, published in 1969; and by his classic best seller, *The Man Who Cried I Am*, a novel published in 1967, which won him international acclaim despite his "pariah" status in his own country, the United States, where he was ignored by many literary critics and other fellow Americans simply because he was black. In the book, Williams explores the exploitation of blacks in a predominantly white society in a plot in which the protagonist, Max Reddick, exposes a sinister plot by western countries to prevent the unification of Africa, and an even more diabolical scheme code-named "King Alfred," a genocidal plan to end the race problem chillingly similar to Hitler's "Final Solution" that entailed extermination of the Jews and members of other "inferior" races.

Now, here is a black man who, in spite of all the racial persecution he was going through right there in the United States, was still bold enough to tell the truth about it, just like millions other African Americans did and still do. Yet another black man, also born in the United States but now far away with us in Africa, could not even admit what was obvious to everybody - including us - that racism was a fact of life in the citadel of democracy where he was born and raised. As a black Peace Corp teacher in Africa, it was obvious he had some interest in the continent and in the well-being of fellow blacks. And we approached him with open hearts.

We wanted to hear what he had to say about racial problems in the United States. We already knew about Dr. Martin Luther King and the civil rights movement and pretty much kept up with what was going on in the United States and in other countries. When Dr. King was assassinated on April 4, 1968, our headmaster, Mr. Sanga, called an emergency meeting of all the teachers and students to break the news. We went back to our classroooms but the only thing we had in mind on that day was King's assassination. I was then 18 years old and in standard 12, my last year at Songea Secondary School.

We hardly missed important news. We read newspapers, and we listened to the radio including the BBC in both English and Kiswahili. And we knew some history, including the history of the United States even if not in detail in all aspects, but enough to talk about the civil rights struggle and other issues.

All the students at our school were black, except two of Indian origin. And we thought the black American Peace Corp teacher would feel pretty much comfortable with us as fellow blacks. And he was pretty much relaxed, smiling a lot during our conversation. He didn't talk much, but he didn't seem to be uncomfortable either.

In spite of all the enthusiasm on our part, anxiously waiting to hear what he had to say, we got nothing from him, except denials, flat denials, about racism in the United States. It was an informal gathering, only a few of us probably no more than ten or fifteen, standing outside that evening. The white teachers who came with him did not in any way interfere with us. And some were talking to another group of students.

It was a frustrating experience trying to get something out of him. We knew he wasn't telling the truth. Yet, our interest in him was genuine since we identified with him as a fellow black who came from a country where some of our people had been taken as slaves and were still being oppressed for no reason other than that they were black, and of African origin, like us. That's how we saw it. I remember he was tall, dark, and slim, and probably in his twenties as many Peace Corps teachers were, fresh out of college.

But, whatever the case, nothing worked. And for whatever reason, he saw it differently, not in terms of racial identification with us - he knew we were black just like he was, simple common sense, even if he didn't like it, which I doubt seriously; he saw it differently in terms of racism in the American context and obviously in terms of how his country, the United States, was viewed abroad especially in Africa, the black man's homeland. He was concerned about the American image. He did not want it to be tarnished, I don't know by whom, since we had nothing to do with that; in fact, America had already tarnished her image by practising and condoning racism especially against blacks.

We were not trying to drag the name of his country in the mud.

He didn't say that, but that's how some of us saw it. He was also very conscious of the fact that all his colleagues were white and he did not want to step on their toes, although many whites in the United States were stepping not just on the toes but on the necks of black people, deriving satisfaction as they saw them groaning in pain.

And that was back in 1965, the same year Watts exploded; also the same year in which Malcolm X was assassinated. He had just been assassinated a few months earlier, in February, before the black Peace Corp teacher and his colleagues came to our school. And it's probably an encounter he never forgot for a long time.

We knew racism was a serious problem in the United States. We knew blacks did not have equal rights as much as we knew black people in South Africa did not have equal rights. There was apartheid in the southern states of the United States. And the whole world knew about that. Even the Soviet Union tried to capitalize on that, exposing the hypocrisy of the United States as a democratic country while at the same denying blacks equal rights as citizens and human beings, rights whites, even white foreigners in terms of human rights, took for granted.

Racism tarnished the image of the United States worldwide. It was a major problem back then in the sixties just as it is today in spite of the progress made to overcome it. Yet, for some inexplicable reason, this black Peace Corp teacher pretended that it was not, if it was one at all. In fact, I remember him flatly denying it.

There probably wasn't any among us who did not notice right away that he was not forthright and cooperative in answering our questions. Most of us were teenagers; the oldest were probably in the early twenties since some students started school late and were therefore a little older than the rest of us. We still knew better; we knew he was being deliberately evasive and was not telling the truth, may be not offend his counterparts who were white and within earshot, although some of them were talking to other students and probably were not even paying attention to what was going on in our group with the black American teacher.

I remember one student, Raymond Mshamu, from Mtwara Region, whose family once lived in my home district when his father was headmaster of Ndembela Middle School about two miles from Tukuyu, the administrative capital of Rungwe District on the Tanzania-Malawi border about 300 miles from Songea Secondary School. Raymond spoke Nyakyusa, my tribal language, he learned when they lived in Tukuyu.

They were members of a different tribe from Mtwara Region, and his facility with language when he learned Nyakyusa demonstrated a capacity and the ability to interact with people of other tribes so common among Tanzanians; the kind of brotherhood that was vigorously promoted by the government of President Julius Nyerere who was our leader until 1985, although he remained the most influential figure in the country even after he stepped down from the presidency.

In general, people of different tribes and races live together peacefully in Tanzania and the government under Nyerere had a policy of assigning people of different tribes to work in districts and regions other than their own in order to break down tribal barriers. And it worked. The same applied to students, and we liked it; an attitude that was also reflected amongst us when we identified with black people in the United States, prompting us to ask the black American Peace Corp teacher questions about racism in the United States.

Since we accepted each other in spite of our tribal differences, it was obvious that we would equally accept blacks in the United States as an integral part of us. People who don't accept members of other tribes, in their own country, are certainly not going to accept people of other tribes in other countries including detribalized Africans such as African Americans. We were different, as are the majority of Tanzanians. I don't know how the black Peace Corp teacher saw us, but we saw him as one of us.

I remember Raymond Mshamu asking him, over and over again, questions about racism in the United States. He told him we hear and read about racism in America, and that we hear and read about Dr. Martin Luther King leading the civil rights movement fighting for racial equality. Still, we got nowhere with him, despite being pestered with all sorts of questions on the subject, repeatedly, especially by Raymond. The fellow just smiled. It was a disarming smile, but not quite. Raymond didn't give up.

He took the lead because of the type of person he was:

aggressive, unrelenting, and very outspoken. He was also older, four years ahead of me and others; at least some of us in that group. He was in his last and senior year, standard 12, in 1965, while I was in my first in the four-year secondary school which was also a boarding school; the equivalent of an American high school. Our high school goes up to standard 14, and only a few students make it that far because of the highly competitive elimination exams every four years. Once you fail, you are out.

It was a frustrating experience, to say the least, with this black Peace Corp teacher. But nothing dampened my interest, or that of the other students, in black America and the United States in general, especially as a country that was also built by our African ancestors who were taken to "the land of the free and the home of the brave" in chains, as slaves, and where their descendants are still not treated as equal citizens almost two hundred years after the end of slavery.

It was not until after I went to high school (standard 13 and standard 14, generally known as Form V and Form VI) that I came into the presence of another African American. There were, of course, a number of black Americans living and working in Tanzania, including some well-known ones such as Bob Moses and Charlie Cobb who had been active in the American civil rights movement in the south.

Tanzania was one of the African countries which attracted a very large number of African Americans because of President Nyerere's formidable credentials as a staunch Pan-Africanist who accepted black Americans and other blacks in the diaspora as fellow Africans; also because of his relentless support for the African liberation movements; and his pursuit of socialist policies in an attempt to break the stranglehold of western countries on our economies. All this was very appealing to a large number of African Americans, including militants such as the Black Panthers and others, as much as Ghana was under Nkrumah until his ouster in February 1966 in a military coup engineered and masterminded by the CIA.

After my encounter with the black Peace Corp teacher at Songea Secondary School in 1965, the next African American whose presence I was aware of, was in 1969 at our high school Tambaza in the nation's capital Dar es Salaam. He was a student

56

there with us and his parents or relatives had been attracted to Tanzania by President Nyerere's policies and leadership just like many other African Americans had been. We lived in the same student hostel for Tambaza High School students only a few yards away from the school and from the beach on the Indian Ocean. But I never interacted with him on personal basis. He was my junior, a secondary school student, while I was in high school (standard 13 and standard 14), and he had his own friends who were not in my circle.

Formerly known as H.H. The Aga Khan High School almost exclusively for Tanzanian students of Indian and Pakistani origin, Tambaza was one of the best schools in the country and most of the students at the hostel were of Asian origin. The school was also fully integrated when I was there, mostly by black African students and those of Asian descent. There were also a few Arab students. The black African students also came from many different tribes across the country. And students in my class were among the first to integrate the school, a mandatory policy the government pursued since we won independence in 1961, as it still does today. The African American student also added diversity to the student body, as a foreigner, although he was black like some of us.

I went to Tambaza High School in 1969 after completing my four-year secondary school education at Songea. I was one of the very few students in the country who qualified to go to high school and the only one who went to Tambaza from Songea. A handful of others from my school, not more than 10 altogether, went to other high schools. It was also when I was at Tambaza that I again seriously considered pursuing further education in the United States, as I did when I was at Songea Secondary School. I just didn't know how I was going to do it. But I was determined to achive my goal.

It was not until after I became a reporter at Tanzania's main news paper, the *Daily News*, formerly the *Standard*, that I got the opportunity to pursue my dream. Again, as in my interest in Lincoln University earlier when I was at Songea Secondary School and even at Tambaza High School where I also had interest in the same school inspired by Kwame Nkrumah, black America became my main focus in pursuit of my goal, and eventually African Americans played a critical role in helping me achieve it.

Coincidentally, another student, Frank Chiteji, from Ruvuma Region where I attended secondary school, was also attracted to Lincoln University and finally went there. And by another coincidence, he ended up living in the same room Kwame Nkrumah did when he was a student there in the thirties. Nkrumah first went to Lincoln University in 1935; Chiteji about thirty years later in the sixties.

Yet, by another coincidence, Frank Chiteji also attended another school in the same state I did, Michigan. He earned his PhD in history from Michigan State University in the late seventies and became a professor. He taught at Ohio State University and, at this writing, was a professor at Gettysburg College in Pennsylvania.

When I met him at Michigan State University in the late seventies, he recalled with pride the years he spent at Lincoln University, and told me he lived in the same room Kwame Nkrumah did. I met him for the first time when I went to visit Kaboko Issa Musoke, a former colleague of mine at the *Daily News* where he and I worked as reporters in the early seventies, and who was Chiteji's roommate at Michigan State University. So, this was another coincidence: two former reporters, Musoke and I, from the same newspaper in Tanzania, ended up going to school in the same state around the same time.

Musoke also earned a PhD, in sociology, from Michigan State University and returned to Tanzania where he became professor of sociology at the University of Dar es Salaam. He also taught at the University of Botswana. And like Chiteji and I, he was also an admirer of Nkrumah. I remember the day I visited them in 1977, I had a debate with Musoke on the merits of Nkrumah's argument for immediate continental unification and his contention that Nyerere's approach towards African unity - by first trying to form an East African federation - was "balkanization on a grand scale" as Nkrumah put it. I supported Nyerere's approach. As Nyerere said in an interview with the *New Internationalist* in December 1998:

"Kwame Nkrumah and I were committed to the idea of unity.

58

African leaders and heads of state did not take Kwame seriously. However, I did. I did not believe in these small little nations. Still today I do not believe in them. I tell our people to look at the European Union, at these people who ruled us who are now uniting.

Kwame and I met in 1963 and discussed African Unity. We differed on how to achieve a United States of Africa. But we both agreed on a United States of Africa as necessary. Kwame went to Lincoln University, a black college in the US. He perceived things from the perspective of US history, where 13 colonies that revolted against the British formed a union. That is what he thought the OAU (Organization of African Unity) should do.

I tried to get East Africa to unite before independence. When we failed in this way, I was wary about Kwame's continental approach. We corresponded profusely on this. Kwame said my idea of 'regionalization' was only balkanization on a larger scale. Later, African historians will have to study our correspondence on this issue of uniting Africa."

Nyerere has been vindicated by history, as African countries in different parts of the continent have taken a regional approach towards integration and eventual unification. In East Africa, we have the East African Community (EAC) whose leaders are seriously considering a forming political federation in 2010. In 2004, they formed a committee to explore and institute mechanism for achieving this goal.

In West Africa, there is ECOWAS, the Economic Community of West African States which is also a political organ and an instrument for peace and security in the region. West African leaders are also working towards creating a common currency, a common market, and eventually a federation.

In southern Africa, there is SADC, the Southern African Development Community, the richest and strongest of the African regional organizations mainly because of South Africa's membership and economic might. It also wants to establish a common market, form a regional parliament and create other institutions to achieve maximum regional integration.

It is a subject I have addressed in one of my books, *Nyerere and Africa: End of an Era*. An entire chapter is devoted to this subject: Nyerere's versus Nkrumah's approach towards continental unification.

Dr. Nkrumah galvanized many Africans into action with his inspiring rhetoric and Pan-African militancy, especially on the subject of African unity, and there is no doubt that he also inspired many African students to follow in his footsteps to attend school in the United States even if they ended up elsewhere besides Lincoln University where he went.

But his ties to Lincoln University, and those of other African students who went to school there and other black colleges and universities, clearly shows that black America has always been in the consciousness of many Africans on the continent because of the common heritage we share with black Americans as an African people in spite of centuries of physical separation since the slave trade; and in spite of some misunderstandings between us which continue to put a strain on our relations, a subject I also address in this book and about which I have some knowledge because of the many years I have lived with African Americans in the United States.

My life with African Americans has been an enriching experience for me spanning more than three decades. And my first, direct contact with them began when I was a journalist in Tanzania.

My first experience as a reporter was with the *Standard*, renamed *Daily News* in 1970, where I was hired in June 1969 when I was still in high school at Tambaza. I got the job in June because it was a holiday, what Americans call vacation, and therefore did not go back to school until July. And my first job as a journalist working full-time after I finished high school was at the headquarters of the Tanzania Ministry of Information and Broadcasting in Dar es Salaam in 1971 where I worked as an information officer. That was before I joined the editorial staff of the *Daily News* where I had worked earlier in 1969 as a reporter of the *Standard*. The name of the newspaper was changed when it was nationalized. President Nyerere became our editor-in-chief but only as nominal head. He played no executive role.

It was when I was at the *Daily News* that I first got in touch with some African Americans in the United States. I did not, back then, have any direct personal contact with any African

Americans living in Dar es Salaam or anywhere else in Tanzania; and there were quite a few of them. The only personal contact I had was with one reporter of *Mohammed Speaks* who was based in Dar es Salaam, our nation's capital, which is also known as Dar. I remember he said he came from Chicago, and he used to come to our editorial office on regular basis to get stories he could use in the black Muslim paper back in the United States.

I also remember another African American who came to our editorial office. That was Robert Williams, an internationally known civil rights leader from Monroe, North Carolina. But I never got the chance to talk to him when he came to our office until a few years later in the United States. I was a student then, at Wayne State University in Detroit, and he came to the city to talk to a group of students who were members of the Young Socialist Alliance. That was in 1975. When I met him, I reminded him of his visit to our newspaper in Dar es Salaam, Tanzania, and he remembered it very well.

Working at the Ministry of Information and Broadcasting in Dar es Salaam had serendipitous benefits which later changed the course of my life forever. One evening, when I was about to go home, I accidentally came across a newspaper, *The African World*, in the office of our chief press officer Mr. Mtoi. The paper had been discarded, but the title caught my attention right away. I had never seen it before and didn't know where it was published; it could have been anywhere: Africa, Britain, the United States or any other place. I thought about Africa first. It was therefore somewhat of a surprise to me when I found out that it was published in Greensboro, North Carolina, and had somehow found its ways to our office in Tanzania.

The paper was, in fact, on the floor, ready to be tossed out by the janitor, together with other papers including local ones at the end of the day. Fortunately, I got it in time just before it ended up in the garbage. It was a treasure, and a discovery, which played a critical role in my life. After glancing at it, I took the paper home and kept it.

What I saw in that paper was the beginning of a long journey that would take me from Tanzania, East Africa, all the way to the United States and change my entire life, for better or for worse.

After I left the Ministry of Information and Broadcasting and joined the *Daily News* in the second half of 1971, I started corresponding with a number of African Americans whose contacts I had found by reading *The African World*. I had already written the people on the editorial staff in Greensboro and asked them to start sending me the paper. And they did so generously.

But it was the issue I picked up from the Ministry of Information and Broadcasting which proved to be critical. In that edition, there was an article about Malcolm X Liberation University in Greensboro which also fueled my interest in Malcolm X as a leader, and in the civil rights struggle in the United States in general. A number of other articles, including one on a young black minister, Benjamin Chavis, in Wilmington, North Carolina, who was then 28 years old and whose photo was also in the same paper I had, and what he was going through at the hands of the authorities because of his political activism; and other stories on police brutality against blacks, all had an equally profound impact on me and widened my mental horizon on civil rights and human rights issues in the American context and elsewhere round the globe.

It was also in the same paper that I saw a photograph of one of the leaders of the Detroit-based Pan-African Congress-USA, Ed Vaughn, and a caption about the organization's scholarship program for African students. There I was, trying to go to school in the United States. And right there in my hands, was a black newspaper with a picture of one of the leaders of a black organization in the United States that was sponsoring African students. It was quite a coincidence. But I did not pursue the matter right away.

Instead of writing the Pan-African Congress in Detroit, I wrote *The African World* in Greensboro and asked for a subscription. My immediate interest then was to learn more about black America, although I was still interested in going to school in the United States.

The publishers were generous enough to send the paper to me free, and I received several issues after that. My colleagues on the editorial staff at the *Daily News* also liked *The African World* very much. I remember Reginald Mhango, who was then a senior reporter and who thirty years later in 2002 became editor of one of Tanzania's main daily newspapers, *The Guardian*, saying:

"This is a very good paper."

While at the *Daily News*, I applied for admission to Malcolm X Liberation University and got a response from the school's president, Owusu Sadaukai (Howard Fuller), saying I had been accepted on a scholarship. I had never heard of this school before until I read about it in *The African World*. Having secured admission, on a scholarship, all I had to do was get a plane ticket to the United States.

I told my editor Ben Mkapa about it, and he agreed to help me. Many years later, Mkapa was elected president of Tanzania (1995 - 2005) with the full support of former President Julius Nyerere who played a critical role in choosing him as the presidential candidate of the ruling party, Chama Cha Mapinduzi (CCM), which is a Swahili name meaning Party of the Revolution. Without Mkapa's help, I would not have gone to the United States when I did, if at all.

I left Dar es Salaam, Tanzania, around 8 p.m.on Friday, November 3, 1972, and arrived in New York the next day on Saturday, November 4, on a flight from London and went straight to Greensboro, North Carolina. I had a telephone number to call and two staff members from Malcolm X Liberation University came to pick me up from the airport and take me to the school.

I also had with me a copy of *Africa* magazine. A black air hostess on the flight from London to New York, PANAM flight 101, asked me if she could have it but I said I couldn't give it to her. I told her I wished I could have given it to her but that was the only copy I had. I also had with me *The African World* which contained a short article about the Pan-African Congress-USA and its scholarship program for African students.

My stay in Greensboro was short. Malcolm X Liberation University was not suitable for me in terms of what I wanted to study. I left for New York City where I stayed for about two months with a relative who worked at the Tanzania Mission to the UN. As fate would have it, I again turned to my copy of *The African World* I had brought with me from Tanzania and remembered it had an address of the Pan-African Congress (PAC) in Detroit. Without hesitation, I wrote the leaders of the organization and asked them if they could sponsor me, while I was at the same time trying to get into the State University of

New York-Stoneybrook. Within a few days, I got a call from Detroit. The director of the PAC scholarship program, Malikia Wada Lumumba, a professor of psychology in Detroit, was on the phone. But I was not there to answer the call.

I had just left and gone to the store around the corner from where I lived on East 52nd when the call came. It was in the evening in November. That was also when I had a rude awakening at the store. It was a way of saying, "Welcome to America," but in a very strange way. I had been in the country for less than a month, mostly in Manhattan except for the few days I spent in Greensboro, North Carolina.

I walked straight into a robbery and did not have the slightest idea of what was going on. A young black man, probably around my age, had a chrome-plated snub-nosed pistol pointed at the head of the manager who was trembling and helping the young robber to help himself, handing him dollar bills. He may have had his admirers, other criminals, who would have felt that was just a soul brother emptying the cash register; a stereotypical view of so many young black men who are collectively portrayed as muggers. But I did not see him as any kind of hero, role model or freedom fighter after I found out what was going on, a few minutes after I had entered the store.

As the customers, coincidentally all white, walked into the store, caught unaware, the robber kept on waiving his pistol ordering them to move on: "Move, move," he shouted. He said the same thing to me as soon as I walked in. But I ignored him and went straight to get a shopping basket. He was on my left, by the cash register, and I turned right to the area where the baskets were. He kept on shouting but I told him I was there to shop and had to get a basket. I thought he was a security guard and it was closing time. But since I was already in the store, I saw no reason why he would try to stop me and not let me shop. So I ignored him.

He also ignored me and probably thought I was out of my mind, or he noticed my accent and thought I was new in the country and didn't know what was going on; especially when everybody else was scared and following his orders to "move, move," except me. Whatever the case, he kept on ordering other incoming customers - "move, move!" I was the only one who was relaxed, while everybody else was scurrying for cover. And I stood out because of that. I also stood out for another reason. Besides, the robber, I was the only black in the store during that time. And I will never forget how he looked like. He was about 5' 9", thin, dark, with a thin, long face, but not very long. And he had an intimidating look but which did not intimidate me at all. It's a miracle I wasn't shot.

After the soul brother spared my life, it's a miracle he did, and had emptied the cash register, he fled outside to a waiting getaway car, with its engine still running. I remember it was a beat-up dull green car, medium size. Within minutes, the police came into the store. They talked to the manager and to other customers and came straight to me. Everybody in the store, including the manager, knew I was the only customer who talked to the robber. Detectives, in trench coats, showed me mug shots and asked me if I could recognize him and identify him in any of the photos. I told them I couldn't. His picture was not there. They gave me a card to call them later if I had any information on the robber and the robbery itself.

When I got back to where I was staying, having bought everything I wanted to buy, I told my relative about the robbery. He said that was New York. I knew exactly what he meant. I learnt fast from just that one experience at the store where I could have lost my life, 6,000 miles away from my home country, Tanzania, and after being in the United States for only about three weeks. But that was not my fate or destiny. I lived to tell the story, and much more.

My relative then told me I had an important call from Detroit and the lady who called asked me to call back collect. I did right away. The caller was Malikia Wada Lumumba, director of the scholarship program at the Pan-African Congress-USA. She had good news for me and told me I had been offered a scholarship. I accepted the offer and no longer pursued plans to try to get into the State University of New York (SUNY) or any other school in New York. Money was a critical factor, and there was no reason for me not accept the scholarship in Detroit.

In addition to the scholarship, the organization also bought a plane ticket for me. Malikia, which in Kiswahili means Queen, told me to pick it up at the airport and fly to Detroit. She also told me there would be someone waiting for me at the airport to pick me up. It was a Pan-African Congress member. I flew to Detroit where my new life in the United States began. But my trip to Detroit had a surprise for me and even for my sponsors, the Pan-African Congress (PAC).

After I boarded the plane in New York for the flight to Detroit, a young lady came aboard and was assigned a seat right next to me. It was such a coincidence. She came from Africa; I also came from Africa. She came to the United States to go to school, I also came to the United States to go to school. She was young, I was young, having turned 23 on October 4, 1972. I never asked her how old she was, but I believe she was a little younger than I was. She was headed to Michigan, I was headed to Michigan. Her name was Yormie Amegashie from Liberia.

She asked me where I was headed. I said Detroit. I asked her where she was going. She said Lansing which, as I learnt later, was only about 76 miles from Detroit; it was also Malcolm X's hometown. She told me her sister was a nurse in Lansing, the state capital, and was going to pick her up from Detroit airport. Unfortunately, when we got to Detroit, her sister was not there. But fortunately, the Pan-African Congress member who had been sent to pick me up was there. His name was Kali and recognized me right away soon after I got off the plane; tragically, he died of cancer in the late seventies after I moved to Grand Rapids, Michigan. He was only 28 when he died.

Before I left New York, I told the director of the scholarship program at the Pan-African Congress in Detroit, Malikia Wada Lumumba who had called me, how I would be dressed: in a dashiki. When I arrived in Detroit, Kali was able to identify me by my attire and came straight to me at the airport and introduced himself. By another coincidence, Yormie also was in African attire.

After she told me her sister was not at the airport, I told her not to worry. I told her I would ask the Pan-African Congress member who came to pick me up if he would agree to take her with us. He did, and told me and her there was no problem. He said Pan-African Congress members would also take care of her until her sister came to pick her up. And off we went.

It was one of the best ways the Pan-African Congress

members demonstrated their hospitality and desire to embrace us, and others, as members of the same African family in a Pan-African context. When we got to the Pan-African Congress house, one of the members of the organization, Akosua Ahadi, offered to take in Yormie right away. She was a teacher and lived alone. And a few years later, she ended up moving to Liberia where Yormie came from; another coincidence.

Yormie stayed with her for about two weeks or so and was very grateful to the Pan-African Congress members for what they had done to help her until her sister came to pick her up. She finally ended up in Kalamazoo, Michigan, where she attended college and wrote me when I was still in Detroit to tell me she was getting married. She also said she would always be grateful to the Pan-African Congress members and would always consider them to be part of her family. We all wished her the best. And I hope she survived the civil war in Liberia if she returned home and was there when the country dissolved in anarchy.

That was Pan-Africanism at its best in a personal way. Here was an organization whose members had gone out of the way to sponsor African students when they didn't have to; took in other African students, including Yormie, who were in need. And there I was, myself, as one of the biggest beneficiaries of the generosity of this Pan-African family based in Detroit but whose roots stretched all the way back to Africa, from where African Americans were uprooted and forcibly transplanted on American soil.

It was an organization that had a lasting impact on my life and those of other African students sponsored by the same same organization. Some of them became national leaders when they went back to Africa after completing their studies in the United States. They were Kojo Yankah from Ghana, one of the first two students to be sponsored by the Pan-African Congress-USA, who became a member of parliament and later a cabinet member under President Jerry Rawlings; and Amadou Taal from the Gambia, who held a number of cabinet-level posts under President Dawda Jawara and was Gambia's chief economist.

One of the first two students to be sponsored, together with Kojo Yankah, was Olu Williams from Sierra Leone who went on to get a PhD in agricultural economics from the University of

Nebraska, Lincoln. I did not know his fate after he returned to Sierra Leone and hoped that he survived the civil war which nearly destroyed his home country in the 1990s. I didn't even know if he was in Sierra Leone during the war until I learnt later what happened to him.

I was in touch with one Sierra Leonean, Kadija Kabba, a close relative of President Ahmed Tejan Kabba, who happened to know Olu Williams. When we first got in touch, I told her I knew one Sierra Leonean from my student days in Detroit, Olu Williams, who was sponsored by the same organization which sponsored me and asked her if she knew him and if he was in Siera Leone and survived the war. She told me that she knew Olu Williams well. But something tragic happend to him. As she stated in her email to me on October 7, 2005:

"I did know Olu Williams and in fact used to call him uncle, 'cause, as you know in Africa, if someone is close to your family, you call them Uncle or Aunt even though they may not be related to you.

He used to work on Consultancies with my Dad; on projects such as - this one particular they did for UNDP in 1995 with a colleague of theirs called Dustan Spencer. His wife is a very good friend of my mum. Unfortunately and sad to say, he died in 2000 and his five-year anniversary has just passed this September, if I'm counting correctly. He did survive the war but was seriously ill by 1998 and 1999."

Kadija Kabba got her master's degree in international studies from Norway in 2005 and we have remained in touch since then, working together on some projects relating to conflict resolution and other issues about Africa.

One of the students I mentioned earlier, Amadou Taal, was not sponsored by the Pan-African Congress but was helped by the organization when we went to school together at Wayne State University and even before then when he was a student at Wabash College in Indiana. He stayed with us at the Pan-African Congress house during summer vacation when he was a student at Wabash College, as did another Gambian student, Mamadou Sohna, who went to the same school. And both lived with us when they enrolled as graduate students at Wayne State University. Mamadou later became a professor in the United States.

Another student sponsored by the organization was Kwabena Dompre from Ghana who also became a high-level government official and worked closely with President Hilla Limann after he went back home.

They all achieved their goals with the help of the Pan-African Congress-USA. And we all lived as students in the same house owned by the Pan-African Congress (PAC). Those were some of the best days of our lives, interacting with our brethren, African Americans. It was a truly Pan-African organization. As Amadou Taal, in remembering those days, said in a letter to me from The Gambia in May 2003:

"Although many of us stayed at the PAC house, which we all enjoyed, we were not all part of the sponsorship programme. This does not, in any way, minimise the contributions of the Pan-African Congress to education of African students from the continent. Indeed, we all appreciated their noble objectives and meaningful efforts in bringing together Africans from different countries to stay and interact under one roof and to share our experiences with our brothers and sisters from the diaspora. The PAC days were a real experience which have contributed in no small measure to our perception of Africa within the context of this globalising world."

My life in Detroit was another turning point in my journey in this world. And it had been one long journey from Tanzania about 6,000 miles away. But it had been a short one in my life of 23 years when I first arrived there. I just hoped that I still had many more years to live in this short journey of ours, as mere mortals, on earth. And Detroit had a lot to offer, especially in terms of Pan-Africanism.

Probably more than any other city in the United States with a predominantly black population, Detroit was a hotbed of political activism that has not been duplicated anywhere else in the country. It was in Detroit where the Black Nation of Islam was founded in the thirties. And it was also in Detroit where the Republic of New Afrika, the Shrine of Black Madonna also known as Black Christian Nationalism, the Pan-African Congress-USA and other black nationalist groups were started. Even Marcus Garvey's United Negro Improvement Association (UNIA), a black-to-Africa movement which was the biggest black organization in American history since the 1920s, was very strong in Detroit. I even met some of the older members of this organization in the early and mid-1970s when they spoke at the meetings of the Pan-African Congress, my sponsor. The Black Panther Party also had a strong presence in Detroit.

Malcolm X also had strong ties to Detroit; hence his nickname, "Detroit Red." His wife Betty Shabaaz also came from Detroit. And he himself spent a lot of time in Detroit when he was growing up in Lansing, about 67 miles away, and made frequent trips to the city when he became a leader in the Nation of Islam, and thereafter. Many of his family members also lived in Detroit, including his eldest brother Wilfred Little Shabaaz. And they are still there today. Also, some members of the Pan-African Congress knew Malcolm X. One of his best friends, Riley Smith who adopted the African name, Kwame Atta, was a leader of the Pan-African Congress when I was in Detroit. And Like many Pan-African Congress members, Kwame visited Africa a number of times and later moved to Ghana with his family.

Malcolm X's brother, Wilfred, was also a strong Garveyite throughout his life in Detroit. As Paul Lee, a Detroit black writer and historian, stated in his article in *The Michigan Citizen*, Highland Park, February 10, 2002:

"Some elder Detroit black nationalists recall the visit of a Black Star steamship in August 1964. Malcolm X's eldest brother, the late Wilfred Little Shabaaz, himself a son of Garveyites, told the author of his pride at meeting the ship's captain and posing for photographs, one of which appeared in *Now*, a black nationalist magazine published by Detroit attorney Milton Henry."

Milton Henry, who took the African name of Gaidi Obadele, and his brother Richard Henry, renamed Imari Obadele, founded the Republic of New Afrika in Detroit in 1968. Both knew Malcolm X whose father was a Baptist preacher in Lansing, Michigan, and a follower of Marcus Garvey. After Malcolm X was assassinated, the Obadele brothers and other black nationalists formed the Malcolm X Society in Detroit to honor him and implement his ideals. Together with the Republic of New Afrika, the Malcolm X Society also demanded reparations for the labor extracted from African slaves and their descendants in the United States.

In fact, it was the members of the Malcolm X Society who called a meeting in Detroit which led to the establishment of the Republic of New Afrika (RNA) in March 1968. Therefore the RNA was a product of the Malcolm X Society which itself was Garveyist in orientation. Robert Williams, the black militant civil rights leader from North Carolina who was then in exile in China was named president of the Republic of New Africa. Milton Henry, renamed Gaidi Obadele, became first vice president, and Betty Shabaaz, Malcolm X's widow who was also from Detroit, was named second vice president. Imari Obadele became minister of information in this Garveyist organization.

Years earlier, Malcolm X's father was one of the strongest supporters of the Back-to-Africa movement advocated by Marcus Garvey. He was killed in Lansing because of his outspokenness against racial injustice. It is believed that Ku Klux Klan members killed him. But nothing could kill the spirit that Malcolm X had in pursuit of freedom for African Americans and remained committed to Marcus Garvey who believed that black people should go back to Africa, the only place on earth where they could be free.

The Black Star Steamship Line was launched by Marcus Garvey to promote trade among black people worldwide, especially between those in the Americas and Africa, and to finally transport African Americans and other blacks back to Africa to settle permanently in fulfillment of his dream of the "Back-to-Africa" movement, and "Africa for Africans." Unfortunately, it is a goal he never realized.

But Detroit remained an activist center in the Marcus Garvey tradition even after Garvey died destitute in London in 1940. The Pan-African Congress-USA based and founded in Detroit in 1970 was one of those organizations which considered themselves to be heirs of Marcus Garvey.

One of the reasons black nationalist groups, and black

activism, thrived in Detroit was the predominance of the black population. When I lived there in the seventies, it was mostly black and the fifth largest city in the United States; it slipped to seventh in the nineties while at the same time the percentage of the black population rose, making it almost 90 percent black, although numerically it lost some people, including blacks, through the years.

It was also in Detroit where I forged the strongest ties with Black America; ties which started when I was still in Tanzania in the early seventies and corresponded with people like Nathan Hare, editor of the *Black Scholar* published in Sausalito, California, and who later became a professor at Howard University; editors of *The Black World*; Owusu Sadaukai (Howard Fuller), president of Malcolm X Liberation University, and later professor of education at Marquette University, Milwaukee, Wisconsin; Les Campbell (Jitu Weusi, Swahili meaning Black Man), a black activist and head of a black nationalist group in Brooklyn which had ties to the Congress of African People based in Newark, New Jersey, led by renowned poet and playwright Amiri Baraka, formerly LeRoi Jones, and other civil rights groups; Kimathi Mohammed of the Marcus Garvey Institute in Lansing, Michigan; and others including those in academia. One was a professor at Tufts University who encouraged me to go to school there. I even talked to him when I was staying in New York but never got the chance to go to Tufts and ended up elsewhere, instead, in Detroit.

When I stayed in New York City for about two months from November to December, 1972, I interacted with a number of African Americans in the black nationalist movement. They included Les Campbell and his group in Brooklyn some of whose members spoke Kiswahili and whom I visited on several occasions. Les Campbell and his colleagues also took me to a gathering at Temple No. 7 in Harlem once headed by Malcolm X. I had been to Harlem before and continued to visit this bustling black "city" thereafter when I stayed in New York. I also attended functions in Manhattan organized by the Congress of African People where Amiri Baraka himself, the leader of this organization, was the main speaker. Guests included African diplomats, among them officials of the Tanzania Mission to the

UN, and I got the chance to meet Baraka.

I was also invited to City College in Harlem by one of the professors, Mrs. Sanga, an African American married to a Tanzanian. She spoke fluent Kiswahili and taught the language at City College, in addition to African and African American history. Mrs. Sanga also, unbeknownst to me then, had ties to the Pan African Congress in Detroit who were to sponsor me later on. But I didn't know then that I would be getting a scholarship from them. I had not even written them when I visited City College.

After I moved to Detroit, Mrs.Sanga came to the city shortly thereafter, accompanying Madame Jean Cisse, the ambassador of Guinea to the UN who had been invited by the Pan-African Congress (PAC) to be the main speaker at one of the organization's forums held every Sunday at their PAC hall. All the meetings dealt with Pan-Africanism and other subjects about Africa and the African disapora in a global context.

Because of the organization's ideological orientation, members were also taught African history. A significant number of them also wanted to learn Kiswahili which they considered to be a truly Pan-African language. Many ethnic groups contributed to its evolution and growth and it is the only major African language that is not identified with any particular ethnic group. It transcends tribalism and ethnic identities; hence its appeal to a large number of Africans and those of African descent in the diaspora. And I played a role in spreading the language in Detroit.

The Pan-African Congress members asked me to teach them the language. We had classes every week at the PAC hall and I taught them free. After all, they had sponsored me; so why not do something in return as a token of appreciation? But my primary interest in teaching the language was to promote unity among the children of Africa, those at home and those abroad, by encouraging them to embrace a language that transcended ethnic loyalties and rivalries which have caused so much misery across Africa through the decades simply because many people of different tribes don't like each other or feel that they are better than others.

The desire to unite Africans, including those in diaspora, was also clearly evident in what the Pan-African Congress did in sponsoring African students. They all came from different parts of

Africa: Ghana, Sierra Leone, Nigeria, and Tanzania. And as I said earlier, the organization also helped two students from the Gambia by giving them free accommodation when they were on summer vacation from Wabash College in Indiana, and when they attended Wayne State University in Detroit. While Amadou Taal became a high government official after he returned to the Gambia, his compatriot, Mamadou Sohna, became a professor in the United States.

Some refugees and freedom fighters from South Africa also stayed briefly at the Pan-African Congress house where all the students lived. One of them was a senior leader of the Pan-Africanist Congress (PAC) of South Africa whom I knew in Dar es Salaam, Tanzania, when I was a news reporter and who was invited to Detroit by the Pan-African Congress-USA. The two groups shared a common philosophy which emphasized the significance of race and racial solidarity to the exclusion of other factors in the struggle for freedom and justice. Neither favored or promoted racial integration, a philosophy that was fundamentally at odds with the beliefs of some of the students and other people who supported both organizations in their relentless struggle against racial oppression and exploitation.

The Pan-African Congress-USA also forged links with African countries at the official level, in addition to sponsoring students like me. Besides the Guinean ambassador to the UN, Madame Cisse, other African leaders who were invited to Detroit included the Tanzanian ambassador to the United States, Paul Bomani; deputy ambassador Hamza Aziz, and Martin Kivumbi, a senior diplomat at the Tanzania embassy in Washington, D.C. They all spoke at the PAC meetings.

One of the main subjects discussed was the liberation struggle in Africa. Tanzanian diplomats were in a unique position to address the subject because Tanzania was the headquarters of all the African liberation movements in Africa and one of the frontline states in the liberation wars in southern Africa. Others were Zambia, Mozambique, Angola, and Botswana. And Tanzanian President Julius Nyerere was the chairman of the frontline states.

The Pan-African Congress-USA also supported the liberation struggle in southern Africa and Guinea-Bissau which was ruled by the Portuguese and some of its leaders, together with other African Americans, went to Africa on a fact-finding mission in some of the countries where the freedom fighters were waging guerrilla war against the colonial forces. One of them went to Angola in 1974 and filmed a documentary on the atrocities perpetrated by the Portuguese against innocent civilians which was shown at Wayne State University. Among those who attended was black US Congressman Charles Diggs from Detroit who also had been to Africa a number of times. One of the countries he visited was Tanzania where he met President Nyerere.

Mrs. Rosa Parks, Mother of the Civil Rights Movement, was also in the audience and I got the chance to meet her for the first time. She and her husband moved from Alabama to Detroit in 1957 and had been living there since then. They fled Alabama after many threats by the Ku Klux Klan and other racist groups and individuals because of what Rosa Parks did to fuel the civil rights movement when she refused to give up her seat on the bus to a white man in December 1955.

I remember the documentary about Angola well. It was filmed by Kwadwo Akpan, one of the leaders of the Pan-African Congress-USA who and his wife years later moved to Ghana permanently, and it provoked an angry reaction from the audience. One of the victims in the documentary was an elderly man with a very large bad wound on his head; a victim of bombings by the Portuguese colonial forces. This ghastly image was seared in my memory, and in the memories of others including a veteran and fiery journalist and editorial writer at the *Michigan Chronicle*, Nadine Brown who could hardly contain her anger after seeing the film. The documentary galvanized the audience which included Wayne State University students, mostly black, and members of the general public.

It is this kind of involvement in the African liberation struggle, and in the redemption and unification of Africa in general, which gave the Pan-African Congress-USA a very high profile among many African Americans in Detroit and elsewhere in spite of the fact that it was not a very large organization and had been formed only recently in 1970. But it remained very active and, together with the Republic of New Afrika also founded in Detroit,

75

organized very successful marches in May every year on African Liberation Day to support the liberation struggle in Africa. And the people of Detroit responded accordingly.

Hundreds and hundreds of them participated in the marches. The authorities were informed in advance and the roads, with the participation of the Detroit police and other law enforcement agencies, were cleared of all traffic on the day of the march throughout the entire route taken by the marchers. Those were the seventies when the liberation wars in southern Africa were most intense. And the racial solidarity demonstrated in those marches and other events was very encouraging to all those involved in the struggle, as were the contributions made.

When I was a student at Wayne State University, the liberation struggle in southern Africa was one of the main subjects discussed by African and African American students. In 1975 at the suggestion of Mamadou Sohna, a few of us decided to form an organization of African students on campus. It was named the Organization of African Students. A significant number of African students and some African American students attended the first meeting and Sohna was elected president; I was elected vice president. Mamadou relinquished his post not long after that, and I was elected to succeed him.

We also had a newsletter, *Ngurumo*, which in Kiswahili means thunder, as a forum for discussion and dissemination of information about the organization. Some students voted for this name because it reminded them of Nkrumah. It sounds like his name, and its meaning, thunder, was best personified by none other than Nkrumah in the minds of many of them. Others said they chose the name because of the significance of Kiswahili as a Pan-African, non-tribal language not identified with any African tribe or ethnic group.

Although our student organization was new, we tried to reach out within Pan-African circles in order to promote Pan-African ideals and unity among Africans. We also invited speakers. One of them was the Kenyan ambassador to the United States who spoke to a large audience of African students and African Americans at Wayne State University in 1975. During that time there were about 200 African students attending Wayne State University. Most of them came from West Africa, especially

Nigeria, Ghana, and Liberia. There were only three of us from Tanzania. The other two, Mark Kiluma and Mayowera, were graduate students and both taught Kiswahili at Wayne State.

On the campus itself, we also tried to forge links with the older and larger Black Students Union of African Americans but did not have a functional relationship. Our relationship was more symbolic than functional because neither side tried hard to build a strong relationship between the two. But as individuals, many African and African American students got along very well on and off-campus.

I remember one particular meeting to which we were invited by members of the Black Students Union in 1975. They were discussing how the students should respond to the anti-busing violence in Boston, Massachusetts, where black students were being attacked by white racist opponents of school busing to integrate schools in that city. Some of the students wanted white students to be involved, others were opposed to that. The trend was towards integration but there were some who did not trust whites to be genuine allies in their struggle for justice and equality.

I was one of the students who went to Boston that summer in 1975 to attend a mass rally condemning the racial violence being perpetrated against black students in that city. It was a free ride. About three buses left Wayne State for Boston. The convoy was organized by student groups on campus, black and white, and was fully integrated. We were a part of a large gathering of students from all over the United States who participated in workshops on race and other subjects held at the University of Massachusetts-Boston. Many other people also went to Boston for the event. I remember the buses which kept on coming into the city from all parts of the country after we arrived there. Students and members of the general public were all on board.

After they all had arrived, a mass rally was held. It was a rainbow coalition and, despite the large number of African Americans from all walks of life and from all over the United States at the rally, a strong presence of white supporters of integration was very noticeable and added to the significance of the event as a defining moment in the history of race relations in Boston. The rally was addressed by Roy Wilkins, head of the

NAACP. Although he was not an orator like Dr. Martin Luther King and Malcolm X, his speech was was very inspiring and gave hope to those who believed in racial integration that they would overcome some day. That was the dream. And it still remains a distant goal even today, despite the progress made across the United States through the decades since the civil rights movement. As the NAACP New York office says in one of its statements: "The NAACP was officially founded in 1910....Ninety-four years later, the work is not yet done. The face of racism changes continuously."

That is not Louis Farrakhan talking.

Although racial integration remains an elusive goal in the lives of many African Africans, many of them, may be even the majority, see it as the only way forward in a predominantly white society. Then there are those who see it as a noble but an unattainable ideal, therefore a waste of time and energy. And there are those who simply don't believe in it. In my relations with African Americans in the course of more than three decades, I have met all three types, and more. They include those who support integration but don't trust whites, not necessarily as individuals but as a race in general because of historical experience through the centuries beginning with the conquest of Africa and subsequent enslavement of millions of her people shipped to the Americas, with millions more lost at sea.

I have seen a lot of anger and bitterness, but also hope and optimism among many African Americans. I have also seen despair. But it is despair tempered with hope and faith in the American dream in the world's richest, most powerful, and most successful country in the history of mankind in terms of material civilization. Yet, material civilization is not the pinnacle of success in man's life if it is not inspired by noble ideals including compassion for the weak and helpless; and if it does not value man's spiritual qualities as the very essence of the meaning of life. As Kwame Nkrumah said in his speech on the motion for Ghana's independence he delivered before the Gold Coast Legislative Assembly on July 10, 1953:

"In our daily lives, we may lack those material comforts regarded as essential by the standards of the modern world; but we have the gifts of laughter and joy, a love of music, a lack of malice, an absence of the desire for vengeance for our wrongs, all things of intrinsic worth in a world sick of injustice, revenge, fear and want....

We feel that there is much the world can learn from those of us who belong to what we might term the pre-technological societies. These are values which we must not sacrifice unheedingly in pursuit of material progress....

We have to work hard to evolve new patterns, new social customs, new attitudes to life, so that while we seek the material, cultural and economic advancement of our country, while we raise their standards of life, we shall not sacrifice their fundamental happiness. That...has been the greatest tragedy of Western society since the Industrial Revolution."

Still, many African Americans, just like many Africans and other people, value material things more than they value anything else. Yet, they don't represent all of their people or what is best among them. Most Africans who emigrated to the United States did so to improve their lives and pursue the American dream. Even African students in the United States go to school in order to get good paying jobs after they graduate and return to their countries or stay in America. They want material things. They want security. And there is nothing wrong with that if they don't compromise principles they cherish as a people and as human beings with a conscience.

But sometimes there is a conflict of visions and perceptions between the two groups. I have talked to a number of Africans who say black people in the United States don't take advantage of the opportunities they have to succeed in life. May be that is because we have so little in our countries in terms of opportunity and development to reach the pinnacle of success. And I have talked to African Americans who say when Africans come to the United States, they are treated better and are favored by whites and think "they are better than us." And there are, of course, those who have little regard for each other; African Americans who look down upon Africans because they come from a poor and a backward continent; and Africans who see American blacks as arrogant. In fact, a number of African Americans, especially black

Republicans and other conservatives like them, as well as others who are not even ideologically inclined, don't want to have anything to with Africa. It goes on and on.

Yet, in spite of all this, in all my thirty years living and working with African Americans, I have noticed that the majority of them - the ones I have dealt with - see us as a part of them, the same black race, the same people, because they don't have the same kind of problem we have in Africa: tribalism. Civil wars and other conflicts in many African countries since independence have been fueled by ethnic rivalries in the struggle for power and resources simply because many Africans don't see themselves as one people like African Americans do. And many African leaders and other unscrupulous politicians and the elite exploit and capitalize on these differences to promote their own interests and win power or perpetuate themselves in office and favor members of their own tribes.

In a number of African countries, even the struggle for independence was carried on along tribal lines by tribal political parties; for example the Northern People's Congress of Northern Nigeria dominated by the Hausa-Fulani; the Action Group of Western Nigeria dominated by the Yoruba; the Kabaka Yekka of the Banganda tribe in Uganda; the Inkatha Freedom Party of the Zulu in South Africa; the African National Congress in Zambia led by Harry Nkumbula which was strongest among the Ila and the Tonga, southern tribes; the United Gold Coast Convention (UGCC) in the Gold Coast led by Dr. J.B. Danquah which was strongest among the Ashanti; the Sierra Leone People's Party (SLPP) in Sierra Leone which was dominated by the Mende, a southern tribe and one of the two largest tribes in the country together with the Temne in the north.

Those are just a few examples of ethnic and regional loyalties and rivalries which have caused a lot of problems, including civil wars, across Africa through the decades.

Fortunately, African Americans have been spared this agony, although in a tragic way. That is because they were enslaved, and their tribal identities were destroyed during slavery. Yet out of all this emerged one people. In Africa, we remain divided along tribal or ethnic lines. This is one of the main reasons why some Africans don't identify with African Americans.

If they don't accept people of other tribes even in their own countries, they are not going to accept black people in the United States as a part of them. Fortunately, many Africans in the United States, at least the ones I have known, don't feel that way anymore than many African Americans do. And many African Americans are very much interested in Africa probably more than Africans are interested in black America. They ask questions about Africa more than Africans do about black America.

But it was probably my life with the Pan-African Congress members in Detroit during my student days that best exemplifies what can be done and achieved in terms of building, maintaining, and strengthening relations between Africans and African Americans who remain one people as children of Africa in spite of centuries of physical separation since slavery. It is this spirit of Pan-Africanism that continues to animate many of our people on both sides of the Atlantic, and it is the essence of our very being as a people who share a common heritage deeply rooted in Africa. Nothing can destroy that. Nothing.

# Chapter Three:

# The Image of Africa in America

THE IMAGE of Africa, not only in America but in other parts of the world, is refracted through a prism that distorts reality about the world's second largest continent after Asia.

To many people, it is still the "Dark Continent." To others, especially people of African descent in diaspora and those sympathetic towards Africa, it is a place bustling with activity, filled with a vibrant people inspired and animated by hope and optimism about the future of their continent. Yet to others, Africa is a fetid swamp of misery, blighted by famine, mangled by war and disfigured by disease, desperate for help and surviving on international welfare. The larger picture is one of gloom on the world's poorest yet potentially richest continent.

When I first arrived in the United States, I had the same feeling many Africans have that I would be confronted with stereotypical images of Africa as a jungle where people live with wild animals as neighbors, rubbing shoulders with them; and where many tribesmen run around naked with spears, or with bows and packs of arrows on their backs, and bones protruding through their noses. But I was, many times, insulated from all this by the people who were around me. They were mostly Pan-Africanists or very defensive of Africa because they saw any negative portrayal of Africa as an insult to the entire black race by white racists and others.

So, I operated within this circle, especially during my first few months in the United States. However, their romantic, hence circumscribed, view of Africa as a blissful place, filled with wonderful people known for their unbound hospitality, did not accurately reflect the truth about this complex continent.

There were also a number of times when I talked to Americans, including blacks, who had a negative attitude towards Africa even during my first weeks and months in America. It was hard for them to believe that there were pockets of "civilization" anywhere in Africa, according to their definition of civilization: cities, cars, refrigerators, telephones, television sets and even radios; schools and hospitals, buses and trains and so on. If some of them believed we had all that, then it was only very little of it. They couldn't be convinced otherwise.

And my coming to the United States to go to school only reinforced those stereotypes; for, if we had schools in Africa, why did I and the rest of the other African students have to come all the way to America to go to school, travelling thousands of miles? If we had medicine and hospitals, why did millions of people over there die like flies? And if we lived normal lives like other human beings, why was there so much starvation in African countries, so much so that we had to beg other countries for food? For example, I remember one incident - there were other incidents similar to this one through the years but I particularly remember this one because I knew the person involved - when one black student from Paterson, New Jersey, whom I met in Grand Rapids, Michigan, in the late seventies when he was attending Calvin College in that city, said this to me: "You are starving over there in Africa. We are the ones feeding you!"

And there was some truth to that, I must admit. Those were the years when we had massive starvation in a number of African countries, with millions starving. But it is also true that even back then, or any time when many people are starving in Africa, *most* Africans across the continent *do not* depend on international relief; they feed themselves. We have hundreds of millions of Africans, about 800 million today, and all those people don't depend on food donations form other countries to survive; anyone just with simple common sense, or even with very little knowledge of Africa, should know that. The *whole* continent is not starving.

Yet, we cannot deny that when others are starving, we are not the ones who help them. Africans don't feed fellow Africans in other countries. The food does not come from other African countries but from America, Canada, European countries, Australia and other countries, because we don't have enough even for ourselves for a number of reasons including primitive farming methods, large families, poor management, bad policies, and corruption.

It is not what this student said which is the main point that I'm trying to make here. It is *how* he said it, and *why* he said it: in a condescending manner to denigrate and belittle Africa. "You have nothing over there," was the attitude, also reflected by the media. I remember one story on a local television station (WOTV, an NBC affiliate in Grand Rapids) in which the anchorwoman said one evening that a used ambulance had been donated and "was being sent to Africa," as if the whole continent was waiting for and would depend on this ambulance. She did not even name the country where it was being sent to. But that was typical of the stereotypical image of Africa where "they ain't got nothin!" as Americans say.

And that was the attitude of the black student I quoted earlier. And he wasn't alone. Many other Americans, millions of them, black and white but especially whites for racist reasons, share this perception. Probably the majority do. They hardly have anything good to say about Africa, besides wildlife and our minerals especially gold and diamonds. Almost everything else is bad. The list goes on and on. And that is something that has continued through the years wherever I have been in many parts of the United States talking to different people about Africa.

Fortunately, that was not the attitude of the majority of the people I interacted with in my first days and weeks in the United States. And that is not the attitude of the majority of the Americans I have dealt with through the years. Many of them know there are a lot of bad things about Africa. But they also know that there are many good things about Africa. And I have been able to carry on serious and intelligent conversations with them for more than thirty years.

It does not mean that all of them are not prejudiced or don't make fun of Africa behind our backs. I am sure many of them do. The main difference between them and their fellow countrymen who hardly know anything about Africa is that they are knowledgeable enough to talk about the African continent and its people and reach intelligent conclusions even if they themselves are prejudiced or don't care about us. At least they know what they are talking about.

And that has been my experience since I first arrived in the United States. The place where I stayed the longest when I first arrived was New York City and the people I dealt with were African Americans who were among the most defensive against any attack on Africa.

They were cultural nationalists and fiercely proud of their African heritage. They were based in Brooklyn, as I explained earlier, where I visited them regularly when I stayed in Manhattan for about two months from November to December towards the end of 1972. It was during the same time that I also visited Washington D.C., at the invitation of two gentlemen from Trinidad whom I first met in Dar es Salaam, Tanzania, earlier in 1972. They were students at Howard University and leaders of a Pan-Africanist Caribbean association based in Washington, D.C.

I had earlier corresponded with them before they came to Tanzania. They were introduced to me by some of the other African Americans I had been in touch with when I was a news reporter and whom I corresponded with on regular basis.

When they came to Tanzania, they stayed with me for more than a month. One of them was Anthony Ferguson, an economics student who went on to pursue graduate studies in the field; and other one was Wilbur.

I remember what Wilbur said when I first met them at an Indian hotel in which they were staying in Dar es Salaam, Tanzania: "We don't want to see anything impede the progress of Africa." His was not a lone voice in the wilderness. He articulated a sentiment shared in Pan-African circles at home and abroad as much as it is today.

After we met in Dar es Salaam, they were also very anxious to meet one professor from the Caribbean, Dr. Walter Rodney from Guyana, who taught at the University of Dar es Salaam. He was an internationally renowned scholar and Pan-Africanist who also wrote a best-selling book, *How Europe Underdeveloped Africa*, when he was a professor at the university.

I took them to Rodney's house on the campus of the University of Dar es Salaam, but he wasn't home on that day; only his wife was. I went back to his house a few days later. He and his wife were there this time and he was sorry he did not get the chance to meet and talk to the two fellows from Trinidad whom I took to his house. By then, they had left for the United States. A few months later, I also did, and arrived in New York on a cold winter day in November but proceeded to Greensboro, North Carolina, my destination, where I met staunch Pan-Africanists at Malcolm X Liberation University.

From Greensboro, I moved to New York City where I interacted with another group of ardent Pan-Africanists who were so defensive of Africa that they did not want to hear anything bad said about their ancestral homeland. When I was invited to Washington, D.C., while staying in New York, I met yet another group of strong Pan-Africanists in the Caribbean association whose members included Ferguson and Wilbur I mentioned earlier, and Valerie Andrew, also from Trinidad and a student at Howard University.

They also invited one Tanzanian whom they knew, Emmanuel Muganda, to meet me at the Caribbean association house where they held their meetings. He worked at the Voice of America (VOA) Swahili Service in Washington, D.C., and later became director of the Swahili program as he still was at this writing. Coincidentally, I happened to know some of his family members in Tanzania where I worked with his brother Alex at the *Standard*, which later became the *Daily News*, in Dar es Salaam; Alex, who worked temporarily as a reporter when he was a law student at the University of Dar es Salaam, later became ambassador. I also knew their sister who also was a journalist at the Ministry of Information and Broadcasting.

My trip to Washington, D.C., also happened to be a crash course in race relations in the United States. As I was getting ready to get on the plane for my flight, I was pulled aside by a uniformed police officer, or whatever he was, who asked me who I was, where I was going, and why. He also asked me where I lived. When I told him the address, Sutton House, 416 East 52nd, Apartment 9-DB, he took a hard look at me and finally let me go.

I was dressed in simple attire and he probably felt that I had no business living there, at such an address. A number of diplomats, including my relative, an in-law who worked at the Tanzania Mission to the UN, and top New York business executives lived in that apartment building which was also within walking distance, only a few minutes, to the UN headquarters and to the offices of our Mission to the UN.

I was dressed in a *dashiki* and had an African hat on, the kind won by President Sekou Toure of Guinea who popularized it (people in Tanzania and elsewhere in Africa called it a Sekou Toure hat or just a Sekou Toure), and felt that the white policeman had singled me out because of the way I looked: black and in "strange" attire. "And dark as I am, too!" in a predominantly white country, I said to myself, "I'm really in trouble, for nothing."

Other black passengers, some dressed in suits, were allowed to board the plane without any problems, except me. I also thought that I had been targeted because he felt I was some kind of black militant, hence my *dashiki* and "funny" looking hat, who was getting ready to hijack the plane to Cuba, or some other destination, as some Black Panther Party members had done.

Earlier in January 1971, a Black Panther Party member, Garland Grant of Milwaukee, Wisconsin, hijacked a Northwest Airlines jet and forced it to fly to Cuba where he sought and was given political asylum but, later, ended up in prison for five-and-a-half years under Castro's regime. He got into trouble with the Cuban authorities mainly because of his attempts to return to the United States. He hijacked a Boeing 727 with 59 people aboard during a flight from Milwaukee to Washington, D.C. He said he wanted to go to Algeria but was told the plane did not have enough fuel to cross the Atlantic. So he decided to be taken to Cuba.

Then several months later, in September 1971, there was another hijacking by Black Panther Party members in an attempt to free their comrades from prison. In August 1972, five Black Panther Party members hijacked a Delta Airlines plane to Algeria and had one million dollars in ransom money. The Algerian authorities confiscated the money and Eldridge Cleaver, then living in exile in Algiers, demanded that the money be returned and that the hijackers be allowed to seek asylum elsewhere. It was also in the same year that Ida McCray Robinson and her partner who was a member of the Republic New Afrika, hijacked a plane to Cuba.

And it was during the same period, in September 1972 about two months before I arived in the United States, that eight Palestinian fighters killed 11 Israeli athletes at the Olympic Village in Munich, Germany. And in the following month, in October, a Lufthansa passenger jet plane was hijacked by other Palestinian militants who demanded the release of their three compatriots captured in Munich. Five were killed by German sharp shooters.

So security was tight in Western countries when I flew from Britain to the United States, with air marshals standing throughout the flight and staring at the passengers back and forth. We arrived at John F. Kennedy International Airport in New York, without incident, around 4 p.m. on November 2, 1972, after a six-hour flight from Heathrow Airport in London. But I also noticed something in the waiting lounge at the airport in New York that I attributed to racism. All the janitors and porters I saw were black. I knew about racism in the United States when I was still in Tanzania, and this only confirmed what I had suspected, blacks doing all the "dirty" work, and given menial jobs, while whites got the best and highest paying jobs.

Then it was my turn, after I had been in the United States for some weeks, to have a taste of racism in a very direct and personal way. That was the incident at LaGuardia Airport in New York City in December when I was getting ready to catch the plane to Washington, D.C. After being subjected to all kinds of indignities, being patted down and asked all sorts of questions, I was finally allowed to get on the plane and arrived in Washington where I was picked up from the airport by Anthony Ferguson, the chap from Trinidad who came to Tanzania earlier that year, with his friend Wilbur.

I happened to be in Washington D.C., not long after Tanzania's independence day, December 9, and members of the Caribbean association had just finished celebrating the anniversary in a spirit of Pan-African solidarity and strong identification with Africa. They even had Tanzania's national flag on display in the house where they used to hold meetings. It was our 11th independence anniversary since the attainment of sovereign status by Tanganyika on December 9, 1961, marking the end of British colonial rule in one of the continent's largest countries.

I was also invited to Howard University by the members of the Caribbean association, including Valerie who lived on campus, where the students I met showed great interest in Africa and felt they had strong bonds with their ancestral homeland.

So, not only did I operate within Pan-African circles right from the time I arrived in the United States; most of the people I interacted with were also very knowledgeable about Africa. For example, I remember when I went to the University of Oklahoma in Norman in 1974, intending to transfer there, I met a Jamaican professor who knew a lot about my country Tanzania and its policies including *ujamaa*. He also knew a lot about President Julius Nyerere.

Talking to him was no different from talking to a Tanzanian in Tanzania who knew about our country as an insider. And as a former journalist in Tanzania, I was pretty knowledgeable about my country and was able to discuss serious subjects with him concerning my country's policies. He also strongly identified with Africa and was therefore the type of person who, like many other Pan-Africanists I met in the United States, would not have liked to hear people saying bad things about the continent, reinforcing stereotypes about black people as members of an inferior race.

Still, through all the years I have lived in the United States, I have met many people who are very ignorant and prejudiced against Africa. I even met some in my first months in America, and many more through the years. And the American media has played a critical role in reinforcing those notions and stereotypes, twisting and slanting the truth about Africa, instead of educating the American public as much as they do about other countries, especially European countries.

Africa is either entirely ignored or smeared. I have seen it on American television and I have read about it in American newspapers and magazines including some of the most influential ones such as *The New York Times* and *The Washington Post*, liberal papers supposedly sympathetic towards blacks and Africa; *The Wall Street Journal*, a conservative paper; *Time* and *Newsweek* magazines and others.

It is true that in general liberal newspapers such as *The New York Times*, *The Washington Post*, the *Los Angeles Times*, the *Detroit Free Press* and others provide "better" coverage than conservative papers such as *The Wall Street Journal* and *The Washington Times* do. Still, there is a tendency by both conservative and liberal newspapers and other publications, as well as other media outlets, to portray Africa in a negative light most of the time. And this fits in perfectly with the preconceived notions and prejudiced views of millions of Americans, especially white Americans, they already have about this "Dark Continent," Africa. I have witnessed all that. And I am not alone.

It also has been the experience of other Africans studying or living in the United States, a country whose people, especially white Americans - not all of them but a very large number of them - are so prejudiced against Africa or harbor such racist and stereotypical views about blacks, and are so blind to reality as it relates to black people that they don't even know or don't want to accept the fact that even their own great nation, this predominantly white nation of immigrants from Europe, also *colonized* Africans just like their kith-and-kin, Europeans, did. The only difference is that instead of colonizing Africans in Africa, they took Africans away in chains and colonized them on American soil where they worked for more than three hundred years without being paid a penny for their labor. As Malcolm X said, "we worked from can't see in the morning to can't see in the evening without being paid a dime."

And as Ezekiel Makunike, a student from Zambia, formerly the British colony of Northern Rhodesia just across the border from my home region of Mbeya in the southwestern part of the Southern Highlands of Tanzania, who went to Syracuse University in the late sixties and later became the director of information in the government of Zimbabwe under President Robert Mugabe, stated in his article, "Out of Africa: Western Media Stereotypes Shape Images" in *Media & Values*: *Global Communication*: *For the Powerful or the People?* in Winter 1993:

"As a graduate student just arrived from Zambia to study at Syracuse University in 1968-9, I developed the habit of scanning the local papers for news from my home continent.

90

It was a pretty futile search. I was increasingly dismayed at the near-total lack of news from any part of Africa being presented to Syracuse readers. I also soon discovered that the little African news that occasionally found the light of day and trickled into the *Syracuse Herald and Journal* was almost always negative. This inspired me to spend some of my free time embarking on a more serious investigation of the news selection.

I requested permission from the news departments of those two daily newspapers to glean through their wastepaper baskets for telex sheets from wire services containing stories transmitted from Africa. I conducted this search for most of an entire week. While indeed not much was offered by the news services, I was nevertheless surprised to find that much of the little that came in was either 'killed' or simply spiked for a more suitable publication date that never came.

When I asked an editor to explain these decisions, he told me that stories on Africa are routinely ignored because of a presumed lack of reader interest. 'You see,' he said, 'America does not know Africa well. It never had a colony on that continent. Thus, unless the story has a strong human interest potential, there is no point in using it, since no one will read it.'

Of course, the editor was both creating a self-fulfilling prophecy and ignoring an obvious fact. The prophecy was simple: White Americans would never become aware of Africa unless they could learn enough about it to be interested, a process the media has a lot to do with.

**American Colonialism**

The fact, at once more complicated and highly relevant to contemporary events, was this: American colonialism against Africans was practiced in the American South in the form of hundreds of years of slavery and second-class citizenship. At the time - the late '60s - millions of descendants of those slaves (over 12 percent of the US population) were beginning to rediscover their African roots. Many of them were (and are still) highly interested in events in Africa. Their history and African background has much to do with current events in the United States.

The 1960s period of my study also coincided with the height of Cold War politics, with the United States then heavily involved in the Vietnam War. Africa was not of the highest concern in the super-power politics of the time. Nevertheless, news from Africa seemed essential to forming a complete picture of important happenings in the world, and this was lacking.

About the same time a lengthy newspaper account of an official visit to Africa by Chou En-Lai, then prime minister of the People's Republic of China, appeared in a major paper. The Chinese had promised technical assistance for the construction of a railway line between central Zambia and the Tanzanian seaport of Dar es Salaam on the Indian Ocean in southeast Africa. It read something like this:

'Communist China has promised to build a railway line from the black-ruled and land-locked Republic of Zambia to the port of Dar es Salaam, capital of socialist Tanzania. This is meant to reduce dependency on trade routes with and through their southern neighbors, white-ruled Rhodesia (now Zimbawe) and South Africa. The two black-ruled African countries train and harbor terrorists fighting to overthrow these white-ruled governments.'

The implication was that Tanzania and Zambia were being taken for a ride because China didn't possess the necessary technology to execute such a feat of engineering. The promise was seen as simply an example of Communist propaganda.

A few years later, after I had returned to Africa and become the director of the Pan-African Literature Centre in Kitwe, Zambia, I was reminded of this conclusion. My journalism students and I attended the inaugural ceremony of the Tanzania-Zambia Railway Line (Tan Zam Railway). We actually were passengers on the initial trip of this 'will never-be-built' line, riding safely over 1,000 kilometers from Kapiri Mposhi near Kabwe in central Zambia to the seaside in Dar es Salaam. With the help of the 'technically backward' Communist Chinese, the feat had actually been completed well ahead of schedule!

Influenced first by colonialism and then by Cold War politics, this contemptuous tone has long shaped and fashioned Western media perceptions of Africa. As I learned very quickly in the US, for American readers or viewers to be interested, news out of

Africa must be negative. It must conform to the traditional stereotypes in its spotlight on grotesque and sensational events. It must show misery, corruption, mismanagement, starvation, primitive surroundings and, as in the case of Somalia, chaos and outright anarchy.

Foreign correspondents in African capitals and their superiors in the media gate-keeping chain seem to have these perceptions ingrained in them. From newsgathering in Africa to publication and broadcast thousands of miles away, stories about Africa are looked at with these negative lenses. Even more unfortunately, reporters and editors with a broader vision run the risk of having their stories disbelieved and unused. Little wonder they learn to toe the expected line.

This dynamic explains why the life of Africa's varied and diverse countries is missing. We hear about famines and coups, but not the rejuvenation of its cities and the cultural vitality of its village life; about oppression and massacres, but not education, economic self-help and political development; about poaching and habitat destruction, but not ongoing active efforts at conservation, reforestation and environmental awareness.

Most telling of all, in Somalia and elsewhere, news reports show outside white people helping black people. They never show black people helping themselves.

As a journalist I understand that 'news' is still defined as a usually negative departure from the norm. I also recognize that in the eternal media race for larger circulations and higher ratings, profits and the bottom line dominate concerns about values and ethics.

As in Somalia, the 'hit-and-run' mentality of Western media makes it easy to briefly light up trouble spots, while the years of exploitation and deterioration that produced them are left in the dark. The 'here today, gone tomorrow' nature of much of international reporting, with star newspersons briefly crowding each other at media feeding troughs, then jetting on to the next venue, doesn't help.

By definition such journalists know little of the language and less of the cultures they cover. They certainly never appreciate the subtleties and nuances of local history and interactions that take years to learn. They are neither accustomed nor equipped to observe, understand or explain developmental situations that may change slowly over time.

As a Zambian, my observations are necessarily 'out of Africa.' But these observations of Western media shortcomings could be applied to many parts of the developing world. Admittedly, the negative patterns of coverage I've described were often conditioned by colonialism and Cold War politics. Unfortunately, they reinforced a pattern of ignorance and distortion that has not changed with the changing political systems. In the case of this news blackout at least, it is still very much a dark continent."

The image of Africa as the "Dark Continent" and living hell on earth, as many people especially racists see it, has always persisted and left an indelible mark on the minds of a very large number of people; I remember Byron de La Beckwith, a white supremacist who shot and killed African American civil rights leader Medgar Evers in Jackson, Mississippi, in June 1963, saying he used to scare and discipline white children by telling them: "I will send you to hell in Africa!"

That is the image of Africa among many people in America, especially whites, mainly because of ignorance but also because of racism. A very large number of whites - "we are the most advanced race," as conservative writer and political pundit William F. Buckley Jr., put it years ago, causing quite a stir even in conservative circles - and many other people including Asians see us, black people or black Africans, as members of "the lesser breed" and being on the lowest rung of the evolutionary ladder; a sentiment that was also forcefully articulated by Japanese Prime Minister Yasuhiro Nakasone in 1986 when he said the United States was getting behind in education and economic performance because of the low intelligence of black Americans; who are nothing but Africans themselves, only born in America. A large number of Japanese agreed with what he said but did not like the way his comments smeared Japan. He should have said the same thing, but in a diplomatic way, or should have used some coded language, was their attitude.

But it is not just in Japan where many people believe that we blacks are not as intelligent as other human beings; there are even those, in many countries, who don't even consider us to be full human beings in many fundamental respects - in terms of mental faculties, genetic endowment, and so on. Even in the United States itself where the Japanese prime minister said blacks are a liability because of their very low intelligence, the vast majority of whites believe that black people are less intelligent than members of other races, according to polls conducted through the years.

And publication of *The Bell Curve* in March 1994, a book by two white conservative scholars, Richard Herrnstein and Charles Murray, in which they claim black people have lower IQs than whites and Asians as well as people of others races because of their weak genes, only reinforced such racist notions with pseudoscientific underpinnings. The charts in the book, relying on data from a number of studies, show that on average black Americans have an IQ of 85, which is near the retarded level. A score of 100 on IQ tests signifies normal or average intelligence. Black people in Africa are in even worse shape. Their average IQ score is 70, which is at the retarded level. It is even lower, below the retarded level, in many black African countries where the average score on IQ tests is 60. Among those with such low IQs are many black Africans with secondary school education.

Those are some of the findings published in *The Bell Curve*. The book became an instant seller for obvious reasons, with millions of whites and others rubbing their hands with satisfaction, gleefully saying: "See? I told you so! They aren't too swift upstairs. You know who!"

But that is only part of the image of Africa, and of Africans in diaspora, of course, as less intelligent people. The other and main part is that of the continent itself as a hopeless continent teeming with wild animals, full of disease and inhabited by primitive savages many - if not most - of whom run around naked, preferring their natural dress; in spite of overwhelming evidence that most Africans wear more than just their skin.

I have been confronted with such stereotypes about our continent through the years and have responded accordingly. But most of the time I have been spared the agony and anguish because of the kind of company I have had. I have not been around very ignorant or openly prejudiced people most of the time I have lived in the United States. The people I have dealt with

95

usually know enough about Africa to dispel such stereotypes. And many prejudiced ones have been discreet enough to hide their prejudice.

Still, many others in general out there are just ignorant, sometimes plain stupid, or racist or simply prejudiced against Africa, for whatever reason, even if they are black themselves; for example those who don't like Africa or who have turned against Africans because of their bad experience with some Africans in the United States.

The stereotypical view of Africa may be a product of pure ignorance in the minds of many people. But such ignorance, and even among those who know better, and all these stereotypes are reinforced by the media including liberal news papers such as *The New York Times*. Liberals are supposed to be friends of "Negroes." Right? Their friendship was probably best demonstrated in the United States during the civil rights movement. And *The New York Times* was one of the papers black civil rights leaders and their white liberal supporters counted on to report accurately on what was going on.

But it didn't happen that way all the time. And it hasn't happened that way all the time in the case of Africa. As Milton Allimadi, a black journalist who worked as a *New York Times* stringer stated in his article "Inventing Africa" in *The New York Times* in 2003:

"When *New York Times* reporters such as Lloyd Garrison in the 1960s and Joseph Lelyveld in the 1980s filed news stories from Africa, editors at the *Times* routinely fabricated scenes and manufactured quotes for their articles. In some instances, the foreign editor colluded with the reporter to manufacture scenes that they believed would conform to the racist stereotypical biases that U.S. readers had come to expect in reports from Africa.

When I brought these examples of racist journalistic concoctions to the attention of *New York Times* editors more than 10 years ago, I was virtually ignored. That's why recent assertions by *Times* editors that (black) reporter Jayson Blair's concoctions and fabrications reflected a 'low point' in the newspaper's 152-year history (5/11/03) were disingenuous. A much lower point had been reached in the 1960s, when the newspaper began covering Africa consistently, as I discovered when I dug up documents from the *Times'* archives in 1992.

At the time, I was a Columbia journalism grad student researching the evolution of the paper's African coverage. As nationalism swept across Africa in the early '60s, *The New York Times* sent Homer Bigart, the famous two-time Pulitzer-winning reporter, to cover the transition. In Ghana, Bigart wasn't impressed by independence hero Kwame Nkrumah, as a letter he sent to foreign editor Emanuel Freedman in January 1960 reveals:

'I'm afraid I cannot work up any enthusiasm for the emerging republics. The politicians are either crooks or mystics. Dr. Nkrumah is a Henry Wallace in burnt cork. I vastly prefer the primitive bush people. After all, cannibalism may be the logical antidote to this population explosion everyone talks about.'

When I first discovered Bigart's letter, I assumed that--even with the prevalent racism of the time--it reflected the ranting of one racist reporter. Then as I read the reports that Bigart filed from Africa that purported to be straight news reporting, I found a near-perfect correlation between the language he used in his letters and the feelings he expressed in the purported 'news' reports. Bigart's favorite terms in reference to Africans included 'barbaric,' 'macabre,' "grotesque' and 'savage.'

Typical of his prose was an article published in the *Times* on January 31, 1960, under the headline 'Barbarian Cult Feared in Nigeria.' Focusing on a reported incident of communal violence, Bigart assumed a jaunty and derogative tone, writing: 'A pocket of barbarism still exists in eastern Nigeria despite some success by the regional government in extending a crust of civilization over the tribe of the pagan Izi.' He went on:

'A momentary lapse into cannibalism marked the closing days of 1959, when two men killed in a tribal clash were partly consumed by enemies in the Cross River country below Obubra. Garroting was the society's favored method of execution. None of the victims was eaten, at least not by society members. Less lurid but equally effective ways were found to dispose of them. According to the police, about 26 were weighed with stones and timber and thrown into flooded rivers. No trace has been found of these bodies. A few were buried in ant heaps. But most became human fertilizer for the yam crops.'

97

## 'Where else but the *Times*?'

Foreign editor Freedman shared Bigart's contempt for Africans and the assignment. In a letter to his African explorer, dated March 4, 1960, Freedman wrote:

'This is just a note to say hello and to tell you how much your peerless prose from the badlands is continuing to give us and your public. By now you must be American journalism's leading expert on sorcery, witchcraft, cannibalism and all the other exotic phenomena indigenous to darkest Africa. All this and nationalism too! Where else but in *The New York Times* can you get all this for a nickel?'

When the savages were nowhere to be found, Bigart and Freedman took matters into their own hands. As independence neared for what was then Belgian Congo, Bigart complained to Freedman in a May 29, 1960 letter from Leopoldville, which is now Kinshasa: 'I had hoped to find pygmies voting and interview them on the meaning of independence but they were all in the woods. I did see several lions, however, and from Usumbura I sent a long mailer about the Watutsi giants.' (Usumbura is a Burundi city now known as Bujumbura.)

The Belgian Congo had experienced the most bloody and brutal history of European colonial rule and exploitation in Africa. During the rule of King Leopold II, an estimated 10 million or more Africans were exterminated and countless more permanently maimed or disfigured, all in the quest for wealth. African slave laborers who did not deliver their designated quota of ivory and rubber had their hands severed, to motivate other slackers. Yet Bigart and Freedman's utmost concern was to find pygmies to malign.

When he failed to find pygmies, Bigart did the next best thing: He concocted them, as indicated by his article published in the *Times* on June 5, 1960 under the derisive headline, 'Magic of Freedom Enchants Congolese.' The article began: 'As the hour of freedom from Belgian rule nears, 'In-de-pen-dence' is being chanted by Congolese all over this immense land, even by pygmies in the forest.'

'Independence is an abstraction not easily grasped by

Congolese and they are seeking concrete interpretations,' Bigart added, before continuing to denigrate the pygmies. 'To the forest pygmy independence means a little more salt, a little more beer.'

## Continued concoctions

Was this some aberrant episode between Bigart and Freedman? Hardly. The *Times* tolerated concoctions so long as the newspaper could get away with it. Even when *Times* reporters complained, editors continued to insert concocted scenes and quotes into their articles.

Consider the case of Lloyd M. Garrison, a descendant of the great American abolitionist, who was the *Times*' first West African correspondent during the 1960s. Garrison covered the Nigerian civil war, but was expelled by the military regime for alleged bias in favor of the Biafran secessionists.

In a letter from Nigeria dated June 5, 1967, Garrison complained bitterly that 'tribal' scenarios had been inserted into the edited version of his story, which had been published on May 31, 1967 in the newspaper: 'The reference to 'small pagan tribes dressed in leaves' is slightly misleading and could, because of its startling quality, give the reader the impression there are a lot of tribes running around half naked,' Garrison wrote to the foreign desk. He protested the numerous uses of the derogative term 'tribes' in his story, and added: 'Tribesmen connote the grass-leaves image. Plus tribes equals primitive, which in a country like Nigeria just doesn't fit, and is offensive to African readers who know damn well what unwashed American and European readers think when they stumble on the word.' Garrison noted that the insertion 'invites the image of savages dancing around the fire.'

Editorial insertions of stereotypes and fabrications into a *Times* reporter's copy extended at least into the 1980s. Consider the case of Lelyveld, who completed two tours as a correspondent in South Africa. In the '60s he was expelled by Pretoria for suspected socialist leanings; he returned as the *Times*' correspondent during the 1980s.

In December 1982 (12/19/82, 12/26/82), Lelyveld wrote a pair of articles about South Africa's segregated education system and its denial of adequate funding to black schools. Editors watered down his reporting, prompting Lelyveld to fire off an angry complaint to foreign editor Craig Whitney. In one letter, dated January 6, 1983, Lelyveld complained that 'virtually all the original reporting' conducted over a one-month period had been omitted. In one story, the subject of white control and racial hierarchy in the education system was completely deleted, he complained. The printed version of the article was like 'a salami sandwich without the salami, just slabs of stale bread'--or, 'if you prefer a baseball image, the wind up without the pitch, in other words a balk.'

When fictitious 'officials' were inserted into another one of his stories, Lelyveld was livid, as indicated in a letter dated April 18, 1983, which he sent to Whitney:

'I wrote the following sentence: 'The idea of a referendum among blacks was never considered for the obvious reason that it would be overwhelmingly defeated.' That became: 'Officials made it clear that the idea of a referendum among blacks . . . etc.' To what officials did the rewrite person talk? How does he or she know they made it clear? This exact phrase has been written in my copy before. Officials make damn little clear     here.'

Lelyveld later wrote *Move Your Shadow*, a sensitive book outlining the corrosiveness of apartheid, which was awarded the Pulitzer Prize. He later became managing editor and retired as executive editor in 2001, before coming back to serve as a transitional editor in the wake of the Blair fiasco.

## 'Occasionally distinguished'

While one can understand why *Times* publisher Arthur Ochs Sulzberger Jr. and the newspaper's top editors would prefer the public to believe that Blair's transgressions are uniquely aberrant, the evidence indicates otherwise. Moreover, Sulzberger and Lelyveld certainly can't pretend they are unaware of this research.

In January 1992, the *Columbia Journalism Review* (*CJR*) agreed to publish excerpts of my master's paper about the *Times'* African coverage. After *CJR* backed out, I obtained a copy of the edited version of my paper. To my astonishment, this is what *CJR* editors had inserted on my behalf before rejecting the article:

'Recently, the *Times* granted me access to its archives,

including correspondences from the 1950s, when the paper sent Bigart to Africa on a temporary assignment. After studying the archival material, I interviewed several present and former *Times* reporters. The following excerpts from that material and from lengthy interviews are not intended as an indictment of the *Times*- -whose African coverage has occasionally been distinguished--but as a means of highlighting a problem that all news organizations need to address.'

Presumably some *CJR* editors feared how the *Times* would react; after all, *CJR* was a possible beneficiary of largesse from the *Times'* foundation, and many editors and reporters hope to end up at the *Times*. So I did the *CJR* editors a favor and sent a copy of my paper to Sulzberger. Eventually I received a letter from Joseph Lelyveld, then the managing editor, on behalf of Sulzberger. He conceded that my research had unearthed articles with 'crude and ugly' language. Yet there was no offer to publish corrections. Later, when I proposed to publish an op-ed article in the *Times* to shed light on its ugly past with respect to Africa coverage, the op-ed editor--Howell Raines--didn't respond.

This February, I published *The Heart of Darkness: How White Writers Created the Racist Image of Africa*, a book that details Western newspapers' history of demonizing Africans, including the *Times'* racist fabrications. I sent copies to Sulzberger and to other *Times* editors before Jayson Blair's lies burst into the limelight. I still await a response from the *Times* and an offer to acknowledge the wrongs perpetrated against Africa."

The stereotypical image of Africa is fostered even by some members of the academic community They are supposed to be enlightened, but that does not mean that some of them are not racist; probably many of them are, although they say they are liberal, hence friends of blacks; more than 90 percent of the professors in the United States identify themselves as liberal. But that does not mean they all like blacks or care about Africa.

I remember one of the professors, Gould, who taught international relations at Wayne State University in the seventies - I don't know if he was a liberal or not - who described Africans as primitive with hardly any knowledge about the institutions of government and democracy, let alone the international system. I was in his class but not for long. And had I stayed in there, we probably would have clashed many times because of his stereotypical views about Africa. I am sure other professors felt the same way even if some of them did not openly express their racist and paternalistic views about black people and our continent.

Stereotypical views of Africa are also common in the political arena, harbored even by some of the most "enlightened" leaders. White conservatives are, of course, notorious for being anti-black and anti-African. And they hardly conceal their feelings. Even many black American conservatives - who don't even want to be called African Americans - are also known to be anti-African, but for a different reason or different reasons which have nothing to do with race. They are black themselves but don't identify with Africa as much as their black liberal counterparts do. They are satisfied with just being Americans, nothing else.

But even white liberal leaders of national stature have been known to make fun of Africa and Africans. I remember, for example, when US Senator Ernest Hollings from South Carolina made fun of Africans in 1993 saying African leaders go to international conferences so that they can "get a square meal," the only time they get the chance to eat well. As he bluntly put it when talking to reporters: "Rather than eat each other, they'd just come up [to Switzerland] and get a good square meal." That is why they liked to attend trade conferences in Europe, he said. His remarks provoked furious responses from a number of African American leaders including Randall Robinson, the head of TransAfrica.

Earlier in the 1980s, American Secretary of State Alexander Haig who briefly served under President Ronald Reagan made fun of the Nigerian vice president when he visited Washington D.C. Reporters said he made fun of him and his entourage, and of their African attire, tapping on the table with his fingers to produce an African drum rhythm while laughing. The implication was obvious.

In the 1970s, Vice President Nelson Rockefeller was reported to have made fun of black US Senator Edward Brooke from Massachusetts saying had the senator been born in the jungle in Liberia, he wouldn't be where he was then.

Those are just a few examples of the way many Americans see us. We are nothing in this world as Africans, especially as black people. We come from "the jungle," and we belong in "the jungle." We were born "primitive," and we will die "primitive." Other examples of this stereotypical view of Africa are even more offensive. And they all, including the mild or less offensive ones, perpetuate a negative image of Africa that is transmitted from generation to generation. Ignorance plays a major role, but not in all cases.

Many Americans know more about Africa now than they did in the sixties and seventies, and may be even in the eighties. The large number of African immigrants and students in the United States through the years has had a profound impact on this, correcting misconceptions about Africa so prevalent in America. But a very large number of Americans still see Africa as a monolithic whole in spite of the continent's complexity and diversity; a perception still reinforced by ignorance and racism, and by the arrogance of the United States, a significant number of whose citizens see their country as the center of the universe towards which everything else gravitates; no need to learn or know about other countries or cultures, they are the ones who should learn about us, is the attitude. And in the hierarchy of nations, or groups of nations, Africa ranks last in the minds of most Americans, a very large number of whom continue to see it as just an amorphous whole, one big place in total darkness. Out of sight, out of mind.

It takes a catastrophe, such as war or famine or a locust invasion of biblical proportions, to thrust Africa into the international spotlight and may be even into the conscience of some people. In the 1980s, it was the famine in Ethiopia and other African countries which did it. In the nineties, it was the genocide in Rwanda which put that small African country on the world map. Most people had never even heard of Rwanda, or the Hutu - the Tutsi have been known for quite sometime - and who as perpetrators of the genocide only reinforced stereotypes of African tribes as savages routinely slaughtering each other. As President Nyerere once said, the only time you hear about peace in Africa is when it is broken.

Then in the early part of the twentieth-first century, especially

103

in 2004, it was the locusts which focused some attention on Africa as have civil wars and other conflicts raging across the continent for decades.

But it is also this kind of image of Africa which even some of the strongest defenders of Africa, outside Africa, see on their television screens and in their newspapers in western countries and elsewhere around the world, with appalling statistics: up to 2 million people dead in Biafra during the Nigerian civil war in the late sixties; more than 3 million dead in civil wars in Sudan since 1983, without even counting those who perished since the war started in 1955; another 3 million dead in civil wars, mostly in eastern Congo in only three years or so since August 1998; 1 million dead in the Angolan civil war from 1975 to 2002; another 1 million dead in the civil war in Mozambique from 1986 to 1992; tens of thousands of men, women and children left helpless with chopped-off ears, lips, limbs, noses and even buttocks in Sierra Leone, brutal tactics employed by the rebels of the Revolutionary United Front (RUF) during the civil war in the 1990s.

And we are not yet done: at least 400,000 people dead in civil wars in Liberia and Sierra Leone in the 1990s alone; starving children and women, a common sight in several African countries through the decades; genocide and rape victims in the Dafur region in the Sudan and about which the rest of the world, including the UN, couldn't care less while the victims are crying for help; burnt villages and children being used as soldiers and sex slaves by the rebels in northern Uganda, as the rest of the world looks the other way; children roasted alive in eastern Congo in 2004 in tribal conflicts between the Hema and the Lendu, and this being only one example of brutality and grisly murders, while the Congolese themselves and the rest of Africa do nothing to stop the carnage; women tortured and raped in the same region and elsewhere in the Congo; an entire nation, Somalia, dissolved in anarchy.

This is the image of Africa even we ourselves, Africans, cannot dismiss as a figment of the imagination or a product of racist stereotypes. It is real, it is shameful, and it is painful. And we can do something about it if we stop fighting, and if we stop hating each other and killing each other. Foreigners are not going to do that for us. Our enemies only capitalize on that to exploit us and reinforce the image of Africa as a hopeless continent, the lost continent, and other distinctive appellations that have been used in different contexts to identify and define us as a people.

Still, that does not justify the denigration of our continent and the insults that have been hurled at us and heaped on us by racists through the centuries. They want us and the rest of the world to believe that Africa has no history, except of cannibalism and tribal wars and naked savages dancing around fires with their spears, bows, and packs of arrows on their backs. We are told that Africa has no civilization except of the rudimentary kind, and even that, nothing but a carbon copy of Europe, and crudely duplicated.

It has also been routinely taught that Africa has no systematic knowledge to speak of, no wisdom, not even common sense among the "primitive natives" except simple sayings and proverbs which amount to nothing - despite their philosophical profundity the European mind "endowed" with depth perception has not been able to fathom. The litany goes on and on; on and on.

It has never occurred to these critics, endowed as they are with 'powerful" mental faculties, that what they say about Africa does not even stand up to scrutiny, is an insult to common sense, and has nothing to do with reality as a whole on this massive land mass. If there are pockets of savagery in Africa, there are pockets of savagery in America, Europe and elsewhere. And empirical evidence demonstrates that, as I have pointed out time and again in my conversations with a number of Americans.

Africa is a huge, complex continent. Africans are no more cannibalistic than other people are, including some whites whose rituals include cannibalism. There are no whole tribes in Africa that are cannibals; otherwise there would be no one left amongst themselves or their neighbors. They only have individuals with aberrant behavior and abhorrent conduct just like white tribes - ethnic groups as they prefer to call themselves - do.

Talk about savagery. Who has fought the bloodiest wars in the history of mankind? Africans? The American civil war was the bloodiest conflict in world history before World War I. It was fought by whites, and to save their union, not to free African slaves. Millions and millions of people, about 8 million, perished in World War I to satisfy greed among the imperial nations, white nations, who had already conquered the world. In World War II, even more people perished; for the same reason: greed among white nations. More than 43 million people died worldwide. They were really European wars but, because Europeans conquered the world, they dragged everybody else into these conflicts and called them World Wars - which had nothing to do with us, except our land and resources Europeans grabbed from us when they conquered us.

And talk about bloodthirsty leadership. It is true that Idi Amin was wicked and brutal and presided over a blood-soaked regime under which no fewer than 500,000 people were killed during his eight-year reign of terror. But what about Hitler? Was he an African? The six million Jews he exterminated was only the tip of the iceberg of what he did and intended to do. Millions more perished in other countries because of his madness which his admirers still glorify as patriotism.

A number of Americans have brought up Idi Amin in our conversations deliberately to tarnish the image of the entire continent as if he is the only leader Africa has ever produced, and as if he was president of the whole continent and not of just one country out of a total of 53. When whites have brought this up, I have responded accordingly and brought up Hilter; and Stalin; and Mussolini, to name only a few, none of whom, to my knowledge, was African let alone black.

The image of the United States itself is not a very good one, either, as an imperial power, dictating terms to other countries and acting as the world's policeman. Yet, Americans never ask themselves who said or how many countries decided that the United States should be the global sheriff. It is true that the United States has quite a reputation as the citadel of democracy. Yet, within this citadel of democracy, in this land of liberty and equality, people of African descent and other minorities have not been treated fairly by the white majority or as equal citizens for no reason other than that they are not white. Still, we Africans are always being lectured on the virtues of democracy by the leaders of the very same country where racism remains a major problem. It doesn't take a genius to know that racism is incompatible with democracy.

So, just as we Africans have trouble with our image, partly because of our own fault but mainly because of what outsiders portray us to be, Americans also have trouble with theirs since the founding their republic, the first since Rome. If America was indeed founded on the twin ideals of liberty and equality, and only on that, the world is still waiting for answers to a few simple questions: Why did this great land of liberty and equality enslave millions of Africans, denying them liberty and equality in the land of the free? What did African slaves do? Who laid the foundation for this republic which became the richest and most prosperous in the history of mankind? And who reaped the benefits?

President John F. Kennedy said in a speech in 1963, not long before he was assassinated, that the Emancipation Proclamation was issued and signed in 1863; yet, "one hundred years later, the Negro still is not free." More than forty years after Kennedy gave that speech, many Americans, black and white, say blacks are still not free, because of racism. And the reason is simple, very simple: It is impossible to have equality where racism exists. Racism is anti-democratic, and inhumane. And that is the image, a tarnished image of the citadel of democracy, America has to deal with.

We Africans do, indeed, have trouble with our image smeared in blood because of the wars on our continent. But our American critics, among many others of course, should also remember that even their own civil war, the American Civil War, was fought not to free the slaves, African slaves, but to save the union. Lincoln said if he could save the union half-free, he would do it. And if he could save it by maintaining slavery, he would do that also. He ended slavery to deprive the south of its economic base in order to force it to surrender and end secession, not to free the slaves. And that is a fundamental reality that must be acknowledged if America is to enhance its image as an embodiment of democratic ideals cherished around the world, including Africa, the so-called Dark Continent.

On this huge, dark land mass, it is said that we are busy slaughtering each other. But out of 53 countries, how many are at war, at this writing in 2005? How many have collapsed or been consumed in a conflagration of rage and hate? How many are teetering on the brink of collapse? Most are not.

So, let's talk about war, especially tribal wars. We have them, yes, just like America waged war against her own citizens of African descent for centuries since the founding of the nation. She killed them during slavery. And she killed them after slavery for one reason, and one reason only: They were children of Africa, hence inferior beings. Klansmen even rejoiced at eating the flesh of the "Negro." As one Ku Klux Klan poem says:

No rations have I
but the flesh of man,
and love niggers best.
Eaten legions,
still go hungry.

All this may have been intended to instill fear in blacks. But it may not be far-fetched to say that some Klansmen and other hate-mongers may indeed have tasted the flesh of the "Negro," even if they did not feast. We may never know for sure, but nothing can be ruled out. However, this is certain: hundreds of bodies of black men, and even black women, decorated trees in the south during the lynching era.

Many of them were roasted alive, and lynching parties were festive occasions attracting hundreds and even thousands of people from miles around. They even caught trains to go to lynching parties, complete with refreshments, and attended by some pastors, men of the gospel. They also brought their children to poison their minds so that they can start at early age to hate "Negroes" and see them as inferior beings; an article of faith that has been transmitted from one generation to the next among millions of whites unto this day.

Other atrocities have been committed against blacks, with impunity, through the centuries in the land of the free and the home of the brave, prompting the Black Nation of Islam leader Elijah Muhammad to say he had seen enough evil of the white man to last him 26,000 years. And as Malcolm X said, "The white man is in no moral position to accuse anyone of hate."

While many Americans may say all that is in past, there are no more lynchings, the rest of the world knows that is not true in all cases. True enough, lynchings are no longer the problem it once was years ago. But they are not gone forever. A young black man was lynched in Alabama in 1981, his body strung up a tree in the city. James Byrd was dragged to death tied behind a truck in

Jasper, Texas, in June 1998. And many racist murders, which amount to lynchings, still go on today. Most of the victims are black, children of Africa. That is raw-naked racism in the citadel of democracy, America, tarnishing its image which cannot be burnished by professions of democracy to the rest of the world, including Africa the ancestral homeland of African Americans, while some of its own citizens don't enjoy full citizenship rights equal to whites simply because they are black.

There is no question that the image of Africa among Americans and others is further tarnished by us because of our inability or unwillingness to do what we should do: stop fighting. Yes, we fight. But so do others. Many Americans, Europeans who are their kith-and-kin and other people, talk a lot about our tribal wars, especially after the Rwandan genocide. Fine. We can talk about tribal wars. We don't deny we have them. But what about European tribal wars? Who talks about them? And why don't whites call them tribal wars when whites fight and kill each other?

What about the ethnic conflicts in Kosovo, in Bosnia, and other Balkan countries? What about the religious tribal wars in Northern Ireland between Catholics and Protestants? Basque nationalists and their brethren, whose identity is unique in the region and who are not related to any of their neighbors - in France and Spain - are no less of a tribe than the Zulu, the Shona, the Ashanti and other African groups are. If they are a nation, the Zulu are also a nation. So are the Ashanti, the Shona, the Bakongo, the Igbo, the Yoruba and other Africans. And they are waging war, a tribal war, against other tribes, fellow Spaniards belonging to different ethnic groups, even if they are entitled to self-determination as a people and as a separate entity with its own unique identity.

Still, they are nothing but tribes, all of them, like African tribes which should also be called ethnic groups if European and American tribes - the Serbs, the Irish, for example - are called or call themselves ethnic groups. Yet, "civilized" people insist on making a distinction between us and them, separating Africans - tribesmen - from the rest of humanity as if we are a sub-species of mankind.

No other people have been so stereotyped, and so insulted, like us. And no other people have been so maligned. And I have personally been insulted a number of times as an African through the years in the United States. I was even asked by a young white doctor - she was probably around my age, 34 or 35 or younger - in the mid-1980s at a hospital in Grand Rapids, Michigan, if I knew what a computer was. I told her I did. She didn't seem to believe me at all. Being black was bad enough. That I was an African, a black African on top of that, only made things worse. I was the embodiment of Africa, ignorant, primitive Africa.

There are many people, especially whites, who are determined to perpetuate this negative image of Africa to justify their racism against blacks. And it didn't just start. As Chinua Achebe states in his essay, "An Image of Africa: Racism in Conrad's *Heart of Darkness*":

"In the fall of 1974 I was walking one day from the English Department at the University of Massachusetts to a parking lot. It was a fine autumn morning such as encouraged friendliness to passing strangers. Brisk youngsters were hurrying in all directions, many of them obviously freshmen in their first flush of enthusiasm.

An older man going the same way as I turned and remarked to me how very young they came these days. I agreed. Then he asked me if I was a student too. I said no, I was a teacher. What did I teach? African literature. Now that was funny, he said, because he knew a fellow who taught the same thing, or perhaps it was African history, in a certain Community College not far from here. It always surprised him, he went on to say, because he never had thought of Africa as having that kind of stuff, you know. By this time I was walking much faster. 'Oh well,' I heard him say finally, behind me: 'I guess I have to take your course to find out.'

A few weeks later I received two very touching letters from high school children in Yonkers, New York, who -- bless their teacher -- had just read *Things Fall Apart*. One of them was particularly happy to learn about the customs and superstitions of an African tribe.

I propose to draw from these rather trivial encounters rather heavy conclusions which at first sight might seem somewhat out of proportion to them. But only, I hope, at first sight.

The young fellow from Yonkers, perhaps partly on account of

his age but I believe also for much deeper and more serious reasons, is obviously unaware that the life of his own tribesmen in Yonkers, New York, is full of odd customs and superstitions and, like everybody else in his culture, imagines that he needs a trip to Africa to encounter those things.

The other person being fully my own age could not be excused on the grounds of his years. Ignorance might be a more likely reason; but here again I believe that something more willful than a mere lack of information was at work. For did not that erudite British historian and Regius Professor at Oxford, Hugh Trevor Roper, also pronounce that African history did not exist?

If there is something in these utterances more than youthful inexperience, more than a lack of factual knowledge, what is it? Quite simply it is the desire -- one might indeed say the need -- in Western psychology to set Africa up as a foil to Europe, as a place of negations at once remote and vaguely familiar, in comparison with which Europe's own state of spiritual grace will be manifest.

This need is not new; which should relieve us all of considerable responsibility and perhaps make us even willing to look at this phenomenon dispassionately.

I have neither the wish nor the competence to embark on the exercise with the tools of the social and biological sciences but more simply in the manner of a novelist responding to one famous book of European fiction: Joseph Conrad's *Heart of Darkness*, which better than any other work that I know displays that Western desire and need which I have just referred to. Of course there are whole libraries of books devoted to the same purpose but most of them are so obvious and so crude that few people worry about them today.

Conrad, on the other hand, is undoubtedly one of the great stylists of modern fiction and a good storyteller into the bargain. His contribution therefore falls automatically into a different class -- permanent literature -- read and taught and constantly evaluated by serious academics. *Heart of Darkness* is indeed so secure today that a leading Conrad scholar has numbered it 'among the half-dozen greatest short novels in the English language.' I will return to this critical opinion in due course because it may seriously modify my earlier suppositions about who may or may not be guilty in some of the matters I will now raise.

*Heart of Darkness* projects the image of Africa as 'the other world,' the antithesis of Europe and therefore of civilization, a place where man's vaunted intelligence and refinement are finally mocked by triumphant beastiality. The book opens on the River Thames, tranquil, resting, peacefully 'at the decline of day after ages of good service done to the race that peopled its banks.' But the actual story will take place on the River Congo, the very antithesis of the Thames. The River Congo is quite decidedly not a River Emeritus. It has rendered no service and enjoys no old-age pension. We are told that 'Going up that river was like traveling back to the earliest beginnings of the world.'

Is Conrad saying then that these two rivers are very different, one good, the other bad? Yes, but that is not the real point. It is not the differentness that worries Conrad but the lurking hint of kinship, of common ancestry. For the Thames too 'has been one of the dark places of the earth.' It conquered its darkness, of course, and is now in daylight and at peace. But if it were to visit its primordial relative, the Congo, it would run the terrible risk of hearing grotesque echoes of its own forgotten darkness, and falling victim to an avenging recrudescence of the mindless frenzy of the first beginnings.

These suggestive echoes comprise Conrad's famed evocation of the African atmosphere in *Heart of Darkness*. In the final consideration his method amounts to no more than a steady, ponderous, fake-ritualistic repetition of two antithetical sentences, one about silence and the other about frenzy. We can inspect samples of this on pages 36 and 37 of the present edition: a) 'It was the stillness of an implacable force brooding over an inscrutable intention' and b) 'The steamer toiled along slowly on the edge of a black and incomprehensible frenzy.' Of course there is a judicious change of adjective from time to time, so that instead of inscrutable, for example, you might have unspeakable, even plain mysterious, etc., etc.

The eagle-eyed English critic F. R. Leavis drew attention long ago to Conrad's 'adjectival insistence upon inexpressible and incomprehensible mystery.' That insistence must not be dismissed lightly, as many Conrad critics have tended to do, as a mere stylistic flaw; for it raises serious questions of artistic good faith. When a writer while pretending to record scenes, incidents and

112

their impact is in reality engaged in inducing hypnotic stupor in his readers through a bombardment of emotive words and other forms of trickery, much more has to be at stake than stylistic felicity.

Generally normal readers are well armed to detect and resist such under-hand activity. But Conrad chose his subject well -- one which was guaranteed not to put him in conflict with the psychological predisposition of his readers or raise the need for him to contend with their resistance. He chose the role of purveyor of comforting myths.

The most interesting and revealing passages in *Heart of Darkness* are, however, about people. I must crave the indulgence of my reader to quote almost a whole page from about the middle when representatives of Europe in a steamer going down the Congo encounter the denizens of Africa:

'We were wanderers on a prehistoric earth, on an earth that wore the aspect of an unknown planet. We could have fancied ourselves the first of men taking possession of an accursed inheritance, to be subdued at the cost of profound anguish and of excessive toil. But suddenly as we struggled round a bend there would be a glimpse of rush walls, of peaked grass-roofs, a burst of yells, a whirl of black limbs, a mass of hands clapping, of feet stamping, of bodies swaying, of eyes rolling under the droop of heavy and motionless foliage. The steamer toiled along slowly on the edge of a black and incomprehensible frenzy. The prehistoric man was cursing us, praying to us, welcoming us -- who could tell? We were cut off from the comprehension of our surroundings; we glided past like phantoms, wondering and secretly appalled, as sane men would be before an enthusiastic outbreak in a madhouse. We could not understand because we were too far and could not remember, because we were travelling in the night of first ages, of those ages that are gone, leaving hardly a sign -- and no memories.

The earth seemed unearthly. We are accustomed to look upon the shackled form of a conquered monster, but there -- there you could look at a thing monstrous and free. It was unearthly and the men were .... No they were not inhuman. Well, you know that was the worst of it -- this suspicion of their not being inhuman. It would come slowly to one. They howled and leaped and spun and

113

made horrid faces, but what thrilled you, was just the thought of their humanity -- like yours -- the thought of your remote kinship with this wild and passionate uproar. Ugly. Yes, it was ugly enough, but if you were man enough you would admit to yourself that there was in you just the faintest trace of a response to the terrible frankness of that noise, a dim suspicion of there being a meaning in it which you -- you so remote from the night of first ages -- could comprehend.'

Herein lies the meaning of *Heart of Darkness* and the fascination it holds over the Western mind: 'What thrilled you was just the thought of their humanity -- like yours .... Ugly.'

Having shown us Africa in the mass, Conrad then zeros in, half a page later, on a specific example, giving us one of his rare descriptions of an African who is not just limbs or rolling eyes:

'And between whiles I had to look after the savage who was fireman. He was an improved specimen; he could fire up a vertical boiler. He was there below me and, upon my word, to look at him was as edifying as seeing a dog in a parody of breeches and a feather hat walking on his hind legs. A few months of training had done for that really fine chap. He squinted at the steam-gauge and at the water-gauge with an evident effort of intrepidity -- and he had filed his teeth too, the poor devil, and the wool of his pate shaved into queer patterns, and three ornamental scars on each of his cheeks. He ought to have been clapping his hands and stamping his feet on the bank, instead of which he was hard at work, a thrall to strange witchcraft, full of improving knowledge.'

As everybody knows, Conrad is a romantic on the side. He might not exactly admire savages clapping their hands and stamping their feet but they have at least the merit of being in their place, unlike this dog in a parody of breeches. For Conrad things being in their place is of the utmost importance.

'Fine fellows -- cannibals -- in their place,' he tells us pointedly. Tragedy begins when things leave their accustomed place, like Europe leaving its safe stronghold between the policeman and the baker to take a peep into the heart of darkness.

Before the story takes us into the Congo basin proper we are given this nice little vignette as an example of things in their place:

'Now and then a boat from the shore gave one a momentary contact with reality. It was paddled by black fellows. You could see from afar the white of their eyeballs glistening. They shouted, sang; their bodies streamed with perspiration; they had faces like grotesque masks -- these chaps; but they had bone, muscle, a wild vitality, an intense energy of movement that was as natural and hue as the surf along their coast. They wanted no excuse for being there. They were a great comfort to look at.'

Towards the end of the story Conrad lavishes a whole page quite unexpectedly on an African woman who has obviously been some kind of mistress to Mr. Kurtz and now presides (if I may be permitted a little liberty) like a formidable mystery over the inexorable imminence of his departure:

'She was savage and superb, wild-eyed and magnificent ....She stood looking at us without a stir and like the wilderness itself, with an air of brooding over an inscrutable purpose.'

This Amazon is drawn in considerable detail, albeit of a predictable nature, for two reasons. First, she is in her place and so can win Conrad's special brand of approval and second, she fulfills a structural requirement of the story: a savage counterpart to the refined, European woman who will step forth to end the story:

'She came forward all in black with a pale head, floating toward me in the dusk. She was in mourning .... She took both my hands in hers and murmured, 'I had heard you were coming.'... She had a mature capacity for fidelity, for belief, for suffering.'

The difference in the attitude of the novelist to these two women is conveyed in too many direct and subtle ways to need elaboration. But perhaps the most significant difference is the one implied in the author's bestowal of human expression to the one and the withholding of it from the other. It is clearly not part of Conrad's purpose to confer language on the 'rudimentary souls' of Africa. In place of speech they made 'a violent babble of uncouth sounds.' They 'exchanged short grunting phrases' even among themselves. But most of the time they were too busy with their frenzy.

There are two occasions in the book, however, when Conrad departs somewhat from his practice and confers speech, even English speech, on the savages. The first occurs when cannibalism gets the better of them:

'Catch 'im,' he snapped with a bloodshot widening of his eyes and a flash of sharp teeth -- 'catch 'im. Give 'im to us.' 'To you, eh?' I asked; 'what would you do with them? 'Eat 'im!' he said curtly. . . .'

The other occasion was the famous announcement: 'Mistah Kurtz -- he dead.'

At first sight these instances might be mistaken for unexpected acts of generosity from Conrad. In reality they constitute some of his best assaults. In the case of the cannibals the incomprehensible grunts that had thus far served them for speech suddenly proved inadequate for Conrad's purpose of letting the European glimpse the unspeakable craving in their hearts. Weighing the necessity for consistency in the portrayal of the dumb brutes against the sensational advantages of securing their conviction by clear, unambiguous evidence issuing out of their own mouth Conrad chose the latter.

As for the announcement of Mr. Kurtz's death by the 'insolent black head in the doorway' what better or more appropriate finis could be written to the horror story of that wayward child of civilization who willfully had given his soul to the powers of darkness and 'taken a high seat amongst the devils of the land' than the proclamation of his physical death by the forces he had joined?

It might be contended, of course, that the attitude to the African in *Heart of Darkness* is not Conrad's but that of his fictional narrator, Marlow, and that far from endorsing it Conrad might indeed be holding it up to irony and criticism. Certainly Conrad appears to go to considerable pains to set up layers of insulation between himself and the moral universe of his history. He has, for example, a narrator behind a narrator. The primary narrator is Marlow but his account is given to us through the filter of a second, shadowy person.

But if Conrad's intention is to draw a cordon sanitaire between himself and the moral and psychological malaise of his narrator his care seems to me totally wasted because he neglects to hint however subtly or tentatively at an alternative frame of reference by which we may judge the actions and opinions of his characters. It would not have been beyond Conrad's power to make that

116

provision if he had thought it necessary. Marlow seems to me to enjoy Conrad's complete confidence -- a feeling reinforced by the close similarities between their two careers.

Marlow comes through to us not only as a witness of truth, but one holding those advanced and humane views appropriate to the English liberal tradition which required all Englishmen of decency to be deeply shocked by atrocities in Bulgaria or the Congo of King Leopold or the Belgians or wherever.

Thus Marlow is able to toss out such bleeding-heart sentiments as these:

'They were dying slowly -- it was very clear. They were not enemies, they were not criminals, they were nothing earthly now, nothing but black shadows of disease and starvation lying confusedly in the greenish gloom. Brought from all the recesses of the coast in all the legality of time contracts, lost in uncongenial surroundings, fed on unfamiliar food, they sickened, became inefficient, and were then allowed to crawl away and rest.'

The kind of liberalism espoused here by Marlow/Conrad touched all the best minds of the age in England, Europe and America. It took different forms in the minds of different people but almost always managed to sidestep the ultimate question of equality between white people and black people. That extraordinary missionary, Albert Schweitzer, who sacrificed brilliant careers in music and theology in Europe for a life of service to Africans in much the same area as Conrad writes about, epitomizes the ambivalence. In a comment which has often been quoted Schweitzer says: 'The African is indeed my brother but my junior brother.'

And so he proceeded to build a hospital appropriate to the needs of junior brothers with standards of hygiene reminiscent of medical practice in the days before the germ theory of disease came into being. Naturally he became a sensation in Europe and America. Pilgrims flocked, and I believe still flock even after he has passed on, to witness the prodigious miracle in Lamberene, on the edge of the primeval forest.

Conrad's liberalism would not take him quite as far as Schweitzer's, though. He would not use the word brother however qualified; the farthest he would go was kinship. When Marlow's African helmsman falls down with a spear in his heart he gives his white master one final disquieting look:

'And the intimate profundity of that look he gave me when he received his hurt remains to this day in my memory -- like a claim of distant kinship affirmed in a supreme moment.'

It is important to note that Conrad, careful as ever with his words, is concerned not so much about distant kinship as about someone laying a claim on it. The black man lays a claim on the white man which is well-nigh intolerable. It is the laying of this claim which frightens and at the same time fascinates Conrad: '... the thought of their humanity -- like yours .... Ugly.'

The point of my observations should be quite clear by now, namely that Joseph Conrad was a thoroughgoing racist. That this simple truth is glossed over in criticisms of his work is due to the fact that white racism against Africa is such a normal way of thinking that its manifestations go completely unremarked. Students of *Heart of Darkness* will often tell you that Conrad is concerned not so much with Africa as with the deterioration of one European mind caused by solitude and sickness. They will point out to you that Conrad is, if anything, less charitable to the Europeans in the story than he is to the natives, that the point of the story is to ridicule Europe's civilizing mission in Africa. A Conrad student informed me in Scotland that Africa is merely a setting for the disintegration of the mind of Mr. Kurtz.

Which is partly the point. Africa as setting and backdrop which eliminates the African as human factor. Africa as a metaphysical battlefield devoid of all recognizable humanity, into which the wandering European enters at his peril. Can nobody see the preposterous and perverse arrogance in thus reducing Africa to the role of props for the break-up of one petty European mind? But that is not even the point.

The real question is the dehumanization of Africa and Africans which this age-long attitude has fostered and continues to foster in the world. And the question is whether a novel which celebrates this dehumanization, which depersonalizes a portion of the human race, can be called a great work of art. My answer is: No, it cannot. I do not doubt Conrad's great talents. Even *Heart of Darkness* has its memorably good passages and moments:

'The reaches opened before us and closed behind, as if the forest had stepped leisurely across tile water to bar the way for our return.'

Its exploration of the minds of the European characters is often penetrating and full of insight. But all that has been more than fully discussed in the last fifty years. His obvious racism has, however, not been addressed. And it is high time it was!

Conrad was born in 1857, the very year in which the first Anglican missionaries were arriving among my own people in Nigeria. It was certainly not his fault that he lived his life at a time when the reputation of the black man was at a particularly low level. But even after due allowances have been made for all the influences of contemporary prejudice on his sensibility there remains still in Conrad's attitude a residue of antipathy to black people which his peculiar psychology alone can explain. His own account of his first encounter with a black man is very revealing:

'A certain enormous buck nigger encountered in Haiti fixed my conception of blind, furious, unreasoning rage, as manifested in the human animal to the end of my days. Of the nigger I used to dream for years afterwards.'

Certainly Conrad had a problem with niggers. His inordinate love of that word itself should be of interest to psychoanalysts. Sometimes his fixation on blackness is equally interesting as when he gives us this brief description:

'A black figure stood up, strode on long black legs, waving long black arms. . . .'

As though we might expect a black figure striding along on black legs to wave white arms! But so unrelenting is Conrad's obsession. As a matter of interest Conrad gives us in *A Personal Record* what amounts to a companion piece to the buck nigger of Haiti. At the age of sixteen Conrad encountered his first Englishman in Europe. He calls him 'my unforgettable Englishman' and describes him in the following manner:

'(his) calves exposed to the public gaze . . . dazzled the beholder by the splendor of their marble-like condition and their rich tone of young ivory. . . . The light of a headlong, exalted satisfaction with the world of men. . . illumined his face. . . and triumphant eyes. In passing he cast a glance of kindly curiosity and a friendly gleam of big, sound, shiny teeth. . . his white calves twinkled sturdily.'

Irrational love and irrational hate jostling together in the heart of that talented, tormented man.

But whereas irrational love may at worst engender foolish acts of indiscretion, irrational hate can endanger the life of the community. Naturally Conrad is a dream for psychoanalytic critics. Perhaps the most detailed study of him in this direction is by Bernard C. Meyer, M.D. In his lengthy book Dr. Meyer follows every conceivable lead (and sometimes inconceivable ones) to explain Conrad. As an example he gives us long disquisitions on the significance of hair and hair-cutting in Conrad. And yet not even one word is spared for his attitude to black people. Not even the discussion of Conrad's antisemitism was enough to spark off in Dr. Meyer's mind those other dark and explosive thoughts. Which only leads one to surmise that Western psychoanalysts must regard the kind of racism displayed by Conrad absolutely normal despite the profoundly important work done by Frantz Fanon in the psychiatric hospitals of French Algeria.

Whatever Conrad's problems were, you might say he is now safely dead. Quite true. Unfortunately his heart of darkness plagues us still. Which is why an offensive and deplorable book can be described by a serious scholar as 'among the half dozen greatest short novels in the English language.' And why it is today the most commonly prescribed novel in twentieth-century literature courses in English Departments of American universities.

There are two probable grounds on what I have said so far may be contested. The first is that it is no concern of fiction to please people about whom it is written. I will go along with that. But I am not talking about pleasing people. I am talking about a book which parades in the most vulgar fashion prejudices and insults from which a section of mankind has suffered untold agonies and atrocities in the past and continues to do so in many ways and many places today. I am talking about a story in which the very humanity of black people is called in question.

Secondly, I may be challenged on the grounds of actuality. Conrad, after all, did sail down the Congo in 1890 when my own father was still a babe in arms. How could I stand up more than fifty years after his death and purport to contradict him? My answer is that as a sensible man I will not accept just any traveler's tales solely on the grounds that I have not made the journey myself. I will not trust the evidence even off man's very eyes when I suspect them to be as jaundiced as Conrad's. And we also happen to know that Conrad was, in the words of his biographer, Bernard C. Meyer, 'notoriously inaccurate in the rendering of his own history.'

But more important by far is the abundant testimony about Conrad's savages which we could gather if we were so inclined from other sources and which might lead us to think that these people must have had other occupations besides merging into the evil forest or materializing out of it simply to plague Marlow and his dispirited band. For as it happened, soon after Conrad had written his book an event of far greater consequence was taking place in the art world of Europe. This is how Frank Willett, a British art historian, describes it:

'Gaugin had gone to Tahiti, the most extravagant individual act of turning to a non-European culture in the decades immediately before and after 1900, when European artists were avid for new artistic experiences, but it was only about 1904-5 that African art began to make its distinctive impact. One piece is still identifiable; it is a mask that had been given to Maurice Vlaminck in 1905. He records that Derain was 'speechless' and 'stunned' when he saw it, bought it from Vlaminck and in turn showed it to Picasso and Matisse, who were also greatly affected by it. Ambroise Vollard then borrowed it and had it cast in bronze. . . The revolution of twentieth century art was under way!'

The mask in question was made by other savages living just north of Conrad's River Congo. They have a name too: the Fang people, and are without a doubt among the world's greatest masters of the sculptured form. The event Frank Willett is referring to marks the beginning of cubism and the infusion of new life into European art, which had run completely out of strength.

The point of all this is to suggest that Conrad's picture of the people of the Congo seems grossly inadequate even at the height of their subjection to the ravages of King Leopold's International Association for the Civilization of Central Africa.

Travelers with closed minds can tell us little except about themselves. But even those not blinkered, like Conrad with xenophobia, can be astonishingly blind. Let me digress a little here.

One of the greatest and most intrepid travelers of all time, Marco Polo, journeyed to the Far East from the Mediterranean in the thirteenth century and spent twenty years in the court of Kublai Khan in China. On his return to Venice he set down in his book entitled *Description of the World* his impressions of the peoples and places and customs he had seen. But there were at least two extraordinary omissions in his account. He said nothing about the art of printing, unknown as yet in Europe but in full flower in China. He either did not notice it at all or if he did, failed to see what use Europe could possibly have for       it.

Whatever the reason, Europe had to wait another hundred years for Gutenberg. But even more spectacular was Marco Polo's omission of any reference to the Great Wall of China nearly 4,000 miles long and already more than 1,000 years old at the time of his visit. Again, he may not have seen it; but the Great Wall of China is the only structure built by man which is visible from the moon! Indeed travelers can be blind.

As I said earlier Conrad did not originate the image of Africa which we find in his book. It was and is the dominant image of Africa in the Western imagination and Conrad merely brought the peculiar gifts of his own mind to bear on it. For reasons which can certainly use close psychological inquiry the West seems to suffer deep anxieties about the precariousness of its civilization and to have a need for constant reassurance by comparison with Africa.

If Europe, advancing in civilization, could cast a backward glance periodically at Africa trapped in primordial barbarity it could say with faith and feeling: 'There go I but for the grace of God.' Africa is to Europe as the picture is to Dorian Gray -- a carrier onto whom the master unloads his physical and moral deformities so that he may go forward, erect and immaculate. Consequently Africa is something to be avoided just as the picture has to be hidden away to safeguard the man's jeopardous integrity. Keep away from Africa, or else! Mr. Kurtz of *Heart of Darkness* should have heeded that warning and the prowling horror in his heart would have kept its place, chained to its lair. But he foolishly exposed himself to the wild irresistible allure of the jungle and lo! the darkness found him out.

In my original conception of this essay I had thought to conclude it nicely on an appropriately positive note in which I would suggest from my privileged position in African and Western cultures some advantages the West might derive from Africa once it rid its mind of old prejudices and began to look at Africa not through a haze of distortions and cheap mystifications but quite simply as a continent of people -- not angels, but not rudimentary souls either -- just people, often highly gifted people and often strikingly successful in their enterprise with life and society.

But as I thought more about the stereotype image, about its grip and pervasiveness, about the willful tenacity with which the West holds it to its heart; when I thought of the West's television and cinema and newspapers, about books read in its schools and out of school, of churches preaching to empty pews about the need to send help to the heathen in Africa, I realized that no easy optimism was possible. And there was, in any case, something totally wrong in offering bribes to the West in return for its good opinion of Africa. Ultimately the abandonment of unwholesome thoughts must be its own and only reward. Although I have used the word willful a few times here to characterize the West's view of Africa, it may well be that what is happening at this stage is more akin to reflex action than calculated malice. Which does not make the situation more but less hopeful.

*The Christian Science Monitor*, a paper more enlightened than most, once carried an interesting article written by its Education Editor on the serious psychological and learning problems faced by little children who speak one language at home and then go to school where something else is spoken. It was a wide-ranging article taking in Spanish-speaking children in America, the children of migrant Italian workers in Germany, the quadrilingual phenomenon in Malaysia, and so on. And all this while the article speaks unequivocally about language. But then out of the blue sky comes this:

'In London there is an enormous immigration of children who speak Indian or Nigerian dialects, or some other native language.'

I believe that the introduction of dialects which is technically erroneous in the context is almost a reflex action caused by an instinctive desire of the writer to downgrade the discussion to the level of Africa and India. And this is quite comparable to Conrad's withholding of language from his rudimentary souls. Language is too grand for these chaps; let's give them dialects!

In all this business a lot of violence is inevitably done not only to the image of despised peoples but even to words, the very tools of possible redress. Look at the phrase 'native language' in the *Science Monitor* excerpt. Surely the only native language possible in London is Cockney English. But our writer means something else -- something appropriate to the sounds Indians and Africans make!

Although the work of redressing which needs to be done may appear too daunting, I believe it is not one day too soon to begin. Conrad saw and condemned the evil of imperial exploitation but was strangely unaware of the racism on which it sharpened its iron tooth. But the victims of racist slander who for centuries have had to live with the inhumanity it makes them heir to have always known better than any casual visitor even when he comes loaded with the gifts of a Conrad."

The image of Africa in America is also found in Conrad's notoriously racist book, *Heart of Darkness*. There are many, indeed millions, of Conrads in America. And they continue to be produced even by some of America's finest schools, clearly demonstrated by the high status accorded his book in universities and colleges across the nation where it is used as standard work of literature, in spite of its blatantly racist message. So why have American professors chosen this book? They have chosen it because it reflects their racist beliefs and portrays what they consider to be the true of image not only of Africa and Africans but of all black people including African Americans.

What is so sad is that it did not start with Conrad. It started long before him when Europeans conquered Africa. And it has been that way since then. America, being an offshoot of Europe, harbors the same racist sentiments and beliefs which, in the minds of many whites, reflect what they consider to be the reality of Africa: "That is how Africans are. They are born that way, and they die that way. It is their nature. Nothing can be done to change it." I have been bombarded with such stereotypes, as have other Africans in the United States, but I don't intend to give up the fight.

Yet, even what is positive about Africa is sometimes stereotypical. Probably the most enduring, "positive" image of Africa abroad is one of exotic entertainment: Africa as a tourist attraction, teeming with wild animals that roam vast expanses of territory, and with natives dancing around camp fires to entertain visitors. That is what draws hundreds of thousands of foreigners to Africa every year.

However, we would like to remind them that "Africa is people," as Chinua Achebe put it in his Presidential Lecture to the World Bank in Washington, D.C. in 1998 in which he bitterly criticized the industrialized nations for imposing severe austerity measures, called structural adjustment programs, on African countries which have caused untold misery and suffering, including starvation, to the very same people whose plight these programs are supposedly intended to alleviate. But it is an image, of a suffering continent, seared in the conscience of only a few in a world where Africans don't count much, if at all, as equal human beings.

# Chapter Four:

# The Attitude of Africans Towards African Americans

AFRICANS don't feel the same way about everything just like other people don't; nor do they think alike anymore than whites, Orientals and others do. But there are some things on which many of them tend to agree or share perceptions because of their common African background and history. One of those subjects is their attitude towards African Americans. But even on this subject one cannot generalize and say that is how *all* Africans feel or think.

The purpose of this chapter is to explore what is perceived to be a consensus among a large number of Africans on how they see African Americans, and what I myself have observed in my dealings with both in the thirty years or so I have been in and out of the United States.

I am here reminded of what I heard after I moved to Grand Rapids, Michigan, from Detroit in 1976. I moved to Grand Rapids to attend Aquinas College in this conservative and predominantly white mid-western city in southwestern Michigan that is also a Republican stronghold as much as it has been for decades.

I was the only African student from Tanzania and the second in the school's history to enroll there. The first one was Enos Bukuku, in the sixties, who went on to become a distinguished eocnomist in the Tanzanian government and professor of economics at the University of Dar es Salaam before he became permament secretary in the president's office and an economic advisor to the president of Tanzania, among other posts.

There were a few other African students and they all came from Nigeria, except one student who came from Sierra Leone, when I was there.

I got to know all the African students well and we interacted on regular basis on and off-campus. Since they were mostly Nigerians, it was they who invited me to their homes, as much as I invited them to mine, to socialize and talk about what was going on back home in our continent.

Now and then, the subject of African Americans crept into the conversation since we were also around them and even went to school with them. We lived mostly in the inner city, which was predominantly black, and we interacted with quite a few of them, inviting them to our homes. The black American students at Aquinas College, most of whom came from Detroit, was another group we dealt with, especially on campus.

But, almost invariably, whenever the Nigerians talked about African Americans, they would use the term *akata*. I didn't know what they meant by that and I never asked them. It didn't take me long to figure out that they were referring to American blacks. I did not detect any hostility towards them, or a condescending tone or atttude when they talked about these cousins of ours in the diaspora. They were always friendly and laughing, although I am not sure I interpreted correctly what the laughter meant most of the time back then.

It was not until years later that I found out what the term *akata* meant when I read an article in the *Detroit Free Press* by a Nigerian reporter, or someone with a Nigerian (Yoruba) name, who explained what it meant: a brutal wild animal or something like that. It is said to be a Yoruba term.

Shortly thereafter, I again stumbled upon the term on the internet when I was reading an article posted by an African American who was a member of a Yahoo discussion group, Mwananchi (meaning countryman or citizen in Kiswahili), which addresses many issues in a Pan-African context and in a very intelligent if not highly intellectual manner; and one of whose members is the acerbic and highly controversial Ghanaian professor of economics, George Ayittey, who teaches at a university in Washington, D.C.

The writer of the article was hurt and deeply offended by the use of the term *akata* by some Africans to describe their brothers and sisters in the diaspora and who had the misfortune of having their African ancestors shipped in chains to America as slaves. The same subject again, later in November 2004, came up for discussion and one of the members of Mwananchi, a Kenyan, had this to say:

"I am not in a position to fully address the issues you raised in your recent posting on the perjorative term "akata" used by others in this or other forums to refer to African Americans. I am an old member in this forum but rarely comment on issues raised by others unless I have something meaningful to contribute.

I am from Kenya and the only information I have on the Yoruba is scant and unhelpful in this discussion. I studied the history of West Africa in high school back in the mid- to late 1980s for examination purposes and other than the gods: Sango, Oranminyan and Oduduwa, there's nothing else I can say about the Yoruba.

However, as America wakes up to the reality of a new wave of immigrants from Africa, it is inevitable that a number of socio-political and economic issues will come to the fore pertaining to the interaction that we Africans have with our African American kindred as well as the rest of the host population. As a well informed African who has spent close to a third of my life in America - and still learning - I am very aware that we all share the burden of ignorance of and on each other as we struggle to be part of this mosaic that makes America what it is.

Up until the late 1990s when a clear increase of refugees from war torn countries started pouring into America, most of the African immigrants came to America on student visas. This is the cream of society back home. As of today, there's clear research that shows that Africans in America are some of, if not, the most educated, well paid and upward mobile group of all immigrants in this country. Many people will dispute this and I for one am not well paid, my high education in America notwithstanding.

However, most of us come here with little understanding of the history and complexities of the African American experience in this country. Beside Martin Luther King and Marcus Garvey, very few Africans - even the educated ones - know about the pivotal role played by numerous prominent and other nameless African Americans in the development of this country. Without understanding the history of the African Americans and their relationship with the White establishment, we will forever be wallowing in the cesspool of misconceptions and hearsay.

On the other hand, very few African Americans have an understanding of the new Africans migrating into this country. It is a sad FACT that there are more black men in prisons in America than there are in colleges. This is due to a myriad of factors that are a daily reality of this American life (sorry, Ira Glass).

To most Africans, our experience in America with African Americans is not a pleasant one. May be this is because of the low educational levels of most of the American blacks that we are likely to meet combined with our scant knowledge of the aforementioned African American experience. I, for one, was once told by a not very well educated black brother to learn to speak English properly. I was not offended because I knew the brother did not understand my accent. The setting was not proper for me to teach him a few basics of socio-linguistics.

Speaking of English, I am not sure he'd ever heard of Pope, Chaucer, Moore, Marlowe or Thomas Hardy and how different they would've sounded to him if he ever heard them speak. I studied these literary giants in school in Africa and have even made a pilgrimage to Canterbury, Kent, to drink a beer in the Marlowe: the very pub where my favourite English poet of all, Christopher Marlowe, a contemporary of Sheikh El Zubeir (Shakespeare) was stabbed to death at the age of 29 back in the 1600s. But this is beside the point.

To the bratha, I needed to learn some English. It is saddening that to most African Americans, according to comedian Chris Rock, Africa is far, far away beyond the oceans! True but not so quite exact. A lot of African Americans have been bought into the stereotyping that Africans have perpetually received from the mass media in the West: that we are all dirt poor, ignorant, uncultured and at various stages of starvation living in the Hobbesian world where life is short, bruttish and nasty. Well, there might be some truth to that but NOT quite entirely.

It is imperative for us to address our differences as black kindred in America in every imaginative way. I personally live in a state that is 97% White. It is the second whitest state in the nation wedged between the first and third whitest states. I have minimal interaction with African Americans unless I go to the club for a drink. I know less than 8 African Americans and yet I have lived in the US for close to ten years. As a student of humanities, I know that my minimal exposure to my African American brethren is something I must personally overcome.

I will recommend anyone in similar circumstances to utilize the many opportunities that are available to us in order to bridge this sea of ignorance. The internet, is a prime example. There are quality TV programs out there too that are very informative on the African and the African American experience. PBS and C-SPAN as well as National Public radio offer a window of opportunity to those of us struggling to achieve this goal. That's how I met some of my favourite contemporary African American thinkers: Eric Mike Dyson, Cornell West and Charles Ogletree.

To those who live in places well-populated with African Americans, try and attend their church services and other social functions and you will all be amazed how wrong we are in our pre-conceived notions of each other. May be with a little understanding of our respective experiences, we will overcome our differences and even celebrate them with those bonds that tie us together as we try to improve ourselves and stake a better claim in this great American experiment.

Well, for someone who rarely posts, this is so long a letter. I would recommend a book by Mariama Ba by the same title: "So Long a Letter" to those who want a glimpse into the life of a Senegalese woman in the last century in Africa.

Let the discussion continue.

Soul bratha,
Engo Makabe."

This posting on the internet by an African from Kenya highlights the profound ambivalence we sometimes have towards each other, while many of us don't try hard enough, if at all, to

130

bridge the communication gap and learn more about each other.

In fact, the use of the term *akata* is at the core of this misconception of what we think and know about each other, fuelled by stereotypes manufactured by the white dominant society which portrays Africans as primitive savages, and black Americans as advanced savages in a civilized white society they seem determined to destroy with their propensity towards violence encoded in their genes rooted in their African origin. And that is the meaning of *akata* which is used to describe black Americans as brutal wild animals, contrasted with African immigrants and students in the United States and even with Africans in Africa.

Yet, for some inexplicable reason, I had never heard the term *akata* before, until I moved to Grand Rapids, although I lived in Detroit and knew many Nigerians including Yorubas some of whom were my schoolmates at Wayne State University. But they probably used the term as much as the ones in Grand Rapids did. And just like the ones in Grand Rapids, the Nigerians and other Africans who may have used the term in Detroit to describe or insult African Americans were not all Yorubas. In Grand Rapids, there was only one Yoruba student who was also my classmate at Aquinas College. The rest of the Nigerian students were Igbos, and they used the term *akata* quite often. I don't know if some of them were just joking or used the term in a different context. But I do know that, for whatever reason these Nigerians used the term, many African Americans who knew what the term meant back then would have been highly offended as much as the ones to day are, had they heard them call black Americans *akata*.

There is no question that to many African Americans who know what the term *akata* means, its use only confirms what they have known or suspected all along: "Africans don't like us; they just don't." In fact, that is one of the subjects that comes up quite often in conversations between Africans and African Americans, with black Americans asking: "Is it true that they don't want us over there?" I have been asked the same question a number of times and have done my best to respond accordingly. I even wrote an article on the subject, published in a school newspaper and quoted in the *Michigan Chronicle*, in the early seventies when I was student in Detroit.

131

And there seems to be some credibility to the charge that may be a significant number of Africans, not *all* of us but probably a large number amongst us, have a negative attitude towards black people in the United States. Some people attribute it to arrogance among Africans who think they are better than American blacks, for whatever reason including cultural differences, loss of identity among black Americans since they no longer have their true African identity that was destroyed during slavery; and even an "identity crisis," as some Africans may see it, contending that black people in the United States really don't know who and what they are: they don't know what part of Africa they came from, and which tribes they originated from or belong to; they are not as African as black Africans in Africa are, because they are racially mixed, with only very few of them, if any, having retained their true biological African identity.

Others, especially African Americans, at least some of them, say Africans are just jealous of them because black people in the United States are better off economically than the vast majority of black Africans most of whom are desperately poor and live in the most backward and poorest continent on earth. There are also those who may feel that Africans are not as civilized as they are. The list goes on and on.

And Africans who despise black Americans forget that it is these same people, whom they make fun of, who opened doors for them to enter the American mainstream when they fought for racial justice. The opportunities African immigrants and students enjoy in the United States today would not have been available had it not been for the sacrifices African Americans made in their struggle against racial discrimination during the civil rights movement, and even before and after that.

Whatever the case, we cannot deny that problems exist, or that a significant number of Africans don't have a negative attitude towards black Americans. And it didn't just start.

I remember reading an interview with Andrew Young by Charlie Cobb, a prominent African American journalist and civil rights activist from the sixties who at this writing was working for a major African news organization, allafrica.com, and who once lived and worked in Dar es Salaam, Tanzania, when I was still there before coming to the United States, which is highly relevant in this context.

Andy Young said when he was a student at Howard University, he met a Nigerian student who was very bright, probably the smartest on campus according to Young, but who also was very arrogant, thinking he was better than black Americans; and asked Young, "When are you going to get civilized?"

Whatever he meant by that, there is no question that he had preconceived notions about African Americans which did not correspond to reality. And coming from Africa, the "Dark Continent," he really had a lot of nerve to ask Andy Young such a question. It would have been very easy for Young or for any other black American to hit right back and bring the Nigerian to his senses: "Look at who is talking!"

If black Americans are not civilized, how civilized are the Africans? And in what ways black Americans are not? Having dealt with Africans for a long time, Young knew how to handle the situation and probably handled it the best way he could. He explained in the same interview that he grew up with Africans in his house, since his parents were used to taking in African students studying in the United States. As he stated in the interview on July 22, 2002:

"My parents always had African students in our home in the 1940s. They felt that they had been educated by American missionaries - New England missionaries - and that part of our responsibility was to educate others. So, our home was almost a boarding house for African students at no charge.

I [also] started in 1974 with Arthur Ashe bringing [African] students to the US. We'd bring them in and keep them in Atlanta for a while at my house and we'd find places for them at Michigan State [University] or Texas Southern or other colleges. We had a kind of Underground Railroad on education....

When I was a freshman at Howard University, the smartest guy in the school was a Nigerian. And he used to say to me very condescendingly: 'You're a bright boy. When are going to get civilized?'

And there is a Nigerian success tradition that is older than the African-American tradition. It is not as successful as ours but it is older. It's like Jamaicans. They have a hard time listening to us as African Americans. They were ahead of us in their decolonization and West Indian thinkers have always been....Well, it's like Stokely [Carmichael] didn't think he had anything to learn from John Lewis. Our view is seen as somewhat neo-colonial."

What Andrew Young said illustrates a very important point concerning the attitude of a number of Africans, and some people from the Caribbean, towards African Americans. It is condescending; it is also paternalistic reminiscent of what Dr. Albert Schweitzer said, although in a very perverted way, about black people: "With regard to the Negroes,...I have coined the formula: 'I am your brother, it is true, but your elder brother.'"

That is a loaded statement with all that it implies. The conclusion is obvious on who stands where and for how long. Chronologically speaking, the younger brother will never catch up with his elder brother. Also remember this: elders are wiser. And therein lies the arrogance of some Africans and their negative attitude towards African Americans: they are the original Africans, true black people; black Americans are not. They come directly from the motherland, African Americans don't; Africa is the repository of knowledge, wisdom and genuine black African culture. Black America is not. Case closed.

Is that why "Africans don't want us over there?," a question African Americans ask often. "Is it because we are not really black or African? Aren't we really the same people?" Those are legitimate questions. But is it really true that we, those of us born and brought up in Africa, really don't want to have anything to do with black people in America?

Whenever I have addressed this subject, I have always assured my listeners, African Americans, that it is simply *not* true that "we don't want them over there, in Africa." I also remind them that African Americans are not the primary target or the only people on the defensive against this kind of attack by some Africans. Many people of different ethnic groups - or tribes, whatever you choose to call them - in many African countries also don't like each other anymore than they do black Americans.

It is not selective prejudice against black Americans only. In fact, when African Americans go to Africa, some of them end up being welcomed and embraced by some of the very same people who are at war with members of other tribes right there in their own countries.

Also just remember this: hundreds of thousands, and even millions, who have died in wars in Africa - for example between the Hutu and the Tutsi in Rwanda and Burundi, the Hema and the Lendu in eastern Congo, the Tiv and the Hausa in Nigeria, the Igbo and the Hausa-Fulani during the Nigerian civil war in the sixties - all these people who have been tortured, slaughtered, and sometimes even burnt alive, are Africans right there in Africa, killed by fellow Africans. They are not African Americans from the United States. It is carnage, it is hate far more brutal and deadly than what is or has been directed against African Americans by some Africans who don't like them.

But whatever hostility exists towards African Americans, overt or covert, it is definitely not an omnipresent phenomenon on the African continent. African Americans have through the years since independence been welcomed in large numbers in Ghana, Tanzania, Nigeria and in all the other African countries. And many of them have settled there permanently. You will find them today.

Yet, there have been some incidents, not many but enough to raise eyebrows, arising from misunderstandings, mistrust and suspicions of one kind or another including negative attitudes, which may have strained relations between Africans and African Americans in some countries. For example, some members of the Pan-African Congress-USA, the group based in Detroit which sponsored me and other African students in the early seventies, were unceremoniously kicked out of Ghana, right from the airport where they were denied entry into the country. That was not long before the organization offered me a scholarship to go to school in Detroit.

I don't know exactly what the reason was, why they were tossed out of Ghana, but I remember some of them saying they were kicked out for no reason at all. What may have come into play here, like in some other incidents involving African Americans on the African continent, is ingrained suspicions towards *all* Americans, black and white or whatever, as some kind of spies or agents of the government, working for the CIA or being involved in some kind of scheme to undermine African countries and governments. And it is not difficult to find "sinister" motives behind any trip by any American to Africa, given the highly notorious track record of the CIA and the American government on the continent through the years.

Ironically, Pan-African Congress members were some of the staunchest supporters of Africa, and of leaders such as Dr. Kwame Nkrumah, president of Ghana, a country from which some of them were tossed out in a very humiliating way. And it defies rational explanation to assume that every American who goes to Africa is on a spying mission for the CIA. But whatever the perception, there is no question that it has had tragic consequences in some cases. Perception is reality, no matter how you look at it.

Yet another reason why Ghanaian officials at the airport in Accra may have been hostile towards African Americans who were not allowed to go beyond the airport but were instead put on the next plane back to the United States is the perennial problem many black Americans complain about in their relations with us: the negative attitude of Africans towards African Americans borne of prejudice against their own people, and for no reason, none whatsoever. It's just hate, is the way they see it.

What happened in Ghana to the Pan-African Congress members reminds me of what happened in my country, Tanzania, in 1974. The parallels are almost exact in terms of treatment. Just as the African Americans who went to Ghana from Detroit were kicked out of the country as soon as they arrived, a number of African Americans who had just arrived in Tanzania were caught in the same predicament, detained and tossed out of the country for security reasons. Like those in Ghana, the black Americans who went to Tanzania were some of the strongest supporters of Africa and of African leaders such as President Julius Nyerere, the leader of the very same country from which they were kicked out. But that is the subject of another chapter in this book.

Suffice it to say, regardless of what happened in Ghana and Tanzania and elsewhere in other African countries where African Americans may have run into problems with the authorities as a case of mistaken identity or deliberate decisions by the authorities of the host countries to kick black Americans out for no justifiable reason, there is ample evidence to show that in general, and in overwhelming cases, African Americans have been welcomed by Africans without any problems and have enjoyed the hospitality extended to them in a way they probably never expected. The best proof of all this is the African Americans themselves who have been to Africa and who live in Africa.

It is true that there has been some distance, in terms of communication and direct contact, that has been maintained by both sides for different reasons mainly because of misunderstanding and preconceived notions about each other. For example, when I was still in Tanzania, I remember seeing groups of African American visitors in Dar es Salaam, the nation's capital, walking up and down the streets, and going into Indian shops - what Americans call stores - without any of the local residents welcoming them or talking to them.

We knew they were black Americans - they were called "American Negroes," or just "Negroes," even by Africans in Tanzania and elsewhere in those days. And we could tell from their accent, the attire, and many times just from the way they looked that they were Americans, and not black Africans born and brought up in Africa. They had their own look, hard to describe but easily detectable by us; their Afro hair style, for example, which most local residents didn't have; and even colorful *dashikis* they wore which most people in Tanzania didn't wear like they do in West Africa. Yet, there was no overt or covert hostility towards them. It's just that neither side took the first step to try and bridge the gap between the two. We were so close, physically and genealogically as well as biologically, yet remained so far apart, face to face.

It was a yawning gap that remained through the years even when I was in Detroit. A couple from Detroit affiliated with the Pan-African Congress-USA, and fiercely proud of their African heritage, went to Tanzania in 1975. They stayed in Dar es Salaam, the capital, and the same city where I went to school and worked as a reporter. When they came back to the United States, they were somewhat disappointed because of their experience in Tanzania.

They said no one welcomed them, the people just glanced or stared at them and stayed away from them. And I understood their frustration.

The deeper problem is that neither side addressed the fundamental issue: lack of communication. Again, as in many other cases, neither side took the initiative to try to bridge the gap although, I concede, it is the local residents, Tanzanians, who, may be, should have taken the initiative or the first step to welcome their cousins from the diaspora. You welcome visitors or strangers into your house, they don't welcome you.

This partly explains why African Americans say Africans don't want them over there. But that is only a part of it. Most of the people who say that have never been to Africa. And many of them don't even know much about Africa. As one cabinet member under President Robert Mugabe said on BBC when President George W. Bush criticized Mugabe for rigging the 2002 presidential election - forgetting what he himself did in Florida in 2000 - and whipped up sentiments among Americans against the Zimbabwean leader: "Most Americans don't even know where Zimbabwe is." Even Americans themselves, including blacks, couldn't dispute the validity of this statement by the Zimbabwean cabinet minister.

Therefore, while African Americans have legitimate reasons to blame some Africans for their negative attitude towards them, they themselves should also admit that there are many African Americans who also have a negative attitude towards Africa for a number of reasons, including being brainwashed by the white man to hate their motherland by always portraying Africa in a negative light on television, in books and newspapers and magazines; and their own lack of interest in Africa regardless of what the white man says.

It is a two-way traffic. One is no more guilty than the other. And it is up to both to bridge the gap. Many Africans and African Americans are doing that. But we still have a long way to go, as has been clearly demonstrated by the stereotypes both sides continue to have about each other, although neither is better than the other.

One of the worst stereotypes is that Africans hate African Americans; conversely, you hear some Africans saying black Americans look down upon them and make fun of them for being backward and uncivilized. There is some validity to all this but, mainly it is a clash of perceptions, and dangerously misleading. As Kwame Essien, a Ghanaian student and president of the African Students Union at the University of North Carolina-Greensboro, stated in his article "Dispelling Myths about Africans and African Americans" in the school newspaper, *The Carolinian*, March 18, 2002:

"I had a great awakening about racial stereotypes when the members of the African Students Union did a presentation during the Shades of Color Conference. The Multi-Cultural Affairs Office deserves applause for the great program. Some of the issues raised by some of the African-American participants were 1. There's the notion that Africans HATE African-Americans. 2. Africans who were born and raised in Africa say that they are the only 'TRUE AFRICANS.' Such stereotypes shows that black students do not know a lot about each other.

I am not speaking for all Africans. Before I address these problems let's say a little about slavery and how it has affected the relationship between blacks in the diaspora.

It is obvious that Africans contributed to slavery, but what most people fail to see is the bigger picture. Slavery was not only intended to exploit free labor from Africans; but it was set up to destroy the black race.

During slavery white supremacists in Europe and America did their best to sever the relationship between Africans and the descendants of slaves. Dr. W.E.B. Du-Bois and others who wanted to bridge the gap between the black freedom struggle in colonial Africa and the civil rights movements in America were terrorized and destroyed by the Central Intelligence Agency (CIA). They wanted to divide us so that they could suppress us forever. *Roots*, the film (and book) by Alex Haley explains this notion.

The white slave owner terrorized Kunta Kinte, the African slave who wanted to keep his African name and culture. Slaves on the plantations were held hostage and stripped of their African heritage because of the threat it posed to the white power structure. Some of the confusion and mistrust among us as black people could be attributed to the legacies of slavery.

To make the situation worse in the twentieth and twenty first century some racist people capitalized on their monopoly over the media to create more divisions among blacks in the diaspora. Whenever you hear about Africa on the news or in the newspapers you see famine, diseases (AIDS, Ebola), civil war or some negative images of Africans. Why do you think nothing positive is said about Africans? Some blacks outside Africa deny their African roots because of such depressing and distorted images.

In Ghana (West Africa) where I was born nothing positive was said about African-Americans; we only heard about the greatness of white America. Think about the twenty first century media propaganda against blacks. African-Americans are portrayed as criminals, violent and lazy while Africans are treated as 'uncivilized' and backward. They want us to believe this. The media should not mislead US. My opinion is that Africans do NOT hate African-Americans. In the African culture we are not raised to hate any human being. Hate is a human problem; we Africans hate Africans too.

Concerning the issue of a 'True African.' It is ignorant for any African to claim that we are the only 'True Africans,' this is a backward ideology. What about children of African immigrants who were born at Moses Cone Hospital? An African is not defined by a birth certificate from an African hospital, neither are we defined by our Mandingo accent. NO African has the right or the license to approve who qualifies as an African. You are an African if you accept that your ancestors were Africans. Don't be surprised; we have some WHITE Africans too.

We Africans owe African Americans for the sacrifice they made during the civil war and the civil rights movements. Desegregation benefited Africans too. Without Nat Turner, Frederick Douglas, Ida Wells, and many others, Africans would not have enjoyed the social privileges we have today in America. All of us need to be open-minded and have a dialogue to help us eradicate the stereotypes and ignorance we have about each other. We cannot blame everything on racism and do nothing to change our situation. Let us continue the legacy of Pamela Wilson, Director of Multi Cultural Affairs (deceased), with a 'UNITY DAY' program to address our differences. Please join the African Students Union to help dispel these myths among us.

As Dr. Martin Luther King said: 'We have to live together as brothers and sisters or perish together as fools.'"

What is sometimes so disturbing about some of these negative remarks by Africans when they talk about African Americans is that they come from different parts of the continent, delivering the *same* message of indifference towards American blacks. And because they are not orchestrated or coordinated, they give the impression that hostility or indifference towards black Americans is a pervasive phenomenon among Africans on the African continent and in the United States as well as in other parts of the world where Africans live. That is simply *not* true.

Yet, conflicting signals now and then coming from some Africans only reinforce the notion or the perception that Africans in general don't want to have anything to do or have nothing to do with black Americans. And it is not just because they are Americans that they don't want them; it is not because these African Americans were born and raised on American soil, although that may be one of the reasons, such as jealousy. These African descendants in the diaspora are even denied their African heritage by some Africans who call them "white." And as Kofi Glover, a Ghanaian professor of political science at the University of Southern Florida, bluntly states: "Whether we like it or not, Africans and African Americans have two very different cultures."

I am not saying that Glover is one of those Africans who say black Americans have nothing to do with their African cultural heritage or are not African at all; I'm simply saying that he is emphasizing what is an indisputable fact: there are fundamental cultural differences between Africans and African Americans. The culture of black Americans is essentially European, *not* African. And they should admit that, however cruel and reprehensible the manner in which this Euro-American culture was acquired by them. They have been immersed and submerged in the culture of their European masters and rulers for centuries, although there are still remnants of African culture across black America.

It is not their fault that they lost their African cultural identity - which many of them are trying to reclaim - but it is also true that when they lost it, they became Europeanized culturally, although

141

they did not and could not become European for the simple reason that they were still an African people. And that causes some misunderstanding between the two sides, with some Africans going to the extreme and calling black Americans not African at all, as demonstrated by the following examples.

When some African Americans went to Kenya - I think they were business executives or some other kind of businessmen and may be even scholars - and said they were also Africans, their Kenyan counterparts, black Africans, said, no, they were not; they were "white Africans" born in America, as reported by *The Economist*, obviously because they lost their African culture and identity after centuries of slavery and living in a predominantly white country of which they had become an integral part.

In Ghana also, a significant number of Ghanaians don't accept black Americans as Africans and even have a term, *obruni* in the Twi language, they use to describe them; the term also means "foreigner."

They call African Americans "white." The word *obruni* is used in that context, meaning white, and may be even in a derogatory sense - or to maintain distance - by some people in the case of black Americans; in spite of the fact, the indisputable fact, that many of these very same black Americans whom they call "white" originated from the same place, Ghana, are members of their tribes - the Fanti, the Ewe, the Ashanti and others - and even of their own families.

They are their blood relatives, no matter how many centuries apart, separated since the slave trade. As Malcolm X said in one of his speeches, "There is no tree without roots, and branches without a tree." And as Ghanaian president, Dr. Kwame Nkrumah, stated: "All peoples of African descent whether they live in North or South America, the Caribbean or in other parts of the world, are Africans and belong to the African nation."

And it is consoling to our brothers and sisters from the diaspora when they find out that not all Africans feel this way and treat them as total strangers or outcasts. They learn this when they deal with different Africans in the United States itself; they also find out about all this when they go to Africa and meet many Africans who welcome them and embrace them.

There are some problems now and then, here and there, but the hospitality extended to African Americans by Africans makes many of them feel at home in Africa; be it in Ghana, Tanzania, Nigeria, South Africa, Kenya, Senegal, Gambia, Zimbabwe, Namibia, Swaziland, Togo, Benin, Uganda or any other black African country. As one African American, Imahkus, who moved to Ghana with her husband, states in an excerpt from her her book, *Returning Home Ain't Easy But It Sure Is A Blessing*, published in *Escape From America Magazine*:

"Ahead of us loomed this enormous, foreboding structure. The sight caused me to tremble; I almost didn't want to go inside. The outer walls were chipped and a faded and moldy white exterior. The sea had eaten away some of the mortar. It was gray and dismal as we climbed the steep steps, following the sign leading to the reception area. When we entered the reception area of the Cape Coast Castle Dungeons a smallish man with a bright smiling face met us. His name was Mr. Owusu and he had been working there as a receptionist and sometimes Guide, for many years.

After introductions were made all around, Mr. Owusu, our guide began the tour around the Castle. Entering the inner part of the castle overlooking a large courtyard, our guide gave us the background history of the Cape Coast Castle Dungeons. This was one of the more than sixty castle dungeons, forts, and lodges that had been constructed by European Traders with the permission of local rulers (the Chieftaincy) and stretched for 300 miles along the West Coast of Afrika to store captured Afrikans, until a shipload of enslaved Afrikans could be assembled, for shipment to the West.

Unbelievable, twenty-seven of those houses of misery were located in Ghana. Various European oppressors had occupied the Cape Coast Castle Dungeons during the Trans-Atlantic European Slave Trade. It began with the Portuguese in the 1500's, followed by the Dutch, then the Swedes, the Danes and finally the English who occupied it in 1665. It remained under their control, serving as the seat of the British Administration in the Gold Coast (Cape Coast) until they re-located their racist regime to Christianborg Castle in Accra in 1877.

Our next stop was the Palaver (which means talking/discussing) Hall, the meeting place of slave merchants,

143

which also served as the hall used in auctioning off our ancestors. The room was huge, the only light coming from the windows which lined both sides of the walls; one side facing the ocean, the other side overlooking the town; a bare room, echoing the voice of our Guide, a haunting echo, which reverberated off the walls, as the Guide explained how they bargained and sold us. When slave auctions were not going on, Palaver Hall was used as a meeting place for the Governor, Chiefs and other visitors. We then moved on to the Governor's apartment and the church, which I felt like burning down!

But nothing could prepare me for what we would experience next. We descended the stairs into a large cobble-stoned courtyard and walked through large double wooden doors, which lead into a long, dark, damp tunnel.

The stench of musty bodies, fear and death hung in the air. There was no noise except the thunderous crashing of the waves against the outer walls and the roaring sound of the water. Deeper we walked, into large, dark rooms which had served as a warehouse for enslaved Afrikan people awaiting shipment to the America's and Caribbean.

This was the Men's Dungeon. As we stood in that large cavernous room the air was still, the little ventilation that was available came from small openings near the 20-foot high ceilings. Our ancestors had been kept underground, chained to the walls and each other, making escape impossible.

The mood of the group was hushed, as several people started crying. We were standing in hellholes of the most horrific conditions imaginable. There were no words to express the suffering that must have gone on in these dungeons. I became caught up, thrown back in time. I was suddenly one of the many who were shackled, beaten and starved. But I was one of the fortunate souls to have survived the forced exodus from their homelands to be sold, branded and thrown into those hellholes, meant to hold (600) people but which held more than 1,000 enslaved Afrikans at one time. The men separated from the women, as they awaited shipment to the Americas. According to our Guide, the chalk marks on the walls of the Men's Dungeon indicated the level of the floor prior to the excavation of the floor, which had built up over years of slavery with feces, bones, filth etc. As the guide continued to describe the horrors of these pits of hell I began to shake violently; I needed to get out of there. I was being smothered. I turned and ran up the steep incline of the tunnel, to the castle courtyard, the winds from the sea whipping my face, bringing me back to the present. I couldn't believe what I had just experienced. How could anyone be so cruel and inhuman?

Following the guide we proceeded across the massive courtyard and down another passage way to the Women's Dungeon, a smaller version of the Men's Dungeon but not so deep underground, it had held over 300 women at any given time.

As we entered that dark, musty, damp room, the sound of the crashing waves was like muffled, rolling thunder. A dimly lit, uncovered light bulb hung from the ceiling on a thin, frayed wire. After standing silently for a time in this tomb, the Guide began to lead the group out. I was the last person left in the room when the Guide turned and said he was continuing the tour.

'Please,' I said, 'I'm not ready to leave, just turn off the light for me and I will join the group shortly.'

As the group walked silently away, the tears would not stop flowing. I dropped to my knees, trembling and crying even harder. With the light off, the only light in that dungeon came through one small window near the very high ceiling, reflecting down as though it were a muted spotlight. Darkness hung in every corner. As I rocked back and forth on the dirt floor, I could hear weeping and wailing...anguished screams coming from the distance.

Suddenly the room was packed with women...some naked, some with babies, some sick and lying in the dirt, while others stood against the walls around the dungeon's walls, terror filled their faces.

'My God, what had we done to wind up here, crammed together like animals?'

Pain and suffering racked their bodies, a look of hopelessness and despair on their faces...but with a strong will to survive.

'Oh God, what have we done to deserve this kind of treatment?'

Cold terror gripped my body. Tears blinded me and the screams wouldn't stop. As I sat there violently weeping I began to feel a sense of warmth, many hands were touching my body, caressing me, soothing me as a calmness began to come over me. I began to feel almost safe as voices whispered in my ears assuring me that everything was all right.

'Don't cry,' they said. 'You've come home. You've returned to your homeland, to re-open the Door of No Return.'

Gradually the voices and the women faded into the darkness; it was then that I realized that some of the screams I'd heard were my own. The eerie light beaming down from the window was growing dimmer as day began fading into night. As I got up from the dungeon floor I knew that I would never be the same again!

'After years of wandering and searching, I have finally found home. And one day, I wouldn't be leaving again.'

The book that you hold in your hands, *Returning Home Ain't Easy But It Sure Is A Blessing*, speaks to the visions of our ancestors and demonstrates the efforts both positive and negative, the humor, the tears and the frustrations of a Diaspora Afrikan family diligently working and struggling within the blessings of being back in our ancestral homeland. It faces the startling realities plagued by those of us who are trying to return home. Realities of the fact that many of our continental Afrikan born brothers and sisters have very little knowledge of the Afrikan people born and raised in the Diaspora that resulted from the Trans-Atlantic (European) Slave Trade.

Ironically, every Ghananian we spoke with wanted to go to the United States. We were coming and they wanted to go. We were like ships in the night, passing each other unseeing and uncaring.

My story contrasts these with those realities of life on the other side. Brothers struggling to survive were being killed on a regular basis while driving taxis in New York City. A few years before we repatriated to Ghana, two men held up my husband with a shotgun, while he was working his taxicab. When they entered the cab and sat down, the man with the gun, who spoke no English, put it to my husband's head, as the other man announced in broken English

'Dis es ah stickup, don' turn roun' or jew dead, Mon.'

They then tied and bound him, before throwing him in the trunk of the taxi. Riding around the Bronx and Manhattan they ended up dumping him on a dark street in the early morning. At a deserted Terminal Market in the Bronx, they ordered him to stay still and not move for 15 minutes. Thank God, he was unhurt that time, but what about next time? Certainly no one could doubt there would be a next time the way things were happening in New York City.

Children were being gunned down playing in the streets and in playgrounds. Safety was a problem even in the school system. These chaotic conditions, among other problems caused us to run like hell from New York, out of the United States and straight home to Afrika.

Here we found our family of four could live in comfort on my husband's pension from the New York City Fire Department. We set about pursuing economic empowerment for ourselves and the development and betterment of our Afrikan family on the continent.

However, since arriving here we have found that there are many jobs that are either reserved exclusively for Ghanaians or require certain monetary stipulations designed for big corporations. My husband, who owned and operated his own taxicab/car service in New York, would have to have a minimum of 10 cars to go into the car service business here. If we could afford to purchase 10 cars, would we need to open a car service? We owned our own Travel Agency in the United States but in Ghana we would have needed ($10,000.00) US Dollars operating capital and a Ghanaian partner, or ($200,000.00) U.S. Dollars to do it alone. In the absence of that kind of up-front cash, we have had to call upon our God given creativity. *Returning Home Ain't Easy* chronicles how we maintained ourselves, re-connected with our extended family, developed business interests to secure a good future for our families, while trying to make a worthwhile contribution to our community.

It has been ten years since our family returned to 'Mother' Afrika leaving behind mayhem, racism, creeping anarchy, bedlam, etc. (That's not to say things aren't far from or are perfect here in Ghana). We've been tricked, accused of being racist, called Obruni (White man and foreigner), but we've also been loved and welcomed home by many of our Ghanaian brothers and sisters. They are anxious to learn about us, as we are about them. Each of us wants to know who the other has become. Who, we have become while we were separated from our 'Mother' land.

147

This healthy exchange makes a stronger bond between us. Together we can set about correcting those wrongs committed against us and remember the strength and greatness of us as Afrikan people. Just as a two-chord rope is stronger than a one-chord rope, our knowledge of the truth of our separation from one another will enable us to go forward as a stronger, united Afrikan front, a power source to be reckoned with spiritually, economically and politically..

One of our great Afrikan Leaders and Statesman, the late Osageyfo Dr. Kwame Nkrumah, 1st President of the Republic of Ghana from 1957 to 1966 said, 'All peoples of Afrikan descent whether they live in North or South America, the Caribbean or.in other part of the world are Afrikans and belong to the Afrikan nation.'

That being so, it is with the blessing and fulfillment of Prophesy that we have returned home on the wings of the wind."

Her experience, of course, contrasts sharply with that of other African Americans who have returned home, to Africa, and who have lived in different African countries, including Ghana. Some of them complain that they have been rejected or ignored by their brothers and sisters in Africa. Others say "all they want is our money, the dollar," nothing else. "We're nothing but bags of dollars for them," as one African American woman who went to the Ivory Coast said. They don't want to have anything to do "with us," as another African American woman, who lived in Ghana, reportedly said, as quoted by *The Wall Street Journal*, March 14, 2001. She got tired of the hostility and negative attitude towards African Americans and returned to the United States.

The story in *The Wall Street Journal* raises a number of questions, in a larger context, as to the relevance of what was reportedly said. Even if it is true that there were indeed some Ghanaians who were not very friendly with the African Americans quoted in the article, out of how many? Are most Ghanaians hostile or indifferent towards African Americans?

There are definitely those who are, just as there are other Africans who feel the same way in other African countries. But to tarnish the image of the entire country simply because some Africans feel the way they do towards black Americans in a negative way, is unwarranted. It also calls into question the motives of the writer. But that is typical of the Western media. They love to portray Africa in a negative light. And they hate to say anything good about the "Dark Continent." That would be too good to be true, is their attitude.

But if nothing good comes out of Africa, and if the vast majority of Africans are indeed hostile towards American Americans, it defies rational explanation why they keep on going there every year, and why many of them have even settled permanently in Africa. As Retha Hill, an African American, put it: "A trip to Ghana is not just a vacation; it is a balm for a broken soul."

African Americans are not the only ones who like going to Africa. Hundreds of thousands of whites from North America and Europe and other people  also go to Africa every year, and definitely not to suffer.

However, those of us who were born and brought up in Africa and are members of indigenous tribes or ethnic groups should not deny the fact that there are some Africans who are either indifferent or hostile towards black Americans, for whatever reason or reasons. And even the few African Americans who complain about the negative attitude of some Africans towards them, should be taken seriously in order to set the record straight, instead of being ignored and dismissed as an insignificant minority.

When I lived in Grand Rapids, Michigan, for, example, I talked to a number of African Americans who said some Africans they dealt with had a very negative attitude towards black Americans, saying they steal a lot and commit a lot of other crimes, "all that crime," as the expression goes; they don't want to work or work hard like Africans do; use drugs, drop out of school, and complain too much about racism instead of helping themselves or trying to do something constructive with their lives. Others said Africans like to associate with whites more than they do with American blacks.

Yet others said some Africans claim whites like them better than they do black Americans for different reasons: Africans are not troublemakers like black Americans are; they are achievers, unlike black Americans; they behave well, unlike American

149

blacks, and so on.

There is also latent anger among many African Americans who blame Africans for capturing them and selling them into slavery. I remember a black schoolmate of mine at Aquinas College in Grand Rapids, Michigan, in 1976, who said to me: "You sold us into slavery. You sold us!"

The list goes on and on.

Now, whether or not all this is true, and I am sure some of it and may be even most of it is true, is not the point. Fantasy or reality, fact or fiction, the point is that don't ignore it. Perception exists and defines reality as much as it affects relations between Africans and African Americans. History also is sometimes distorted to fit one's perception.

Our critics, including some black Americans, ignore or don't know that most Africans did not participate in the slave trade as raiders or traders. Instead, millions were victims themselves right there in Africa, having lost their relatives, and had their livelihood and entire villages and communities destroyed or wiped out, forcing them to live in a chronic state of uncertainty for decades and even for centuries, in many cases, because of this diabolical traffic engineered and masterminded by the white man who also was the biggest beneficiary.

Even many African slave raiders were victims themselves, forced to capture others or get killed if they didn't. And don't forget that many Africans resisted enslavement and fought against the slave raiders and traders.

Therefore most Africans were against slavery and the slave trade. Only a few, in fact very few, captured and sold into slavery people from their own communities. Most of those who were sold by fellow Africans were war captives or members of other tribes not on friendly with or outrgiht hostile to their tribe or tribes.

Many African Americans, out of anger or because of ignorance, overlook those historical facts, thus helping fuel misperceptions and perpetuate misunderstanding between them and us. When some of us try to explain all this and put things in their proper historical perspective in order to understand how slavery was conducted, by whom and why, and who was guilty, that some of our African American brethren think we are just being defensive of the criminal and reprehensible conduct of our

150

ancestors and are justifying the enslavement of our people, selling them to the white man.

No, we are not erecting barricades, and we don't have a fortress mentality as if we are under siege resisiting onslaught by our brethren, African Americans, many of whom still ask us why we sold them into slavery. Nothing is going to be solved unless we start to communicate effectively and on sustained basis. And such communication entails dispassionate analysis of all the issues involved including the role of Africans in the slave trade.

Therefore constructive dialogue is the only solution, or at least one of the solutions. And it entails tolerance on both sides. Response to every question raised by either side is also critical to a better understanding between the two sides, as much as it is with regard to the article in *The Wall Street Journal* of March 2001 which, even if it contained some truths, deliberately distorted reality and omitted some facts in order to conform to the stereotypical image not only of Ghana but of Africa as a whole.

One of the responses came from an association of African Americans living in Ghana, published on newsinghana.com, under the title, "African-American Association of Ghana Angry with *Wall Street Journal* publication":

"A publication in the March 14 edition of the Wall Street Journal, the most widely read business newspaper in the world, has been described as an attempt by American neo-colonialists to stop the transfer of wealth from the US to Africa.

According to the article, some African Americans who moved their families and their businesses to Ghana with the hope of linking up with their ancestral homeland feel unwelcome and betrayed because Ghanaians are only interested in their money.

The article said Ghanaians see African Americans as an arrogant breed that have a lot of money and should be taken advantage of.

Reacting to the damning article at a press conference in Accra, the President of the African American Association of Ghana (AAAG), Victoria Cooper said Ghana should demand an apology and a retraction of the story, which could stop potential tourists in the US from visiting Ghana and affect the successful organization of this year's Pan African Historical Festival, PANAFEST.

Miss Cooper, who was quoted in the article as saying that the African-American community in Ghana felt betrayed by the failure of parliament to pass the bill on dual citizenship, denied making any such statement in the interview with the white writer of the article, Paschal Zachary.

Flanked by other members of the AAAG who were mentioned in the article, Miss Cooper, who works for Price Waterhouse Coopers in Ghana, said she is considering legal action against *The Wall Street Journal*.

According to her, she has already asked the editor of the paper to retract the story. 'I have still not heard anything from them ever since I told them to retract the story. I am still monitoring the paper and will resort to other means if they fail to do so. America is a country ruled by law and I will make sure the publication does not tarnish my image,' she added."

The article by *The Wall Street Journal* provoked furious responses from many quarters, obviously because it distorted the truth, did not present the whole picture, and tarnished the image of the entire country and an entire people who were portrayed as hostile towards their kith-and-kin from the African diaspora.

It was written by Gregg Pascal Zachary and entitled, "Tangled Roots of African Americans in Ghana, The Grass Isn't Always Greener," a title that sent mixed signals to its readers, especially those interested in Africa in general, not just in Ghana. As he stated in the article, reproduced here in its entirety:

"ACCRA, Ghana -- Kwaku Sintim-Misa, a popular comedian here, likes to tell a joke about the African American who emigrates to Ghana.

'Brother, I've found my roots!' the African American crows. A local shakes his head, wondering why anyone with a coveted United States passport would choose to move to Ghana. 'Move to the Motherland?' the Ghanaian cries, 'I want to escape the Motherland.'

Mr. Sintim-Misa's story gets laughs because it rings true. Last year, the number of Ghanaians applying to legally enter the U.S. tripled. In the same year, Ghana's currency lost nearly two-thirds of its value against the dollar. So many skilled and educated

Ghanaians have fled that Mr. Sintim-Misa has the impression that 'nobody wants to live in Ghana anymore.'

Nobody, that is, except African Americans.

Promised Land

U.S. officials estimate that 1,000 African Americans live in Ghana, mostly in its capital, Accra, and that an additional 10,000 visit as tourists each year. By many accounts the country attracts more black Americans than any other in Africa, and by a wide margin. In recent years, hundreds have decided to relocate, drawn by beautiful beaches, a tropical climate, low living costs and, most of all, a sense that this historic heart of the slave trade is an ancestral homeland.

Mona Boyd, an Arkansas native married to a Ghanaian, runs a car-rental agency in Accra. Ada Willoughby, a retiree from Tennessee who moved here in 1995, remains even after her husband's death from cerebral malaria. Michael Williams was the head of the African Studies program at Simmons College in Boston when he came here looking for a wife. He married a Ghanaian woman, Afua, in 1995 and stayed on to run an exchange program for U.S. students. Another professor, Lisa Audrey, bought a house and, keeping her post at Ohio University, teaches part of the year at Ghana's leading university.

The country's appeal is not always obvious. Electricity and water supplies are often interrupted. Malaria is rampant. Wages are meager by U.S. standards. Given the number of people leaving, the arrival of enthusiastic African Americans might be expected to delight Ghanaians.

It doesn't. Far from seeing African Americans as kin, most Ghanaians lump them together with other Americans, calling the whole lot *obruni*, which in the local Twi language means "white" or foreigner. With better education and deeper pockets, African-Americans strike many Ghanaians as arrogant. 'When they get into any situation they want to take over, and we are not like that,' says R. William Hrisir-Quaye, an official with Ghana's commission on culture.

Indeed, many black Americans living in Ghana find they aren't particularly welcome -- and wonder whether they need a new civil rights movement to secure a place in their adopted home. Ghana forbids American residents from taking most government jobs. Hospitals charge them higher fees. Americans can't vote in elections or participate in local politics. It is virtually impossible for them to obtain citizenship, or permanent 'right of abode,' even after marrying a Ghanaian. The infamous slave castles along Ghana's coastline impose entrance fees on Americans that are 30 times as high as those paid by locals.

All this annoys Yvetta Shipman, who moved here from Atlanta five years ago with her husband, gave birth to a child, named FreeSoul, and started a business exporting locally made clothes. The 37-year-old Ms. Shipman realized a longtime dream by moving to Ghana and connecting with her heritage. In Ghana, she made friends and gradually learned local ways, but still felt like an outsider, she says. After three years, she tired of Ghanaians seeing her 'not as a black sister, but as a dollar sign,' and moved back to the U.S.

The gulf between Ghanaians and African Americans seemed to narrow a bit two years ago when Ghana's President Jerry Rawlings stood alongside President Bill Clinton during a visit to the U.S. and declared that any black American who wished to live in Ghana was welcome and eligible for citizenship.

Mr. Rawlings's declaration -- his way of demonstrating solidarity with American blacks -- was widely reported at the time, igniting a record level of interest in Ghana among African Americans. But Mr. Rawlings failed to make good on his promise of citizenship. Neither he nor John A. Kufuor, who succeeded him as president in January, will talk about the possibility of giving citizenship to African Americans. The required legislation failed to win approval under Mr. Rawlings and is now considered dead. 'We feel very betrayed,' says Victoria Cooper, who heads the African-American Association of Ghana and is a partner in the Accra office of PricewaterhouseCoopers. 'It's like we've been hoodwinked. Ghanaians want our money, but they don't want us.'

Frustration Bubbles Up

One February afternoon, frustration erupted. The U.S. ambassador, Kathryn B. Robinson, drove nearly three hours on a

154

crumbling, pot-holed road in order to address the African Americans who live in the historic slave-trading communities of Cape Coast and Elmina. While the gathering was billed as an annual visit to report on Ghana, Ms. Robinson's actual purpose was to meet the vocal African Americans here. In an outdoor restaurant, called Mable's Table, set against a breathtaking stretch of rocky Atlantic coast, the ambassador peered out at 30 residents, all but four of whom were black.

The crowd at Mable's was diverse. Nathaniel Ha'levi, from Mount Vernon, N.Y., owns the restaurant with his Ghanaian wife and is a self-styled Black Hebrew who counts among his ancestors an ancient tribe of African Jews. John Childs is a retired teacher from Philadelphia who lives here year round but admits that 'without my pension I'd be on the next plane out.' Imahkus Robinson, dressed in a headscarf and an African dress, stages re-enactments of slaves being sent to the New World for African-American tourists. Gladys Rice, a nurse from Detroit, runs a health clinic, supported by her U.S. church. All share a belief that Ghana is a special place for African Americans and that this is where they belong.

The ambassador and her two aides steered the discussion away from emotional issues, but Ms. Robinson's husband, Okofo, a retired New York firefighter, complained about his humiliating experiences trying to renew his visa. Ghanaians have threatened him with 'deportation,' he insisted, perhaps as a way of getting him to pay a bribe. Since he considers himself 'a surviving descendant of Africa,' why can't he be a citizen of Ghana?

Others agreed that the visa process is unfair and that citizenship is overdue. The ambassador was sympathetic but said this was a matter for Ghanaians to decide. And that's a problem since most Ghanaians feel they owe nothing to African Americans, seeing slavery as the legacy of Europeans and Americans, not Africans.

'The African role in the slave trade is not an issue in Ghana,' says Audrey Gadzekpo, a newspaper columnist in Accra. 'People here are totally detached from any guilt or responsibility for their ancestors selling other Africans into slavery. It's like there's some collective amnesia.'

Some African Americans are determined to end this amnesia.

In eastern Ghana, Kwadwo O. Akpan, who moved from Detroit here with his wife and two children a decade ago, sits under a straw gazebo, watching three men saw a piece of wood. One holds the wood, the other saws, and the third watches. From his seat, Mr. Akpan, who is 56 years old and has taken a local name, can see a banana plantation and the man-made Volta Lake below.

He calls this spot Rosa Park Lake View, in honor of the African-American civil rights pioneer. Around him, seven houses are going up slowly. Mr. Akpan wants to build a total of 50 homes by the end of the year. 'This is a personal quest,' he says. The homes are to be sold to African Americans and other descendants of Africa. Prices, ranging from $19,000 to $30,000, are low because Mr. Akpan has persuaded local leaders to give him a tract of land as compensation for the misdeeds of African slave traders hundreds of years ago.

Unprecedented Gesture

In all of West Africa, the gesture accorded to Mr. Akpan is apparently unprecedented. In the village Akwamufie, a short drive from where he sits, a council of chiefs granted him use of this land. One chief, Nana Darko II, who is Mr. Akpan's closest ally, says his presence represents 'a revisitation of our people who left these shores. Why not accept our own people back?'

When Mr. Akpan first approached him six years ago about creating an African-American community amid rural poverty, Mr. Darko replied, 'Everyone wants to go to the U.S. Why do you want to come here?' Mr. Akpan explained that for some African Americans Ghana is a spiritual home, preferable to the U.S.

Mr. Darko appreciates Mr. Akpan's aims and effort but admits, 'this is still very difficult for me to understand.'

As difficult to fathom is the pace of work set by Mr. Akpan. In blazing midday heat, he issues a fresh batch of complaints to Mr. Darko, who supervises the local construction workers. Mr. Darko shrugs. 'African Americans expect us to have the same output as them,' he says, yet pay scales are vastly different, with Americans accustomed to earning in an hour what Africans earn in a day or a week.

Mr. Akpan, meanwhile, must keep expectations from running

156

out of control. The locals, who are normally limited to such jobs as harvesting bananas for a dollar a day, hope he will be followed by hundreds, perhaps even thousands, of well-heeled African Americans. Prosperity should come in their wake, they think. Yet such a torrent seems unlikely given the remote location of Mr. Akpan's settlement, 90 miles over poor roads from Accra.

Still, Mr. Darko hopes his community will benefit from African-American interest, though how this will happen remains a mystery. 'We've never done anything like this,' he says, 'so we don't know how it goes.'

Persuading Ghanaians to experiment may be the best hope for African Americans. In Elmina, the seaside town where the ambassador spoke, Eric Thompson produces vegetarian foods, prodding Ghanaians to diversify their starch- and meat-heavy diets. In a rented bungalow a hundred yards from the ocean, he and several Ghanaian women every morning whip up an array of yam balls, fruit cakes, banana breads and ginger-laced soy milk -- a menu that was never seen in these parts before his arrival. The food is sold to businesses and restaurants along the coast.

The 40-year-old Mr. Thompson, who goes by the name of Shabazz, wears his hair in dreadlocks and sports a small tattoo above the bridge of his nose. He moved here four years ago from Atlanta, where he ran a record store in a neighborhood so rough that he never worked without a handgun. When a friend was gunned down, he decided to leave for Ghana, where he hoped to find tranquility as well as roots.

Way With the Locals

Mr. Thompson has proven adept at winning over locals, making common cause with the leading physician in town and even some village herbalists who dispense drinkable 'bitters' that help with a variety of ailments. And he is preparing to build a small school in Elmina where he plans to teach local children about nutrition.

One recent morning, he pulled his pickup truck into the University of Cape Coast, parking near a student cafeteria. The manager was a recent convert to vegetarianism, and Mr. Thompson plied him with his latest culinary creations. 'Try these,'

157

he said, handing the manager a bag.

Mr. Thompson wants to turn the campus bus stop into an open-air cafe where commuters could munch on his vegetarian goodies while waiting for a bus. Nowhere in Ghana is this done, and the cafeteria manager, a small smiling man named Freddie, knows that a higher-up must make this revolutionary decision. He agreed to make the case to his boss. Mr. Thompson flashed a big smile and hit him with a high-five rather than Ghana's traditional finger-snap handshake. 'I'm counting on you Uncle Freddie,' he said.

This is a rare moment of delight for Mr. Thompson, who still anguishes over his decision not to follow his wife, Ms. Shipman, back to the U.S. two years ago. He wants to visit his wife and their son this spring, but he now has a problem. Having returned to the motherland, he is legally unable to leave. His last visa to live in Ghana expired a year ago. Until he normalizes his status by paying a fine or giving additional explanations for his visa violation, Ghanaian authorities won't let him leave the country.

Mr. Thompson is struck by the oddity of this situation, as he considers Ghana his home. 'I have a lot left to do here,' he says. 'It isn't always easy, and I wonder why I stay sometimes. But I am building a community and I want it to last.'"

Victoria Cooper, president of the African American Association of Ghana, denied making the statements she was quoted to have made in the interview with the *Wall Street Journal* reporter Gregg Pascal Zachary, implying the quotation was manufactured. Whatever the case, manufactured or not, one also wonders if the rest of the statements quoted and attributed to African Americans living in Ghana were also manufactured and, if they indeed were, what their response was. If they did not dispute what is attributed to them in the story, it means they said what the reporter said they did.

One of the African Americans quoted in the *Wall Street Journal* report, Kwadwo Akpan, was one of the leaders of the Detroit-based Pan-African Congress-USA, the organization that sponsored me and other African students in the seventies as I explained earlier. I learned that he and his family moved to Ghana in 1991 but I have not been in touch with him since the late seventies after I moved from Detroit to Grand Rapids, Michigan. So, I cannot confirm the veracity of the statements attributed to him or dispute what Gregg Pascal Zachary said in his report from Accra, Ghana.

But I do know that Kwadwo Akpan was then, and still is at this writing, a leader of an African-American Community in Ghana, called Fihankra, and was installed as its chief in 1997. He is a very outspoken person and a committed Pan-Africanist who would not have kept quiet if Zachary lied about him in his report in *The Wall Street Journal*. He was always very defensive of Africa, as was his wife who also worked as a reporter and features writer at the *Detroit News*, one of the nation's largest newspapers, and would have responded accordingly. As one of the main African-American leaders in Ghana, he probably did not like the tone and slant of the article. But I am not sure he, or any of the other African Americans quoted besides Victoria Cooper, disputed everything that Zachary said in his report.

Some of the strongest responses to the *Wall Street Journal* report came from Ghanaians living abroad. I got the chance to read quite a few of them and would like to reproduce some of them here to put things in proper perspective. As Dr. Kofi Ellison stated in his commentary, "Whose Tangled Roots, Zachary's or Ours?," in *Profile Africa* on March 30, 2001:

"Ghanaians in the diaspora, are still fuming over an article that was published in the March 14, 2001, edition of *The Wall Street Journal*. The article, written by Gregg P. Zachary under the headline: "Tangled Roots: For African Americans in Ghana, The Grass Isn't Always Greener", sought to highlight the lives and activities of the hundreds of African Americans who have 'emigrated' to Ghana.

That would be an interesting reading considering that at least a thousand African Americans have 'permanently' settled in Ghana, and nearly ten thousand African Americans visit Ghana yearly. Indeed, Ghana is the destination of choice for African-American tourists who visit Africa. African-American oriented Radio stations, newspapers, and churches in Washington, D.C., and other major American cities tout successful visits to Ghana or as they say, 'the motherland,' thus fueling more interest! Ghana has been assisted in so many ways by African Americans since independence.

However, the article elicited mainly protests and opprobrium from Ghanaians and African Americans alike. For Ghanaians, the article was deemed derogatory for its emphasis on the negative aspects of our underdevelopment: 'rampant malaria', 'electricity and water interruptions', and 'corruption'. By emphasizing African-American frustrations with the provision of services in Ghana, among other issues, the African Americans felt Gregg Zachary's article could antagonize their hosts; and undermine tourism!

Thus, both the Ghana government, and the African American Association of Ghana (AAAG) had to disown much of what was written. Mrs. Victoria Cooper head of the AAAG, and Mr. Akbar Muhammed, the AAAG spokesman, called for a retraction.

Ghanaians in the diaspora were similarly outraged. Short of calling for Gregg Zachary's blood, Ghanaian Internet sites encouraged people to flood *The Wall Street Journal* with e-mail letters and telephone calls to protest the 'biased' reporting. Such was the outrage that Gregg Zachary (who lives in London) had to personally engage in written discussions with Ghanaian contributors at a Ghanaian Internet forum where he was grilled as to his motives for, to use a Ghanaian proverb, pointing his left finger in the direction of our father's village!

Needless to say, much of the debate was not civil; and as happens on that particular website, the debate degenerated into the unprintable!! As I write, Gregg Zachary was also expected to appear on an Accra (Ghana) Radio station for further discussions on the issue on Friday, March 30th.

Indeed, Ghanaians in the diaspora had every reason to be incensed at the way the article portrayed events in our great country, especially when one considers the outlet used to air our dirty laundry. *The Wall Street Journal* is the most important business and financial daily in the world, and it is also the most widely read newspaper in the field. By unwittingly portraying Ghana negatively, and Ghanaians as unfriendly and hostile to 'foreigners', especially of a group that wishes to live and invest in Ghana; the article could do irreparable harm to Ghana's image in so many areas.

Rather than emphasizing the negatives aspects of Ghana's under-development, a problem that our newly democratically elected government has vowed to tackle, Gregg Zachary could have delved into some of the many positive aspects of Ghana and Ghanaians which I am sure he benefitted from during his visit. Were Mr. Zachary so inclined, he could have done a ton of good to his readers who would be interested in exploring investment opportunities in Ghana.

Among African countries, Ghanaians stand out as a peaceful, hospitable and friendly people. This view of Ghana is supported by reports coming from investors and tourists alike. As the Americans are wont to say, image is everything. Irreverent remarks such as the one in *The Wall Street Journal* (WSJ) must be countered in order that Ghana's image is not sullied. Americans and other Western countries spend millions of dollars on advertising, lobbying, and image-makers to ensure that their credibility as secure edifices of stability and free enterprise remain unchallenged. The universal condemnation of the article by the Ghanaians in the diaspora must be seen in that light.

The security of investments and ease of transfer of funds to and from Ghana is comparable to what obtains in many developed countries. For the discerning investor, the high cost of life and property insurance in neighboring countries - brought on by armed robbery, kidnapping and civil strife - is another incentive in investing in Ghana. It is significant to note that the WSJ article's only mention of death in the African-American community in Ghana, was caused by natural factors, and not as a result of a drive-by shooting, or car-jacking which the immigrants were accustomed to in the United States of America.

The writer interviewed African Americans who said they felt betrayed by the unfulfilled promises of citizenship promised them by the government of Ghana. That promise of citizenship refers to a statement of the moment made by President Jerry Rawlings during a Press Conference with president Clinton at the White House last year. President Rawlings did not consult the Ghana Legislature on the matter, and thus the promise lacked any legal basis. Neither are the issues of African Americans being denied citizenship in Ghana, or having problems in renewing their resident visas (permits), peculiar to that group only. Ghanaians who have become naturalized citizens elsewhere face similar problems. One hopes the new government will address these issues. But it must take a complete fool to believe Gregg Zachary when he writes that one African American is stranded in Ghana because his visa expired; and he cannot therefore leave Ghana!

The article quotes one Yvetta Shipman, (formerly of Atlanta), regarding her frustrations at not being accepted as "a black sister" after three years sojourn in Ghana! A debilitating aspect of the African-American imagination of Africa, and hence Ghana, is the romanticism, and sometimes the naivete that attends their view of Africa.

It is not as if our African-American 'cousins' are returning to Ghana after a few years' trip to America; to be recognized by uncles, aunts, and other relations. At least four hundred years has lapsed since the initial 'forced migration' (to borrow historian Joseph Inikori's phrase on the subject of the Trans-Atlantic Slave Trade) to America. It shouldn't take a dose of reality to understand that it is the children of the 'new immigrants' who will be truly Ghanaian, just as say anyone born and bred from, Asuonwun in Asante! African immigrants in America report similar frustrations in their relationship (or lack of it), with African Americans in the United States of America. And Ghanaians have also suffered from some of the indignities that African Americans have been subjected to in the United States of America.

A noted example is the treatment meted out to the late Mr. Komla Agbeli Gbedemah. As Ghana's Finance Minister, Mr. Gbedemah travelled to the United States to conduct official government business. According to a *New York Times* report of October 9, 1957, Gbedemah was refused service at a restaurant in Dover, Delaware; because of his skin color. It did not matter that Mr. Gbedemah had officially hosted the then U.S. vice-president, Richard Nixon, and the official U.S. delegation to the Ghana independence celebration at a feast in Accra in March 1957. One of the greatest Americans of any color, W.E.B. Dubois lived, died, and is buried in Accra! We have ties that bind.

But African Americans must show restraint in their expectations while in Ghana, as further affirmation of their commitment to Ghana, and Ghanaians. They must not be seen as retreating to the United States (as some of the 'immigrants' have reportedly done) at the least perceived injury to their pride and sense of purpose; and then spread unfounded rumours about life in Ghana!

Furthermore, African Americans return to Ghana, not as Black people imbued with African ideals and culture. Rather, African American return as know-it-all Americans; and products of centuries of being brainwashed about Africa. Most of them still subscribe to the racist Western view of Africa as a jungle inhabited by Tarzans gallivanting from tree to tree! African Americans have also bought into the romanticism of being descended from "Nubian" (i.e. African) Kings and Queens. It is inevitable therefore that some of them would expect to be treated as Princes and Princesses upon their return to the 'motherland'! That is not reality.

Should our African-American 'cousins' shear themselves of whatever romantic pretenses they harbor about Ghana (and indeed Africa), and resign themselves to the reality of a 'Third-World' situation, that is completely 'unlike America', perhaps the initial culture shock will subside into a more mature relationship. That way, even some of the 'most alienated and bitter cultural migrants' from America will indeed find a home in Ghana. Above all, Ghana should endeavor to attract the upper-crust of American society to invest in Ghana (Black or White!); and not rely only on the 'Black Hebrews,' 'Nation of Islam' zealots, and retirees looking for sun and fun, who flocked to Ghana under Rawlings!!

Neither do African Americans have a humanitarian record once they are accorded citizenship in Africa. The last time African Americans were granted outright citizenship in Africa, the effect was the diminution of the African as savage and uncivilized, worthy only to be colonized, and treated as second-class citizen. That happened in Liberia since the 1820's when freed slaves made their home in those parts. In 1926, the League of Nations had to censure the (African-) Americo-Liberian (as the freed slaves and their descendants called themselves) government for operating a system of forced labor on the 'natives', that was akin to slavery. It took the Samuel Doe coup d'etat in 1980 to right the wrongs in Liberia.

African-Americans can be a great source of investment in Africa, but there is no greater example than by their lack of similar investment in black neighborhoods in America!!

As a developing country, Ghana is afflicted by all the symptoms of under-development, yet the tendency to emphasize the negative aspects by the Western Media is mind-boggling. Gregg Zachary's attempt to introduce Ghanaian guilt in the slave trade in his article on the lives of African-American immigrants in Ghana is typical of ongoing attempts by the West, to shift 'the slave trade blame-game to Africans to assuage European and American guilt. It follows among others, earlier American TV documentary pieces on slavery such as those by Arthur Kent on the History Channel, and Henry Louis Gates, Jr., on public television's PBS Channel.

The gist of the new argument is that 'without African participation, the Trans-Atlantic Slave Trade could not have been possible.' That is simply hogwash. It is as if the Europeans sought African agreement before building the ships, the chains, the Forts, and all the instruments needed to effectuate the nefarious trade. Or as if Europeans sought African views at Berlin 1884 when the partition and colonization of Africa was discussed and planned. Did African concerns matter in these two wholly European enterprises, intended to benefit Europeans and Americans?

The Slave Trade was a European enterprise into which Africans were dragged as bit players! Six years ago, a delegation of Ghanaian Chiefs led by Nana Oduro Numamapau, the Paramount Chief of Asumenya in the Asante Region did in fact travel to the USA to deliver an apology to an African-American group for Ghanaian chiefs' role in the slave trade.

It can only be surmised that African guilt in the slave trade is being employed in order to drive a wedge between the African Americans and Ghanaians, in this instance. Thus, the article could have the unintended consequence of destroying the fledgling tourism business in Ghana, by casting Ghanaians as ancient slave traders, and currently hostile to the descendants of slaves who have returned to the 'motherland'!

As a people, Ghanaians relish debates, criticisms, and differing opinions. We are our own harshest critics. Several of our idioms and proverbs such as 'Ti Kro Nko Agyina,' 'Dua Kro Gye Mframa a Ebu,' all speak to the dangers inherent in not accepting advise and criticism. Ghanaians are aware that much of our roads are savaged by pot-holes; that our public health system is in disarray; and that corruption inhibits the deliverance of prompt service in the public sector. Such issues are debated and written about endlessly in the Ghanaian newspapers, and discussed on radio and television. Indeed, the government is taking adequate measures to redress these problems. Hence, Gregg Zachary's article is pointless and retrograde, in its portrayal of Ghana in rather negative tones at a time when Ghana is at the forefront in Africa's march to progress and development; activities to which investors such as the readers of *The Wall Street Journal* have been invited by the new Ghanaian administration to participate.

The new millennium presents new opportunities and challenges for Ghana. Ghana has just had peaceful elections, and inaugurated a new a president to office. The country enjoys peace and stability which are sine qua non to political and economic development. Gregg Zachary and *The Wall Street Journal* could have emphasized these positive aspects as a good service to its numerous readers who may wish to invest in, or visit Ghana.

By deciding to focus on the trivial, and rehashing non-existing tensions, Gregg Zachary provided a disservice to his readers by continuing the inordinate and pernicious practice among the Western media to ignore everything but the negative in Africa. Such a view can only derail Ghana's attempt to entice foreign investors to assist in the development of the country. And that would be unfortunate!!!"

Yet some of the things Zachary said in his article seem to have been supported or substantiated by some Ghanaians, and even by a significant number of African Americans themselves, especially the cold reception some African Americans have been accorded upon their arrival and when staying or living in Ghana. As Ishmael Mensah, who did not dispute all, if any, of what Zachary said, stated in his article, "Marketing Ghana As A Mecca For The African American Tourist":

"There is talk of African-Americans feeling unwelcome to Ghana as well as allegations of mistreatment. They claim Ghanaians are intolerant to African Americans and treat them as foreign tourists to be exploited though they are their own kith and kin. As one African-American lady Nehanda Imara, puts it 'we were not greeted at the airport with open arms, and are perceived as *obrunis*.'

Other factors that have contributed to this perception is the Citizenship Bill of 2001 with an additional provision which would have given African-Americans and Africans in the Diaspora 'the right of abode' which was only passed in 2002 by the NPP government. Even under this new bill, it takes seven years for them to apply and get the right of abode so as to be able to live and work in Ghana without having to resort to visa renewals.

African Americans have also accused Ghanaians of denying them government jobs, the right to vote as well as charging them higher hospital bills. In 2001, *Wall Street Journal* reporter Pascal Zachary talked about his first-hand experience with the above claims in his article "Tangled Roots for African-Americans in Ghana, the Grass isn't Always Greener" . Though this received wide condemnation from the African-American Association of Ghana (AAAG) and numerous Ghanaians in the Diaspora, the damage that this article caused to the image of Ghana, cannot be underestimated."

Mensah seems to agree with Zachary and other observers including a number of African Americans themselves, one of whom he quotes in his article, that there are indeed some Ghanaians - hence other Africans - who don't embrace their cousins from the diaspora. He does not explain why, but obviously they don't feel any kinship with them; they are culturally different; they are distant from each other physically and spiritually; they each live in their own world; they have their own problems to contend with, and so forth.

Some of this was brought into sharp focus by a Ghanaian who wrote to *African Spectrum* in April 2001 in response to a number of critics of Zachary's article and to African Americans themselves who had complained of mistreatment or rejection by Ghanaians in Ghana:

"When Ghanaians meet Americans, whether at home or abroad, they do not draw a distinction between White and Black. We do not feel any more emotionally drawn to American Blacks

166

than Whites, because the forces that have shaped African-American history, politics and lifestyles are different from what we Africans have been through. That is why when African Americans expect us to treat them as sisters and brothers, they find us disappointing - we see them as Americans, pure and simple.

In fact, some African Americans don't even want us to treat them as 'fellow brothers or sisters.' They simply do not want to be reminded of their African roots. They are offended when we Africans try to establish a link between their history and ours, and relate to them as comrades. They want to be left alone, so to speak, because as they say, America is the only country they have known - they have nothing to do with Africa. 'If people don't refer to Europeans who migrated from Europe to America as European Americans, why do they want to call us African American?,' they are often heard asking.

If all African Americans would show greater interest in their African roots as other ethnic groups that have migrate to America, probably it would draw the attention of Africans to the bonds that exist between us. We would be sensitized to the need to draw closer to them and see them as sisters and brothers.

Unfortunately, that is not the case. When African Americans display contrasting perceptions about Africa, as they are doing now, it would dissipate the efforts of the well-meaning African Americans to draw Africans closer to them. This contrasting attitude makes some of us defensive at best, and at worst we become aloof, and standoffish.

Some African Americans are even hostile to Africans living in the United States. Some of them look down upon us as inferior people from a less developed part of the world; some are angry with us because of what they call the collaborative attitude of our ancestors who sold them into slavery. The latter school of thought thinks that our stay here in America affects their chances for education and employment because we compete with them for the few positions available.

What is more worrisome to them is that many Africans come to the US as students to study in colleges. Even those who do not come as students eventually find colleges to go to. With such a high desire for college and professional education, some African

Americans are concerned that Africans will steal the limelight from them.

Ms. Dee Robinson's (the Ambassador to Ghana) husband is a member of a diplomatic family; so I wonder why he would have problems with his visa. An ambassador's husband is unlikely to be threatened with deportation, even under a military regime. I don't see how I can reconcile this allegation with what I know to be the current arrangement that the government of Ghana has for members of the diplomatic corps and their families.

I want to comment also on the allegation that an African-American woman who had immigrated to Ghana returned to the US out of frustration because Ghanaians would only relate to her as a dollar sign and not as one of them. While this is an unfortunate thing to have happened to this woman, I would like to stress here that she suffered that fate not because she is American. What she went through happens to even native Ghanaians living abroad who return home to visit. Because we live in 'the white man's land' we are considered 'wealthy.'"

There is also some evidence showing that not every African American living in Ghana disputed the essence of what Gregg Pascal Zachary said in his article in *The Wall Street Journal*.

One of them was a professor at the University College of Education of Winneba who implied he had bad experiences with some Ghanaians, may be quite a few of them, simply because he was an African American.. As he stated in his letter to Zachary published in *African Spectrum*:

"Thank you so much for your article. It is very eye opening. I am an African American who currently resides in Ghana. Your article hits home a lot of my experiences....

I am not proud of these experiences, but it is easier to cope with them when you realize that this not something to take personally. I use these misunderstandings as an opportunity to 'lecture' to Ghanaians I meet about my decision to be here. I explain it is a cultural decision and not a financial one. I have mixed emotions about this being a permanent home for me, because of emotional loyalty and financial abuse.

This article has given me a lot to think about, as it reflects some of my past conversations with some of the people you have mentioned in your article.

Is it possible to love Ghana in spite of the people, or can you only love Ghana only because of the people?

Thanks again for the insight."

The African American professor who wrote this leaves the unmistakable impression that he has had some bad experiences with a number of Ghanaians which have jolted him into reality about life in a black African country where many black Americans automatically assume they will be wholeheartedly embraced by their African brothers and sisters when they "return home."

The problem with this kind of reasoning is that it does not correspond to reality. Many African Americans have a romantic view of Africa. But when they get there, they quickly find out that it is not the idyllic place they thought it was when they were still in the United States. Compounding the problem is the fact that probably the majority of Africans in black African countries *don't* see black Americans as "returning home," to Africa, but merely as foreigners coming to Africa in spite of their ancestral ties to the continent.

It does not necessarily mean that they are hostile towards them - some are, of course, just as they are towards other foreigners and even towards members of other tribes in their own countries. It simply means that they don't feel any special kinship with African Americans because they have been separated for so long, prompting many Africans to conclude that black Americans lost all their African identity and are therefore no longer African.

To many African Americans, of course, this is tantamount to rejection by their own people, the very same people they embrace as their kith-and-kin yet who want to maintain distance from them. A lot of this frustration, and even anger, on the part of African Americans comes from the high expectations they have of Africa, and of the people themselves; expectations which do not correspond to reality or match the performance - in all areas across the spectrum including personal relationships between black Americans and Africans - they expect to see when they arrive on the continent.

169

What the frustrated African American professor said should be viewed in this larger context, especially when he asked: "Is it possible to love Ghana in spite of the people, or can you only love Ghana only because of the people?" It is a sentiment articulated in nationalistic terms - in this case in a Pan-African context - and reminds me of what French Prime Minister Monsieur Clemenceau once said when he talked about loving France without loving Frenchmen.

There are ideals we aspire to, but, sadly, they remain ideals. One of those ideals is the acceptance and unification of all Africans and people of African descent in the diaspora as one and the same people. Attitudes, however negative towards each other, can never change this reality. It is a fundamental truth, it is an immutable fact. We have already taken the first steps towards achieving this goal, and we have made some progress. But it is one long journey. We still have a long, long way to go.

# Chapter Five:

# The Attitude of African Americans Towards Africans

AFRICAN AMERICANS are not a monolithic whole anymore than Africans are. But there are some things that bind them together and shape their attitude, or attitudes, towards Africa.

There is a perception among a significant number of Africans, backed up by empirical evidence derived from personal experiences with black Americans, that their brothers and sisters, or cousins, in the United States, don't want to be closely identified with Africa, if at all, and have a negative attitude towards their ancestral homeland and its people.

There are several reasons for this. Probably the most important one is that black Americans *are*, first and foremost, Americans, not Africans in terms of national identity and upbringing; although they are also Africans in the genealogical sense.

They were born and raised in the richest, most developed, and most powerful country in the history of mankind and are a product of American culture in terms of mentality, attitudes, values, and the way they look at the world even if some black nationalists in the United States may deny that with regard to mentality and culture. It is true that black Americans constitute "a nation within a nation," as black American sociologist E. Franklin Frazier argued in his classic work, *Black Bourgeoisie*. But that is because of racism and segregation. Therefore Black America, as a nation within a nation, still is a product of white America.

Anyway, by contrast, as opposed to black Americans, Africans come from or live in the world's most backward, most diseased, and poorest continent - as conventional wisdom goes - which also is the ancestral homeland of African Americans whether they like it or not.

The contrast between the two is glaring, and ruthlessly public, often thrust into the international arena and spotlight when people around the world, including black Americans, see on their television screens and in newspapers and magazines, millions of Africans starving, dying of AIDS and numerous other diseases many of them preventable, and desperately pleading and begging for help from other countries including some in the Third World such as India and Brazil.

All this has had a profound impact on African Americans and their image as Americans, yet at the same time as Africans, as well, inextricably linked with their kith-and-kin living in misery on the African continent. It is an image many of them are ashamed of. But it is also reality, a harsh reality, they cannot evade or escape and from which they will never be able to escape although many of them may desperately try to do so. And they include the educated, not just the uneducated.

Even many African Americans who identify themselves with Africa have an ambivalent attitude towards their motherland, and ask themselves, like Countee Cullen did, "What is Africa to me?," in his poem "Heritage":

"What is Africa to me:
Copper sun or scarlet sea,
Jungle star or jungle track,
Strong bronzed men, or regal black
Women from whose loins I sprang
When the birds of Eden sang?
One three centuries removed
From the scenes his fathers loved,
Spicy grove, cinnamon tree,
What is Africa to me?"

The difference is that Cullen, who died in 1946 at the age of 43, wrote that poem in expression of his love for Africa, even if his passionate love for his motherland was somewhat tempered by the negative image of Africa he had known when growing up and during the rest of his short life.

And there are many African Americans today who feel the way he did. But there is another group of African Americans who are torn apart by two images of Africa. They are attracted by its beauty, and a longing for their roots, reinforcing their romantic image of Africa; yet they are repelled by the harsh realities on the continent, the poverty, the hardship, and even by the primitive condition of the people themselves, so close yet so far, separated for centuries.

I remember in the early 1980s talking to an African American woman in Grand Rapids, Michigan, who was married to a Nigerian. After she went to Nigeria and came back, she said she couldn't live in Nigeria or anywhere else in Africa because she was not used to the lifestyle and the inconveniencies.

I talked to another one who once lived in Liberia and moved back to Grand Rapids after the 1980 military coup, disgusted with the place because of what the new military rulers did, executing Americo-Liberian leaders and wreaking havoc across Monrovia, the capital. As an African American, she easily identified with the Americo-Liberians far more than she did with the "natives," if at all. And she did not put in historical perspective the injustices perpetrated against the indigenous people which prompted a 28-year-old sergeant, Samuel Doe, and 16 of his compatriots from the Liberian army, to seize power after 150 years of Americo-Liberian hegemonic control of the country to the detriment of the native population.

Yet, when she first went to Africa, she had a very romantic view of the motherland as do the majority of black Americans who go there. Compounding the problem was the hardship one experiences living in a poor and underveloped Third World country like Liberia. The same applies to the rest of the countries on the continent, the poorest of the poor in the entire world.

Many African Americans who intended to settle in Africa or live there for an indefinite period of time have been known to turn right back, after only a short stay, vowing never to return except, and that is may be, for short visits. They did not expect to see what they found and saw when they arrived there; a place so attractive, and alluring, with its majestic beauty, yet sometimes so forbidding even to the most hardened soul, except the inordinately ambitious to defy the odds.

That is what prompts many Africans to ask black Americans: "What did you come here for? We are desperately trying to get out of here and go to America or some other place, and you are dying to come here!" And it is not before long that the harsh reality settles in: "It was a mistake, a big, terrible mistake, to come here. I wish I had known. I would never have left the United States."

But that is only part of the story, in fact not even half of it. A higher percentage of African Americans who go or intend to go to Africa don't have such a negative attitude towards their motherland. Many of them go there, even if not to stay. It is a pilgrimage, a physical and spiritual journey, to the motherland they have never known or seen since they were forcibly uprooted from there and transplanted on American soil permanently. Yet, even some of these returnees also feel out of place when they are in Africa. For cultural and historical reasons, they don't seem to fit in.

In spite of all this, probably an even higher percentage of African Americans, most of whom don't intend to leave the United States and go back to Africa to visit or to stay, have some kind of emotional attachment to the land of their ancestors regardless of how much they hear about this "Dark Continent" as a miserable place: desperately poor, backward, primitive, and intolerable. One clearly sees this in the support African Americans have given to Africa through years, especially during the liberation struggle, and in defending their motherland whenever it is negatively portrayed in the white-dominated media in the United States and elsewhere around the world; and when African interests are ignored by white American leaders and other vested interests.

And they probably could do more if they were not under white control. They operate in a milieu that is not of their making, and in a society whose interests do not necessarily coincide with theirs. White interests are paramount.

Yet African Americans have tried to overcome these barriers in order to help Africa. It is a positive attitude that should be acknowledged. Unfortunately, Africans have sometimes not reciprocated this feeling the way they should. As the late Nigerian scholar, Professor Claude Ake, who died at the age of 57 in a mysterious plane crash near Lagos in November 1996, said in an interview with an African journalist Walusako Mwalilino published in *West Africa Review*:

"Walusako Mwalilino:
'Let's talk about African Americans vis-a-vis Africans. What's your assessment of their reactions towards Africa? Are they playing a positive role regarding what's happening in Africa today? I bring this up in view of the repeated [anti-apartheid] demonstrations in front of the South African Embassy, for instance. But right now, where there have been a lot of killings in Liberia and many other African countries, the African American voice is very muted towards these happenings in African countries. Why do you think that is so? Or, am I expecting too much from them?'

Claude Ake:
'Well, I think so, because you have to look at the matter in its historical context. African Americans are doing their best in the circumstances. I think that if they could do better, they would. I do not believe...the kinds of contradictions people think...exist, [really] exist. You have to look at this whole thing in terms of the general situation of oppressed people. We are oppressed people, both Africans and African Americans. And it is much more difficult for the weak and oppressed to rally in their own defense than for the strong and the privileged to organize their own defense. That is part of the very definition of being weak.

Now, African Americans suffer discrimination, they are marginalized, they have no serious access to the media, particularly television. They have some marginal influence over some rather obscure radio stations, but no major network. They have no control over any major national newspaper. They have no control over any chain of corporations. It is only recently that they have had a governorship [of Douglas Wilder in the State of Virginia]. So their general condition, under the admission of *The New York Times* and in some of the surveys that have been done and published recently, they have been losing ground. Their health condition has deteriorated to that of the people in

Bangladesh. And it has come to the point where, a newspaper like *The New York Times*, is writing about the young black male being an endangered species; of many more [black] people being in prisons than in universities. And so the years of reaction have meant a loss of even some of the marginal gains they have made.

So these are people under pressure - under tremendous amount of pressure by a system that is not only not yet given them their due, but is actually conspiring in their regression. So they're struggling to hang on against all these disadvantages in a society in which you have to have the strength to stand for yourself or nobody will stand for you. And you can see how this frustration is internalized in violence within the black community.

Yet, in spite of all this, they take interest in Africa as much as they can. Those of them who have a little leverage, like Jesse Jackson -- without minding the consequences of this [to] their political fortunes here in the United States, and on occasions where they could focus their energies profitably, as in the struggle against apartheid in South Africa -- they have done so admirably. And the visit of [Nelson] Mandela [in June 1990] was an incredible display of solidarity. So I think that we should give them credit.

Of course, compared with what other people do here for the groups in other parts of the world from which they come - for instance, like the support for Israel [by Jewish Americans] - Africa is very far from getting that kind of support. You cannot really compare. I mean, given the disadvantages [of African Americans], I really think that it is superficial to blame somebody who is marginalized, struggling in regression, that they are not doing [enough]. They are doing within the circumstances.

Now you also have to consider the other side: Africans, too, have an obligation to do for black Americans. It is not a one-way street. And Africa has not done anything for black Americans. Because, the prestige of black Americans - their ability to walk erect here - depends also partly on what we do in Africa. And what we have done in Africa in 30 years [since the independence period] is to fumble our opportunities. Instead of helping African Americans to stand erect, we are making them ashamed to be like us. And I think that a very important part of this equation is to straighten ourselves in Africa; and, in the process of doing so, try also to support the African Americans. So, it should not be a matter of one person trying to distance himself from the other or become an embarrassment, but one of recognizing our common cause, disadvantages and our marginality, and knowing that whatever any of us achieves helps the other person to have greater self-esteem, to be better respected by others, and to move forward collectively.

Walusako Mwalilino:

'In specific terms, how can African leaders assist black Americans?'

Claude Ake:

'African leaders can assist black Americans, first of all, by stopping fumbling! The African Americans don't need people sending them distraught news from Africa; they need good news from Africa. That is the first thing. That would be enough! They want to read about good news, of good examples, of people who are trying hard, of people who are confronting difficulties with courage and dignity and intelligence.

We need more examples of the Botswanas and their [economic] experiments, of progress, of prudence in management, of humanitarian concerns.

Let us give them good news so that they can be proud of the places they have come from. And when they're proud of themselves and their history, their sense of efficacy here [in the United States] will be enhanced. The material connections can come later. What they need is good news from Africa: that we should help ourselves and strengthen ourselves. Nobody likes to come from a background in which you are ashamed. And part of the reason why they can be put down here, so decisively, is precisely because we are creating a background of shame [for them].'"

And it is understandable, in a way, why they would be ashamed of such a background. If Africa was developed like Europe is, or was moving forward like some parts of Asia and even Latin America are doing, an even larger number of African Americans, probably almost all of them, would be proud of their motherland. And they would be telling the rest of the world: "See? How our motherland is doing and how it looks like? And how our people are doing over there? Just fantastic! We *are* on the move as a people. And we keep on moving."

But that is not the general attitude among the majority of African Americans, and for good reason. Even many Africans born and raised in Africa are ashamed of the place. Just talk to them. Hundreds of thousands of them already live in the United States permanently. They fled from Africa. And they share the *same* attitude towards their motherland just like many African Americans do. They are ashamed of the place because, they say, we could do better and have the same genetic endowment members of other races do.

Even many black American college students, who are supposed to be enlightened, show disdain for Africans on campus and act as if they have nothing to do with them, in spite of their common identity and heritage as children of Africa regardless where they were born. And it's no just in predominantly white colleges and universities where this goes on; it goes on in black schools as well. As one Ghanaian who attended Morehouse College, an elite college for black male students in Atlanta, Georgia, stated on amazon.com in October 1999 in his review of a book written by Philippe Wamba, *Kinship*: *A Family's Journey in Africa and America*, which also examines relations between Africans and African Americans, among other subjects:

"Born in Ghana and having lived in the US for 18 years, I share almost all of Wamba's sentiments. At my alma mater, Morehouse College, the flagship black institution, Africans were mostly looked upon with disdain.

As a practicing physician in rural Georgia now, I am exposed to very poor blacks who hail from generations of poverty and illiteracy. Almost all descended from the slave plantations that dotted this area. All of Wamba's experiences are drawn from African Americans with education (Harvard students, etc). Even among this educated group, the knowledge of Africa is minuscule.

Imagine the level of knowledge in this area in the deep south. It has never ceased to perplex me how a group of people will be so lost as to their origins. One might argue that point that, so what? What difference does it make if someone does not identify with his or her ancestral homeland?"

There is no question that many African Americans don't. That is their general attitude. But Philippe Wamba was not of them. A product of two cultures, or "two" black worlds, Philippe Wamba was born in the United States but grew up in Tanzania. His mother was an African American. His father, Ernest Wamba dia Wamba, was a Congolese who once was imprisoned by President Mobutu Sese Seko of Zaire (renamed Congo) because of his political activities and opposition to Mobutu's despotic and kleptocratic regime. He attended school in the United States, returned to Zaire, and moved to Tanzania where he became a professor at the University of Dar es Salaam. He later became the head of one of the major opposition groups which eventually toppled President Mobutu in May 1997.

Like his father and his mother, Philippe Wamba, who died in a tragic car accident in Kenya in 2002 at the age of 31, was proud of his African heritage as much as he was of his African-American background. But that is not the general attitude among the vast majority of African Americans; theirs is an ambiguity, of this dual identity as Africans in diaspora and as Americans born and raised in America. Some accept it, some don't. Many Africans feel the same way towards their brethren in the diaspora.

So, when we talk about the attitude of African Americans towards Africa, or the attitude of Africans and of African Americans towards each other, we are talking about their attitudes in a larger context, as opposed to those of individuals. But such generalization can sometimes be grossly misleading in many individual cases. That is because not everybody feels that way. I know, for example, many members of the Pan-African Congress in Detroit who were not ashamed of Africa but were, instead, very defensive of their motherland; and for good reason.

Whites have used the backwardness of Africa to demean and belittle, discredit and dehumanize, and insult African Americans, telling them they have no history or culture to be proud of, and should be glad their ancestors were taken from the jungles of Africa giving their descendants the chance, the golden chance, to be born in the land of milk and honey, in this sweet land of liberty, "'tis of thee I sing."

But as Malcolm X said: "We have not enjoyed any American

fruit, only thorns and thistles." And as he said on another occasion: "I don't see any American dream; I see an American nightmare." And he had a very positive attitude towards Africa, reminding other African Americans who were ashamed of their motherland: "You left your mind in Africa." And the general attitude of a significant number of African Americans towards Africa remains largely negative.

Yet our knowledge of the general attitude of a people, even if it is grossly misleading in  many individual cases, is based on observation and cumulative knowledge derived from individual attitudes across a broad section of that particular people. For example, we talk about the general attitude of whites towards blacks based on observation and the pervasiveness and persistence of racism.

Therefore, the majority of whites are racist, is the inevitable conclusion based on empirical evidence: racism is a fact of life. It is brutal, it is pervasive and penetrates every social fabric of the American society, contrary to what black American conservatives - they don't even want to be called African Americans, just Americans - say, contending that racism is no longer a serious problem in the United States, and that black people are their own number one problem because they lack values conducive to achievement. It is a subject I have addressed in one of my books, *Black Conservatives*: *Are They Right or Wrong?*: *The Black Conservative Phenomenon in Contemporary America*: *Contending Ideologies*: *Conservatism versus Liberalism.*

As in the case of white attitudes towards blacks, the general attitude of Africans and of African Americans towards each other is also derived from general observation and from our experience with individuals in both groups whose attitudes, we believe, reflect a broad consensus among a very large number of people in those groups and may be even the majority.

Therefore, there is some validity to the conclusion reached, for example, the belief among a significant number of Africans that many African Americans have an ambivalent attitude towards Africa: they identify with it but are uncomfortable with the image of Africa as a backward continent and may be they are even ashamed of it as their ancestral homeland.

Yet, even negative attitudes of individuals which do *not* reflect

180

a broad spectrum of consensus among their people, Africans or African Americans, *do* show that there *are* problems in relations between the two groups that need to be addressed. These problems are caused mainly by lack of communication and misunderstanding between the two peoples - who are really one and the same people - and by distortion of truth about Africa by the media and other detractors of Africa, especially racists, more than anything else.

A look at some of these conflicting attitudes between the two groups may shed some light on this intractable problem for a greater understanding and possible resolution of this perennial conflict. It may not be the biggest problem Africans and African Americans face in the world, bit it is a problem nonetheless. And unless the problem is solved, all talk of racial solidarity in a world where we mean nothing to the rest of mankind - because and only because we are weak and powerless - is no more than empty rhetoric.

And what is so sad is that some of these attitudes towards each other have not changed through the decades. As Tracie Reddick, a black columnist, stated in her article, "African vs. African American: A Shared Complexion Does Not Guarantee Racial Solidarity," in *The Tampa Tribune*:

"When Anthony Eromosele Oigbokie came to American in 1960, he heard racial slurs - not from Klansmen in white sheets - but from dashiki-wearing blacks.

'Just because African-Americans wear kente cloth does not mean they embrace everything that is African,' says Oigbokie, a Nigerian business owner in Tampa. 'I caught a lot of hell from the frat boys at Tuskegee University,' a historically black college in Alabama.

'They were always trying to play with my intelligence. This was a time when folks were shouting, 'Say it loud: I'm black and I'm proud.' Yet, when I called someone black, they would say, 'Why are you so cruel? Why are you calling us black?' If they saw me with a girl, they would yell to her, 'What are you doing with that African?'

Three decades later, not much has changed. Africans and black Americans often fail to forge relationships in the classroom and

181

the workplace. They blame nationality, ethnicity, culture, economics and education.

'A shared complexion does not equal a shared culture, nor does it automatically lead to friendships,' says Kofi Glover, a native of Ghana and a political science professor at the University of South Florida. 'Whether we like it or not, Africans and African Americans have two different and very distinct cultures.'

'That's a fallacy,' retorts Omali Yeshitela, president of St. Petersburg's National Peoples' Democratic Uhuru Movement, a black nationalist group whose name means 'freedom' in Swahili. Yeshitela is from St. Petersburg and was formerly known as Joe Waller.

Whether blacks live on the Ivory Coast or the Atlantic Coast, Yeshitela contends, 'we're all the same. There are no cultural differences between Africans and African     Americans.'

Na'im Akbar, a psychology professor at Florida State University, sides with Glover. 'The only way we'll ever begin to appreciate each other is to recognize and embrace our cultural differences,' says Akbar, who was born in America. Slavery is the tie that binds, but the legacy also keeps the two groups apart. Some local blacks argue the closest they've ever come to Africa is Busch Gardens. The fact that African leaders profited from selling others is a betrayal many blacks refuse to forgive or forget.

'A lot of us do harbor a lot of hostility toward Africans,' says Tampa poet James Tokley. 'Many Africans have no idea what our ancestors endured during slavery.' Glover agrees that while some Africans suffered under colonial rule and apartheid, not all can relate to the degradation of slavery.

In Ghana, he says, 'we did not experience white domination like the Africans in Kenya, Zimbabwe or South Africa. We do not understand the whole concept of slavery, or it's effect on the attitude of a lot of African Americans, mainly because we were not exposed to it. To read about racism and discrimination is one thing, but to experience it is something else.'

Much bad blood stems from interactions between Africans and whites, Oigbokie says. For example, he ate at some segregated restaurants in the 1960s. 'A lot of African Americans were upset that white people would serve me but not them,' he says.'They felt the system gave us better treatment than it gave them.' Many black Americans are ignorant about Africans, Oigbokie adds. They share comic Eddie Murphy's joke that Africans 'ride around butt-naked on a zebra.' 'They think we want to kill them so that we can eat them,' Oigbokie says, laughing. 'I remember a black person once asked me if I knew Tarzan. I told him, 'Yes, he is my uncle."

Glover, who also teaches African studies at USF, says these perceptions are rooted in all the negative things we've been taught about each other. 'A lot of African Americans were taught that Africa was nothing more than just a primitive, backward jungle from whence they came,' he says. Meanwhile, Africans have picked up whites' fear of blacks. 'Our perception of African Americans is that they are a race of people who carry guns and are very, very violent.' Africa's tribal wars often-times mirror black-on-black violence in America, and some ask how is it possible to form friendships with all this intra-racial friction.

'I have seen us come together in great magnificence,' Yesihitela says, citing, as an example, Marcus Garvey, founder of a back-to-Africa movement in the 1920s. 'He was very successful in bringing about the unity of African people.' Africans admire the American struggle for civil rights. Yet, when some come to America and discover black is not so beautiful, they insist on maintaining a separate identity. 'When indigenous African people come to the United States, they adopt an attitude of superiority...about individuals who could very well be of their own blood.' Tokley says.

Some African customs, such as female circumcision, shock Americans. Other traditions have been forgotten, or, in the case of Kwanzaa, invented in America. Africans tend to have a strong patriarchal system, with differences in attitudes about family and work. 'The women's liberation movement has barely caught up to Africa,' says Cheikh T. Sylla, a native of Senegal and the president of a Tampa architecture firm. 'That's why I think many unions between African men and African-American women don't tend to last. Most African-American women are like, 'I'm not going to put up with the notion that you are the absolute head of the household." says Sylla, who does not mind his American wife's feisty ways. Sylla says he's baffled by blacks' unwillingness to take advantage of America's many opportunities and their willingness to blame most problems on race.

'When most Africans come here, their first priority, by and large, is education,' he says. 'Right here you have a tool that allows you to open doors within American society.' 'There was no king in my family or any other type of royalty in my lineage. I had to work to earn every single penny I won, and it was brutal. The African-American experience is so profound that at times I don't think I can appreciate it. I understand it must be recognized as a matter of history, but it cannot be held as a justification for one's inability to      succeed.'

In 1990, the median household income of an African immigrant was $30,907, according to the Center for Research on Immigration Policy in Washington, D.C. That compares with $19,533 for black Americans. Africans who immigrate to the United States come largely from the educated middle class of their countries. The research center reports 47 percent are college graduated and 22 percent have a professional specialty. Only 14 percent of black Americans graduate from college. 'Most of the friction between African people centers around the class issue,' Yeshitela says. He says when blacks and Africans fight over jobs, they are buying into a conspiracy to keep them at odds. 'I don't like the artificial separations that won't allow the two of us to get together. It is not in our best interest to always be at each other's throat.' Especially since the two groups are in the same boat now, Akbar says.

'If you visit Nigeria or Ghana, the masses of the people are locked in the same circumstances as poor African Americans,' he says. 'Both groups seem content to do nothing other than what they are currently doing. However, the denial among Africans comes from living in a place where all the bodies that surround them look the same as they do. That makes it easier for them to fail to see that the folks who are controlling the whole economy of Nigeria are the oil barons - and they don't look anything like (black)   Africans.'

Another point of contention, Akbar says, is that blacks appreciate their heritage more than Africans do. 'We have to convince them to preserve the slave dungeons in Ghana or to continue the weaving of the kente cloth.' Tours to Africa are booming. Feeling rejected at home, many middle-class blacks turn

184

to Africa, Yeshitela says. 'But in the final analysis, culture won't free you. Any ordinary African will tell you a dearth of culture is not the source of our affliction. We're faced with a situation where 3 to 10 percent of the total trade in Africa happens in Africa. The rest is exported from Africa. The future of all black-skinned people centers in Africa. That is our birthright and someone else has it. The struggle we have to make lies in reclaiming what is rightfully ours.'"

While a significant number of African Americans are genuinely proud of their heritage, there is another large number of those who are not, even if they don't deny their African origin. And there may be a general impression that black Americans who are most ashamed of Africa are those least knowledgeable about the continent, forming negative impressions from Tarzan movies and other shows on television which portray Africa in a negative way, even if what they depict is true; for example, famine stalking the land. They also hear negative stories about their ancestral homeland.

Yet, even those who know enough about Africa, including many who have travelled to the continent, harbor stereotypes not very much different from those of their less knowledgeable brethren. In fact, their "in-depth" knowledge of the continent, including first-hand knowledge derived from their trips to Africa, gives them some sort of credibility - among other black Americans in America - as authorities on the motherland, passing on their stereotypical views as empirical facts. And that is a tragedy, not only in terms of negative portrayal of Africa, but also in terms of relations between Africans and African Americans that are tempestuous at times.

This reminds me of what one African American said to me when I lived in Grand Rapids, Michigan in the early eighties, about his experience with Africans in Africa. When he was a college student in the seventies, he went to West Africa at least twice - may be even three times - and visited Ghana, Togo, Benin, and Nigeria. He said he liked his ancestral homeland and even adopted an African name from Ghana.

He met people from all walks of life who were very friendly, and he liked all that, except one thing: their nasty habit of not washing their hands, or washing their hands in the same bowl of water they passed around as the water got dirtier and dirtier until it turned almost brown; getting ready to eat from the same dish, dipping with their fingers small lumps of *fufu* (West African stiff porridge, what we in East Africa call *ugali* in Kiswahili) into a bowl of stew with some meat in it: fish, chicken, or whatever.

When he got back to the United States, he returned with images of Africa that left an indelible mark on his mind. And what he saw was enough for him to judge virtually all Africans the same way. As he put it: "The people were very friendly. But you guys, I don't know. They didn't wash their hands or washed them in the same bowl. Their hands were dirty."

He said he saw all that during his trip to West Africa. I asked him if all the people - if any at all - he met in West Africa did not wash their hands, or washed their hands in the same bowl of water, before eating. Yet nothing could dissuade him from his blanket condemnation of "all" Africans as unhygienic, a people with a nasty habit of not washing their hands. I conceded that it is true that people in African countries, including Tanzania where I come from, wash their hands in the same bowl, and they do pass it around to others for them also to wash their hands before they all start dipping into the same dish. It signifies brotherhood, and humility putting none above the rest, although I did not defend the practice on hygienic grounds.

But not *all* Africans do that, probably not even the majority. In fact, I remember asking him point blank: "Are you saying *all* the people you met in West Africa, in *all* the countries you visited, did not wash their hands, or washed their hands in the same bowl of water, before they ate?" He did not want to concede the obvious, that it was not true that not even all the people he met in West Africa did not wash their hands or washed their hands in the same bowl of water before they started eating.

Yet, that is the stereotypical view he had of *all* of us Africans as a primitive, backward people, with poor hygiene and nasty habits of not washing our hands and much more; probably not going through the whole ritual even after attending the call of nature, just taking off, instead.

Now, because he had been to Africa, twice at least, it would have been very easy for many black Americans in America who had never been to Africa to *believe* him. And they probably did; not all, but probably many of them, if not the majority, thus reinforcing and even confirming their negative stereotypes of all Africans as a backward people with all kinds of nasty habits they - as civilized Americans - had nothing to do with. After all, here was someone who had been to Africa twice, at least, and was speaking with "authority," from "experience," and from what he saw there. It was first-hand knowledge, I concede, but twisted.

It is these kinds of stereotypes even among educated and highly knowledgeable African Americans which have many Africans thinking "black Americans think they are better than we are." And it's very damaging to relations between the two.

Even some black American children have a tendency to make fun of African children in school and in their neighborhoods because of what they hear at home, from friends, and from what they see on television. It is mainly the parents' fault. They don't teach them about Africa and don't have anything good to tay say about Africa; not in all cases but in quite a few of them. And the problem is nationwide. African children complain about that in New York City, which probably has the largest number of African immigrants; in Washington, D.C.; in Detroit, Michigan; in Los Angeles, California; in Texas and many other parts of the country.

I have cited some of those cases in appendices at the end of the book. And the following example also illustrates the seriousness and complexity of the problem with regard to poor interaction and lack of communication between Africans and African Americans even among adults from whom stereotypes about Africa among African Americans filter down or get passed on to their children: A Kenyan student in Dallas, Texas, was often called "baboon face" by a number of black American students who also made it clear that they did not want to identify with him. As Angela Uherbelau stated in her article she sent from Cape Town, South Africa, entitled "African Americans in South Africa," published in the black newspaper, *Amsterdam News*, New York, July 28, 2005:

"Busie Ntintili, 28, is South African by birth but spent almost 20 years in the United States. After Ntintili's father was briefly jailed for his political activism in 1977, the family was granted U.S. visas. They moved to Texas where Ntintili's father studied theology.

Starting a new life, Ntintili realized in elementary school in Dallas that ethnicity could be just as divisive an issue as race. 'I went to school with a student from Kenya and the kids called him 'baboon face' and 'African boy," she remembered. 'In the 80's, one did not advertise one's 'African-ness' because I was looked down upon, especially by Black American kids.'

Growing up in Texas and then New Jersey, Ntintili rapidly assimilated into American culture, but always hoped to move back to South Africa. Her return in 1999 was more difficult than she thought it would be. Speaking English with an American accent - and not knowing any African languages - set her apart South African Blacks just as her nationality had set her apart from the Black community in the U.S.

After six years back in South Africa, Ntintili feels more spiritually connected to her native country now than she ever did to the United States. She has learned Xhosa (the language of her ethnic group), can understand some Zulu, and earns a living writing for a popular South African TV soap opera.

Her cross-cultural experiences have given her a unique understanding of both countries, but she gets frustrated by American Blacks that 'come home' to South Africa and don't really try to forge a connection. 'I heard that when Ja Rule came to perform here last year, he was asked if he planned to visit Soweto for musical inspiration,' Ntintili remembered. 'He said: 'Is that a new club?"

By contrast, other Black American celebrities have dug deeper, the most notable of which is Oprah Winfrey."

The black American students who made fun of, and looked down upon, African students at the school in Dallas were not typical of all the black students. But they were a significant number. And may be even the majority of them felt the same way even if they did not openly express those feelings. And there's no question that examples of this kind of behavior abound, reinforcing stereotypes about Africa even among young black American students. And it is symptomatic of a deeper, underlying problem, denying Africans humanity and portraying them as a sub-species of mankind at best, and as monkeys at worst.

I have had the same kind of experience myself with a number of blacks, young and mature, lower class and middle class, who have made fun of me as an African as much as they have the rest of our people in Africa and the entire continent. And they have done so in different ways, with a few pretending that they are just joking.

But we know better than that. Whenever we hear those kinds of jokes, we know that the people who are cracking those jokes mean what they say. It makes no diference they are fellow blacks, many of whom don't even want to be called African American.

I vividly remember that it was in 1988 at a meeting in New Orleans that black American leaders leaders, Jesse Jackson and others, officially adopted the term "African American" to be used as the official designation, instead of "Black American," to describe American blacks.

Malcolm X was probably the first prominent black leader to use the term "African Americans" in his speeches and interviews and in the sixties; he also used the term "Negro," which was commonly used in those days, although he also saw it as demeaning and questioned its relevance: "Where is Negroland?," he asked in one of his speeches. Black people came from Africa. They were therefore Africans. The only difference was that they were born in the United States.

Therefore he used the term "Africans, sometimes," to describe black Americans who even in the sixties, with all the great political awakening and consciousness about Africa among many blacks, were often called "Negroes." And many of them seemed to have been satisfied with that or had simply reconciled themselves to the fact that - that is what they were. In fact, Dr. Martin Luther King used the term "Negro" in his writings and in his speeches, including his landmark "I Have A Dream" speech he delivered in Washington D.C., in August 1963.

Besides Malcolm X, Stokely Carmichael - later renamed Kwame Ture after he moved to Guinea in 1969 where he lived for almost 30 years until his death in November 1998 - is another leader who used the term "Africans" to describe black people in the United States and elsewhere in the diaspora. And as Malcolm X said to his audience in one of his speeches, "You are nothing but Africans."

But beyond black nationalist circles, and even there among only a few people like Malcolm X and Stokely Carmichael as well as others including black American Pan-Africanist leaders such as Kimathi Mohammed of the Marcus Garvey Institute in Lansing Michigan whom I got the chance to know since I first met him at the Pan-Africanist Carribean association in Washington D.C. in 1972 - the term "African American," let alone "African," never came to be widely used or accepted by the vast majority of blacks in the United States who still called themselves "black Americans" or simply "blacks" in most cases, and sometimes "Afro-Americans." And the reason is simple. They are Americans.

But that does not mean that they are not African as a people of African descent. As Nelson Mandela said in a speech to a black audience in Harlem not long after he was released from prison: "We are all children of Africa."

Still, had black people been given the chance to vote on whether or not they should be called "African Americans," I doubt the majority of them would have voted for it. They probably would have been preferred to be simply called Black Americans; not only because that is what they really are, in terms of upbringing and national identification, but also in order for many of them to maintain distance from "backward," "primitive" Africans. And a very large number of them are ashamed of Africa and their African origin and see Africans as some kind of distinct "sub-species" although they are of African origin themselves.

This kind of attitude, the denigration of Africa, is prevalent among whites and people of other races. And that is understandable because of racism, although it is wrong. But even black Americans who identify themselves with Africa and don't mind being called African Americans should admit that this kind of attitude is also prevalent among many black Americans - educated and uneducated - who think they are better than "those savages in the jungle" over there in Africa; a concession that may help facilitate constructive dialogue between the two groups and may be even help heal whatever wounds have been inflicted on each other, and by our enemies, through the years, in fact since slavery and the conquest of Africa by the imperial powers. But the insults, and the arrogance, must be acknowledged.

And many African immigrants are acutely aware of this, which is one of the reasons - by no means the only one - why a significant number of them don't associate with African Americans as much as they should, if at all.

Equally damaging is the attitude among some black Americans - yes, African Americans whether they accept the term or not - to make fun of Africans as a people "who have nothin' over there. They ain't used to nothin'. Nothing good. I mean nothin'."

Africans in the United States who are successful, with good jobs, homes and cars, have now and then been subjected to such indignities. Some of this comes from jealousy. But it is true that a significant number of Africans have overheard some black Americans talking about them in a very negative way, saying "they're in paradise now. They had nothing where they came from," or something like that.

I have heard that myself more than once, and so have many others. Probably some black Americans, just like many whites, won't even believe that I have written many books which are found in university libraries in many countries around the world and are used as college textbooks. "Who, him? Wrote what? That so-and-so from Tanzania? From the jungle? He don' even know no English!" Whatever the double negative means, so commonly used by many Americans of all races, not just black Americans as many whites would like to believe, making fun of them saying: "Blacks don't know English."

It is also interesting to note that many Africans in the United States, especially those born and brought up in Africa, say black Americans don't know English.

We were taught King's English by the British in Africa, a colonial legacy. And our teachers, including African teachers, were very strict. They enforced rigorous intellectual discipline. Most of the students of my generation in Tanzania, what was then Tanganyika, started learning English in standard five in middle school and continued to do so in secondary school. Our teachers were African and British who were later joined by American Peace Corp teachers. I was also taught English literature by British teachers when I was in secondary school from standard 9 to standard 12, and in high school from standard 13 to standard 14.

And it is true that many African Americans speak broken

English called "Ebonics." By contrast, Africans who were taught English in Africa speak and write standard English, although not all of them have thorough command of the language. But even those who don't, can tell that a significant number of black Americans including some with college education, the very same people who make fun of Africans calling them ignorant, don't speak standard English.

Many of them can't even write a single sentence with lucidity although they have spoken English since they began to speak. I knew some of them. I helped them when they wrote papers in college. And most of them spoke "Ebonics," sprinkled with standard English only now and then, here and there.

Even many blacks who speak standard American English drift into "Ebonics," a linguistic anomaly wrongly attributed to their African heritage, especially West Africa where the majority of the African slaves came from, contending that there are linguistic patterns in West African languages which match and reflect the grammar and structure of "Ebonics." And just like many of their brethren who routinely speak what is also known as black English, they are proud of "Ebonics." As Reuben Abati, a Nigerian journalist who was then studying at the University of Maryland, stated in his article, "An African in America is Baffled by 'Ebonics,'" published in *The Baltimore Sun*:

"Nothing prepared me for the uniqueness of American English and colloquial American speech. Six months after arriving in the United States, I am still in a state of linguistic shock.

To come here from Nigeria, I had to take a test of English as a foreign language at the American Embassy in my country. If I had failed, I wouldn't be here. Which is why I am surprised to discover that there are Americans who cannot speak standard English. To survive in America, I have to understand a broad range of American colloquialisms, and a strange tongue called 'Ebonics.'

Americans speak of the *elevator* instead of the *lift*; instead of *boot* they say *trunk*; for *railway station* they substitute *metro* or *train* station; the college *bus* is called the *shuttle*; instead of *petrol*, Americans say *gas*. I have often referred to the small space I share with two colleagues as a *flat*, but I am told it is an

192

*apartment*. When I refer to my colleagues as *flatmates*, I am told they are *roommates* although we do not live in the same room.

Several times, I have heard an American sprinkle a conversation with 'Oh, my God' and I have always responded with 'Sorry,' thinking that he or she was in some form of pain. I have since discovered that Americans call on God as a matter of habit, to express surprise, joy, regret, all at once. But I am not stubborn. I am learning and adjusting. I have realized that the success of my 10-month stay in this country depends on my being able to understand the people. There is perhaps no point complaining.

When I tell Americans that they confuse me with their pronunciation, they tell me I have a funny accent. Or that they have problems understanding the English I speak. Yet I speak simple, standard English as handed down by Her Majesty, the Queen of England's government to the former colonies. The problem is probably with the English language. Every society that inherited it from the English has had to infuse it with local color and experience.

But Ebonics stretches my patience and frustrates me. Often, I meet African-Americans and because they look so familiar I experience an instant racial bonding. I feel like talking with them to let them know that meeting and seeing them makes me feel at home, as if I am in the midst of my own family.

But this natural identification collapses immediately when the African-American begins to speak Ebonics. On several occasions I have heard my brothers and sisters in the diaspora say: 'Yo!' 'She say, he say.' 'We was.' 'I is.' 'I be.' This is supposed to be English, but it is not English.

At such moments, the genetic coding fails and I am forced to note the difference between nature and nurture. To me, Ebonics is totally unrecognizable, and those who argue that it has a West African origin are merely contriving a thesis to justify nonsense.

True, West Africans speak a kind of English called 'pidgin English,' but it is the language of the illiterate, a tribute to incompetence, and it bears no resemblance even to Ebonics. Those who speak pidgin English in West Africs and other parts of Africa would rather speak standard English.

The novelist James Baldwin may have made a case for Ebonics: It may well work as literature and music. African-

Americans are also probably entitled to a lingistic 'inside baseball' [NB: *a reference to the "insider-jargon" of American baseball that only those who know the sport well would understand*]. But they should not be encouraged to cling to a dialect that is bound to increase their alienation from their brothers and sisters in Africa, their fellow Americans and the rest of the English-speaking world.

The success of African-Americans and all black people who speak and write good, proper English proves the point that Ebonics is not in the genes. It is certainly not in the African gene."

But, with all their ignorance, many black Americans - not all but this particular kind - *still* think that they are better than Africans in every conceivable way. And that includes highly educated Africans many of whom have post-graduate degrees. They see them as nothing, simply because they are African, "from the jungle."

I have dealt with Americans of all races and I know, as much as other Africans in the United States do, that there is no end to stereotypes about Africa and Africans. Even if you tell people who harbor such stereotypes that there are, for example, more than 30,000 Nigerian doctors practicing in the United States alone, saving countless lives mostly American, they won't believe it; none of it.

I am here again reminded of what the African American who went to West Africa said to me in the early eighties in Grand Rapids, Michigan, with regard to all this, as stereotypes go. He sometimes pretended to be joking. But I knew he always meant what he said about Africa even if in a sleek way; he tried to be very smooth whenever he brought up the subject. Sometimes he was just rude and crude. And he found it to be amusing, of course.

I remember him saying one day: "You don't have this in Africa, do you?" He was talking about chicken, some chicken, and rice! One of the most common dishes we have all over Africa even in villages where many people are desperately poor.

This reminds me of the *mopani* worms some whites talk about in a commercial on American television, telling some Africans (supposedly from Zimbabwe, Botswana or South Africa where some people eat these worms) to taste and eat  some chicken, instead of *mopani* worms, as if they have never eaten chicken all their lives, and as if we have no chicken in Africa. It is the same old stereotype about Africa being backward and primitive, and a place where people have nothing!

The African American in question also knew full well that we have chicken and rice all over Africa. He himself ate rice and chicken many times when he was in West Africa, by his own admission.

The point I am trying to make is this: It's not that he didn't know that was true. He knew it was true. People eat plenty of rice and chicken in Africa. Even the blind know that. But he had something entirely different in his mind. He was still trying to portray Africa in a negative way as a place where the people "have nothin'. Ain't used to nothin' good. Nothing!" And he compounded the felony with his rendition of "America the beautiful, from sea to shining sea," and ended on a sweet note: "You guys love it here, don't you?"

The conclusion is obvious. We have run away from hell in Africa to live in paradise in America.

But Africans have earned it the hard way. Unfortunately, many of them are not accepted probably by just as many African Americans for different reasons. As Joseph Takougang, an African immigrant himself and associate professor of African history at the University of Cincinnati, stated in his essay "Contemporary African Immigrants to the United States: A Historical Perspective" in *The Western Journal of Black Studies*:

"Another problem faced by African immigrants is the lack of acceptance by some of their African American counterparts. African immigrants are perceived by some African Americans as responsible for the fact that their ancestors were sold into slavery. There is also the accusation that African immigrants see themselves as better, if not superior to their African American counterparts.

Unfortunately, this perception has led to an uneasy relationship between some African immigrants and their African American brothers and sisters that continues to divide and paralyze Blacks in America thereby making them ineffective political and economic forces in national politics."

There are more than 1 million African immigrants in the United States today, at this writing (in 2006), according to census figures. And they are probably the most highly educated group of immigrants and one of the most successful in the professions and in the economic arena, defying the odds against them, as is the case in Britain, contrary to conventional wisdom. And that is one of the main reasons why a signficant number of American blacks are jealousy of Africans. They say African immigrants take jobs away from them. But that is not true. The argument is irrelevant.

Africans are highly educated. They have needed skills and they don't take jobs away from highly educated black Americans. Educated black Americans get jobs as much as educated Africans do. Blacks who complain the most don't have skills comparable to what African immigrants have in general.. They are some of the least educated people in the United States, unlike African immigrants.

There are, however, some highly educated Africans who complain about discrimination against them by American blacks when they seek employment. They say there are a number of highly educated black Americans who resent their presence on American soil for a number of reasons including jealousy.

Africans who complain about such discrimination include professors and newly minted PhDs who say they were denied teaching jobs at black American colleges simply because of what they are: black African.

One Nigerian scholar, in his message posted on a Nigerian discussion forum on the internet in July 2005, said black American college administrators like to hire Arabs and Ethiopians, with "Caucasian features" as he put it, while ignoring people like him with "Negro" features.

It made absolutely no sense to him, and to many others, since the people they preferred to hire were not even related to them and don't even look like them. Ethiopians, let alone Arabs, don't have "Negro" features, he emphasized. He reminded American blacks that none of their slave ancestors came from Ethiopia or any of the Arab countries in North Africa and that if they wanted to identify with African people, they should do so with Yorubas, Igbos, Ashantis, Ewes and other West Africans. They should

196

focus on West Africa because that is where most African slaves shipped to America came from, he said, as he ended his short lecture.

It was a powerful emotional appeal. But it probably fell on deaf ears among a large number of black Americans, including administrators at black colleges whose employment criteria are not exclusively racial.

But in spite of such complains and others, many Africans in the United States are glad they came to "the promised land," the land of milk and honey like no other on planet Earth. Those who are highly successful in America would probably not have reached the pinnacle of success had they stayed in Africa, prompting many Americans, including black Americans, to say we ran away from hell in Africa in search of paradise in America.

And there is some truth to that, we must admit; not necessarily that life is hell in Africa, and America is heaven on Earth especially for us. It is true in the sense that most Africans who live in the United States believe that they have better opportunities to succeed in America than they do in Africa.

And the majority of them do realize their dreams: be it earning college degrees and getting good paying jobs or doing whatever they want to do, although a significant number of them don't get the jobs they deserve, commensurate with their skills and level of education, including some with PhDs, for different reasons including racism and anti-foreign sentiments.

But they are found across the spectrum of the job market. As one African immigrant, Sam Omatseye, stated in the *Rocky Mountain News*, March 19, 2000: "Africans permeate all aspects of Colorado life. They are doctors, lawyers, professors, engineers, students, cab drivers, clerks, security guards and chefs."

Many of them end up taking menial, low-paying jobs just to survive, while their relatives back home in Africa automatically assume that they are "rich" and expect them to send them plenty of money and gifts from paradise America, the land of milk and honey. That is just a myth. It does not correspond to reality. Nothing could be further from the truth. People don't just scoop up money in America. Life can be hard, in fact very hard, in this land of magnificent bounties even for Americans themselves, let alone foreigners who are not always welcome.

But it is also true that nobody has forced them to stay in America. "Why are you here, then, if life isn't better in America than it is in Africa? Who forced you to come or stay here?" And they *are* legitimate questions. We have to admit that. It's not impenetrable logic, but pretty tight, with empirical evidence against those who refute the validity of this argument: that things are better than they are in Africa for African immigrants who have settled in the United States. As Americans, black and white as well as others, love to say: "America is number one! Love it or leave it!"

But Americans should also remember that Africans have to the right to live in America, if they want to, because it was our ancestors, African slaves, who built America. And they know it's true. But they gloss over that by focusing on the stereotypical image of Africa as "hell on earth."

Whether any of that is true or not is besides the point in this context. It is the stereotype that is drawn from all this, especially by African Americans of *all* people, that is relevant to what I am saying. Africa is portrayed as the very antithesis of America, the opposite of everything America has achieved; although it is worth remembering - especially for African Americans who are descendants of African slaves - that it was Africans, *not* Europeans, who laid the foundation of the United States and built this country in its early years with their slave labor, and continued to do so through the years.

The foundation they laid eventually made the United States the richest and most powerful country on earth, with more than 50 percent of the entire world's wealth, while they got nothing, absolutely nothing, in return; not even a mule and 40 acres of land they were promised after the end of slavery. In fact, it is highly unlikely that America would even have survived as a nation had it not been for the labor extracted from African slaves who "worked from can't see in the morning to can't see in the evening, without being paid a dime, not a dime," as Malcolm X said.

But all that is ignored, or gets lost in the confusion caused by stereotypes about Africa fostered by many American blacks as if those stereotypes and the denigration of Africa are more important than relations between Africans and African Americans. Utter nonsense!

# Chapter Six:

# Misconceptions About Each Other

RELATIONS between Africans and African Americans have been reinforced and impaired by a number of factors through the years.

On the positive side, natural bonds between the two "peoples" - who are really one people - have been the most critical factor in maintaining and strengthening this "tempestuous" relationship. On the negative side, misconceptions about each other have been some of the most damaging, sometimes even impairing the credibility of those who are genuinely interested in fostering and maintaining a strong relationship between Africans and African Americans on both sides of the Atlantic.

One of the biggest misconceptions is that we don't care about each other or even like let alone love each other.

I asked one of the African Americans who moved to Ghana a few questions on this subject. She was living in Ghana when I asked her these questions towards the end of November 2004, the same month I started writing this book and when I was working on this chapter and she was more than willing to answer any questions I had.

Her name was Imahkus Okofu, author of *Returning Home Ain't Easy, But It Sure Is A Blessing*, about her return to her ancestral homeland Africa. She was born and raised in the Bronx, New York, and lived in Jamaica before moving to Ghana in 1990, permanently, with her husband. These are her answers to my questions:

Q: "What are some of the challenges have you met?"

A: "Language, culture, historical differences and the perception that all Africans from the diaspora, especially Americans, are rich. Getting over the romanticized notion about Africa. It's a hard crash into reality."

Q: "What is the general attitude of Africans on the mainland towards African Americans, especially when they return to the motherland?"

A: "Some are very happy to see us, are proud and want to help us adjust. But many are angry and confused because (1)They say we were fortunate as our ancestors were taken as slaves and as a result we got to be born in America. (2) They don't understand why we left the land of golden opportunity (America) to come to Ghana where they are suffering. (3) Many want to go to America and can't."

Q: "What do yout think about Gregg Pascal Zachary's article, "Tangled Roots: For African Americans in Ghana, The Grass Isn't Always Greener," in *The Wall Street Journal*, March 14, 2001? It caused quite a stir. But I don't know if all the people quoted in the article, besides Victoria Cooper, disputed what was said or denied saying what the writer said they did."

A: "Several people mentioned in that article responded to *The Wall Street Journal* and to date have received no response. This so-called journalist with his warped mentality to the degree that he should be put into the category of agent provocateur in trying to discourage Afrikans of the diaspora from looking towards Afrika with the thoughts of returning and re-uniting this Afrikan family.

As a couple of individuals (my husband and I) that this 'white boy' wrote about, we can honestly say that a lot of what he said was unfounded, untrue and terribly distorted. He also failed to mention in his article how he had been treated and accepted as a journalist in our community. Nor did he expound on his vocal discourse of 'wishing he had been born black.' And let us not fail to mention his sneaky, underhanded affinity towards Afrikan sisters. He has been banned from our community and all others should take careful notice of this snake."

Q: "Is it true that some African Americans are disgusted with Africa - the cold reception, etc. - and have decided to return to the

United States?"

A: "Our reception has been anything but cold. Extremely friendly, even with underlying motives. Afrika is not for every Afrikan descendant born in the diaspora. As the title of my book states, 'Returning Home Ain't Easy.'

There are a few, and I do mean *a few*, who have returned to the diaspora. But for the most part, those who have repatriated have stood the test of time, dating as far back as 1956 when The Honorable Osagefyo Kwame Nkrumah first invited brothers and sisters to come home to motherland Afrika/Ghana; and also keeping in mind the affirmation of The Honorable Marcus Garvey 'Africa for Africans, those at home and those abroad.' Those descendants who visited Afrika and chose to return to America are the Africans      'abroad.'

The networking between the continent and the diaspora is extremely important. so, those Afrikans 'abroad' must support those of us repatriated Afrikans on the continent as much as possible, for we are here to make a way for those who desire to come.

Those Afrikans born in America as a result of the Trans-Atlantic Arab-European slave trade, descendants of kidnapped Afrikans, are the ones that are working to be a part of the re-building of Mother Afrika and the uniting of the Black Afrikan family globally.

There are those of us kidnapped Afrikans born in the diaspora who also hear the message from The Honorable Marcus Mosiah Garvey that we have to reclaim and redeem Mother Afrika. Of course, there are those who do not want this to happen, but 'Up You Mighty Race You Can Accomplish What You Will' (as Marcus Garvey said)."

Q: "What happened to the citizenship bill for African Americans President Jerry Rawlings talked about at a press conference with President Bill Clinton in Washington in 1998? Is it true that it's dead?"

A: "For all intents and purposes, it is unconscious. It is up to us to re-awaken the sleeping giant. Dual citizenship was only given to Ghanaians. We received something called Right of Abode and it is not citizenship. We will have to fight hard for this one. Sorry, Jerry let us down, I'm afraid.

Stay strong. The Struggle Continues But Victory Is Ours!
One Love, One God, One Heart, One Blessed Afrikan Family.
Seestah Imahkus and Nana Okofo Iture Kwaku I Ababio."

Although she tried to clear up some of the misconceptions Africans and African Americans have about each other, a commendable effort, there is no question that some of the African Americans who lived in Ghana - as well as in other parts of Africa - and returned to the United States disagree with her assessment of the situation on the continent, especially in terms of relations between Africans and black Americans.

There are Africans who don't want to be bothered, just as black Americans don't; there are those who are genuinely friendly and interested in helping our brethren from the diaspora to settle in Africa; there are Africans who pretend to be nice to African Americans, calling them "my brother," "my sister," just to raid their pockets or use them to get to the United States in order to escape "hell" in Africa; and there are some who are outright hostile, just as some African Americans are, especially those who don't want to be identified with "primitive savages" on the "Dark Continent" as their brethren.

And there are many factors we have to take into account in order to understand why we have misconceptions of each other and why relations between Africans and African Americans are sometimes not as good as they should be.

We have to be brutally frank that our perceptions of each other are quite often refracted through the prism of prejudice. There are many Africans in Africa and in the United States who simply don't want to bothered or be indentified with African Americans because they don't see them as fellow Africans. They see them as just Americans, nothing else, not even as distant cousins. As one African American woman in Detroit stated in her message posted on the internet on a Nigerian discussion forum, Mobile Nigeria Forum, in March 2005:

"For years even after traveling to Africa, I have watched strange relationships between native Africans and other Africans living all over the world.
A few years back, I  had the opportunity to travel to West

Africa: Ghana. While visiting in a local cafe, I desired to strike up an conversation, and I was told by a gentleman there, 'Listen I don't care who you say you are, you are American and go back home.' I walked off confused.

Yet again, someone else had the same attitude towards me, but this time I replied, "do not be mad at me because my great grandmother made the the trip through unthinkable atrocities across the Atlantic". It wasn't until after this statement, that I was offered a seat.

It has always bothered me as an American what should I call myself. I believe my heritage is in the West African area, but what am I to do? But this I do know: I refuse to let anyone tell me that I am not African - for I am.

My question to you is: What must we all do to improve relations between native Africans and others descendants living in other countries?"

Some Africans cite cultural differences as the main reason why they don't accept American blacks as fellow Africans. And it is true that black Americans have been exposed to the full radiation of a predominantly European culture and therefore, through no fault of theirs, their culture is more European or Euro-American than African.

Then there are those who say black Americans lost their African identity a long time ago through slavery and racial intermingling, creating a new identity of their own which is neither European nor African; an argument Dr. Martin Luther King also made in one of his speeches and published in his book, *Where Do We Go From Here: Chaos or Community?* As he unequivocally stated, "The Negro is not an African." He went on to say that "the Negro" is neither African nor European but a hybrid of both.

I remember when I was a student in Detroit in the early and mid-seventies, some African students used to say black Americans were not African. One of them, a West African student, went even further and bluntly stated: "You know we don't like them." Another one, a Nigerian student who had just arrived in the United States said: "They are not African. I don't accept them and will never accept them as Africans."

There were others who shared those sentiments. But there were also those who didn't. And that is still the case today across the United States and in many parts of Africa. Many black Americans, of course, don't care about Africans anymore than Africans do about them.

There are also realities which are ignored when people ask why relations between Africans and African Americans are sometimes not very good. One of those realities is the misconception many blacks in the United have about Africa. Even those who should know better seem to ignore the fact that Africa is not a monolithic whole, and that Africans are not one people in several fundamental respects.

Africa is not one country. It is a continent, huge and diverse, with about 800 million people who belong to more than 1,000 different ethnic groups and also to different races. To say, for example, that Ethiopians and Somalis in East Africa and Fulanis in West Africa (who probably originated from Ethiopia as the Somalis did as linguistic evidence shows; so do common physical features Fulanis share with Ethiopians) belong to the same race as the Ashanti in Ghana or the Yoruba and the Igbo in Nigeria or the Zulu and the Xhosa in South Africa is to ignore reality.

Somalis and Ethiopians and Fulanis are African, it is true, but they are not "Negro." Nor are the Moors or Berbers with curly straight hair. They belong to different races and some of them, typical Berbers for example, look white. Their languages also are very different. Amharic, for example, the main Ethiopian language is related to Hebrew. Other Ethiopian languages, in Tigre and other parts of Ethiopia, also have Semitic roots or elements.

Even just the way most Ethiopians look - many with curly straight hair, thin faces and pointed noses, others with light complexion, what have been described as black "Caucasian" features - should be enough to raise questions regarding the claim that they have the same racial identity as Bantus and "Negroes." No, they don't! Emperor Haile Selassie himself looked like a Jew. So do many other Ethiopians.

Yet many, if not most, African Americans lump all Africans together and in fact insist that Ethiopians and Somalis are the same as Zulus or Ewes or Ashantis, members of the same race!

And in their determined attempt to identify with Africa, some African Americans point to their own features saying they look like Ethiopians and Somalis, ignoring the fact that they look that way because of their Caucasian heritage; they have European genes, and not just African, since slavery and from voluntary racial intermarriage between blacks and whites in the United States through the years.

And when they are not fully accepted as black people or as Africans by blacks in Africa or from Africa, they say Africans just don't like them or just don't want to identify with them or with black people in or from the United States. And many of them don't. They don't even see them as black people but as a product of mixed races; which is an indisputable biological fact even according to mixed blacks themselves except that they choose to identify with only their African heritage even if they are mostly of European ancestry.

And there are such people even in Africa itself, in fact many of them, born and raised in Africa who are a product of mixed races, African and European, African and Arab and other races or all combined. And they are Africans just like the rest of the Africans on the continent and elsewhere because they are citizens of African countries. Many of them have black African blood in varying degrees just like black Americans or African Americans do; although there may be some black Americans who are even more African in terms of genes than some of the black Africans themselves who say none of the American blacks are African like black Africans.

Still, none of them - racially mixed black Americans and racially mixed black Africans - can be denied their African heritage.

If a black African has a sister who has children with a white man, he cannot honestly say that those children are not his nephews and nieces like those born to another sister whose husband is a black African. They are all his nephews and nieces, and not half-nieces and half-nephews simply because they are half-black or simply because their father is white.

And that is analogous to the African identity of racially mixed black Americans. They have African heritage, and they are entitled to it as much as their brethren are. And they have relatives in Africa just like other black Americans do, relatives their ancestors left behind when they were captured and sold into slavery.

But even racially mixed Africans are not considered just black, for obvious reasons, because of their mixed parentage. In East Africa, especially in Kenya and Tanzania where we have a very large number of people of mixed races, they are called *chotara* in Kiswahili, which means half-caste, a British term we learned from the British who taught us English since the two countries were British colonies.

The term *chotara* is not a derogatory term. It is used only for identification purposes even if it has some derogatory connotations in the minds of some people. In South Africa, such people are called Coloureds and like to identify themselves as such, in many cases to deliberately maintain distance from blacks whom they consider to be inferior even if they don't say so, especially after the end of apartheid. But during the apartheid era, they were classified as superior to black people. Many of them still feel the same way today.

Now, when African Americans whose features distinctly show that they are racially mixed find out that they are not accepted as black people when they go to Africa, unlike in the United States where they are identified as such, they assume that black Africans just don't want to accept them. They have the same experience with a number of Africans even within the United States itself who don't see them as really black.

But they forget that even within Africa itself, people of mixed races are not considered black as I have just explained, although they are accepted as fellow Africans. For example in South Africa, they wouldn't be calling themselves Coloureds if they thought they were black. And many of them don't even want to be called black just like many light-skinned blacks in the United States did not want to identify themselves with blacks, until the civil rights movement started to gain momentum in the fifties and sixties and they started to drift with the current for their own interest since they saw that blacks were then making progress in the struggle for racial equality. So they had to identify with the only group which would accept them because of their common African heritage in spite of the fact that mixed blacks also had a

206

lot of European blood in their veins.

Therefore it is not rejection but different perceptions of who and what people are which keeps some African Americans and Africans apart, although we can't deny that there are those who simply don't want to accept black Americans - racially mixed or not - as fellow Africans just as there are black Americans who don't want to identify themselves with Africans as the same people.

The problem of racial identity manifests itself even in subtler forms in Africa among the elite. Unlike the uneducated, many educated Africans claim to have transcended racial and tribal loyalties for the sake of national unity. Jerry Rawlings, the former president of Ghana whose father is Scottish and his mother a member of the indigenous Ewe ethnic group found mostly in eastern Ghana and across the border in Togo, was elected on this platform. Many people, the elite and laymen alike, supported him eschewing racial solidarity and ethnic loyalties. But there were still those who did not accept him as a fellow black African. The phenomenon is not unique to Ghana or any of the other African countries.

In South Africa, Walter Sisulu, one of the most prominent leaders in the anti-apartheid struggle who was also very close to Nelson Mandela, was not just black. His mother was a Xhosa and his father British. Yet he was fully accepted by most black Africans as a fellow African and was revered as a leader with the same stature as Nelson Mandela, Oliver Tambo, and Govan Mbeki - some of the most the most prominent black African leaders in South African history.

In Tanzania, my country, Dr. Salim Ahmed Salim lost the presidential nomination in 2005 as the candidate of the ruling party CCM (Chama Cha Mapinduzi which means The Party of the Revolution or The Revolutionary Party), which was guaranteed to win the election as has always been the case since independence, mainly because he was an Arab.

His racial identity became a subject of discussion even in the media, with some people raising concerns about his "eligibility" as an Arab to be president of a predominantly black country. As Professor Teddy Maliyamkono, a black, at the University of Dar es Salaam said about Dr. Salim's quest for the presidency, many people in Tanzania - meaning black people - were "not ready for an Arab-looking person" to be president.

Even Dr. Salim's explanation at press conferences and other meetings that he was also partly of black African origin, Nyamwezi and Manyema, two tribes in western Tanzania with the Manyema also straddling the Tanzanian-Congolese border, did not help his candidacy.

Yet he was highly popular among many people and was one of the three finalists, coming in second, although a distant second, in the number of votes cast by the ruling party's delegates at the nominating convention, ahead of a black African candidate, Professor Mark Mwandosya, who came in third.

The nomination went to the country's highly popular minister of foreign affairs, Jakaya Kikwete, a black African whose election as president was a virtual certainty. Yet, through the years since Julius Nyerere, the country's first president, stepped down in 1985, it was generally accepted that Dr. Salim would be the next president of Tanzania and was in fact even endorsed by Nyerere to be his successor.

Salim himself said Nyerere asked him to run for president in 1985 but he declined because there was so much opposition to his candidacy. He also said he declined again to seek the presidency in 1995 because he felt that it was the turn of someone from Tanzania mainland to lead the country; Salim comes from the former island nation of Zanzibar, Pemba island in particular.

But it was his identity as an Arab, probably more than anything else, which derailed his candidacy. Even delegates of the ruling party from Zanzibar, the isles where he came from, were resolutely opposed to his candidacy for the same reason, contrary to what the founding father of the nation, Mwalimu Nyerere, taught about racial tolerance and equality.

Therefore much as racial identity plays a major role in the acceptance and non-acceptance of many African Americans as fellow Africans or as fellow blacks by many black Africans in Africa and in the United States where many of them live as immigrants or as students, it plays an equally major role within Africa itself among Africans themselves of different racial backgrounds.

One example of how many Africans see black Americans

differently involved a female African American student who went to the University of Dar es Salaam in Tanzania in the 1990s on an exchange program as I explain elsewhere in this book. She said when she walking in the streets of Dar es Salaam, the nation's former capital and now its commercial center with more than 3 million people, some people stared at her and even children called her "half-caste"; in spite of the fact that there are many people of mixed races in Tanzania, between Africans and Europeans, and between Africans and Arabs for an even longer period of time spanning centuries.

There is another divisive element among black Africans themselves: tribalism. And it is a potent force. Tribalism in African countries is probably an even bigger problem since it involves more people, tens of millions of Africans, interacting with each other or in conflict with each other sometimes on daily basis.

The Hutu-Tutsi conflict which cost about 1 million lives in Rwanda in 1994, and about 500,000 in more than 10 years in neighboring Burundi since 1993, is just one example. In Nigeria in the sixties, about 2 million Igbos perished in a civil war led mostly by the Hausa-Fulani.

The civil war in southern Sudan which ended in 2005 claimed more than 3 million lives, mostly black since 1983, at the hands of the Arabs and was therefore mostly racial. But even among black ethnic groups themselves in southern Sudan, there have been conflicts through the years costing untold numbers of lives in spite of the fact that they were at the same time fighting a common enemy, their Arab oppressors, the same ones who have committed genocide against members of black tribes in Dafur region in western Sudan.

The ethnic and cultural diversity itself of this vast continent is enought to boggle the mind. And many African Americans are disappointed when they find out they can't fit anywhere in Africa in terms of ethnic and cultural identity. When they get there, they realize that Africa is not one, but many in one. They also have a distorted and romantic view of Africa and automatically expect to be embraced, even with hugs and kisses, by Africans as their kith-and-kin finally returning home after centuries of separation since the slave trade.

Some Africans accept them, and even embrace them with hugs and kisses, while some don't. Africans experience the same thing when they go to the United States, although they probably fit in easier when they move into black communities because blacks in America constitute a single ethnic group and are not fragmented along tribal lines the way we are in Africa. And many of them see African immigrants and students in the United States just as fellow blacks.

But even when they settle in black communities in the United States for obvious reasons, including acceptance by black Americans as fellow blacks and avoiding white neighborhoods because of racial hostility, many Africans still don't easily mingle with African Americans. And there are several reasons for that.

One is non-acceptance or indifference by some black Americans. They don't want to mingle or associate with Africans. They don't see them as a part of them; they don't want to be identified with "primitive" people; they think that Africans don't like them or accept them as their people with the same African origin and heritage; they are not sure how Africans are going to respond to their overtures; some say Africans are arrogant and think they are better than American blacks; and some of them don't like Africans because they say they sold them into slavery.

Another reason why many Africans don't mingle with black Americans is that they are perfectly comfortable within their own world even when they are far away from home and live in the United States. They are a part of the black community in the United States, yet so far apart in terms of social interaction in many cases.

They like to socialize with fellow Africans because they are more comfortable to be with "their own kind"; they have their own groups they identify with, fellow African immigrants and students in general or people from their own countries including their own ethnic groups - for example there are many Igbos and Yorubas in many parts of the United States, including large numbers of them within the same cities where some of them have even formed organizations. Many Africans also have state and national organizations.

Africans in the United States also don't mingle or associate with black Americns because they don't consider them to be

African.

They also see them as "lazy" and "prone to crime" instead of doing something constructive with their lives and always complaining about racism in a country which has so many opportunities almost for anybody to succeed in life as long as one is willing to sacrifice and work hard and save money, even if it's a dollar at a time - it adds up eventually.

The work ethic is strong among Africans, as it is among other immigrant groups, while it's lacking in the black community among many black Americans. That is the erroneous assumption many Africans have about black America, ignoring the fact most black Americans have jobs and work hard; with the shiftless and the riff-raff among them being only a minority.

But that is the belief they have, and it is prevalent among a large number of Africans in the United States, although not all, I should emphasize. I have dealt with  fellow Africans, many of them, for many years in the United States, and those are some of the observations I have been able to make in my dealings with them.

And many of them have been frank about it in the company of fellow Africans. There are even those who tell American blacks how they feel about them, however rude and cruel this may be. Therefore there is no question that many Africans have a negative attitude towards black Americans. As Chike Okafor, a Nigerian immigrant in the United States, stated in his article (posted on the internet), "Dilemma of Nigerian Kids in the Diaspora":

"I read an article not too long ago about African stereotypes toward African Americans. The article contended that Africans regarded African Americans as inferior, poor, uneducated, lethargic, crime prone, poor English, and the list goes on. In fact, the last stigma resonates with the thesis of this article.

I have also been in a number of discussions with our resident brothers and sisters in the United States of America who perceived Africans as arrogant, selfish, pompous, crass, and the most troubling, looking down on them with scorn.

I have often tried to reconcile the prejudice held by these two communities. In one instance, I reasoned with an acquaintance that these stereotypes were a result of lack of understanding and knowledge of each other.

I have argued that the elite western media takes to heart and adore its role in preventing African Americans from knowing their heritage by continuously planting the seed of discord among the two communities. The elite western media were able to do the damage through selective content reporting on Africa. I have argued that the western media is not friendly to Africans or African-oriented issues. For instance, it is a common knowledge that about 90 percent of the western media reports on Africa were negative, five percent were on safari (animal watching) and the remaining five percent can be apportioned to other issues.

It is no secret that the bulk of the information that African Americans read or see were presented through the eyes of others; in this case the western European dominated media. As mentioned previously, remember that at least 90 percent of the reporting on Africa are negative. An example of such reporting are ethnic warfare and killings (Sierra Leone, Liberia, Zimbabwe, Somalia, Sudan, Burundi), famine (Ethiopia), corruption (Nigeria), and Aids (Kenya, South African president's position on the issue) and the list goes on. So it is easy for one to see how negative opinions can be easily formed about Africans.

Alternatively, if one wants to know the truth, one has to travel to Africa. Unfortunately, to do so is very expensive and not too many African Americans can afford the cost of such trip. To compound the situation, African leaders have not made any serious effort to encourage such trips especially through real tourism.

Those African Americans who have been to the African continent have a different perception about Africa and its people. They tend to be more susceptible to a rational opinion in discussion of African affairs. Moreover, I have equally held that Africans in the Diaspora have not done enough to bridge the gap. What they did was to incorporate the existing stereotypes held against African Americans into one word - Akata.

What is Akata? In Yoruba language of southwest Nigeria where it originated, it meant black Americans of African descent. Fair enough. However, the Africans in the Diaspora have turned the term to mean something more negative or derogative.

They have used it derogatorily to imply all the symptoms

212

embodied in negativity such as lethargic, penury, unmotivated, kleptomania, drug head, welfare queen, drunkard, uneducated, killers, broken homes, illiterates and rapists.

However, what they have missed in the process is that they, the Africans in the Diaspora have contributed to the growing population of the Akatas, a phenomenon that occurred through childbirth. Most of the new generations of Diaspora kids are more confused than the African American that have been subjected to unfounded scorn and derogatory remarks."

And that is a fairly objective assessment I share with this fellow African from Nigeria. Yet, little has been done to dispel the myths we have about each other. Both groups, African and African American, continue to fuel misperceptions of each other to the detriment of both, and as many people from both sides continue to maintain distance from each other. Africans in the United States are no less inhibited in all this, as I have explained earlier, and are probably further encouraged to do so because they are far away from home and see themselves as "isolated," and as strangers, in a foreign country - which is thousands of miles away from Africa.

There are other reasons why Africans maintain distance from African Americans. Like most immigrants and foreign students, they came to the United States to succeed in life and have little time for anything else including forging strong ties with black Americans simply because they are fellow blacks or people of the same African origin. They are busy with their own lives just like most black Americans are busy with theirs and don't care who has moved nextdoor or has come from Africa and moved into their neighborhoods. Each to his own.

Africans also see black Americans as arrogant who don't want to have anything to do with them or with Africa and therefore maintain discreet silence when they are around them or when they live in the same neighborhood where they also maintain distance from them. This is not true in all cases but in many of them. Both sides can testify to that, while others will dispute this, sometimes out of racial solidarity which, from my observation in many cases, is more apparent than real.

And the fact that many Africans don't seem to be bothered by the legacy of slavery in the United States, since their ancestors in Africa never experienced it and memories of the slave trade are in the distant past, only compounds the problem of this "tempestuous" relationship between Africans and African Americans.

And, tragically, neither side has taken strong initiatives to bridge the communication gap or improve relations between the two groups.

In all the years I lived in the United States, mostly in black communities, I was not aware of any concerted efforts by groups of Africans or African Americans to improve relations between them, although now and then meetings have been held by some people and a few groups through the years, even if only sporadically, to discuss issues of mutual interest.

Still, those who may contend that this has been going on across the the United States, on sustained basis for years, will be hard-pressed to come up with empirical evidence to support their argument. Ask them where those groups are in Michigan, where I lived for many years, doing this on regular basis. Where are they? I knew one, the Pan-African Congress-USA, which sponsored me and other African students in Detroit in the seventies but it was eventually dissolved, with members going their separate ways.

Go anywhere in the United States where Africans have settled in significant numbers, and come up with some evidence to show that they and black Americans in those places work together on regular basis to establish strong ties between them, help each other, and pursue a common agenda to achieve common goals. You'll probably come up empty-handed besides a handful of speeches here and there made by some Africans and black Americans, "full of sound and fury, signifying nothing." In many cases, it's all rhetoric without substance.

Even black churches, which should be some of the leading institutions in forging strong ties between black Americans and African communities in the United States, don't seem to be doing much in this area. I lived in Detroit, a predominantly black city with many black churches, large and small, and I didn't see any evidence of this.

And one of the biggest reasons for this failure is that the primary interest of black churches and other black institutions

214

including social and civic organizations, and of the black American community itself, is black America. And it is understandable. That is their constituency, not Africa or African immigrants. And that is because black Americans *are* Americans more than anything else in the practical sense.

Still, they and the Africans in their midst or around them can work together on the basis of racial solidarity to pursue common goals in a country, and in a world, which does not make a distinction between them but sees them simply as one people and as children of Africa.

While it seems that efforts are being made at the international level, with African-American groups establishing ties with and working in African countries, not much is being done at the local and national levels between Africans and African Americans within the United States even in pursuit of racial solidarity without which achievement of any other common goals is virtually impossible. Even African and African-American student groups on college campuses don't always work together, if at all in most cases.

So, whose fault is it? Both sides.

But there are somethings which have been done, even if on a limited scale, in pursuit of common objectives. Even those who are genuinely interested in the well-being of each other still don't know some of the things which both sides have done to foster racial solidarity and support the struggle for justice we as people, black people, have been denied probably more than anybody else.

I remember, for example, reading about an African American graduate student at an American university who wanted to know if Africans in the United States and those in the motherland had ever been concerned or played any role in supporting African Americans in their struggle against racial injustice including lynchings. He asked this question obviously because most black Americans don't know or don't believe that Africans have ever shown any interest in their plight or helped them in the struggle for racial justice and equality. Although it is a misconception, it is accepted as truth.

Most people may not know about this, and there may not be much documentation on the subject, but it is a fact, a documented historical fact, that Africans have supported their kith-and-kin in the United States for decades and in the best way they could, given the constraints under which they have had to operate. There are, and there have been through the decades, operational limits beyond which, as foreigners, Africans on American soil and in Africa cannot go in their support for the black American struggle for equality and    justice.

During the civil rights movement, African governments took strong interest in the struggle for racial equality in the United States and issued a formal statement condemning racial injustice against people of African descent in the United States. The statement was in the form of a resolution linking racial discrimination in the United States with apartheid in South Africa and was issued by the African heads of state and government who met in Addis Ababa, Ethiopia, in May 1963, to form the Organization of African Unity. And it was incorporated into the OAU Charter:

"The Summit Conference of Independent African States meeting in Addis Ababa, Ethiopia, from 22 May to 25 May 1963; having considered all aspects of the questions of apartheid and racial discriminations; unanimously convinced of the imperious and urgent necessity of co-ordinating and intensifying their efforts to put an end to the South African Government's criminal policy of apartheid and wipe out racial discrimination in all its forms,...(also) expresses the deep concern aroused in all African peoples and governments by the measures of racial discrimination taken against communities of African origin living outside the continent and particularly in the United States of America,...intolerable mal-practices which are likely seriously to deteriorate relations between the African peoples and governments on the one hand and the people and Government of the United States of America on the other."

And in the following year, after the OAU summit of African heads of state and government met in Cairo, Egypt, in July (1964), African leaders addressed the subject of racial discrimination in the United States. This was after Malcolm X spoke at the conference and appealed to African  leaders to raise the matter at the United Nations. If apartheid in South Africa

216

could be addressed by the UN, he saw no reason why racial discrimination against people of African descent in the United States could not be accorded the same treatment.

About nine African countries including Ghana, Guinea, Tanzania and Egypt agreed to take up the matter and bring it before the UN General Assembly but did not do so for a number of reasons including diplomatic and political problems and strong opposition from the United States government.

When Malcolm X went on a trip to several African countries in July 1964, State Department officials in Washington complained about his activities, saying he was causing a lot of trouble for the United States in Africa where he also strongly condemned American involvement in the Congo and in the assassination of Patrice Lumumba. And the assassination of Malcolm X himself several months later on February 21, 1965, after his African trip, sealed the fate of this subject since he was the only major African American leader who consistently worked to have it brought before the UN.

But even before then, and even much earlier, Africans had been involved in varying degrees in the struggle for racial equality in the United States just like African Americans had been in the independence struggle and liberation movements in Africa.

In the late 1950s, the leaders Ghana and Guinea, the first two black African countries to win independence - Ghana from Britainin 1957 and Guinea from France in 1958 - addressed the issue of racial discrimination in the United States. The diplomats from these two countries raised the issue at the UN at least once.

And not long after Tanganyika (renamed Tanzania in 1964 after uniting with Zanzibar) won independence, the Tanganyikan ambassador to the UN, and other diplomats at the Tanganyika Mission, worked with African Americans including Malcolm X who, after his African trip in July 1964, was picked up from the airport and taken in a car with diplomatic plates that were traced to the Tanganyika Mission to the UN. This is contained in a memo written by the FBI who had been watching Malcolm X all the time and had agents at the airport waiting for him to follow his movements.

The FBI also said after Malcolm X arrived in New York, he was taken to the residence of Tanganyika's ambassador to the UN.

And in a photograph on one of Malcolm X's speech albums, one of the people shown is Muhammad Ali Foum, a Tanzanian diplomat to the UN. At this writing, Foum was still a high ranking Tanzanian and also an African diplomat representing the African Union (AU) in different forums including peace missons on the continent.

In another photo, Malcolm X is seen talking to Abdulrahman Mohammed Babu, a leading Tanzanian cabinet member and one of the most influential African and Third World leaders who worked closely with President Julius Nyerere for many years. The picture was taken when the two met in Harlem. Babu died in 1996. He remained a formidable political figure and renowned academic intellectual in international circles until his death even after he felt out with Nyerere and left Tanzania to go into exile in the United States where he became a professor.

All that is more than just anecdotal evidence of African support to black Americans in their quest for racial justice in the United States. It is enough proof showing that a number of African countries have been actively involved in the struggle for racial justice in the United States and have always strongly identified with African Americans as an African people themselves; although their support has been limited for a number of reasons including threats and strong opposition by the United States, and also due to the fact that it is not easy for outsiders to play a major role in the domestic arena of other countries.

Yet, in spite of all this, some Africans in Africa devised various means to support their brethren in the United States in their quest for racial justice. For example, trade unionists in Ghana in the fifties, aware of what was going on in the United States in terms of race relations, periodically sent letters to America's largest labor organization, the AFL-CIO, condemning racial injustices including lynchings and other travesties of justice.

And even further back in the forties, many Africans in Africa closely followed what was going on in the United States. Nigerian newspapers under Nnamdi Azikiwe - who later became Nigeria's first president after independence in 1960 - and black American papers worked together, covering events on both sides of the Atlantic, especially in the mid-late forties. For example, there was extensive coverage of the Nigerian general strike of 1945 and the Enugu coal miners' strike of 1949 in black American newspapers which prompted black American organizations to ask the US State Department to intervene on behalf of the Nigerian workers whose rights were being violated by the British colonial government.

Even US federal intervention in the southern states was largely motivated by foreign policy considerations to win the friendship of African countries in the super-power rivalry with the Soviet Union and rob the Soviets of a powerful propaganda weapon they used against the United States to portray it as hypocritical nation which professed democracy while denying racial equality to people of African descent on its soil for no reason other than that they were black and African. Concerns about America's image at home and abroad was a much more powerful motivation than the quest for justice and concerns about the plight of American blacks as victims of racial injustice.

As African countries emerged from colonial rule in the late fifties and sixties, African leaders paid close attention to what the United States was doing in terms of advancing the cause for racial equality. And the *Daily Graphic* in Ghana reported extensively on what went on in the United States during the civil rights movement; an interest motivated by racial considerations and racial solidarity between Africans and African Americans.

The paper, which was the organ of the ruling Convention People's Party (CPP) led by President Kwame Nkrumah, even sent a correspondent to Little Rock, Arkansas, to cover the school desegregation case, and the accompanying violence, all of which attracted international attention. The *Daily Graphic* correspondent was also assigned to cover race relations across the United States in general.

I also remember when I was a news reporter in Tanzania in the early seventies, our newspapers, especially *The Nationalist* owned by the ruling party TANU (Tanganyika African National Union), had many stories about the struggle for racial justice in the United States, including the plight of the Black Panthers such as Angela Davis and George Jackson.

The editor of *The Nationalist* was Benjamin Mkapa, simply known as Ben Mkapa, who also wrote strong editorials on the subject. He later became my editor at the government-owned

*Daily News* in Dar es Salaam, the nation's capital, and helped me to go to school in the United States. In 1995 he was elected president of Tanzania. He was re-elected in 2000 for a second five-year term which was also his last as stipulated by the constitution.

And like the founding father of the nation Mwalimu Julius Nyerere, Mkapa was also a committed Pan-Africanist who was fully aware of the imperative need for unity of all African people including those in the diaspora.

This should help to dispel the myth that Africans don't want to have anything to do with African Americans.

But there is another dimension to this problem, the misconception that Africans don't want to identify themselves as black, or that they don't want to call themselves black, especially when they are in the United States, in order to maintain distance from black Americans who are collectively known as blacks in the American context. And there is some truth to this, also arising from a misconception on the part of many Africans - by no means all - that black Americans are low-class and lack positive values including values conducive to achievement, an image reinforced by the media and the predominantly white racist society.

But it persists, nonetheless, and is taken for granted as a fact of life by many Africans including those who should know better after living in the United States for many years. As Charles Mudede, the son of African immigrants from Zimbabwe, stated in his article, "Out of Africa: Young African immigrants Must Choose Between Being African or African American" published in TheStranger.com in 2001: "Black Americans represent an underclass and to adopt their ways - and be their color at the same time - is to adopt their terrible fate."

That's a pretty loaded statement. And to understand what he is saying, it is important that it should not be taken out of context, as the author himself explains in his article reproduced here in its entirety so that we don't lose perspective on the subject:

"Young African immigrants must choose between being African or African American. Their parents pull in one direction and their peers pull in another.

The bus that runs up and down Rainier Avenue carries two

types of East African youths. The first type is distinguished by their traditional clothes and Islamic politeness and diffidence. They never speak loudly, and are always found near the front of the bus for either safety or propriety's sake. Then there's the second, newer type of East African youth. This type always sits deep in the back of the bus, decked out in FUBU, Johnny Blaze, Ecko, and Mecca with sneakers as thick as Neil Armstrong's moon shoes.

In the winter they wear puffy space jackets, their ears sealed in bulging Sony headphones. In the summer, they wear NBA vests and long, baggy shorts or white undershirts with polka-dot boxer shorts puffing out of their sagging 'raw denim' pants. If they are girls, they have colorful nails done up at Hollywood Nails; if they are boys, they have tight braids or do-rags, and no amount of scrutiny can separate them from African Americans. Only when they speak is the truth revealed.

'I can always tell the difference between the two right away,' Dinknesh says to me in the library of her high school. She came to Seattle in 1999 from Ethiopia, and though her accent is thick, she has a steady command of English. 'If I go to the mall,' Dinknesh says confidently, 'I can tell who is African American and who is African. For some people it's not easy, but I know the difference.'

I explain to her that I can never tell them apart, especially with the East African youth. If they come from Nigeria or Zimbabwe or Zaire, I know right away they are African, and not because their features are more recognizable (more Bantu, as an ethnologist might bluntly put it), but because they always get the codes wrong or messed up. They are either a year behind the trends or their pants aren't sagging in the proper, lackadaisical manner, or worse still, and I have seen this several times, they are wearing a generic version of Tommy Hilfiger--a brand name that's already a thing of the past for African American youth.

'I can understand how you might not tell the difference with the [Ethiopian] boys; they are harder [to distinguish]. But the African girls, you can tell right away,' Dinknesh says.

Dinknesh is a case in point: She is East African, but in terms of appearance, clothes, bright jewelry, and fancy fingernails, she's all African American. And though she doesn't say it directly, she's proud of the fact that in just under three years, she has managed to blend into the American foliage. 'Many African Americans are surprised when they hear me speak,' says Dinknesh. '[Before I speak] they think I'm an American or even someone they know. But I'm Ethiopian, and proud of who I am, and of my African heritage.'

A hard line runs between Dinknesh's appearance, which is connected with her American future, and her internal life, which is still connected with her African past. The surface and the center do not hold well in Dinknesh and others like her; they speak two separate social languages, which they have yet to reconcile or make sense of. For many young East African immigrants, this conflict has produced a crisis. Dinknesh's successful assimilation of black American clothes and style will, according to popular and academic reasoning, probably be more detrimental than beneficial to her future in America. Black Americans represent the American underclass, and to adopt their ways (and be their color at the same time) is to adopt their terrible fate.

All East African youths who look like African Americans are conscious of this; it's frequently emphasized by their parents. To look like African Americans, who are the very definition of limited opportunity in this society, is to reject the grand myths of success that obsess the immigrant parent. Dinknesh and other East African immigrants like her are making a choice that will relegate them to the bottom of this oppressive society.

Classic Assimilation

The old model of assimilation--the classic assimilation model-- goes something like this: Immigrant arrives in a big, northern industrial city like New York City, with a leather suitcase in hand. The immigrant then moves into a ghetto, gets a low-paying job, works long hours for his/her kids, who do their homework in a tiny kitchen smelling of Old World foods. The kids, the second generation, then go to college, graduate with honors, and become doctors, lawyers, and presidents of the United States of America.

As Kathryn Harker writes in her invaluable study, 'Immigrant Generation, Assimilation, and Adolescent Psychological Well-Being' (Social Forces): 'According to this model, first-generation immigrants, who are foreign-born and socialized in another

222

country, should rarely be expected to achieve social and economic parity with the native-born American population because they must often overcome barriers such as discrimination, a new culture, and a new language. However, the second generation, U.S.-born children of immigrants, [or] foreign-born immigrants who migrated to the U.S. while very young... [are] expected to narrow the gap between themselves and the native population in terms of social outcomes.'

The classic model of assimilation, however, applies only to European immigrants, who can lose their ethnic identity and become white, and thereby identify themselves with the ruling class. 'Life is easier for you if you assimilate, and become more white American, that is true,' says Mimi Rosinski, who is 19 and came to America from Poland 14 years ago. Like the Polish immigrants who arrived in this country in the early part of the 20th century, Mimi has gone through the first phase of the transformation from European to white American; her son will complete the transformation and become all-American.

'You get shit for being different in school, and so you become like them. It also makes it easier for you to get a job if you're American, and to get to places you want to be in this society,' says Mimi. 'But then there is the whole other problem of becoming Americanized, even if it is white American. In the end, parents don't like it. At least my parents didn't like it. They now say I'm too Americanized and liberated, and I've lost touch with my Polish roots. But they are the ones who let me become American. They didn't teach me anything about being Polish. I think they first thought it was good and were even excited about it, then [later] they thought it was bad and ruined the unity of the family.'

Despite its currency in the popular imagination, the classic assimilation model has been in sharp decline since the passage of the Hart-Cellar Immigration Reform Act in 1965. That law abolished 'national origins' quotas that favored European immigrants above all others, and channeled immigrant flows through more democratic processes. Today, 90 percent of immigrants come from Asia, Latin America, and Africa, and they've invented a plethora of new assimilation and adaptation models to meet their specific needs.

For blacks in particular, the classic assimilation model is

223

nothing more than a bad joke. Unlike Latin Americans and even some Asians, blacks don't stand a chance of becoming white and benefiting from the institutions and connections available to white people. In fact, all they can become is another type of traditional American: black American. But this form of assimilation doesn't offer the same opportunities that white assimilation offers European immigrants.

So to succeed in the United States, modern African immigrants have to adopt the very opposite of the classic assimilation model. To survive in this country, they work hard to preserve their cultural distinctions rather than blend in with African Americans. To blend with African Americans is to engage in downward assimilation, as sociologists call it, a process by which new immigrants are absorbed into 'impoverished, generally nonwhite, urban groups whose members display adversarial stances toward mainstream behaviors, including the devaluation of education and diminished expectations.' (Center for Migration Studies of New York.)

In New York City, for example, the retention of foreign accents and culture has helped West Indian blacks get jobs. 'Given the strong negative stereotypes attached to black Americans, maintaining their distinctiveness [is] particularly important for West Indian blacks,' writes sociologist Kyle D. Crowder. 'Recent research indicates that West Indian immigrants are well aware of the stigma attached to being black in America, and, especially among first generation West Indians, there is a strong motivation to maintain their distinction as West Indian ethnics.'

This was certainly the case for me. I'm the son of Zimbabwean immigrants, and when my family lived in a black community near Sharptown, Maryland, my mother took extraordinary measures to keep my sister and me separated from local black Americans. My mother allowed only the children of whites, other Africans, and upper-class African Americans of the sort to be found in *Ebony* magazine to hang out in our rooms. But most of the African American boys and girls I knew--and conducted secret friendships with under my mother's radar--were like Kicky, who lived across the street from us. Kicky's mother was a part-time server in a cafeteria at a special school, and his father was somewhere in Tennessee serving time. My mother not only banned Kicky from our house, but also from the sidewalk in front of our house.

## Our Parents

'Where have I heard that before?' laughs Hali Mah-Mohamed, after I tell her the things my mother used to say about African Americans. 'I hear that all of the time. Even the little bad things that happen, she blames them on African Americans. She is always saying they are drug dealers, they don't want to work, they do nothing but bad things.'

Like Dinknesh, Hali, who is 18 years old and moved here from Uganda six years ago, looks more African American than African. Her friend, Tirzah Ngaga, who is 19 years old and moved here from Kenya four years ago, also looks American, though a part of her makeup--the penciled eyebrows; her long, pulled-back hair--recalls Nairobi's 'high life' culture. We're sitting in the Rosebud, and the girls seem to forget me for a moment, locked, as it were, in a conversation about their guardians.

'Remember when you braided Makoni's hair at my house, and he was there with three of his friends?' Hali asks Tirzah.

'Yeah, I remember that,' Tirzah responds, sipping her cappuccino.

'My mother just freaked out when she saw the boys, because they looked African American,' says Hali. "'Who are those African Americans?' she asked me. I told her that they were not even African American but from Ethiopia, and they were my friends. But she still freaked out, saying I should stay away from African Americans 'cause they are bad people, and a bad influence. They do drugs, and go to jail.' Hali shakes her head as she recounts her mother's impossible reasoning.

'Even if they were African American, what does it matter anyway?' Tirzah adds, raising her voice in protest. 'My sister does the same thing. In fact, she is always judging African Americans. She never stops saying that they are not good people and I will get into trouble if I hang out with them. But how can you judge something you don't understand? She does not know any African Americans, so how can she call them all bad?'

'Parents are always like that. They just label everyone as the same and that is it,' concludes Hali.

A few days before meeting Tirzah and Hali, I met again with Dinknesh, who has been in the United States for two years, and a handsome young student named Hayat Yemer, who has been in the United States for four years. Seventeen years old and from Ethiopia, Hayat's face has the noble air of basketball superstar Kobe Bryant. Whispering in the library of Chief Sealth High School in West Seattle, we discussed their parents' attitudes toward their appearance, which is black American.

'Our parents have problems with [it], but this is the way we must look because we are now in a new country,' Hayat says confidently. 'When I play basketball with my friends we speak English, and I like to speak English. It is the professional thing to do.'

'I don't feel whites. You know,' says Dinknesh, laughing, '[whites] don't like me and my skin color, and I don't like them. So why should I try to look and act like them?' I ask her if she gets along with African Americans, seeing as she has rejected white Americans. 'My people have a problem understanding them,' she says. 'That is why we don't get along. They talk too fast, and pronounce words like 'ask' like 'axes.' So we don't know what they are talking about. Plus they don't like us. And they also think we don't like them.

'When I was at the mall the other day, some African American guys who thought I was American came up to me and started talking. [But] when they heard me speak they backed away, saying African women don't like African Americans. But I said it's black Americans who don't like Africans, especially black American girls. The girls don't like us because they are jealous of us--at least that is what I heard. They are jealous because of the hair and they recognize our beauty. So they are worried that their men will chase us instead of them.'

'All you have to do is work hard and everyone will respect you,' Hayat says, feeling that Dinknesh has gone off the deep end, and is now in private territory. 'I know African Americans have problems working and also with family [life]. Their fathers are never around, and drugs are everywhere. But if you work hard, get a job, and don't abuse the freedom we have in America, then everything will be okay.'

## The Survivors

Most immigrants avoid thinking too deeply about what's really going on in America. The whole weird and complex structure of their new society is broken down into basic parts: parts that work and improve their lot, and parts that don't work and don't improve their lot. All other possibilities are thrown out the window. Immigrants can't help but be so blunt because their world is a panicked world. They arrive in America fleeing desperate circumstances--war, famine, crazy dictators.

Once they arrive, deportation always seems a phone call away. They are usually forced into poor neighborhoods riddled with crime and bad cops, and if they have a job it's rarely stable or meaningful. This is why so many black immigrants hold such low opinions of African Americans, the very people they should identify with. Immigrants want to improve their lives as fast as possible, and they don't see many black Americans living the lives they want to live in America.

Indeed, most black immigrants are as suspicious and critical of whites as black Americans, but they don't have the luxury of voicing their grievances. For example, my mother's criticism of black Americans was equally matched by her criticism of white Americans, particularly Republicans. She hated Ronald Reagan with a passion, and thought that Republicans were the cruelest, most selfish people on Earth. The day Reagan was shot was not a dark day in the Mudede home. But my mother would never express this harsh criticism in public, because she didn't want to jeopardize her already shaky status as an American.

What mattered to her first was achieving some sort of security, and not the larger problems of the racism and capitalism in America. (When we were back in Africa, many years later, she let everyone know how much she despised Ronald Reagan. Even the daughter of the American ambassador to Zimbabwe, who visited my sister regularly, was told that her father's employer was a very bad man. My mother's brother, who was educated in the middle of Idaho, spoke about Europeans in terms that would have pleased Louis Farrakhan after he returned to Africa.)

## The Real Future

East African youths like Dinknesh are in transition; they may look black American, but their core is still African. Their children, however, will be African American in the deepest sense. Because America is the way it is, these African American children will experience the full brunt of America's brand of racism. The happy life their grandparents dreamed about when they arrived here from 'war-torn Africa' will become, for them, a nightmare of police harassment, job discrimination, and limited social and economic prospects. Dinknesh's parents are trying to block the path to this bleak future by sustaining and imposing their Africanness.

As for my own mother, she succeeded. Despite my absorption of black American culture from hiphop to black literature, I maintained my African/British identity, and never became an African American. But now I have two kids, who, despite being mixed (white/black), are considered black in this society--the sad legacy of the 'one drop rule' (during slavery days, it was held that one drop of black blood made you 100 percent black). Will I react like my mother if my son comes home from school in sagging pants, saying nigger this and nigger that? At present, I really don't know. And maybe I don't want to contemplate such a terrible question."

So, in a very strange way, though not totally inexplicable, this blackness, this black identity of ours, attracts and repels at the same time. It draws many Africans towards black Americans because of the natural ties they share as people of African origin; yet it repels them from their brethren precisely because they have the same identity as blacks, not because they are fundamentally different in terms of origin. But it is reciprocal. Many black Americans feel the same way. It is the fear of admitting "I am what you are" because of the negative image they have of each other.

But there is still another dimension to this, at least in the American context, which explains why some Africans don't want to be called black. "Are you black?" "No, I am African. I come from Africa, not from the United States." That is because the term black in the American context is generally used to mean black American as opposed to foreign-born blacks.

228

Therefore many Africans don't want to be called black or be identified as black because they don't want to be confused with American blacks. But there is also an underlying motive, powerful, and even if not necessarily sinister. They don't want to forge links with them. They just want to remain and to be known as Africans, with their own distinct identity or identities solidly anchored in their African heritage. That is the line of reasoning, convincing or not, rational or irrational. It is a powerful motive, nonetheless, among a significant number of Africans in the United States.

But while some of that is true, it is *not* true that Africans don't want to identify themselves as black people or don't accept their black identity because they hate to be mistaken for black Americans; there are, in fact, many who would like to be black Americans and even do their best to talk and sound like black Americans, something they wouldn't be doing if they were ashamed of being identified as such.

Yet, there is no question that Africans usually don't call themselves black people. I myself remember this very well when I was growing up in Tanganyika, later Tanzania, in the sixties. We simply called ourselves Africans. Even during colonial rule, we did not have the equivalent of the *Black World*, or *Black News* or any other organ to articulate our nationalist sentiments and aspirations in racial terms in our quest for freedom and independence, the way black Americans do, appealing to color (blackness) as a binding force in their struggle against white domination and oppression. We had, instead, *Mwafrika*, a newspaper for Africans, black Africans yes, but African, not black, as our common identity. We had the same paper in Tanganyika and in Kenya whose name in Kiswahili simply means an African - man or woman.

And the main reason we Africans usually don't call ourselves black in Africa the way African Americans do in the United States is that we have ethnic or tribal identities our brethren in the diaspora don't. They lost all that during slavery.

Except in Tanzania and may be in Botswana, Africans in other African countries usually identify themselves *first* on the basis of tribal identity, as Kikuyu, Ashanti, Ewe, Shona, Ndebele, Yoruba, Igbo, Zulu, Venda, Xhosa, Toro or Luo before they say they are

Kenyan or Nigerian next, or African, let alone black. As Mwashuma Nyatta, a Kenyan student at Harvard University in the 1990s, bluntly put it when quoted in an article "Black Identity on Campus" on Africana.com: "I am more Taita than I am Kenyan, and more Kenyan than I am black." His tribal identity, Taita, comes first.

That is one of the fundamental differences between Africans and African Americans who are bound together by their blackness in a predominantly white society. Therefore, whereas, for example, Kamau is a Kikuyu first, or Olutola or Adelabi is a Yoruba first, and next a Kenyan or a Nigerian before he even identifies himself as an African, a black American is black *first* and *last*, or American next.

And when black Americans complain about racism that is being perpetrated against them by whites, thus using or seeking refuge in their collective black identity in a predominantly white society in the American context, Africans in Africa have to contend with tribalism by fellow Africans who belong to other tribes and whose members favor their own people as much as whites do against blacks and other minorities.

Therefore, the tribe, or tribal identity, unites Africans in the same way skin color or race or blackness unites black Americans. Skin color between rival or competing African tribes is irrelevant. It does *not* unite Africans because tribes divide them and unite their own members. Africans *know* they are black. But they are *not* united by their blackness, except in conflicts or confrontations with white racists; for example as happened in apartheid South Africa. But even then, black people in South Africa identified themselves mainly as Africans, not as blacks, as opposed to Europeans or people of European origin with their own non-African identity and whose domination and oppression helped Africans to transcend their tribal loyalties and rivalries since they were facing a common enemy.

Yet, ethnic loyalties remained paramount in many cases in apartheid South Africa as they still are today; for example, the Zulu and their Inkatha Freedom Party (IFP) against the Xhosa who "dominate" the African National Congress (ANC); some of their enemies and detractors even call the ruling party, La Xhosa Nostra.

230

In Nigeria also, ethnic divisions were a major problem even during the struggle for independence, in spite of the fact that all Nigerians faced a common enemy: the British colonial rulers. The Hausa-Fulani of Northern Nigeria had their own party, the Northern People's Congress (NPC); the Igbo dominated the National Council of Nigeria and the Cameroons (NCNC); and the Yoruba, one of the country's three largest ethnic groups, led and dominated the Action Group (AG). However, in many cases across Africa, Africans temporarily submerged their ethnic and regional differences to form a united front in their struggle for independence.

After Europeans left at the end of colonial rule, different tribes or ethnic groups started to compete for power along tribal and ethnoregional lines, plunging a number of countries into chaos and even civil war, the kind of turmoil and virtual anarchy unheard of among black Americans who constitute a single ethnic group, black, in Black America - if it was a separate nation - as opposed to the Igbo, Hausa-Fulani, Yoruba and the rest of the ethnic groups, 250 altogether, which make up Nigeria as one nation.

Yet, many African Americans including college students have not come to grips with this fundamental reality or been able to comprehend its complexity because they see all blacks just as one people; overlooking the ethnic diversity that is so typical of Africa, and ignoring the big role tribes or tribal identities play in African lives.

Some Africans have transcended that. However, they are only a minority. The vast majority appeal to ethnic loyalties and capitalize on ethnic allegiance to promote their own interests to the detriment of national unity.

But even those who have transcended tribalism simply identify themselves as Africans, whether they are in Africa or in America, because that is their collective identity. It is a misconception for American blacks to say assertion of this African identity is a rejection of black identity black Americans share with black Africans.

All these misconceptions will continue to keep Africans and African Americans divided, or confused, unless the two "peoples" sort them out and try to understand exactly what they mean, bearing in mind that they can build a strong relationship by focusing on what they have in common and not on what divides them.

But they must also seek unity in diversity because of the fundamental cultural differences between the two, thereby respecting each other's identity instead of trying to submerge both identities to create a monolithic whole which is unsustainable because of the differences that exist: in outlook, in our backgrounds and other ways.

They must also realize that they have more similarities than differences, and far more than they realize. But they have not capitalized on what they have in common and on what unites them, thus fuelling suspicion that they don't care about each other.

And that is tragic, especially in a world where Africans and people of African origin will remain on the periphery of the mainstream if they don't unite and work together to protect and promote their common interests and well-being.

# Chapter Seven:

# African Americans in Tanzania: Black Panther Leader Pete O'Neal and Others

TANZANIA is one of the African countries which have attracted a significant number of African Americans through the years since independence.

When Tanganyika won independence from Britain in 1961 under the leadership of Julius Nyerere, before it became Tanzania in 1964 after uniting with Zanzibar, it encouraged African Americans to go to Africa to help develop the continent. As Nyerere said in an interview with Ikaweba Bunting of the *New Internationalist* in December 1998: "I gave our US ambassador the specific job of recruiting skilled Africans from the US diaspora. A few came, like you. Some stayed; others left."

When the interview took place, Ikaweba Bunting had lived in Tanzania for 25 years. He was still living in Tanzania when I was writing this book and was one of the African Americans who had lived the longest on the African continent.

Another African American who has lived even longer in Tanzania is former Black Panther leader Felix "Pete" O'Neal, simply known as Pete O'Neal.. He has lived in Tanzania for more than 30 years, and his story is one of the subjects I address in this chapter.

Many African Americans still go to Africa every year, continuing their pilgrimage to their ancestral homeland. Some stay, while others return to the United States. The majority enjoy their stay in Africa, in spite of the problems they face; for example, lack of social amenities they enjoy in America.

There are those who say they have been warmly welcomed by Africans, even if they have not been fully embraced; and there are those who say they have been ignored or rejected, yet remain optimistic in their outlook, as was the case of Kianga Ford, a student at Georgetown University who went to the University of Dar es Salaam in Tanzania as a participant in the international student exchange program from 1992 - 1993. As she stated in "Minorities Abroad," a report from the Office for Study Abroad:

"People rarely ask me why I went to Africa. Occasionally, someone may question why exactly Tanzania. They assumed, as I'm sure that I did at some point, that I had gone to return to the 'motherland.'

Tanzania found me a minority of one, one 'black American' female student feeling looked at - the only one, to my knowledge, in the country. When I walked down the street, I was always followed by dozens of eyes and there was the echo from people that could hazard a guess, 'ah, black American...black American....'

Even in a country with centuries of Arab influence and more shades of brown than you can imagine, school children followed me and chimed, 'half-caste.' One old man near the Serengeti, more in grunt than in English, told me my very existence was a sin.

In short, there was no homecoming party waiting for me. It was a beautiful country for no expectations. Everyone will not see things as I did. Some of you may feel completely embraced in your journeys home, and whatever the outcome, they are worth it. If there is one thing that I could say to those of you 'in search of...,' it is, please, travel with an open mind. Expect nothing. Be open to anything."

While others may have had similar experiences, in Tanzania or elsewhere in Africa, that is not typical of the majority. A higher percentage of those who go Africa say they were delighted and enjoyed themselves in their ancestral homeland. And many of them go back to visit, some of them several times or as long as they can afford it.

Some countries have drawn more people than others for different reasons. West African countries attract larger numbers of African Americans every year because the majority of them believe that is where they came from, although a significant number of African slaves who were taken to the United States and other parts of the New World also came from Congo and Angola; and from East Africa, especially from what is Tanzania and Mozambique today, mainly because the anti-slavery patrol ships were more active on the West African coast more than anywhere else around Africa after the slave trade was declared illegal by the United States Congress in 1808. But it never stopped and went on even in the 1830s and thereafter, even if sporadically.

Besides historical reasons as the ancestral homeland of some African Americans, there are other reasons why Tanzania has attracted a large number of black Americans through the years: As a black African country, it is considered to be a homeland of African Americans just like the rest of black Africa is collectively embraced by American blacks as their ancestral homeland since they are descendants of many different African tribes or ethnic groups and don't even know exactly where in Africa they came from. Tanzania also has always attracted a large number of African Americans because of its Pan-African commitment and the leadership of President Julius Nyerere who was greatly admired and highly respected by many African Americans as he still is today.

That is one of the main reasons why Black Panther leader Pete O'Neal sought refuge in Tanzania after he fled from the United States. Other African Americans attracted to Tanzania for the same reasons, Nyerere's leadership and Pan-African commitment as well as Tanzania's role as the headquarters of all the African liberation movements, were some of the members of the Pan-African Congess (PAC), an organization founded by African Americans in Detroit, Michigan, in 1970, and which sponsored me as a student in the same city in the early seventies.

One of the  PAC members moved to Tanzania in the mid-seventies and acquired some land to live there permanently. Two also went to Tanzania in the mid-seventies and worked as engineers for two years. One worked in Moshi,  on the slopes of Mount Kilimanjaro in northeastern Tanzania. He also got married to a Tanzanian woman from Moshi. The other one worked in Dar es Salaam on the east coast.

Pete O'Neal also settled in northern Tanzania, in an area called Arusha not very far from Moshi. And he maintained an uncompromising position on the principles of the Black Panther

Party throughout his life in Tanzania. As he stated in an interview with Jeremy O'Kasick, published as "A Panther in Arusha," in an East African weekly newspaper, *The East African*:

"I am in debt to the revolutionary concept of the Panthers. I live that concept here in Tanzania. I need that belief structure to survive. And I'm not going to let it go for you, for anybody else, for exile, for the police, for nothing."

Besides Pete O'Neal, other African American political activists who lived in Tanzania for a number of years included Charlie Cobb and Bob Moses. Both had been active in the civil rights movement in the south in the sixties where they worked with people like Stokely Carmichael before going to Tanzania.

And Tanzania's pivotal role as a frontline state in the liberation struggle in southern Africa, and as the headquarters of all the African liberation movements, attracted black militants and other political activists from the United States and the Caribbean more than any other African country in the sixties and seventies, with the exception of Ghana under Nkrumah who was overthrown in February 1966 in a military coup masterminded by the CIA.

Howard T. Barnes, a CIA agent working undercover at the American embassy in Accra, Ghana, played a critical role in directing the coup and paying large amounts of money to Ghanaian army officers including one of the ringleaders, Akwasi Afrifa.

The CIA also plotted to attack and blow up the Chinese embassy in Accra, and kill everybody inside, during the military takeover, but dropped the idea. However, eight Soviet advisors were killed during the coup and the CIA seized a lot of Soviet military hardware and secret documents with the help of the coup plotters in the Ghanaian army.

The CIA was also involved in many assassination attempts on Nkrumah. By April 1965, there had been seven attempts on his life and he made it clear that he believed the American government was behind those attempts.

It was also around the same time that the CIA tried to undermine Nyerere's government in Tanzania in order to overthrow him.

Declassified documents from the CIA and the National Security Agency provide compelling evidence of America's direct involvement in Nkrumah's ouster. And the CIA's role in Nkrumah's downfall was also confirmed by John Stockwell, a senior CIA agent and former chief of the Angola Task Force at the CIA, in his book *In Search of Enemies: A CIA Story*. He was sued by the federal government for telling secrets.

It was also around the same time, in the mid-sixties, that the CIA tried to undermine Nyerere's government in Tanzania in order to overthrow him. As in Nkrumah's case, directives came from the White House and the American State department to cary out these subversive activities with the help of local agents in both countries. And Tanzania's role as the headquarters of the African liberation movements, all of which got diplomatic and military support from the Soviet Union, China and other eastern-bloc countries in their struggle against western-backed white minority racist regimes in southern Africa, did not please the West including the United States.

But in spite of the fact that Tanzania was the headquarters of all the African liberation movements, and a place which attracted many liberals and leftists from many parts of the world including black militants from the United States such as the Black Panthers (among them Black Panther Party leader Pete O'Neal and his wife Charlotte who have lived in Tanzania since 1972), and Malcolm X who also visited Tanzania and met President Nyerere and attended the OAU conference of the African heads of state and government in Cairo, Egypt, in July 1964 (where he almost died when his food was poisoned, probably by CIA agents who followed him throughout his African trip); our country still enjoyed relative peace and stability, not only during the euphoric sixties soon after independence, but during the seventies as well, when the liberation wars were most intense in southern Africa, with Dar es Salaam, our capital, as the nerve center.

Therefore, besides the raids by the Portuguese from their colony of Mozambique on our country; a sustained destabilization campaign by the apartheid regime of South Africa whose Defence Minister (later President) P.W. Botha said in August 1968 that countries which harbor terrorists - freedom fighters in our lexicon - should receive "a sudden knock," a pointed reference to

237

Tanzania and Zambia, and by the white minority government of Rhodesia (Prime Minister Ian Smith called Nyerere "the evil genius" behind the liberation wars), all of whom had singled out Tanzania as the primary target because of our support for the freedom fighters; the influx of refugees from Rwanda, Burundi, and Congo into our country; and Malawian President Kamuzu Banda's claims to our territory; in spite of all that, Tanzania was, relatively speaking, not only an island of peace and stability in the region but also an ideological center with considerable magnetic pull, drawing liberal and radical thinkers from around the world, especially to the University of Dar es Salaam which became one of the most prominent academic centers in the world with many internationally renowned  scholars who strongly admired Nyerere and his policies.

Among the scholars drawn to Tanzania was the late Dr. Walter Rodney from Guyana who first joined the academic staff at the University of Dar es Salaam in 1968 and, while teaching there, wrote a best-seller, *How Europe Underdeveloped Africa*; the late distinguished Professor Claude Ake from Nigeria who died in a mysterious plane crash in his home country in 1996; Professor Okwudiba Nnoli, also from Nigeria (secessionist Biafra); Professor Mahmood Mamdani from Uganda and one of Africa's internationally renowned scholars; Nathan Shamuyarira who - while a lecturer at the University of Dar es Salaam - was also the leader of the Dar-es-Salaam-based Front for the Liberation of Zimbabwe (FROLIZI)  headed by James Chikerema, a Zimbabwean national leader. Shamuyarira went on to become Zimbabwe's minister of foreign affairs, among other ministerial posts.

Many other prominent scholars from many countries around the world, and from all continents, were also attracted to the University of Dar es Salaam. C.L.R. James from Trinidad & Tobago, one of the founding fathers of the Pan-Africanist movement who knew Kwame Nkrumah when Nkrumah was still a student in the United States, and who introduced him to George Padmore when he went to Britain for further studies before returning to Ghana (then the Gold Coast) in 1947 with Ako Adjei, was also attracted to Tanzania. So was Kenyan writer Ngugi wa Thiong'o, disenchanted with the Kenyan leadership, and

Ghanaian writer Ayi Kwei Armah, an admirer of Nkrumah and Nyerere, who has also called for the adoption of Kiswahili as the continental language just as Wole Soyinka has.

Besides Malcolm X, other prominent black American leaders who came to Tanzania included Stokely Carmichael (originally from Trinidad) who as Kwame Ture lived in Guinea for 30 years until his death in November 1998. When in Dar es Salaam, Stokely used to stay at the Palm Beach Hotel, not far from the Indian Ocean beach and our high school hostel, H.H. The Aga Khan, in an area called Upanga; while Malcolm X and Che Guevara used to go to the New Zahir restaurant. But while Malcolm X was in Tanzania only for days, Che spent about four months in Dar es Salaam.

Angela Davis of the Black Panther Party and others in the civil rights movement including Andrew Young, Jesse Jackson, and Robert Williams who organized some blacks for self-defense in North Carolina, also came to Tanzania.

I also remember when Robert Williams came to our editorial office at the *Daily News* in Dar es Salaam. I saw him again in 1975 when I was a student at Wayne State University in Detroit, Michigan, USA. He came to Detroit and spoke to Wayne State University students who were members of the Young Socialist Alliance (YSA). I was at that meeting as an observer and reminded him of his visit to our newspaper office in Tanzania, which he remembered very well, as we went on to talk about a number of subjects including the influence of President Nyerere in a Pan-African context.

Some of the prominent leaders in the American civil rights movement who lived in Tanzania for a number of years include Charlie Cobb and Robert (Bob) Moses. They were active in Mississippi and other parts of the Deep South during the turbulent sixties when they almost got killed. Bob Moses was one of those who got a thorough beating in Mississippi for trying to organize blacks to vote. The White Citizens Council, founded in Greenville in Mississippi, the Ku Klux Klan and other racist groups could not tolerate that. Cobb had similar close calls. Both eventually moved to Africa. After they returned to the United States, they continued to be involved in civil rights activities and organizing communities for their collective well-being.

They co-authored *Radical Equations: Math Literacy and Civil Rights* and developed an algebra curriculum also designed to mobilize communities to achieve common goals.

Launched in 1982, the Algebra Project now operates in many cities and communities across the United States, and their book, *Radical Equations*, describes the project's creation and implementation. The project involves entire communities to create a culture of literacy around algebra, a crucial stepping-stone to college math and opportunity, especially for blacks and other minorities who lag behind in preparation for college work because of the low quality of education they get in inner-city schools.

Bob Moses, who was a secondary school teacher in Tanzania, began developing the Algebra Project after becoming unhappy with the way algebra was taught to his teen-age daughter. He saw algebra as a major obstacle for black students trying to go to college.

Charlie Cobb was a field secretary for the Student Non-violent Coordinating Committee (SNNC), once headed by Stokely Carmichael, in Mississippi from 1962 to 1967 where he developed the idea for the Freedom Schools that SNNC operated. The schools taught basic literacy skills to black children and became a model for many new approaches to education still used across the United States today. He also helped found the National Association for Black Journalists and became a senior writer for allafrica.com, the web site of AllAfrica Global Media. The site posts hundreds of news stories about Africa everyday from more than 80 African media organizations and its own reporters.

The years the two civil rights activists and many others spent in Tanzania helped strengthen ties between Africa and Black America, and is strong testimony to Tanzania's hospitality to oppressed people from around the world who found sanctuary in Tanzania during Nyerere's tenure.

The relationship between Tanzania and Black America has also been demonstrated in many other ways. For example, as we saw earlier, when Malcolm X returned to the United States from Africa, FBI agents were waiting for him at the airport in New York. He was seen going into a car with a diplomatic license plate which was traced to "the new African nation of Tanzania," according to an FBI memo. The car took him to the residence of the Tanzanian ambassador to the United Nations, trailed by FBI agents the same way Malcolm X was followed by CIA agents throughout his African trip.

President Nyerere also forged ties with Black America soon after independence when he instructed the Tanzanian ambassador to the United States to recruit skilled African-Americans to work in Tanzania to help the country meet its manpower requirements and as act of Pan-African solidarity.

There are also schools and other institutions in black communities in the United States named after Nyerere and other African leaders such as Nkrumah, Lumumba and Mandela. And Kiswahili, Tanzania's national language, is the most popular African language among African-Americans; much of this popularity attributed to the influence and stature of Mwalimu Julius Nyerere as an eminent Pan-Africanist who was embraced by the African diaspora as much as Nkrumah was. Many African Americans came to Tanzania because of Nyerere and his policies. Others viewed their trip as a pilgrimage, a spiritual journey, and a return to the motherland in the spirit of Pan-African solidarity.

One of the African Americans who was among the earliest to settle in Africa was Bill Sutherland, like Dr. W.E.B. DuBois and George Padmore, both of whom he knew and worked with in Ghana where they also lived and died. He came from Glen Ridge, New Jersey, and lived in Tanzania for decades. He knew and worked with Nyerere and was still in Tanzania when Nyerere died. Influenced by Mahatma Gandhi as a youth, he became a pacifist and worked for the Quaker-affiliated American Friends Service Committee after he graduated from Bates College in Maine. From 1942 to 1945, he was in a federal penitentiary as a war resister.

He first went to Africa in 1953 and settled in Ghana where he worked closely with Kwame Nkrumah. And through the years, he met or worked with many other African leaders including Nyerere, Kaunda, Lumumba, Tom Mboya, Mandela; others in the diaspora such as Frantz Fanon, and Malcolm X whom he interviewed extensively; as well as the leaders of the liberation movements in southern Africa, all of whom were based in Tanzania. In his book he wrote with Matt Mayer, *Guns and Gandhi in Africa: Pan-African Insights on Nonviolence, Armed*

*Struggle and Liberation in Africa*, Sutherland has a lot to say about Nyerere whom he knew and worked with for more than 30 years.

He moved to Tanganyika after he fell out with Nkrumah and left Ghana following his criticism of Nkrumah's increasingly dictatorial tendencies and abandonment of nonviolence in the struggle for African liberation. When he settled in Dar es Salaam, he became involved in politics - as he had always been - and worked in the office of Prime Minister Rashidi Kawawa who became vice president of Tanganyika under Nyerere, and later second vice-president of Tanzania; with the president of Zanzibar, Abeid Karume, serving as first vice-president as stipulated by the constitution of the United Republic of Tanzania.

As with Nkrumah, Bill Sutherland also disagreed with Nyerere on the same subject of non-violence and quotes him in his book. As Nyerere explained his support for armed struggle to liberate southern Africa: "When you win, the morale of the African freedom fighters will go up and the morale of their opponents throughout southern Africa will go down. I said that's what we should do, demonstrate success, which we did."

Sutherland also quotes Nyerere as saying that although the struggle for Tanganyika's independence was non-violent, he was not opposed to the use of violence if that was the only way to win freedom. Therefore his opposition to violence or support of armed struggle was not based on principle but dictated by circumstances. As Nyerere told Sutherland about the non-violent struggle for Tanganyika's independence: "The nonviolence of our movement was not philosophical at all...My opposition to violence is [to] the unnecessary use of violence."

And Zambian President Kenneth Kaunda, once a pacifist himself, asked Sutherland and co-author Matt Meyer if they had ever run a country on pacifist principles. As he put it: "Have you tried running a country on the basis of pacifist principles without qualification or modification, or do you know anyone who has?" As Sutherland states in the book, the discussion went well into the night, "but the upshot was that nobody had a clear and definable answer. We were not really able to respond to Kaunda."

I remember talking to Bill Sutherland in Grand Rapids, Michigan, USA, in the summer of 1977 when he spoke about the liberation struggle in southern Africa. He also talked about other African subjects including Idi Amin, saying Amin did many of the things he did just "for a little bit of publicity," as he put it. He also happened to know well some of the people, including national leaders, I knew in Tanzania.

I was still a student then, in the United States, following closely the events in Africa including the liberation wars in southern Africa. We agreed on almost everything except the armed struggle. I supported it. But even he as a pacifist was ambivalent about it, especially in the context of southern Africa.

He understood the necessity of armed struggle but, as a pacifist, could not as a matter of principle support the use of violence. I saw it as the only viable option; a concession he grudgingly made in conversations with the freedom fighters in Tanzania and elsewhere, and even with Nyerere and Kaunda, although they also agreed to diasgree. Yet he also realized that he could not really oppose the use of violence in southern Africa, considering the nature of the situation. Nor could he justify the use of non-violence in a situation where the oppressor did not have the slightest compunction shooting and killing unarmed, defenseless, and innocent men, women and children for no other reason than that they were demanding basic human rights, including the sanctity of life pacifists themselves invoke to justify non-violence.

Yet, he was a dedicated Pan-Africanist who made Tanzania his home, a country which became the most relentless supporter of armed struggle in southern Africa. And he settled in Tanzania because of Julius Nyerere who was already, even back then in the 1950s, becoming increasingly influential in African affairs, especially in the liberation of our continent from colonialism and imperialism.

A number of revolutionary thinkers from Latin America, Europe, and Asia were equally drawn to Tanzania and lived in Dar es Salaam which was the center of ideological ferment and provided an environment conducive to cross-fertilization of ideas stimulated by Nyerere's policies and ideological leadership. And Tanzania's prominent role in the African liberation struggle and world affairs because of Nyerere's leadership put the country in a unique position on a continent where few governments looked beyond their borders, with most of them content to pursue goals in the narrow context of "national interest," which really meant securing and promoting the interests of the leaders themselves.

Tanzania was therefore an anomaly in that sense, on the continent, as a haven and an incubator for activists and revolutionaries from around the world. And it remained that way as a magnet throughout Nyerere's tenure.

It was also his leadership more than anything else, which played a critical role in forging and shaping the identity of our nation and in enabling Tanzania to play an important role on the global scene, far beyond its wealth and size, especially in promoting the interests of Africa and the Third World in general. The fact that Nyerere himself was chosen as chairman of the South Commission, a forum for action and dialogue between the poor and the rich countries on how to address problems of economic inequalities in a global context, is strong testimony to that. And it was in this crucible of identity, a country that would not be what it is today had it not been for Nyerere that my own personality was shaped.

Many other people who were not Tanzanians were also profoundly influenced by Nyerere's leadership and the country's policies. They include African Americans who not only admired Nyerere as an icon of liberation and the pre-eminent Pan-Africanist leader of his time after Nkrumah died in 1972; they were also highly impressed by Tanzania's socialist policies of *ujamaa*, which means familyhood in Kiswahili. Some of them even adopted Nyerere's socialist principles of *ujamaa* to implement in the American context. For example, the Republic of New Afrika founded in Detroit in 1968 incorporated into its ideology some of the principles formulated by Nyerere in a Pan-African context.

When I was still in Tanzania working as a news reporter, I saw many African Americans in the capital Dar es Salaam. They came to our country in significant numbers every year. They came to visit. But there those who came to stay including some who established the Pan-African Skills Center to contribute to the country's development. Among those who came was Owusu Sadaukai, president of Malcolm X Liberation University in

Greensboro, North Carolina, who was also deeply involved in the liberation struggle in southern         Africa. When he came to Tanzania, I was making plans to go to school in the United States, and left a few months after I met him in Dar es Salaam.

I left Tanzania on November 2, 1972, and first went to Greensboro, North Carolina, where I stayed for a few days at Malcolm X Liberation University, a school Owusu started in 1970. His other name was Howard Fuller, but he was known in Pan-African and  black nationalist circles by his adopted African name, Owusu Sadaukai.

He was then a black nationalist firebrand and staunch Pan-Africanist. I don't know if he's still a black militant today, although I seriously doubt it, since he once served as superintendent of the Milwaukee Public Schools and as director of the Milwaukee County Department of Health and Human Services; establishment positions  in the American system he may not have been given had he remained an "outsider," a firebreathing black militant as he was in the seventies when I first met him.

He also came to Detroit where he and I were the main speakers at a conference about Africa attended by African Americans and Africans in 1975. I spoke about the significance of the Tanzania-Zambia Railway (TAZARA) in a Pan-African context. Known for his oratorical skills and fiery rhetoric, he was considered by a number of people in the United States to be the next Malcolm X, although he never went that far. The racist US senator from North Carolina, Jesse Helms, described him as "the most dangerous man" in the state of North Carolina. That was when he was president of Malcolm X  Liberation University in Greensboro.

I also vividly remember when he addressed students and faculty members at the University of Dar es Salaam in 1972, an event covered by Jenerali Ulimwengu, a fellow reporter at the *Daily News*, who later became chairman of Habari Corporation and publisher of a number of Swahili newspapers. I was still in Tanzania then.

Ulimwengu came back to the office very impressed by him, saying Owusu kept on saying, "We are an African people! We are an African people!" It was an expression he used a lot when he also addressed black American audiences - African Americans -

to emphasize that they were also Africans. In fact, Malcolm X said that even earlier, in the sixties, in his speeches. I remember one of his speeches in which he told a black American audience, I think in New York or Detroit, that "You are nothing but Africans." And he used it more than once. He also used the term African Americans, which is now - since 1988 - being officially used to identify black Americans.

Anyway, Owusu Sadaukai is now (in 2004) a professor of education at Marquette University in the city of Milwaukee, Wisconsin, and uses his former name, Howard Fuller, which he may never have officially changed as is the case with many other African Americans who use African names. And he remains an activist of national stature especially in the area of education for blacks in the inner cities and elsewhere.

Back in the seventies, Owusu was also national chairman of the African Liberation Day Support Committee formed to mobilize support across the United States for the liberation struggle in southern Africa and in the West African Portuguese colony of Guinea-Bissau.

In 1971, he visited Mozambique, Guinea-Bissau, and Angola to observe and support the liberation struggle going on in those countries against Portuguese colonial rule. When he returned to the United States, he began to make plans for African Liberation Day (ALD) demonstrations to show support for the liberation struggle on the African continent. The demonstrations became an annual event in many cities across the United States and were held in May every year. And I participated in all of them when I lived in Detroit. Dr. Walter Rodney, who then taught at the University of Dar es Salaam, was one of the speakers at some of those events in different parts of the United States.

When I met Owusu for the first time in Dar es Salaam, Tanzania, in 1972, we talked about my interest in attending his school, Malcolm X Liberation University in Greesnboro. I had already written him and he wrote me back saying he would be in Tanzania soon. We met at the Pan-African Skills Center which was established in Dar es Salaam by African Americans, and he promised me a scholarship to attend his school. I already knew about Malcolm X Liberation University after I read about it in *The African World* and wrote the school expressing my interest in

246

enrolling there. But I changed my plans after I got to North Carolina and ended up in Michigan, instead.

By the way, there are a number of accredited academic institutions in the United States named after Malcolm X. They include two four-year colleges, one in New York City and the other one in Chicago. And although Malcolm X was vilified for years during his life time and after he died, mainly by the federal authorities and by many whites who didn't like him or deliberately twisted what he said, he was eventually accepted as a major civil rights leader and one of the most influential in the twentieth century and was even honored when his picture was used on an American postage stamp in the late 1990s in commemoration of his legacy.

Malcolm X also had profound influence on the Black Panthers including Felix "Pete" O'Neal who ended up in Tanzania, coincidentally, in the same year I left for the United States. Even today, Malcolm X's influence on O'Neal's life is as strong as it was in the sixties and early seventies before he and his wife Charlotte, also a Black Panther, moved to Tanzania in 1972. And a huge picture of Malcolm X is one of the most visible items one sees at the O'Neals' residence near Arusha in northern Tanzania.

Also their life in Tanzania is one of the most important chapters in the history of African Americans in Africa, as much as it is in the history of the Black Panther Party and its stormy relationship with the authorities in the United States who were hostile to the Black Panthers and other black organizations, including Dr. Martin Luther King's, fighting for racial equality in the citadel of democracy. And it was this hostility which forced Pete O'Neal and his wife to flee the United States and seek asylum in Africa, first in Algeria and then in Tanzania where they settled in the small village of Imbaseni in the lush foothills between Mount Meru and Mount Kilimanjaro; Meru is the second highest mountain in Tanzania after Kilimanjaro.

At Imbaseni, O'Neal and his wife established the United African Alliance Community Centre (UAACC) in 1990, a charitable organization offering free lessons in a number of areas and that has been involved in small development projects. As he stated in an interview with BBC correspondent Daniel Dickinson, "Panther Pursues His Goals in Africa," Novermber 3, 2003: "I am not going to apologise, because I think it was a reflection of the way we represented ourselves in that particular setting and at that time. Now, when I look back, I must admit that there is something in me which is a little bit satisfied that I had the heart and determination to speak out publicly without fear."

On the small-scale development projects in Imbaseni, O'Neill, 63, said in the same interview: "We dug a bore hole here which means women no longer have to walk for up to eight kilometres to get water. This is fulfilling and if you want to juxtapose this with my goals as a very good young man in the States - when I thought that happiness came from expensive clothes and rings and big cars - that's nothing, this is true happiness, man."

By the end of 2003, the UAACC had trained more than 2,000 young people using Tanzanian volunteer teachers. The center is supported solely by donations from friends and family members in the United States. And a documentary film, "A Panther in Africa," was produced in 2004 and acclaimed for its portrayal of O'Neal who remains one of the most controversial, and most well-known, leaders of the Black Panther Party which was hounded into extinction by the FBI in the early seventies.

The former Black Panther leader explained that his work in Tanzania was an extension of the goals of the Black Panther Party, but without the guns and the rhetoric. As he said in the BBC interview: "It's 100 percent a continuation of the work we were doing as members of the Black Panther Party without the politics - I never hesitate to tell people that. I am very proud of that history. We have taken it to another level by providing opportunities for education and and enlightenment here in this setting. But it's the same spirit."

He applied for Tanzanian citizenship and got it. He said he had no plans to return to the United States. He received a letter from the American embassy in Tanzania saying it is possible he would be arrested if he returned to America. He was convicted of gun-running, a conviction he maintains was politically motivated because of his activities as chairman of the Black Panther Party in Kansas City, Missouri, from 1968 to 1970.

He was arrested on October 30, 1969, for transporting a shotgun across state lines from Kansas City, Kansas, to Kansas City, Missouri, and sentenced to four years in prison. When he was arrested, he did not even have the gun. The police had confiscated his gun nine months earlier from a fellow Black Panther. It was reported that the gun was sold after that, and the police had to trace it to O'Neal as the original owner for them to file charges against him.

When he was out on bail in 1970, he overheard a police officer say the only way O'Neal was going to leave prison was in a coffin. The implication was obvious: the police were going to have him killed in prison. He fled the United States in the same year while awaiting an appeal.

He fled to Algeria via Sweden with his 19-year-old wife, Charlotte, and finally settled in Tanzania. They were helped by some members of the communist party in New York City who obtained fake passports for them. And a new life, in exile, began. As he said in an interview with Jeremy O'Kasick published in *The East African*: "Three weeks to the day after that [US Senate] hearing, they came back and got me. There's no doubt in my mind that the government wanted me to go down after I raised hell at that hearing. And what did they get me on? They got me on a gun charge that was so bogus that it was pathetic....The government lied, they connived, and they conspired, like they did to bring down so many Panthers. "

He said a friend of his had taken the gun from his house, crossed the state line and was then arrested. He went on to say: "I said I didn't carry that gun across state line. Man, I carried more guns across that state line than you can count. I have had police friends carry guns for me. You see, Kansas City is one town divided by a state line. The cops actually sold the gun and the FBI had to get the gun from someone else, so they could arrest me!"

The gun charge originated from what he said before. He once on national television and other forums accused the Kansas City police chief of providing weapons to racist right-wing organizations, prompting the United States Senate to hold a hearing on the matter. O'Neal went to the Senate and disrupted the proceedings saying the senate committee charged with investigating the matter had deliberately disregarded valid evidence he had obtained. He became a marked man. Shortly after that hearing, he was arrested for illegally transporting a gun across state lines and sentenced to prison. He knew it was time to go.

That was more than 30 years ago.

By the end of 2003, O'Neil had already tried three times to have his gun-running conviction overturned, without success. As he stated in the same interview: "Clearing my name is important, as it will right a wrong. But I will not return to the States. I love Tanzania. I love the Tanzanian people and this is where I want to continue to work, grow and die. So I won't see 12th Street again."

Although he may never see the United States again, and the 12th Street in Kansas City where he was born in 1940 - which is also the city's historic street because it was also home to musical legends such as Charlie Parker, Countie Basie, Big Joe Turner, and Mary Lou Williams - O'Neal still serves his former country in a number of ways as a coordinator of the Study Abroad program for a number of American universities in Tanzania; and also runs an international exchange program under which he sends Tanzanian youth to the United States while bringing American urban youngsters to Tanzania for cultural enrichment.

The UAACC in Imbaseni, a non-profit organization, also offers computer classes and English lessons for local people and others, and has bed-and-breakfast services for travellers, in addition to managing an exchange program for Tanzanian and American students.

Charlotte O'Neal was also born in Kansas City, Missouri, in 1951. She married O'Neil in 1969. The O'Neal's have two children, Malcolm who was 38 at this writing in 2004, and Ann Wood, 35. Charlotte is a self-taught artist and the programs director of the UAACC in Imbaseni. She is also a published poet and writer, and her art has been shown many times in Africa and in the United States since 1987.

Their home in Tanzania has had many visitors through the years. One of them was Elmer Geronimo Pratt, former deputy defense minister of the Black Panther Party who was falsely accused and convicted of killing a white woman and served 27 years in prison for this wrongful conviction before he was cleared of the charges and walked out of prison, a free man, in June 1997. He sued the FBI and won millions of dollars in settlement with the help of the renowned black lawyer Johnnie Cochran who also successfully defended O.J. Simpson in 1995 against charges that he killed his former white wife and her male companion.

Elmer Pratt, by then known as Geronimo ji Jaga, visited the O'Neals in Tanzania in August 2002, more than 30 years since he and O'Neal last met in the United States. When O'Neal was chairman of the Kansas City chapter of the Black Panther Party in Missouri, Elmer Pratt headed the Los Angeles chapter of the Panthers before he became the party's deputy defense minister under Huey P. Newton, co-founder, with Bobby Seale, of the Black Panther Party in Oakland, California in October 1966 when the two were students at Merritt College in that city.

Jaga also heads a group for Africa's development, the Kuji Foundation, and has supported projects, including a water project, undertaken by his colleague Pete O'Neal and his wife at Imbaseni in Arusha in northern Tanzania. He and his wife also built a house in Tanzania, next to the O-Neals. They also live in Tanzania.

When Johnnie Cochran died in March 2005, Jaga was in Tanzania. And he still had that revolutionary spirit he and his fellow Panthers were known for in the sixties, as clearly shown when he wrote an article in memory of the African American lawyer who helped get him out of prison. As he stated from his home in Arusha in northern Tanzania in the article, "Geronimo Pratt Remembers Johnnie Cochran," posted on the internet:

"Alisema Kwamba Atakuja
(He said he would come)

I woke up this morning at 4 am, wide awake. Something led me out of my bed, and out the door of my shamba home here in Tanzania. I walked outside and looked into the Afrikan sky and wondered what this strange feeling was that had come over me. It wasn't bad, it was just a feeling that something was amiss. I just couldn't put my finger on it. I walked back inside and went to the computer and right away i saw Johnnie's face, and i knew it was Johnnie who woke me up.

Johnnie, who last time we spoke had told me, 'G, I'm coming. I told you I was coming. I am coming to the mama land with you!!!' And true to his word, he is right here with me. I can feel his presence grow stronger as the sun ascends over these sacred lands of the Great Rift Valley where life began. He is talking to me now. 'Look out for Chief.' 'Tell Ed to be cool.' 'Tell Stu not to worry.' 'Take care of Ginny.'

It's not easy to try and put into words one's feelings at a time like this. So many words and pictures come to mind that it is very hard to put them in order and transcribe them. What i can say is this: Johnnie was a beautiful brother, who even after becoming well versed in the ugly reality of Cointelpro, always remained a calming influence for me, encouraging forgiveness for all those puppets that were being exploited by the system. Despite the sick, sadistic practices of the government and its stooges, as documented in their own records, Johnnie continued to believe in the goodness of everyday people, who were being used as he used to say, 'For they know not what they do.'

Johnnie would want us all to keep forgiveness in our hearts, but to remain vigilant of these rats, who are now going to come out of the woodwork and claim friendships with Johnnie and sing his praises just to promote themselves and their egos. Johnnie never bought into the ego trip, and was always willing to give his time and energy to represent the most underrepresented in society. He was a man with a heart as big as Yogi Pinell's.

Johnnie and i connected long before he began defending members of the Black Panther Party against police repression in Los Angeles. We both came out of the Mississippi Delta and the great tradition of struggle by Africans in the south to liberate ourselves from oppression. We were born into this glorious history of resistance to the slavocracy, from the Bras Coupee Uprising and many other insurrections, to the Afrikan Blood Brotherhood and the Garvey Legionnaires in the 1920s to the Deacons for Defense during the civil rights movement. Johnnie and i were comrades in struggle, sometimes employing different methods but fighting for similar goals, the freedom and self-determination of Afrikan people in particular and all oppressed people in general.

The tradition of struggle continued in Los Angeles where Johnnie 'Chief' Cochran Sr. was one of the first men in Los Angeles to support the Free Breakfast for Children's program of the Black Panther Party at the Second Baptist Church with Rev. Kilgore. Soon after, his son, Johnnie Cochran Jr. began defending the members of the Black Panther Party in court against the racist police and other agencies who set out to destroy our movement as part of the federal government's illegal Cointelpro pogrom.

People were surprised, but not us, that Johnnie was willing to come to the fore of our struggle for Reparations. In 1975, while i was imprisoned on san quentin's death row, he and i began to dialogue via mail about the legal predicates regarding the money owed the descendants of African slaves. Johnnie was impressed with the arguments being made under international law, and the legitimacy of our right to reparations as was being taught by the great legal minds of Imari Obadele and Chokwe Lumumba.

His commitment to our struggle and his eager willingness to begin to engage in the struggle for reparations for Mama Afrika, who was raped first by colonialism and slavery, makes me suspicious of the suddeness and speed in which this healthy, picture perfect man, was taken from us by this strange illness. Johnnie also recognized that there were many other political prisoners in the United States such as Sundiata Acoli, Leonard Peltier, Mumia Abu-Jamal, Mutulu Shakur, Marilyn Buck, and too many others to list here. Johnnie was just as supportive of them as well. He would agree that we needed to go beyond domestic law, which is inherently racist, and use international law to escape the many racist trappings of domestic law that have been instituted since the early days of the slavocracy.

We had spoken about him joining me in Afrika to work on some of the issues facing our people here, and he had told me it was his next quest. He was anxious to address the problems of orphans, HIV/Aids, poverty, genocidal sorties, and patterns of economic exploitation that have continued since the days of colonialism. Johnnie wanted to come and pay homage at the Altar of Mt. Kilimanjaro, but he also wanted to meet two of our greatest heroes, Pete and Charlotte O'Neal. Johnnie was amazed at contradictions surrounding Pete's case, and the fact that he, Assata, Don Con and Cetewayo had to remain in political exile clearly and only because of the FBI's war against the Black Liberation Movement.

Many of Johnnie's detractors like to claim he played the race card in the OJ trial by exposing the misconduct, racism and ineptitude of the Los Angeles police. But those critics fail to accept the truth that Johnnie knew all to well; the Cointelpro card. This dirty, pernicious, secret, illegal war, that victimized even

Johnnie when the police pulled him out of his car and had him prostrate on the ground in front of his children. His past experiences on my case and many others having shown him how deliberately and shamelessly the police would manufacture evidence, lie on the stand, and generally use all sorts of nefarious tactics to get a conviction. Johnnie stood up and refused to blindly accept the testimony of police or other government agents. Unfortunately too many people still refuse to acknowledge the corruption and injustice that is rampant within the so-called justice system in America. But Johnnie knew it, and fought against it at every opportunity.

But Johnnie is home now. Another great son of Afrika has returned to the Ancestors. He has been a great son. A father, a brother, a friend and a comrade. We can all feel a little more secure knowing that while our brother is no longer able to look after us individually in the courtroom, he now watches over us collectively alongside Bunchy, Red, Toure and all the other Freedom Fighters who have gone before him.

Johnnie fought not only for justice, but also for peace. And he has finally found his. I could talk all day about my beautiful brother, but I know he didn't wake me up for that this morning. I can hear him calling me now, telling me to get up, get out, and continue to 'Fight the Good Fight!'

Pamberi ne Chimurenga!
(Ever Onward to Liberation)

geronimo ji Jaga
Tanzania, East Afrika
Wednesday, March 30, 2005."

Cochran, well-known for defending O.J. Simpson and winning an acquittal for him, will also always be remembered as the man who helped free Geronimo Pratt from prison when he won a multi-million dollar suit against the FBI on behalf of his client.

In interviews years later, including one on the nationally televised news program "NBC Today" not long before he died, he said winning the case for Geronimo Pratt was his biggest achievement and happiest moment in court. And as Pete O'Neal said in an interview with *The East African*:

"Everything we do here in Tanzania is a refined version of what we were doing in the late 1960s with the Panthers. Geronimo and I have been through a hell of a lot since those days. But that hasn't deterred us from trying to impact individual lives and hope that we're making some kind of contribution to the larger picture."

Pete O'Neal's story is an integral part of the history of African Americans in Tanzania. But a part of this history is also a sad chapter in the history of relations between Africans and African Americans.

In 1974, when O'Neal and his wife had been in Tanzania for about two years, the Sixth Pan-African Congress was held on the campus of the University of Dar es Salaam, Tanzania's leading academic institution. It was the first Pan-African Congress to be held on African soil after the last one, the Fifth Pan-African Congress which was attended by future African leaders such as Kwame Nkrumah and Jomo Kenyatta, was held in Manchester, England, in 1945. It was held in Nkrumah Hall, named in memory of Dr. Kwame Nkrumah, under the stewardship of President Julius Nyerere.

On the eve of the conference, there were between 700 and 800 African Americans living and working in Tanzania. However, their numbers dwindled after an incident that came to be known as the Big Bust.

When Pete O'Neal and his wife first arrived in Dar es Salaam in 1972 from Algeria, Tanzania was a haven for African Americans including revolutionaries such as Che Guevara who stayed in the nation's capital for at least four months after the failure of his Congo mission. It was when he was Dar es Salaam that he wrote his famous book, *Congo Diaries*.

Also several members of the Black Panther Party visited or lived in Tanzania during that time; as did their mentor Malcolm X, earlier in July 1964, when he stayed in Dar es Salaam for some time and met President Julius Nyerere at Nyerere's residence in Msasani on the outskirts of the capital. As O'Neal recalled those days in the early seventies up to 1974:

"There was a huge (African-American) population. It was amazing. There was an excitement here. There were so many African Americans here (in Tanzania) and everybody had at least some kind of vague sense of revolution. They definitely felt Pan-Africanism. And everybody wanted to be a part.

You had your cultural nationalists. You had your Pan-Africanists. Old Garveyites. Here's a bit of trivia, too: There has always been a large presence of African Americans in Tanzania who are from around the Kansas City area, whether back in the day when there were 800, or today, when there are less than 50, because the Tanzania ambassador to the US went to the University of Kansas to make a speech in the 1960s, welcoming African Americans to participate in nation-building at home."

The departure of African Americans from Tanzania, to the point where there was nothing left one could call an African American community as had existed before, coincided with the decline of Tanzania's economy in the late seventies due to a combination of factors including failed socialist policies; lack of incentives to production among the workers and peasants who were not rewarded accordingly for their labor and products; the war with Uganda under Idi Amin from October 1978 to April 1979 which cost Tanzania's fragile economy more than $500 million; exorbitant oil prices; a hostile international environment and terms of trade unfavorable to Third World countries; drought, poor management of the economy, corruption, and other factors.

But that is *not* what caused the exodus. The Big Bust did, as reported by various sources through the years, including *The East African* in 2003:

"On Friday, May 24, 1974, two young African Americans passed through Dar port Customs with a six-tonne container full of machinery and various goods that had arrived on a ship from New York City.

The two had intended to take the goods to Kirongwe village, Mara, as a part of a nation-building skills project. As Customs officials inspected the containers, however, they apparently discovered several guns and bullets that had not been declared on

256

the manifest.

According to the government-run Kiswahili daily newspaper, *Uhuru*, dated May 28, 1974, the Americans were immediately detained for interrogation.

'So here come Americans bringing in these things and bureaucrats and security officials immediately jumped to the conclusion that the African Americans in Tanzania were a fifth column working for the CIA to overthrow the Tanzanian government!' O'Neal explains.

'This seed of doubt was planted into the minds of a few people. It went way up to the top. And it became the idea that there could be an aircraft carrier in the Indian Ocean. So, they busted people. They started busting a lot of people. Just about every African American was under house arrest or they were in jail and in detention.'

O'Neal's account of the events is supported by a book titled *Guns and Gandhi in Africa* by Bill Sutherland. An African American and a personal friend of the late Mwalimu Julius Nyerere, Sutherland had worked with the Tanzanian government since the mid-1960s, often acting as a liaison between the government and the African-American community in the country.

As he tells it, he personally spoke with the president and the former vice-president Rashid Kawawa to try to resolve the situation. There was also an outcry in the US for the release of the prisoners.

As June and July wore on, however, African Americans continued to be incarcerated, placed under house arrest, shuffled and interrogated between prisons in Arusha and      Dar.

'If any African American had a gun around, or even a walkie-talkie, they were imprisoned,' Sutherland writes in the book.

'It was quite a tragic moment. Tanzania had represented, for the African-American community, what Cuba represented for the left in general: a sign of hope and possibility. After these incidents, there was tremendous disillusionment.'

After about four months, no further evidence was discovered to support the CIA collusion theory and all of the African-American prisoners were released, in part due to an effort by Kawawa.

Nyerere never made any further comment on the incident,

other than saying that he felt his security forces had overreacted. Sutherland points to the division within the (ruling party) Tanganyika African National Union (Tanu) at the time over the presence and nation-building work of African Americans in the country.

While Nyerere and several other politicians welcomed African Americans, a number of Tanu officials were outwardly resentful of their work, believing it unbalanced the nation's power structure.

Other accounts maintain that certain Tanu officials orchestrated the Big Bust as a means of diverting attention away from the historic Sixth Pan-African Congress, which began just three weeks after the first African Americans were arrested at the port.

One thing is definite: shortly after the Big Bust, many African Americans started to leave the country.

'Yeah, soon thereafter the exodus started,' O'Neal says. 'And you compact that situation with the war with Idi Amin and the falling economy; by the early 1980s, nearly everybody was ready to leave.'"

And there is some validity to those charges outlined by Sutherland. For example, Africans in many countries on the continent say black Americans are "aggressive" and when they come in, they try to "take over," an accusation also heard in South Africa after the end of apartheid.

O'Neal and his wife are some of the very few African Americans who stayed in Tanzania after the Big Bust. And he recalled with nostalgia the good old days in his interview with Jeremy O'Kasick in 2002 and published in January 2003 as "A Panther in Arusha" in *The East African*: "This is not the Tanzania of old. And revolutionary spirit, it no longer exists. But I am hopeful that the foundation that was laid when that spirit was at its highest will serve Tanzania well. Although it's changing, it is still an island of stability in a sea of turmoil."

He was one of the African Americans who decided to spend the rest of their lives in Africa. There were others such as Dr. W.E. DuBois in Ghana, Bill Sutherland in Tanzania, and many unknown ones through the years in different African countries, yet who were no less committed and whose Pan-Africanist spirit and their love for the motherland was no less intense than that of the luminaries. As he stated in the interview from his home in Tanzania in 2002:

"Can I see myself ever going back to Kansas City? I've asked myself that a thousand times. I don't know how to answer. I can't envision it. To go back there now would be a culture shock that I don't know if I could handle.

Let's get one thing straight: I am not sitting here planning to return to the US. I don't know anything about the United States. There are Tanzanians that know more about it than I do. What would I do if I went back to the States? I am 62 years old. My life here has a meaning. There, I would go and probably hold on to Charlotte's shirt tail all the time." After he became a Tanzanian citizen, chances are that he will probably never see America again.

But, while the African-American community in Tanzania virtually vanished by the late seventies because of the Big Bust in 1974, a number of African Americans were still interested in the country as they still are today. Probably most of them did not know about the Big Bust and still don't today.

However, their interest in the country has had the unintended benefit of reversing the migratory trend of the seventies which saw what was probably the biggest exodus of African Americans from an African country in the history of post-colonial Africa; ironically, from a country that had been, and still is, one of the strongest advocates of unity among Africans and people of African descent, especially during the era of President Nyerere. And Tanzanian officials have also encouraged African Americans to move to Tanzania, especially in this era of globalization. According to a report by Joseph Mwamunyange, "Dar es Salaam Tells African Americans: Come and Retire Here," in *The East African*, March 31, 2003:

"Tanzania has invited African Americans to come invest in Tanzania in various economic ventures, especially retirement homes for their compatriots around Lake Victoria and along the country's 800-plus km Indian Ocean coast. The Director of

Investment at the Tanzania Investment Centre (TIC), Daniel Ole Naiko, told *The East African* that Tanzania was prepared to offer land to Americans willing to invest in the country, saying Tanzania had many untapped investment opportunities.

'We already have a variety of options for the African Americans once they come and decide to invest in our country,' said Ole Naiko. He said local government authorities had earmarked over 370,000 hectares in various parts of the country for Tanzania's proposed 'Land Bank,' adding, 'TIC will facilitate investment in these areas; I believe the African Americans who were here a couple of weeks ago were impressed with what they saw.'

Mr Ole Naiko was responding to requests by a group of African Americans that had visited Tanzania a couple of weeks ago to make on-the-spot assessments of investment opportunities in East Africa. He said there are several other opportunities in mining, agriculture, fishing, tourism, transportation, construction, IT technology, telecommunications and more.

The chairman of Africa United Against AIDS Globally (AUAAG), Tiahmo Rauf, who led the team, said, 'Many African Americans would be interested in investing in Tanzania, but what is needed is for Tanzania and its people to fully advertise what is on offer. The investors I am talking about are not necessarily those who invest billions of dollars, but as individuals could invest from around $100,000 (Tsh100 million) upwards; this would be a good start.'

He further said there were over 40 million African Americans with a total income of over $60 billion, and many of them would be happy to create a 'Florida-style' retirement resort in East Africa and invest in economic ventures. Mr Ole Naiko responded by saying, 'We are ready to negotiate with them to come up with tailor-made packages that suit them and are acceptable to us.'

The AUAAG delegation included Steven Lattimore, who reports for American Urban/ Southern Radio; Aldoph Mongo - a freelance writer and media/political writer; and Monica Morgan - a photographer for *Jet*, *Ebony* and *Essence* magazines. The others were Reginald Smith and Jerod Smith representing American Urban TV and MBC, Tiabi Gill, international education director for AUAAG in the United States, and Dr Abdallah Mohamed,

East Africa co-ordinator for AUAAG in Kenya, Uganda, Tanzania and Ethiopia.

Ole Naiko told the delegation that TIC was in the process of readying local businesses to receive the potential investors. The delegation said their association was making arrangements to initiate a constant flow of African American visitors beginning June or July this year. Thereafter 35 tourists will visit East Africa every month, with the hope that their numbers will increase as time goes on.

The group of African-American journalists, who are also involved in the fight against AIDS, visited Kenya before moving on to Tanzania. In Kenya too, the African Americans were offered pieces of land along the Lake Victoria shore for building retirement homes for African Americans.

Mr Rauf asked the Tanzanian and Ugandan governments to consider doing the same. However, Mr Ole Naiko said Tanzania had more Lake shore land on offer around the other shared lakes of Tanganyika and Lake Nyasa. Mr Ole Naiko also assured Mr Rauf that Dar (Dar es Salaam) would open up its Stock exchange to foreigners the moment a draft Bill was passed by the National Assembly later this year. The American visitors said some members of their delegation had bought shares on the Nairobi Stock Exchange while in Nairobi.

A member of the delegation, Ms Tiabi Gill, told *The East African* that African Americans in the age group from 25 to 35 were keen to know more about and travel to Africa. 'They so much want to travel to Africa, but they are short of information on what they should expect when they come here,' said Miss Tiabi.

The AUAAG was instrumental in organising a musical tour to Kenya, 'Celebrate Life,' which included the renowned African American musical group Kool and the Gang. Their concert drew a crowd of over 500,000 people. The AUAAG tour of Kenya and Tanzania was intended, among other things, to enlighten the Americans on the many different tourist attractions and investment opportunities available in East Africa, and to encourage them to visit as a way of helping the region cope with the economic difficulties that hinder the fight against Aids.

The AUAAG delegation expects to educate and inform Americans about the 'untold story' of the flora and fauna of

Tanzania and of East Africa in general. This was the first time that such a large number of American journalists had visited Tanzania with the aim of promoting business opportunities and highlighting the effects of the Aids pandemic on the economies of Tanzania and Kenya. AUAAG is a US-based organisation dedicated to fighting the AIDS pandemic in Africa by sensitising American citizens, especially the African-American community, to contribute towards the fight of the scourge."

But like all the other people of African descent who decide or intend to return to the motherland permanently or for long periods of time, or even for short visits, they should be prepared for the challenges they are bound to face when they get to Africa. Many of those challenges are mental, emotional and psychological, including the rude awakening to the harsh reality that Africa is *not* what they envisioned it to be and is totally different from the romantic image they had of their motherland.

However, they are not insurmountable obstacles, and they have not discouraged many African Americans from going or moving to Africa. People of African descent go to Africa every year. They include some of the people whom I know and who moved to Ghana and established a settlement of African Americans in a country that blazed the trail of the African independence movement when it became the first black nation on the continent to emerge from colonial rule under the leadership of Kwame Nkrumah.

# Chapter Eight:

# Back to the Motherland: Fihankra
# An African-American Settlement in
# Ghana
# and other Diasporans

MANY AFRICANS in the diaspora have always had a strong interest in Africa as their ancestral homeland from which they were forcibly uprooted and removed during the slave trade and transplanted in the New World.

Through the years, a significant number of them have taken a step further and returned to Africa not only to reclaim their roots and heritage but to live permanently. They include some members of the Pan-African Congress, an organization founded and based in Detroit, Michigan, which sponsored a number of African students, including me, to study at colleges in the United States in the early and mid-seventies.

In the early nineties, a group of African Americans formed a community called Fihankra in eastern Ghana. One of the leaders was Kwadwo Akpan who was also a leading member and leader of the Pan-African Congress-USA in Detroit. He moved to Ghana with his family in 1991.

On December 9, 1994, coincidentally Tanzania's (specifically Tanganyika's) independence day, several Ghanaian and Nigerian chiefs met in Accra, Ghana's capital, to perform traditional rituals to atone for the misdeeds of some of the African ancestors who participated in the slave trade; although the initiators and conductors of this diabolical traffic in human beings were Europeans who went to Africa to capture Africans and take them into slavery in the New World.

They were also the biggest beneficiaries of this trade, in Africa and in America. Africans did not ask them to come and enslave them; nor did they ask them to build the slave castles along the coast to facilitate the transportation of Africans in chains to America. However, whatever role Africans played in this transaction was the subject of atonement on that historic day in Accra presided over by traditional chiefs from different parts of Ghana and Nigeria.

During the ceremony, attended by more than 3,000 people including a number of government officials, Nana Kwadwo Oluwale Akpan, whom we simply called Kwadwo Akpan in Detroit when he was one of the leaders of the Pan-African Congress-USA, was appointed paramount chief of the Fihankra community of Africans from the diaspora. In 1995, the community was given more than 30,000 acres of land by the people of the Akwamu traditional area in eastern Ghana to establish the Fihankra community.

The community is located near the banks of the River Volta, between Accra, the capital, and Tema, the nation's main seaport, and is surrounded my rolling hills and lush tropical vegetation. The houses built in the Fihankra community cost from $20,000 to $40,000, at this writing, and can be bought by Africans from the diaspora who want to move there. There are many African Americans who want to go to Africa for different reasons. There are those who want to "go back" to live there permanently. Others want to retire there, start a business, help build Africa, or simply visit.

The land was given to African Americans and other diasporans not only because they are entitled to it because of their African roots, but also to encourage others to move to Africa, live with their people from whom they were forcibly separated for centuries, and help develop the motherland. The land is free to any diasporans who want to live or invest in Ghana.

Once fully developed, it is going to be a full-fledged self-sustaining community with all the basic necessities and services needed to lead a complete life. Many plots are available not only for houses but also for schools, clinics, shopping malls, offices and other facilities.

Although modern conveniences such as shopping malls, once completed, may give the Fihankra community the appearance of an urban setting transplanted from the metropolitan West, the settlement for all intents and purposes is intended to fit in its African environment, with the establishment of farms and traditional institutions to reflect the African way of life.

The community is intended to be an integral part of Ghana. Fihankra members were further encouraged in pursuit of this goal when in March 2000, Ghanaian President Jerry Rawlings signed a new immigration law which was passed by parliament in November 1999, giving Africans from the diaspora resident in Ghana rights previously accorded only to Ghanaians.

The rights, collectively known as Right of Abode under the new law, include entering Ghana without a visa; remaining indefinitely in Ghana; and working in Ghana either as a self-employed or as an employee without a work permit. As Alban S.K Bagbin, chairman of the parliamentary committee which submitted the bill to parliament, stated: "This bill reflects the sentiment of both the parliament and the office of the president. We look forward to the increased investment and cultural exchange that is likely to evolve between ourselves and our brothers and sisters from the diaspora."

But there was some disappointment among many diasporans. When President Rawlings visited the United States in 1998, he announced at a press conference with US President Bill Clinton in Washington that Ghana would grant dual citizenship to African Americans and other Africans from the diaspora who wanted to move to Ghana. He said during the televised press conference that if he as a black man could be a citizen of Ghana, he did not see why other blacks, descendants of African slaves, could not be.

The announcement was received with a lot of excitement among many Africans and other Africans in the diaspora. However, the Ghanaian parliament did not go that far and, instead, gave diasporans limited rights short of full citizenship under the 2000 immigration law.

In spite of the disappointment, some members of the Fihankra community were optimistic. As Kwadwo Akpan stated: "While the immigration law may not represent all that Diasporans had hoped for, Fihankra International believes that each step forward moves us closer to our goal of re-integrating Africa with its Diaspora. Toward that objective, this law is a most significant step ahead while there will be continued dialogue to further improve relations between Diasporans and the government of Ghana."

Although the establishment of the Fihankra community was a major achievement, one of the challenges that lie ahead is the full integration of its members into the Ghanaian society. But it requires mutual involvement and commitment by the indigenes and the diasporans.

The indigenous people of Ghana should fully embrace their brethren from the diaspora, instead of rejecting them, ignoring them or maintaining distance from them as some of them have done. And the diasporans who live in Ghana must also avoid isolating themselves or giving the impression that the community they have established is some kind of island of western material civilization in the midst of poverty-stricken rural Africa, exclusively for them, and different in lifestyle.

The community is not "little America" or "little Europe" in Africa. It is, and must always strive to be, an African community in Africa. Otherwise prophets of doom will be vindicated in their belief that attempts by diasporans to forge geniune links with their brothers and sisters in Africa, and integrate themselves into the traditional African society, are no more than empty rhetoric. As one African American who visited Ghana said in his comments on G. Pascal Zachary's article, "For Black Americans in Ghana, the Grass Isn't Always Greener" in *The Wall Street Journal*, posted on Christine's Genealogy web site, April 5, 2001:

"I just recently returned from my first (and hopefully not my last) trip to Africa (Ghana to be exact) and I would say that I agree with the overall premise of the posted article.

However, I did not go to Africa with the expectations of being accepted by the locals as a 'Brother.' Rather, my goal was to bring the captured genes of my ancestors back to their native land. I am sure that many generations of my family tree, ached to return to their home land and I felt obligated and pleased to be able to bring them home.

No White American or Native African can deny me the affinity that I have with Africa. My DNA contradicts such nonsense.

So, the fact that Ghanaians saw me as an American and not as a 'Brother,' did not disappoint me one bit. In fact, many Africans have problems accepting Africans of different ethnic groups. For example, many Fanti members have resentment for the Asante, in Ghana. Also, attempted acts of genocide committed by one tribe against another in some parts of Africa are well known. Furthermore, I grew up in an all Black inner-city neighborhood and when a Black kid from the suburbs came in the hood, I would see him as basically being "White" (notwithstanding blue-blackness).Therefore, African Americans visiting or living in Ghana should stop being so naive.

I also believe that Americans can be a corruptive influence on African culture and society. We have basically been reared as Europeans (although very poorly) and not as Africans. And if they (Ghanaians) are not careful, we (African Americans) can have the same effect as "White Colonizers" of the past. I believe that it is the African Americans who should humble themselves to Africa and its culture and not try to make it like Detroit.

In regards to the grass not being greener for Black Americans in Africa, the same can be said for Ghanaians in America. Many find that the streets of America are not paved with gold and that life, as an 'individual,' can be very complicated here in America. I know many Ghanaians who are contemplating repatriation.

As humans, we all long for what we don't have and the grass of others often seems greener. However, the end should not always be moving to where the grass is greener; rather, we should cultivate our own lawns so that we no longer have to envy others."

It is obvious that not every African American who has been to Ghana disagreed with the main thrust of Zachary's article in *The Wall Street Journal*.

Yet, in spite of whatever problems black Americans face in Ghana, and whatever other problems lie ahead for both Ghanaians and their brethren from the diaspora, there is no question that the establishment of the Fihankra community of African diasporans in Ghana is of major symbolic and practical significance in the quest for Pan-African solidarity overflowing continental boundaries, and in terms of encouraging others to move to Africa to live permanently and contribute to the development of Africa. And it has taken place in a country that has always attracted signficant numbers of African Americans and other diasporans through the decades, although mainly as visitors and not as immigrants.

When viewed in a larger context, for example, in terms of total population of African Americans in the United States, the numbers of this reverse, voluntary migration - as opposed to the enslavement of millions of Africans who were taken to the Americas during the slave trade - don't seem to be impressive. There are almost 40 million African Americans in the United States today.

Yet, African Americans who live in Ghana at this writing are only a few hundreds, about 1,000 or so, and not all of them immigrants who have decided to live there permanently. More Africans emigrate to the United States every year, at least tens of thousands, than African Americans do to Africa.

However, the impact of this migratory trend, "back to Africa," should not be viewed in terms of numbers alone but also in terms of commitment to the well-being and development of the continent among many African Americans even if the majority of them don't move "back" to the motherland but, instead, stay in the United States while making a contribution to Africa's development through investment, educational projects and in many other ways.

Still, however small, and it's not that small, there is no question that there is a steady pattern of migration of African Americans to Africa, especially to Ghana and a few other West African African countries such as Liberia.

In East Africa, Tanzania, especially in the seventies, had the largest number of African Americans, about 800, living there; roughly equal to the total number of those who live in Ghana today, in a country that traditionally has attracted probably the largest number of African diasporans than any other on the continent, especially since the days of Kwame Nkrumah whose influence among African Americans as an African leader was unmatched, except may be by Nyerere's among black political activists and academic intellectuals.

Ghana has always been a black star in the constellation of nations because of Nkrumah's stature and influence. Although he is gone, people still invoke his name and memory, bringing attention to Ghana even when the country has had poor leadership as was the case in the late sixties and early and mid-seventies during inept military and civilian rule until Jerry Rawlings, a strong admirer of Nkrumah and with a strong and charismatic personality of his own, emerged on the political scene in 1979 as a military ruler and became one of the most dynamic African leaders in post-colonial Africa.

It was also during Rawlings' tenure that Ghana went a step further than any other African country and gave African Americans rights that had been exclusively reserved for Ghanaian citizens in terms of residence and employment. And as far back as 1992, when Rawlings won his first term as president, after leading Ghana as a military head of state, a significant number of African Americans were already living in the country; many of them drawn to this part of Africa for historical reasons as their ancestral homeland.

At least 25 percent of all the African slaves taken to America are believed to have come from what is Ghana today, formerly the Gold Coast. Others have moved to Ghana for personal, economic and political reasons. As Elsie B. Washington stated in an article, "Cousins: African Americans in Ghana," in *Essence*, October 1992:

"If you asked each of the approximately 300 African Americans who reside in Ghana why they choose to live in this small West African nation, you'd hear some common reasons emerge.

Some of them are intensely personal--such as the search for a better environment in which to raise children. Others are political--dissatisfaction with the state of affairs in the United States.

Talk with them, and you'll note a certain serenity. African Americans who call Ghana home have wound down, cooled out--are less on guard. Visit one of their homes, and you'll experience their joy at being in a history-making Black nation, surrounded by people who are pulling together to build a strong society and a secure future.

Some of the 300 are 'lifers,' among them Dr. Robert 'Uncle Bobby' E. Lee, a dentist who settled in Ghana in 1957 with his wife, Sarah, who was also a dentist, and their two sons.

Lee still remembers the jubilation he, Dr. Martin Luther King, Jr., and other Black visitors shared on Ghana's Independence Day. Benjamin Harrison Robinson, Jr., and his wife, Imahkus Vienna, who arrived last year, are also in Ghana for good. They are working on several development projects in their village near Cape Coast and are happy for the chance to give their "time, energy and resources" to help the people of Ghana. A close friend who, like Robinson, has been made a regional chief (women chiefs are called Queen Mother) is Malkia Brantuo. She also manages a seaside hotel and runs a school in Cape Coast.

Often the love affair with Ghana begins with the encouragement of a friend who is familiar with the country from her own travels. That was the case with Bryan O. Lowe, whose first trip was in 1987. Now he and his sister, Dorothy Lowe-Wilbekin, spend half of each year in Ghana; they return to Brooklyn for the other half to raise funds for the physically challenged.

Business and employment opportunities bring other African-Americans to Ghana. Daniel McGaffie serves as a public-affairs officer for the United States Information Service, while his wife, Nell, earns her baccalaureate at the University of Ghana. McGaffie sums it up for the African-American community when he says, 'I feel at home in Ghana, as if I belong here.' "

Although only about 1,000 African Americans live and work in Ghana, mainly in the capital Accra, about ten times that number, at least 10,000 black Americans, visit the country every year. That is more than any of those who go to any other African country.

Despite some negative experiences - such as rejection by some of the indigenous people who call African Americans *obruni*, meaning white; denial of jobs; higher taxi fares, and higher costs for hospital visits and treatment - a large number of African

Americans are still attracted to Ghana, with the tropical climate and the beaches being another attraction as much as it is for many other African countries; so is the low cost of living contrasted with that of the United States.

However, just like in any other black African country, conflicting perceptions and profound cultural differences between Africans and black Americans in Ghana complicate relations between the two groups. They have different perceptions and expectations of each other. Many of them also see each other as different, with more differences than similarities between them, perceptions and misconceptions of each other which also often lead to indifference even towards plight afflicting one group or the other.

That is one of the reasons why in the United States, for example, you don't see or hear about well-organized groups of African Americans lobbying or campaigning for African causes at the national level and on sustained basis the way Jews do for Israel, or even the way Arabs do for the Palestinian cause or for the well-being of their people in the entire Middle East.

All that is symptomatic of an underlying problem in relations between Africans and African Americans. As Professor Femi Ojo-Ade, a Nigerian teaching at St. Mary's College of Maryland in the United States who also taught at universities in Nigeria and other countries and once served as a Nigerian diplomat, said about relations between Africans and African Americans in a lecture he delivered at Olabisi Onabanjo University, Ago-Iwoye, Nigeria, in March 2005, entitled "Living in Paradise: Africans in America":

"Whether we like it or not, there is a divide, a deep one, a dangerous one, that may either break or make our destinies in a world that refuses to fully accept our humanity....

The relationship between Africans and African Americans living in America is more often than not a source of sorrow. The title of a newly published book by Godfrey Mwakikagile, makes the point quite clearly: it is a matter of *misconceptions, myths, and realities*.

The misconceptions and misunderstanding are based upon myths. African Americans accuse Africans of selling them into slavery. To counter that heinous act, they claim that the best and brightest from Africa were sold (read: saved) from the jungle into Civilization.

For their part, Africans accuse African Americans for being more American than Africans; for being uneducated, uncouth, and unfriendly. They claim that whites treat them better, and make them feel more welcome, than do African Americans. This latter claim is particularly widespread among intellectuals. It is not unusual to hear an African employed in a historically black college complain that his black brothers and sisters are deliberately alienating him. On the contrary, those on white campuses claim that they are treated with some dignity....

It is remarkable that, in present-day America, there is no African American lobby on behalf of Africa, similar to the commitment of Jews for Israel, for example. When one recalls the past cooperation between diasporic and continental Pan-Africanists, and the work of the likes of W.E.B. DuBois, Kwame Nkrumah, and Wole Soyinka, one remains nonplussed by the current inertia within the black community. There is enough blame on both sides of the Atlantic to build a skyscraper of shame and sorrow; of missed opportunities for constructive engagement and exchange."

Compounding the problem is the indifference of a large number of Africans towards the legacy of slavery which is a constant reminder to African Americans of their subordinate status in a predominantly white society which remains essentialy racist even long after the abominable institution of slavery was abolished. They don't have memories of slavery as much as African Americans do. It's all in the past, the distant past, while the legacy of slavery is very much an integral part of daily life for black Americans in the United States, and even when some of them move to Africa.

And many Africans feel they had nothing to do with slavery. Their ancestors did. They don't feel guilty about it, and they are not sorry about it, as many African Americans expect them to be. As Kofi Glover, a Ghanaian professor of political science at the University of South Florida states, slavery is a divisive issue between Ghanaians - and other Africans as well, of course - and African Americans.

272

He goes on to say the differences Africans and African Americans have over slavery could even strongly discourage or prohibit African Americans from ever making Ghana their permanent home, regardless of whether or not they have been given the right to settle there, as they indeed were, when President Rawlings signed the new immigration law which included a provision of Right of Abode for African Americans and other descendants of Africa in the diaspora.

Yet, the new law giving them permanent residence and other rights previously reserved exclusively for Ghanaians is not going to bridge the gap between Africans and African Americans. That is something the people themselves have to work on.

And the differences are real and profound. They cannot be glossed over. As Professor Kofi Glover states: "Whether we like it or not, Africans and African Americans have two very different cultures." On the differences over slavery, he has this to say: "[Ghanaians] did not experience white domination like the Africans in Kenya, Zimbabwe, or South Africa. We do not understand the whole concept of slavery, or its effect on the attitude of a lot of African Americans, mainly because we were not exposed to it."

When African Americans hear this, many of them automatically conclude that Africans don't care about them and "don't want us over there." Yet, the context in which such sentiments are articulated, as Kofi Glover did, should be fully understood; *why* he said what he did, and exactly *what* he meant by that.

It's not enough to take it at face value, superficially, without probing the essence of what he articulated.

However, no matter how well-intentioned or innocent some comments and remarks by Africans may be when they talk about African Americans or about slavery, there are always people who will pounce on that to further their own  agenda or objectives; whether it is to keep African Americans and Africans divided, discourage African Americans from moving to Africa, or simply to articulate a position from an African perspective on slavery which African Americans don't share, yet which can be twisted for ulterior motives by anybody who wants to do so.

This reminds me of what Gregg Pascal Zachary said in his

article in *The Wall Street Journal* in March 2001 about African Americans in Ghana where he said they felt they were not welcome because of the hostility towards by them by Ghanaians.

No matter which side you are on about what he said, and regardless of the merits or demerits of the essence of his article, there is no question that it sparked an important debate on the contentious subject of relations between Africans and African Americans. Many people responded to the article in different forums, as we saw earlier.

And there were others from different perspectives, including "Unbiased Article?: For African Americans in Ghana, the Grass Isn't Always Greener - Seeking the 'Motherland,' They Find Echoes of History and A Chilly Welcome - Mr. Thompson's Yam Special," in *The African Independent*:

"By G. Pascal Zachary
Staff Reporter of *The Wall Street Journal*
14 March 2001
*The Wall Street Journal*
A1

ACCRA, Ghana -- Kwaku Sintim-Misa, a popular comedian here, likes to tell a joke about the African-American who emigrates to Ghana.

'Brother, I've found my roots!' the African-American crows. A local shakes his head, wondering why anyone with a coveted United States passport would choose to move to Ghana. 'Move to the Motherland?' the Ghanaian cries, 'I want to escape the Motherland.'

Mr. Sintim-Misa's story gets laughs because it rings true. Last year, the number of Ghanaians applying to legally enter the U.S. tripled. In the same year, Ghana's currency lost nearly two-thirds of its value against the dollar. So many skilled and educated Ghanaians have fled that Mr. Sintim-Misa has the impression that 'nobody wants to live in Ghana anymore.'

Nobody, that is, except African-Americans.

U.S. officials estimate that 1,000 African-Americans live in Ghana, mostly in its capital, Accra, and that an additional 10,000 visit as tourists each year. By many accounts the country attracts more black Americans than any other in Africa, and by a wide margin. In recent years, hundreds have decided to relocate, drawn by beautiful beaches, a tropical climate, low living costs and, most of all, a sense that this historic heart of the slave trade is an ancestral homeland.

The country's appeal is not always obvious. Electricity and water supplies are often interrupted. Malaria is rampant. Wages are meager by U.S. standards. Given the number of people leaving, the arrival of enthusiastic African-Americans might be expected to delight Ghanaians.

It doesn't. Far from seeing African-Americans as kin, most Ghanaians lump them together with other Americans, calling the whole lot *obruni*, which in the local Twi language means 'white' or foreigner. With better education and deeper pockets, African-Americans strike many Ghanaians as arrogant. 'When they get into any situation they want to take over, and we are not like that,' says R. William Hrisir-Quaye, an official with Ghana's commission on culture.

Indeed, many black Americans living in Ghana find they aren't particularly welcome -- and wonder whether they need a new civil rights movement to secure a place in their adopted home. Ghana forbids American residents from taking most government jobs. Hospitals charge them higher fees. Americans can't vote in elections or participate in local politics. It is virtually impossible for them to obtain citizenship, or permanent 'right of abode,' even after marrying a Ghanaian. The infamous slave castles along Ghana's coastline impose entrance fees on Americans that are 30 times as high as those paid by locals. . . .

Shooting "Back to Africa" Bullets
March 24, 2001

Last week, on March 14th to be exact, I got shot. I glanced at the cover of *The Wall Street Journal* and got shelled, hit hard with well-crafted propaganda. I know that's a heavy word and as soon as you use it, people immediately box you into a safe, neat corner. They are less threatened that way. But paper (or digital) bullets are no joke. And they don't take you out gangsta-style. They heat sink your brain and expand into unattributable hearsay, innuendo and subtle opinion-altering pieces of mind shrapnel.

The article, entitled: 'For African-Americans in Ghana, The Grass Isn't Always Greener' and written by Journal Staff Reporter G. Pascal Zachary, is built on one notion: that African Americans living in Ghana, as well as those who visit, are not welcome by Ghanaians.

'Far from seeing African-Americans as kin, most Ghanaians lump them together with other Americans, calling the whole lot *obruni*, which in the local Twi language means 'white' or 'foreigner,' reports Zachary. 'With better education and deeper pockets, African-Americans strike many Ghanaians as arrogant.' 'When they get into any situation they want to take over, and we are not like that,' says R. William Hrisir-Quaye, an official with Ghana's commission on culture.'

As a journalist and university lecturer who has visited and written extensively about Ghana, I am very familiar with Ghana's complexities, both positive and negative. I also know unfair, inaccurate journalism when I see it.

I personally know several of the people Zachary interviewed in his piece and like most journalists, know the formula for spinning stories. It mysteriously lies between the sly use of quotes, text and context, maligning by omission and, of course, corporate editorial and advertising mandates. The deadline driven, newsstand-rocking copy is then processed with assembly-line expediency. Just call it shake n' bake journalism. Ready to eat anytime.

Although there are truths in his story, it fails miserably to provide a balanced, objective view of the relationship between African Americans and Ghanaians or for that matter, shed any light on the many accomplishments of Ghana itself.

Take for instance, the fact that the country recently held peaceful democratic elections and successfully handed over power to a democratically elected government after a nearly twenty-year regime. But is that newsworthy? Will that sell like controversy?

The article has already created an outcry among progressive black folk everywhere. Take for example Zachary's quoting of Audrey Gadzekpo, a Ghanaian newspaper columnist in Accra and women's rights advocate. After setting a hostile tone in the beginning of his piece through assorted one-sided vignettes and quotes, Zachary drops in a quote by Gadzekpo to fortify his ill intentions.

Here's the quote: 'The African role in the slave trade is not an issue in Ghana. People here are totally detached from any guilt or responsibility for their ancestors selling other Africans into slavery. It's like there's some collective amnesia.'

The thing is, Gadzekpo is making an objective analysis of the legacy of slavery and how Ghanaians have come to interpret or misinterpret it. Her quote, which was stated in the historical context of slavery itself, is innocuous, matter-of-fact. But when slyly inserted into a conversation about reconnecting to Africa, it is interpreted as injurious and uncaring.

In fact, it is possible that the Zachary did not even interview Gadzekpo -- who received some of her schooling in the US and returned to Ghana -- for this piece but simply cut and paste this quote to suit his aims. If so, that's lazy, unethical journalism to say the least.

'I question the credibility of any reporter who quotes people out of context,' says Richard Osei, a Ghanaian living in San Francisco. 'It is extremely disturbing to read the 'negative' spin one reporter can put on a country, or for that matter, the entire continent. As usual, the reporter specifically chose to write this 'riveting' article at the expense of fueling animosity among Africans and African Americans and despite the fact that Ghana continues to make a historic democratic turn.

Even the tone of the article potentially could fuel a downtown in Ghana tourism," says Osei, an entrepreneur with his business sights on Africa. The WSJ piece also reports that Ghanaians see African Americans not as brothers and sisters but only as 'dollar signs.' To highlight this view is one thing but to ignore the fact that all Americans, regardless of race, who visit marginalized nations are seen as 'dollar signs' is to reveal an insidious agenda. Think about it. Who wins and who loses by this 'divide and rule' strategy?

Some 35 years after Kwame Nkrumah, Ghana's first president, published his landmark book,*Neo-Colonialism: The Last Stage of Imperialism*, his words still ring true: '...the financial preponderance of the United States is felt more and more through its influence over international capitalist journalism. Under this guise, a flood of the West, directed against China, Vietnam,

Indonesia, Algeria, Ghana and all countries which hack out their own independent path to freedom.'

The article also completely ignores issues of capitalism, imperialism and colonialism. But I'll flip it to you another way. This divisive line of thinking is tantamount to a camera zooming-in on two people bickering over a fender bender at a busy intersection. But if we pull the camera back for that all-telling longshot, we see the real deal: the damn traffic light is broke. Who else, but America, is directing the world's traffic?

They say the first basic rule of propaganda is to deliver deceptive information through a generally accepted, 'reliable' source. But this one-sided, divisive, racist, anti-black, anti-Africa article ties a more efficient lynch knot than the Klan could have ever dreamed of. It's so transparent it ain't even funny.

'Unfortunately we still don't have a lot of sophistication in how we respond to the media,' says Nehanda Imara, a college administrator. Imara, an African American, who lives in Oakland and is building a home in Ghana, says the mainstream media wields the same power as the police in black communities. 'The white media ain't gonna give us nothing but a headache.'

In the sixties, the FBI's Counter Intelligence Program (COINTELPRO) used misinformation and espionage to weaken black political resolve. Today, it seems most corporate newsrooms, largely still devoid of representative percentages of people of color and beholden to dollar deadlines, are creating more havoc in the black community than J. Edgar Hoover could've ever concocted himself.

The writer crafted the following lead for his article: 'Kwaku Sintim-Misa, a popular comedian here, likes to tell a joke about the African-American who emigrates to Ghana. 'Brother, I've found my roots!' the African-American crows. A local shakes his head, wondering why anyone with a coveted United States passport would choose to move to Ghana. 'Move to the Motherland?' the Ghanaian cries, 'I want to escape the Motherland.'

And of course nowhere in the piece is there any mention of the sobering hows and whys out of which such a joke could be created in the first place. But hey, I love a good, politically incorrect joke anytime but come with something stronger. Make me wince. Perhaps this is all the writer could cull from the brother's act to suit his needs.

'These African Americans who have made this move should be applauded and encouraged not ridiculed,' says Michel Bowman-Amuah, a Ghanaian in Denver. 'Just because some educated Ghanaian's seek a different lifestyle in the USA does not in anyway indicate that living in Ghana is intolerable or that Ghanaians are any less satisfied or patriotic about their country. Let us celebrate the diversity of ideas and encourage this movement of people to Ghana, because it is only through such efforts that we can truly exchange information and breakdown myths and cultural barriers that inhibit dialogue between Americans in general and Native Africans.'

Don't get it twisted. A romantic view of Africa (or America, for that matter) just won't cut it. We owe it ourselves to be as constructively critical toward Africa as we would with our family members. I truly believe the blood of the universe is on the side justice in Africa and joining in the struggle to understand our (all people of African descent) relationship to the continent is what time it is. Has been.

White Supremacy, capitalism, neo-colonialism and other assorted schisms aside, it really ain't that complex. Either you feel connected to and love black people everywhere or you don't -- straight up and down.

Surly Martin Luther King, Jr., who gave a speech of brotherhood at Kwame Nkrumah's inauguration in Ghana in 1957, and W.E.B. Du Bois, who spent the last years of his life in Ghana and is buried there, would charge us to think higher, broader about Africa.

By learning to approach the media with more sophistication -- whether when reading a cover story, being interviewed, or forwarding that hot, 'unbiased' and accurate email to others -- we can always choose to be the players instead of the ones gettin' played.

Cheo Taylor Tyehimba

Gateway to West Africa ?
Stacey Barney, Blackelectorare.com

Tuesday, March 26, 2002

Early in 2001 Ghana's government was poised to pass new legislation that would grant Ghanaian's living abroad dual citizenship that included the right to vote. This was a move designed to woo the skill, talent, education, and money of many of Ghana's expatriates back to the country in efforts to help aid the waning economy.

Now, with the help of bi-partisan support, Ghana's Parliament moved a step closer to passing the new Citizenship Bill with an additional provision that would allow Africans within the Diaspora 'the right to abode' - the very same right to abode promised to African Americans by former Ghanaian President Jerry Rawlings in 1999 during a visit to the United States.

For Ghana the right to abode clearly represents a hoped for boost to the economy with American dollars, but for African Americans, and other members of the African Diaspora, this 'right to abode' would undoubtedly mean the ability to live and work in Ghana without having to renew costly and inconvenient visas and work permits; although the right to participate in politics and the right to vote seem to be altogether another matter.

But certainly for the thousand or so African Americans already living in Ghana this 'right to abode' or 'right to return,' as Ghana's Minority House Leader, Mr. J.H. Mensah, calls it, is a welcome step in the direction of full-fledged citizenship, and a de facto dual citizenship status for those who may not be verifiably Ghanaian, but are certainly visibly of African descent.

If passed, Ghana would be the first and only African nation to provide the right to return to Africans in the Diaspora. Furthermore, if passed this could also be a significant first step in fulfilling W.E.B. Dubois's dream of true Pan-Africanism, with Ghana, the very country in which Dubois spent the last years of his life, leading the way.

It could mean this if Ghanaians and African Americans could find a way to accept one another as brother and sister related first and foremost by the shared color of skin, and it could mean this if, and only if, African Americans are truly ready to reconnect with their point of origin.

In addition to approximately 1,000 African Americans

280

currently living and working in Ghana's capitol city of Accra, the number of African American visitors to Ghana is close to 10,000 each year. Furthermore, in comparison to other African nations, Ghana attracts far more African Americans than any other nation on the continent. This is due primarily to mild weather, beaches, a low cost of living, and the sense that Ghana could be a spiritual homeland for many African Americans.

However, Ghana also has at least one very big detracting attribute - an apparent intolerance for African Americans. While it is true that many African Americans have had much success in making a home of Ghana via fulfilling employment or entrepreneurship opportunities, and especially marriage to Ghanaian citizens (as is the case in the U.S. for many Africans living and working here), and many more describe their visits to Ghana as a reconnection to the mother land, there are others who have been deterred by a Ghanaian regard for African Americans as obruni, the Twi word for White or foreigner, as well as societal treatment that includes such norms as the denial of government jobs, the right to vote, and higher costs for hospital visits.

These conditions make some African Americans, who go to Ghana seeking the spiritual home that cannot be attained in the United States, feel as little more than an American dollar sign.This is a depiction of Ghanaian attitudes towards African Americans that the Ghanaian government and the African American Association of Ghana (AAAG) vehemently reject.

*Wall Street Journal* reporter G. Pascal Zachary experienced this first-hand in regards to his 2001 article titled, 'Tangled Roots, for African-Americans in Ghana, the Grass Isn't Always Greener.' In this article Zachary spoke of the mistreatment African Americans living in Ghana receive at the hands of Ghanaian citizens.

The AAAG condemned the article as derogatory, and accused Zachary of threatening, not only a 42-year relationship between Ghana and African Americans, but also tourist revenue (hmm.), and at the worst possible time - a time when many African American tourists were preparing to attend the Pan-African Festival.

'Americans are terrified by anything that takes their comfort away,' said Mr. Akbar Muhammed, spokesperson for the AAAG.

281

Muhammed, according to the Ghanaian News Agency (GNA), also asserted, 'the...reason for the article was to discourage...40 million African Americans...[from shifting] a large chunk of their over 500 billion dollar annual investments in the U.S. to Africa.'

But, despite the AAAG's denial of the claims Zachary made in his 2001 article or the supposed motivations behind Zachary writing his account of African American experiences in Ghana, it isn't hard to imagine African-Americans feeling unwelcome in an African nation.

Think of the perceptions that many African Americans have of Africans. Think of the ignorance many African Americans still have of the African continent. Think of Eddie Murphy's joke that African's 'ride around butt-naked on a zebra.' Think of Will Smith's recent statement that he didn't know Africa had beautiful women until he'd gone there. Think of the treatment many Africans receive from African Americans right here in the United States.

Tracie Reddick reported for The Tampa Tribune on the treatment Anthony Eromosele Oigbokie, a Nigerian business owner in Tampa, Florida received at the historically Black college, Tuskegee University in her article 'African vs. African-American: A Shared Complexion Does Not Guarantee Racial Solidarity':

'Just because African Americans wear Kente cloth does not mean they embrace everything that is African. I caught hell from the frat boys. They were always trying to play with my intelligence. This was [at] a time when folks were shouting, 'Say it loud, I'm Black and I'm proud.'...If they saw me with a girl, they would yell to her, 'What are you doing with that African?'

Thirty years later, Africans and African Americans still do not form easy bonds or relationships. African American women who marry African men often find they have difficulty contending with strict patriarchal expectations of womanhood, while Africans find themselves in awe of African Americans who have the tendency to blame the White man for everything, and at the same time do not take advantage of the opportunities the United States has to offer.

Kofi Glover, a native of Ghana and a political science professor at the University of South Florida told Reddick, 'Whether we like it or not, Africans and African Americans have two very different and very distinct cultures.'

Glover goes on to describe slavery as a divisive bond between Ghanaians and African Americans that could perhaps prohibit African Americans from ever establishing a permanent homestead in Ghana - right to abode or no right to abode. '[Ghanaians] did not experience White domination like the Africans in Kenya, Zimbabwe, or South Africa. We do not understand the whole concept of slavery, or its effect on the attitude of a lot of African Americans, mainly because we were not exposed to it.'

For many African Americans who are still living with the brutal consequences of slavery, this is a hard truth to face - that one who is also Black does not identify with the pain of slavery. Think of the relationship African Americans have with the term Uncle Tom.

The treatment that Zachary speaks of in his article may be uncomfortable - as uncomfortable as any discussion on the psychological bones hanging in one's closets; nevertheless it has brought to the foreground the question of how Africans and African Americans perceive one another - a question the prospect of dual citizenship exacerbates.

In the best circumstances, Africans and African Americans see one another as family, an extension of the other. However, the experiences of Oigbokie and African Americans who have lived in Ghana only to return to the U.S. disillusioned suggest that this is not always the case, nor does everyone agree it should be.

Glover says the perceptions that Africans and African Americans hold of one another stem from 'all the negative things we've been taught about each other. A lot of African Americans were taught that Africa was nothing more than just a primitive, backward jungle from whence they came, [while Ghanaian] perceptions of African Americans is that they are a race of people who carry guns and are very violent.'

What if anything can help Africans and African Americans traverse this rift, making Ghana's right to return more than a token reconciliation? Perhaps remembering that we are, in fact, first and foremost bound by skin color. The differences between Africans and African Americans as observed by Omali Yeshitela, former president of St. Petersburg's National People's Democratic Uhuru Movement, are false. She says, 'Most of the friction between African people centers around the class issue. I don't like the artificial separations that won't allow the two of us to get together. It is not in our best interest to always be at each other's throat.'

But what is in our best interest? Unlearning damaging ideas about ourselves, and those who look like us? Yes. Embracing the differences in faith of a larger similarity? Yes. Ghanaian citizenship? Are we even ready for the right to return? Kente cloth and Kwanza is one thing, but moving to another continent is quite another.

Ghanaian citizenship for Americanized Africans is a frightening prospect. To embrace Ghanaian citizenship requires African Americans to embrace the paradox of both what is foreign and what is not. Africans are supposed to be those backwards, Black jungle bunnies-everything that White society has told us that we are, and everything that we have told White society we are not. How do we put aside this fear and ignorance in order to know ourselves?

How do Ghanaians put aside all that they know of us - guns, drugs, violence, and money to burn - to embrace brethren that could well be family?

It seems clear that in order for Ghana's Citizenship Bill to have the effects W.E.B. DuBois might have liked to see, false sensibilities need to be disarmed. Furthermore, along with the realization of citizenship - a right to return, there must be a realization that the problems of Black peoples are the problems of all Black peoples. A realization wherein we refuse to see them as those foreign Africans and they refuse to see us as those foreign Americans.

Until then, dual citizenship represents just two words put together to make it easier on visitors to Ghana who have traditionally had to spend too much time filling out paperwork for visas and work permits. Words that for Ghana lend a needed boost to the economy of a country whose people welcome the obruni dollars if not the obruni themselves.

That's a sad reason to return home.

Stacey Barney

Africa and the World
A. Akbar Muhammad
Web posted, April 17, 2001

We need each other- Pt. 1

While traveling and writing about Africa and what is happening on this great continent, I have encountered many opinions. I try to deal with people on their various levels and I also try never to be a reactionary.

However, I could not help but to react to an article, which appeared on the front page of *The Wall Street Journal* Wednesday, March 14, titled, "Tangled Roots: For Black Americans in Ghana, the Grass Isn't Always Greener." Since I have lived in Ghana for 10 years as well as traveled to many parts of Africa, I must respond to such a derogatory article written by Pascal Zachary.

*The Wall Street Journal* is one of the most conservative newspapers in America, from what I know of it. Its focus is on business issues. However, the only business that was highlighted in this article was the establishment of a vegetarian restaurant in the Cape Coast and Elmina area, and the adventures of the owner.

The writer mentioned that the Black American community is drawn to Ghana 'by beautiful beaches, tropical climate, low living costs and most of all a sense that this historical heart of the slave trade is an ancestral homeland.' I thought it odd for a paper like *The Wall Street Journal* not to have mentioned the Ghanaian stock market, its gold or even it's tourism. Perhaps, I thought, it would at least mention that many are interested in the opportunities to conduct business in Africa.

Many Black Americans have made a conscious decision to move to Africa to escape the blatant, harsh racism that exists in America. Another incentive is the lack of opportunities in America to use their God-given talents and skills, which were learned while living in America. These same skills and talents are very useful on the African continent. I know that *The Wall Street Journal* is not a major voice for the plight of the Black

285

community. However, it is interesting that this point was missed altogether.

The writer talked about malaria, knowing that many of the readers of the article have not studied tropical diseases. Some people only know it as a name, some kind of sickness that you get in the tropics. He mentioned how electric and water supplies are often interrupted. His point, I ascertained, was to list all the reasons that one should not have the desire to travel to Africa, Ghana in particular.

The writer mentions that the Black Americans are lumped together with white Americans and are called *obruni* or white by the Ghanaians. He also mentions that many Ghanaians see the African Americans as arrogant, which is absolutely correct. However, what I would like to add is that many of the Black Americans who are trained, taught and shaped in white America have taken on the arrogant attitude of the Americans that is seen all over the world. Since we have been under the tutelage of white America for over 400 years, we have taken on the same arrogance. This is why we need Africa as much as Africa needs us.

We have the opportunity to learn some valuable cultural lessons. Our first lesson we should learn as Black Americans or Africans from the Diaspora is a lesson in humility and cultural nuances.

We must learn something about the continent from which we were snatched. We must critically examine the effects and the horrors of slavery. We need to throw off the shackles of the arrogance taught to us by a very arrogant slave master.

Those of us who may have read this article may have understood the real message was designed to discourage the movement of Black capital investment in Ghana that would create the kind of financial marriage that is direly needed on the African continent."

Although Akbar Muhammed, a spokesman for the Nation of Islam led by Louis Farrakhan, contends that G. Pascal Zachary did not tell the truth in his article in *The Wall Street Journal* when he said African Americans feel unwelcome in Ghana, even quoting some of the people who expressed this sentiment, there is no doubt that there are many black Americans who will find it hard to believe that they are welcome in Ghana or anywhere else in Africa when people like Kofi Glover, a Ghanaian professor, and other Africans say they don't feel the same way about slavery like Americans blacks do. And the impression is unmistakable when they read or hear what Glover said: Africans don't understand slavery like black Americans do because they were not exposed to it.

It may be insensitive, and it may even sound cruel, especially to African Americans. And it is, to many people, one way or the other, or both. But it must also be looked at in its proper context. The context is historical and contemporary. Ignore one, you lose perspective.

Therefore, what Glover says must be viewed not only in its proper context but also from the contemporary perspective of Ghanaians - and other Africans - to understand *why* they articulate such sentiments regarding slavery.

As an African myself, born and brought up in Africa, in Tanganyika later Tanzania, I can say this to African Americans who intend to go to Africa or those who have not been there long enough to know what's going on: Expect the unexpected, and be ready for anything. Also, expect to be welcomed, and even to be embraced, by some Africans; and be prepared to meet those who are indifferent.

I use the term "indifferent," instead of "hostile," deliberately. I am not saying there aren't any Africans who are hostile towards Africans, for different reasons, including jealousy, with many of them wishing they were born in America or they could go to America to live.

There are such people, including those who see black Americans as no more than dollar signs or bags of dollars as some of these returnees from the diaspora have complained in Ghana, Nigeria, Ivory Coast and other countries.

We must admit that there are such people who are hostile towards African Americans, although the ones who see them as bags of dollars are not necessarily hostile; they are some of the most friendly human beings you will ever meet, for obvious reasons.

But hostile ones are a very small minority, from my experience and the experiences of others. The higher percentage of those who are not friendly are basically indifferent, rather than hostile, towards African Americans - and other foreigners - and simply ignore them. This includes those who reject African Americans as their brethren.

They even talk to them in a friendly way, sometimes very friendly. But they tell African Americans, "You are not Africans. You are Americans." Others say, "You are no longer African. It has been centuries since your ancestors were taken from Africa." And there are even those who call African Americans, "white Africans," for example, in Ghana where some people call them *obruni*, meaning white in the Twi language, something I *never* heard in Tanzania, calling them *wazungu*, which means whites in Kiswahili; *mzungu* is the singular form, meaning white or European.

But it does *not* mean they hate African Americans when they describe them that way, or when they simply say, "you are just Americans." It only means that there are fundamental differences between Africans and African Americans in terms of perception. And whether we like it or not, perception is reality.

I am reminded of a similar incident when I was a student in my home country, Tanzania. That was in 1969 when I was 19 years old in standard 13 (what Americans would call grade 13) at Tambaza High School in Dar es Salaam, the nation's capital. It was formerly H.H. The Aga Khan High School exclusively for students of Asian origin, mostly Indian and Pakistani. It was integrated after independence but the students were still mostly of Indian and Pakistani origin; they were Tanzanians, of course.

One day, some black Indians came to visit our school. The visit was arranged by our headmaster, Mr Lila (pronounced as Leela). In fact, it was he who brought them and introduced them to us. They came to our classroom and Mr. Lila said those were Africans whose ancestors were taken to India centuries ago as slaves and came from what is Tanzania today; other African slaves were, of course, also taken from East Africa, mainly Tanzania and Mozambique, to the United States, Brazil and other parts of the Americas, not just from West Africa as some people may be inclined to believe because of geographical proximity. But it is true that the majority of the African slaves taken to the

United States came from West Africa.

Anyway, when we saw these black Indians, or Africans from India, we were excited, bewildered, and even shocked. We had never seen black Indians (with so-called kinky hair) or African Indians before, although we had studied in history that Africans from our region were taken as slaves to India, Indonesia, China, and other parts of Asia, and not just to Arab countries and the Americas, centuries ago. In fact, the East African slave trade preceded the West African trans-Atlantic slave trade by centuries.

Arabs carried on the slave trade for about 1,000 years and have been in East Africa for about 1,300 years, just as long as they have been in North Africa which they conquered in the 600s A.D. In fact, there were small Arab and Persian (Iranian) settlements in what is Tanzania today even before the Christian era (B.C.), and some Asian influence from China, India, Indonesia and other parts of Asia around the same time. But Greeks, the ancient marines, were the first to come to the region even before the Asians and the Arabs did.

Therefore, the context had been set for centuries before the full-scale invasion and conquest of East Africa by foreigners which came later, first by the Arabs, then the Portuguese, the Germans, and the British, with significant Asian influence including trade mainly with the coastal regions. The black Indians who came to our school were a product of that, as descendants of African slaves taken to Asia.

And they looked very Indian, in terms of attire, and sounded very Indian. They did not speak Kiswahil like we did but one of the Indian languages. Most of the students in my class saw them as just Indians, although black Indians. They did not say these black Indians had nothing to do with Africa; they just felt that they were Indian in terms of history and culture after all those centuries.

We were also sympathetic towards them, knowing the history of slavery, and the fact that they were descendants of African slaves, our people. Therefore, we identified with them, in a way, although we also knew that there were some fundamental differences between us in terms of culture and outlook because of centuries of separation. Yet that did *not* mean that they had no biological ties to Africa. We knew they were an integral part of us, biologically, and there was no hostility towards them.

When we look at their situation and that of African Americans, or black Americans, the parallels are almost exact. When I was in Tanzania, as a student and as a news reporter, I never met or talked to *one* person, a black Tanzanian or any other black African including refugees from southern Africa, who was hostile towards African Americans. I never even heard of that from anyone, saying so-and-so said this and that about African Americans in a hostile way or derogatory manner.

We saw them in the streets of Dar es Salaam, our nation's capital, and quite a few people admired them. But I also noticed that there was a communication gap. Neither side tried to reach out, and touch someone, or talk to someone, on the other side. That was the general perception, or observation, although I am sure there are those who did and even formed solid friendships, especially between African Americans living in Tanzania and local Tanzanians. In fact, I know of one such relationship.

One of my friends in Dar es Salaam who also comes from my home district of Rungwe in the Southern Highlands of Tanzania, and whom I went to school with, had an uncle, his father's younger brother, who was a high-ranking government official. He held some of the highest posts, including an ambassadorial post, under President Nyerere since independence. His uncle was a very close friend of Charlie Cobb, the African American and former civil rights activist in the United States during the civil rights movement, when Cobb lived and worked in Dar es Salaam. And this was not the only close relationship between Africans and African Americans in Tanzania.

There were hundreds of African Americans living in Tanzania, mostly in the capital Dar es Salaam, during that time. And they were there for a number of years. They would not have stayed there had the local people been hostile towards them. One of them was a member of the Pan-African Congress-USA from Detroit who worked as an engineer in Dar es Salaam for two years before returning to the United States. I talked to him when he returned to Detroit in the mid-seventies and he never said he experienced any hostility from Tanzanians.

Another Pan-African Congress member who moved to Tanzania and was given some land also never complained about any hostility when he wrote me from Tanzania. He loved Tanzania and the people. I was still in Detroit then. That was also in the mid-seventies, although I don't know if he stayed in Tanzania or not. It has been more than 30 years since we last communicated.

When I first got to Detroit and was new in the country, I was asked by some African Americans in school and elsewhere in the city if it was true that we did not want them in Africa. I said, "No," it was not true; at least from what I knew. When I was in Tanzania, I *never* heard Tanzanians or anybody else from other parts of Africa living in Tanzania who said, "We don't want them here"; a common saying I have heard through the years in conversations with African Americans in the United States, saying we, Africans, "don't want them over there." When I first heard this, it bothered me because I knew it wasn't true. I never even heard that from my fellow African students from different countries whom I knew or went to school with in the United States.

But there *was* an indifferent attitude towards African Americans among some of these African students, mainly because of cultural differences and the way the media portray black Americans as low-class, committing a lot of crime, and lacking values conducive to achievement.

Therefore, in the absence of any evidence of hostility towards African Americans among the majority of Africans in Africa, and even among the majority of Africans in the United States, there is no reason for anyone to say or believe that people of African descent in the diaspora are not welcome in Africa. And individual stories tell a lot because, cumulatively and coming from different parts of the continent through the years, they show what kind of reception African Americans have been accorded upon their arrival or during their stay in Africa. This is one of them, from the *Penn African Studies Newsletter*, January/February 1997, of the University of Pennsylvania:

"Veniese Wilkinson, a Penn senior African Studies major, and Carla Land, a Penn senior Entrepreneurial Management major, spent the 1996 Spring semester in Ghana on a study abroad program.

Veniese Wilkinson and Carla Land so enjoyed their semester abroad in Ghana that they both say they definitely want to go back. They commented on how gracious and helpful the Ghanaians were. Wilkinson noted, 'When they see a stranger they think, 'this person needs help." Land told a story about a time she was lost and asked for directions. When she got lost again, she turned around to find that the woman who had given her directions had followed in her car. She then picked Land up and drove her to where she was going.

Land pointed out that there aren't many stories about crime on the news. Many of the TV shows are produced in Ghana and contain little violence; every story has a good ending with a moral. In addition, CNN is broadcast on national TV; so Ghanaians are often more educated about world news than Americans.

During their semester, Wilkinson and Land spent several weeks living with families in Cape Coast where they studied Fanti and heard lectures. They also lived for a week in a village, spent several weeks traveling, and lived in Accra for four weeks with an older Ghanaian woman while they did their independent study projects.

Land worked with a small women's magazine that had been in existence for about a year. She wrote articles for the paper and conducted a survey at the University of Ghana to learn what the women students' cultural attitudes were. She was intrigued because the magazine seemed to reflect American culture rather than Ghanaian culture, with articles about weight-loss and self-esteem. Land thinks this reflected the interests of university women, but not the interests of Ghanaian women in general.

Wilkinson studied development organizations in Ghana, focusing on women's organizations. There are a lot of organizations trying to better women's lives, but in some ways they are stifled by the government. Without friends in the government organizations, it's difficult to accomplish anything. Wilkinson noted that every other day there seemed to be a meeting so that the women would say, 'Here we go again to another 'talkshop." Wilkinson also noticed that everyone referred to the Beijing conference, often saying, 'Well you know, since Beijing....'

As African-Americans in Ghana, both said that many times people thought they were Ghanaian. That meant that they didn't get tourist treatment, but it also meant that people would assume they knew things that they didn't. Wilkinson said that some days she told people that she was an American, because she wanted them to know who she was and that what they said wasn't necessarily going to make sense to her. They found that many Ghanaians didn't know the history of slavery. Some thought that many Africans had gone to America and died. Land noted that sometimes people thought her mother was a Ghanaian who had immigrated to the U.S.

A particularly interesting event during their semester was their attendance at a girl's puberty rite. One of the women in their group wanted to develop a puberty rite for African-American women, and to prepare she underwent a Ghanaian rite herself. Before the event, their friend was bathed, and then dressed in expensive powder, perfume, and clothes. She changed her outfit three times during the event, which displayed the wealth of her 'family.' Her 'mother' also talked with her before the ceremony.

During the ceremony there were times for socializing, feasting, and parading around the village. Symbols of fertility such as eggs and chicken organs were important. Her body was painted with open circles representing sugar cane for a sweet life. This ceremony lasted for a day, but it can last as long as a week if there is food to feed the guests.

Visiting a number of historical sites was also a highlight. One place was Cape Coast Castle, where slaves were held before being shipped to the Americas. Funds for restoring the castle came from the U.S., and Wilkinson felt it had been restored into a U.S. park for American tourists, which took away a certain reality.

Wilkinson particularly enjoyed their trip to Kumasi, which was the capital of the Asante Kingdom. A museum with wax figures depicted the history of the Asante. Her favorite wax figure was the one of the Asante Queen Mother, a short woman holding an enormous rifle. When the British were coming to invade Kumasi, the men were cowering, but she insisted on fighting. The British eventually exiled her to the Seychelles Islands which showed their fear of her power."

Yet, in spite of such exhilarating experience and exciting stories, we must also acknowledge that there are Africans who have an indifferent attitude towards black Americans, and vice versa. I remember what a couple in Detroit told us in the mid-seventies when they got back from Tanzania after spending some time there. They said the people in Tanzania did not speak to them, they just looked at them or just stared at them, as if they were nothing to them or some strange-looking people. They did not identify with them.

That is sad, especially if you are a foreigner, but it's nothing new. People in Tanzania and elsewhere in general don't always speak to each other, either, especially if they are strangers. And in the case of African Americans, the problem gets worse if the local people in African countries are able to identify them as black Americans; which they usually do and are pretty good at it, just by looking at them.

Some of them don't see black Americans as an integral part of them. This is indifference. And one may argue that indifference is tantamount to rejection, especially for African Americans who expect to be welcomed and embraced by their African brethren when they return to the motherland. They feel that they have been rejected, not just ignored.

But that is *not* the attitude of even those who are indifferent towards African Americans. They have not rejected them. One may say, by not welcoming them, they still have rejected African Americans, and that's why they are indifferent towards them. And it may be true. But the main reason *why* they are indifferent is that they don't care, or it doesn't bother them, if black Americans visit or live in Africa, or not. They really don't care either way, and they just go on with their lives, as much as African Americans do when they are in Africa, and when Africans - students and immigrants - are in America. They just go on with their business.

This can, of course, be discouraging to African Americans more than it is to Europeans or Asians, for example, who are not related to Africans. Black Americans expect to be welcomed and embraced by their African brothers and sisters. They are their kith-and-kin, whether one accepts this or not. Nothing can dissolve genealogical ties.

But the question is this: How *many* African Americans

experience this or feel this way? And why do African Americans keep on going on to Africa, every year, in fact every month, if they are indeed rejected by their African brethren? Even those who have been there before go back. Why? It's not because they forgot their luggage or something else and they are going back to pick it up. They go back for another visit, and another, and another. It goes on, and on. Why?

The answer is obvious, as has been clearly demonstrated in many ways, and by permanent settlements such as Fihankra, an African-American community in eastern Ghana, and by the presence of a significant number of Africans from the diaspora in this West African country and other parts of Africa. They have gone "back home." As President Robert Mugabe said in 2000 to a large black audience, estimated to be about 10,000 in Harlem, New York, where he was introduced by the black Nation of Islam leader Louis Farrakhan: "Come back home!" And in the words of Nelson Mandela in the early 1990s soon after he got out of prison and spoke to another large audience, also in Harlem: "We are all children of Africa."

It is a sentiment that was articulated years earlier by the first president of Ghana who blazed the trail for the African independence movement, Dr. Kwame Nkrumah, when he said: "All peoples of African descent whether they live in North or South America, the Caribbean or in other part of the world are Africans and belong to the African nation."

African Americans are finally going "back home." There is no place like home.

Yet, even at home, there are problems that must be addressed. Simply because it is home does not mean that it is paradise. And although African Americans know that Africa is not paradise on earth - there's none down here, not even America which many people consider to be mankind's heavenly home - many of them still have unrealistic expectations and get disappointed when they get to the motherland.

They should *not* expect everybody to welcome them or embrace them simply because they have returned to the motherland. They should also remember that Africa is *not* America in terms of living standards.

But they should also be treated on equal basis with the local people. They should not be charged more, for anything, than Africans are, simply because they are Americans and therefore "rich."

In Ghana, for example, where African Americans complain about being overcharged for goods and services, indigenous Ghanaians should answer a few questions to set the record straight:

Do you ask Ghanaians who have lived in the United States, when they return to Ghana, to pay more for medical treatment and for taxi service and for other goods and services than other Ghanaians simply because these returnees lived or live in America and are therefore assumed to be rich? What about wealthy Ghanaians who live in Ghana? Why don't you also charge them higher for goods and services than other Ghanaians, as much as you do African Americans?

What about Africans from other countries who live in Ghana and who have more money than some Ghanaians? Do you overcharge them also, the same way you do to black Americans? Why just black Americans? If you do so because they are rich, you should do the same thing to rich Ghanaians and other rich Africans visiting or living in Ghana.

It is also a fact that not every black American, in America or in Africa, is rich. And when African Americans face this kind of discrimination, don't blame them when they say they are not welcome in Ghana, or in Africa. Not all of them say that. But there are those who do when they face this kind of discrimination by their African brethren, of all people.

Yet, it's not very surprising. We have discrimination in Africa of the most blatant kind, tribal discrimination, members of one tribe discriminating against members of another tribe or other tribes. And there are Africans who see African Americans as just another tribe, or simply as outsiders, and not as a part of them; therefore a target for discrimination.

Faced with these kinds of problems, some African Americans are bound to be frustrated and feel unwelcome in Africa.

Compounding the problem is the underdeveloped nature of African countries. Many black Americans are aware of these problems, of course, even before they go to Africa and do their best to cope with the situation. However, there are those who can't cope with this and return to the United States.

I am sure it also happened in my country, Tanzania, where there were about 800 African Americans in the early and mid-seventies, in spite of the economic hardship under socialism. But there's no question that some of them left because of economic hardship even before the Big Bust of 1974 which led to an exodus of black Americans from this East African country, as we learned earlier, a country led by Mwalimu Julius Nyerere whom they admired so much.

When I was writing this book, I asked one African American who had been to Tanzania what he thought or knew about the presence of black Americans in this East African country, my homeland, and if he knew of any of the problems they had with their African brethren and if it was easy to talk to them about the subject.

I also asked him a few other questions on a number of subjects including the role of African Americans at the Sixth Pan-African Congress held in Dar es Salaam, Tanzania, in 1974 (coincidentally, the same year of the Big Bust that led to the exodus of African Americans from Tanzania) when I was already in the United States, and about the rumor or report that Dr. Walter Rodney, an African diasporan from Guyana who taught at the University of Dar es Salaam during that time where he also wrote his best-selling book, *How Europe Underdeveloped Africa*, was barred from the conference. I told him I was highly skeptical about that, knowing Rodney and the close ties he had with Tanzanian officials and the leaders of the African liberation movements based in Dar es Salaam.

His name was Seth McGovern Markle, a graduate student at New York University who was working on his PhD. His dissertation was on the same subject, of African Americans in Tanzania, and this is what he said to me in response to my questions in his letter of December 14, 2004:

"I've been dong research on this topic for about 2 years now and I have similar questions as you do that I've yet to find answers for. I've been to Tanzania the past two summers.

Currently, there are quite a few African Americans living there, but only a handful from the days of *ujamaa*. The Big Bust was one of those reasons. I believe after the "bust" a lot of African Americans got disillusioned and returned to the U.S. But there were other reasons as well. Some just wanted to stay only for a couple of years. Some felt culturally alienated and home sick. The reasons are many.

In regards to the Big Bust, the story is sketchy. I, too, have read that article in *The East African* and that's all the information I have of the event, so I don't have much to offer there.

What I do know, however, is that there were conservative wing in TANU who did not warm up to the African American presence. They thought they were brash, arrogant, aggressive, etc. So it was this contingent which really tried to get African Americans out. Similar to what happened in Nkrumah's Ghana, African Americans were charged with being members of the CIA.

African Americans were never 'barred' from 6PAC, they were just seated on 'observer status' which caused an uproar. And Walter Rodney was not barred, he just did not attend, although he did write a quite provocative paper on Pan-Africanism which was circulated around the conference.

In terms of perceptions. It was a mixed bag. Some were well-received, others were not. Some built very close relationships/friendships with Tanzanians, South Africans, Cubans, etc. As you know, it really all depends on who you talk to or read about and my research has not gone that far as of yet.

If you are interested in talking to African Americans in Tanzania it's actually much more easier if you go there and ask around. Although, I must say they are very difficult to talk to, very protective, at times distrustful of people who are interested in their experience.

So its no exaggeration when I say that its a tough road to travel. I haven't developed a relationship with them to the extent that I would like, but I'm still working on it.

I can tell you this though, contacting them by email is pretty useless. The O'Neals live in Arusha and you can go by their community center and try to talk to them. A lot of African Americans are there now, hang out at the U.S. Club and an Ethiopian Restaurant called Addis in Dar.

I think relations between African Americans and Tanzanians are interesting. Constantly shifting and evolving. It's a process of communicating and understanding differences.

As you may know, African Americans tend to imagine Africa in a way that oftentimes is romantic, oftentimes not the "real" Africa. Also, African Americans tend to be too focused on race/racism. I found that Tanzanian's tend to look at African Americans as either Americans, or as an ethnic group. The latter is quite interesting and I think needs to be explored more fully.

The major issue for African Americans is defining their role in Africa's struggle. Should it entail bringing their skills over? Should it entail lobbying the US Government on African issues? There is no single right answer. I do believe the dialogue needs to continue.

Julius Nyerere had a profound impact on African Americans in the 60s/70s. African Americans learned how to speak Kiswahili, trying to developed their own tweaked *ujamaa* programs in the US, the list goes on and on. And some moved there to participate in the national building projects to the best they knew how."

In Ghana, there was a similar "bust" involving African Americans who were, rightly or wrongly, accused of working for the CIA and trying to undermine Dr. Nkrumah's government, leading to their expulsion from that country, as Markle said in his letter to me. And to make things worse, it was a black American, the United States ambassador to Ghana, Franklin Williams, a schoolmate of Kwame Nkrumah at Lincoln University in the 1930s, who played a major role, together with the CIA, in overthrowing Nkrumah in Ghana in February 1966.

It would, of course, be utterly naive to assume or believe that there are no American government agents or spies among African Americans who go to Africa, or that they are *all* spies simply because they are American. There are those who are, but most of them are not. In fact, you find some African Americans who care about Africa more than some Africans born and brought up on African soil do. There are Africans who work for the CIA and other foreign intelligence agencies and governments against their own countries.

Mobutu was not the only one. There were African Americans including Malcolm X who cared about the Congo and Africa as a whole more than Mobutu did, if he ever did at all. Even before the country won independence, he was already on the CIA payroll. And he played a critical role in the arrest and subsequent assassination of Patrice Lumumba. He was once his private secretary before he became head of the army, appointed by Lumumba.

Therefore to assume that every African cares about Africa, simply because he or she is an African, is equally naive and plain stupid. And probably most Africans know that.

Yet African Americans have sometimes been falsely accused of being spies, a blanket charge and condemnation that has led to their expulsion from some African countries including Ghana and Tanzania, ironically from the very same countries that have the strongest appeal among many blacks in the United States and elsewhere in the African diaspora. It happened in the sixties and in the seventies in those two countries, and it may have happened after that in other African countries as well. But expulsion is not the only factor in the departure of African Americans from African countries. And it is rare.

In contemporary times, there are African Americans who have left Ghana, of their own volition, and returned to the United States for different reasons including economic hardship. Other African countries, including Tanzania, have experienced the same phenomenon. But this does *not* mean that the majority of black Americans have had bad experience in Africa. There are those who have and those who haven't. And it seems the majority have a favorable impression of Africa even if they have had hard times and continue to face hardship.

To understand the black American experience in Africa, and make a realistic assessment of the situation, it is important to construct a proportional perspective on reality. And that means *not* ignoring critics or dismissing everything they say as propaganda or a mischievous attempt to sow seeds of discord between Africans and African Americans, even if they tell the truth, or some truth. However unacceptable, accept it if it's true. Otherwise you are sweeping dirt under the rug.

It also means not believing everything people, friends and foes alike, say about Africa without verifying whatever is said or written. The article by Gregg Pascal Zachary in *The Wall Street*

300

*Journal* about Ghana is relevant in both cases. And it caused a firestorm for the same reasons. As Kwadwo Kyei stated in his column, "No One Said Ghana Was A Paradise," in *African Spectrum*, May 2001:

"In recent weeks Ghanaians have demonstrated an uncharacteristic patriotic zeal. Like wounded tigers, our people have leapt to the defense of our country in the wake of a gratuitous newspaper attack on her, leaving no doubt about our loyalty to the land of our birth. And we have G. Pascal Zachary to thank for waking up the patriot in us.

Zachary's recent article in the *The Wall Street Journal* entitled 'Tangled Roots' has touched off a firestorm of indignant responses from Ghanaians around the world including some fellow Spectrum writers. At the risk of overdoing it, it is now the turn of this column to share its modest point of view on an issue that threatens to sow a seed of discord between Ghanaians and African-Americans.

The article in question describes the frustrations of African-American immigrants in Ghana: from difficulties with immigration to problems getting accepted into the Ghanaian mainstream to discriminatory treatment when it comes to paying for goods and services. Incidentally, for another group of immigrants, African immigrants in America, almost all these problems seem to have a rather familiar ring to them.

Considering its origin - *The Wall Street Journal*, a newspaper that seldom, if ever, has kind words for Africa - there is the temptation to dismiss the article as just another obnoxious attempt by a conservative publication to discredit an African nation in the eyes of black America and the rest of the world. May be that was the intent. What else would please the enemies of the black race more than a state of alienation between Africans and black Americans? But whether it was or not, Zachary's article affords us an opportunity to set the record straight on the issue of African-Americans resettling in OUR common motherland.

The article reveals an important characteristic shared by nearly all immigrants: the tendency to indulge in unrealistic expectations about their new or adopted homelands. As is often the case, people migrate in search of a better life, whatever it is that

301

constitutes a better life for them. Many leave their native lands because economic opportunities elsewhere are better; others leave because either the social or cultural or political or religious climate in their native countries is not conducive to their personal wellbeing.

Whatever their motivations to leave, and since they start out with such great expectations, most immigrants are bound to get disillusioned by their initial encounter with the hard facts on the ground in their new homes. Then it begins to dawn on them that, after all, the grass is not greener on the other side.

The grass certainly is not greener in Ghana, and for that matter, anywhere else in Africa. Ghana, like nearly the rest of Africa, is in the throes of a desperate struggle for survival. Our economy is in a shambles; our political system has been in disarray for some time. Ghana is a nation trying to find its feet, a process that has been going on during the last forty years. The entire world is privy to this fact.

Therefore, it seems a little naive on the part of those who wish to make Ghana their home to expect in many respects, any more than they knew about the country before they decided to relocate there. Many of the sentiments the African-Americans poured out to Zachary are actually frustrations born of impatience as well as largely unjustified feelings of disappointment that their El Dorado turned out to be just another struggling Third World nation.

Nevertheless, a particular grievance of the African-Americans merits serious attention. It is indeed a shame that our brothers and sisters in the Diaspora who return to the land of their ancestors should become victims of extortion just because they are perceived as wealthy people from another land. This is patently unfair. Requiring a particular group of people to pay more for goods and sevices merely on the basis of where they came from smacks of the same kind of discriminatory practices against blacks and people of other races and cultures that American white racists have long been accused of. The American bigots practice racial discrimination; the Ghanaian extortionists practice cultural discrimination. Either behavior is inexcusable.

Contrary to the opinion held by others, I believe that charging so-called wealthy foreigners higher prices is not the same thing as assessing an individual a higher rate of income tax due to his clearly documented and verifiable more-than-average earnings. Some of the 'wealthy' African-Americans in Ghana may not be wealthy at all for all we know. Not every black American who hops on a plane to go to Africa is rich.

And even if they all were, making them pay more at the point of transaction is a practice that cannot be defended under any circumstances, especially when affluent Ghanaians are not subjected to the same treatment. Taxation is the only legitimate means by which society can compel the really well-heeled among us to give back some of their wealth for the good of all. If so-called wealthy African-Americans in Ghana are compelled to give back something by any other means, it is nothing but extortionary and discriminatory. And they have every right to be upset about it.

Beyond this blatant unfairness, however, the validity of the African-American indictments against Ghana as catalogued in the *Wall Street Journal* article is very much in dispute. Some returnees may feel "hoodwinked" by the promise of dual citizenship that didn't materialize, but the proposal is far from dead as the Journal article mischievously proclaimed. While it is unclear why the measure failed to win endorsement in Ghana's parliament, to say that it is dead is to betray a lack of appreciation of the depth of Ghana's commitment to Pan-African solidarity.

As the first black African nation to free itself from colonial bondage, Ghana under its first president, Dr. Kwame Nkrumah, very early recognized its special responsibility to bring black people all over the world together, both physically and psychologically. Toward this end, Ghana actively sought to encourage black American and black West Indian emigration back to the shores where their ancestors came from. Furthermore, Ghana organized and sponsored numerous international conferences of black people from all parts of the world.

A very significant outcome of this policy was the decision by two of the most illustrious personalities in the African Diaspora, W.E.B. DuBois and George Padmore, an American and a West Indian respectively, to relocate in Ghana. Over the years, other less famous black people from across the Atlantic have followed in their footsteps.

In time, dual citizenship in Ghana for black Americans will become a reality. It would be so historically out of character for

303

Ghana not to follow through on this. Meanwhile, the door is still open for African-Americans to acquire Ghanaian citizenship through the normal channels, except that they would have to trade in their much-coveted U.S. citizenship for the Ghanaian equivalent. The portion of Zachary's article describing the problems of African-Americans in this area should be taken with a grain of salt, for it is highly inconceivable that any administration in Ghana would deliberately create impediments in the way of eligible black Americans seeking to become citizens of Ghana.

Equally suspicious is the story of a man who was being prevented from leaving Ghana because he overstayed his visa. Didn't it usually work the other way round: people getting kicked out of a country for overstaying? No nation, not even an impoverished one like Ghana, has any desire to keep illegal immigrants within her borders.

Other complaints of the African-Americans are just as unsustainable. The gripe about not being allowed to vote or run for public office in Ghana even sounds silly. Since when did non-citizens become eligible to vote or run for public office in any country? Without a doubt, black Americans, in spite of the denials of a handful of lost souls - the despicable Uncle Toms - are kith and kin of the African people.

However, the laws of modern nation-states have no use for emotionalism. These laws look at things strictly from a technical angle, so that, notwithstanding one's ancestry, one has to have citizenship status in order to participate or share in all the goodies reserved for the citizens of a particular nation.

By and large, the African-American experience in Ghana doesn't seem to be such an unmitigated disaster, even judging by the account of the Journal article. Many of the immigrants are engaged in profitable businesses of their own; others are employed in fields such as teaching and other professions. Local chiefs have generously donated lands to some of the entrepreneurs for real estate development and other commercial uses.

How does any group of people become any more mainstream than this in another country? These facts speak for themselves and make nonsense of any attempt to paint Ghana with the brush of inhospitality and even hostility toward African-Americans.

The welcome mat is still in place for African-Americans and other black people as well as other foreigners who want to make Ghana their home. For newcomers, the most important thing to remember is that Ghana is no paradise on earth. If they love her, they should go in with a mindset that borders on the sacrificial; they should be prepared to help in the great national reconstruction effort now taking place.

Their rewards will manifest themselves in their own good deeds toward their new homeland."

Ghana, and the rest of Africa, may not be paradise; and will probably not attract the majority of African Americans, may be not even 100,000 of them, to go back to the motherland to live there permanently. But it definitely *is* home to those who have decided to leave America and return to Africa.

There may be thorns and thistles on the welcome mat at the door, now and then, here and there. But the door is wide open. What once was  the Door of No Return, out of which went captured Africans who were shipped to America into slavery, never to return, has now come to symbolize, for African Americans, a return to Mother Africa - from whose loins they sprang, to paraphrase Countee Cullen.

# Appendix I:

# What Africans and African Americans Think About Their Relations: Voices From Within

## Black Identity on Campus
## Harvard University

### Tanu Henry

Harvard University sophomores Chartey Quarcoo and Harrel Conner share the same taste in music, have the same friends and even live in the same residential suite. But the roommates remain miles apart when it comes to the notions they hold about black identity in America.

Quarcoo grew up in Brooklyn and has a Ghanaian father and Panamanian mother. And although he considers himself African American, he also self-identifies as African and Latino. "Both my parents are immigrants," he said. "I do not have the same culture as another black person from Memphis, for example."

Conner, on the other hand, is from Memphis. And while he and his roommate have a lot in common, he feels that as a black American, his outlook is different from that of his black classmates of non-American origin. Because black Americans are often ambivalent about their American citizenship and cannot trace their roots to a single country in Africa, Conner feels that African Americans contend with unique "feelings of homelessness."

"Unlike other black groups that have been displaced, we can only claim a continent," he said. "We cannot claim a specific country."

The clash between Quarcoo and Conner's perspectives on identity are emblematic of a growing trend at universities such as Harvard, where the percentage of black students hailing from immigrant communities in the U.S. is growing. As the university admits more and more black students who think of themselves as "African" or "West Indian" rather than as "African American" or even "black," some African American students are beginning to feel underrepresented in the university's diverse black community. And the changing makeup of the black student community at Harvard and other prestigious institutions has led to debates about the changing nature of "blackness" in America.

"I feel that the percentage of African Americans in the student body should reflect the percentage of African Americans in American society," said Woody McClellan, a senior from New Jersey. His opinion is shared by many of Harvard's African American undergraduate students, who say that it often seems as though black Americans are becoming a minority within a minority on campus.The Harvard University admissions office reports that approximately 10 percent of the student body is black, a slightly smaller percentage than in U.S. society at large, where blacks make up 12 percent of the population. But the university does not compile statistics on the ethnic subdivisions among black students, a fact that seems central to recent debates about black identity on campus, which set conceptions of an ethnic umbrella encompassing all "black" students against more narrowly defined black sub-communities.

According to Conner, only 25 percent of the black students at Harvard can trace their family roots to African American slaves. And that percentage includes biracial black Americans. "When you [exclude] the numbers of biracial students, the number drops to less than 10 percent," he added.

The distinctions between the various black subgroups at Harvard are manifested in the variety of separate campus organizations. As the Harvard African Students Association (HASA) tends to draw African students, the Black Students

Association (BSA) has traditionally been an African American organization. Similarly, the Caribbean Club gathers students of West Indian ancestry, the Black Men's Forum (BMF) targets African American men, and groups like the Haitian Alliance serve particular national communities. Although many students belong to more than one organization, most have little time for multiple extra-curricular commitments.

Because African Americans at Harvard are increasingly outnumbered by the children of African and West Indian immigrants, Conner, along with several other African American undergraduates, has been flirting with the idea of establishing a club exclusively for American blacks. Tentatively titled the "Harvard Society for the Descendants of American Slaves," the organization would reflect the particular perspective of blacks in the United States. If the group is organized, Conner feels the BSA - which now comprises a mixture of American blacks, West Indians, and Africans - can become an overarching alliance composed of students from all the black clubs at Harvard.

"The goal of an African American organization should be to promote black American culture but we should be careful so that it does not become divisive," said Kira Tiana Freelon, a sophomore member of the BSA from Chicago.In addition to segregating themselves in different organizations, black students from different parts of the world often tend to be divided by their different conceptions of race and identity. Some African American students say they feel offended that some African and Caribbean students do not primarily identify themselves as blacks. Many also feel that students from other parts of the African diaspora do not understand the racial history of the United States.

"They look at slavery as distant and removed, but in my opinion, the legacy of slavery still affects contemporary society," said Conner. Unlike some of his classmates, Conner is all too aware of the legacy of black inequality in America; his mother was a sharecropper who eventually became the first person in his family to go to college, while his grandfather spent most of his life sharecropping to pay off the financial debts owed by Conner's great grandfather, who was also a sharecropper. While Conner acknowledges that non-Americans might be unfamiliar with black America's history of struggle, he feels that African students at

308

Harvard are less willing than African Americans to make efforts to understand the other's culture.

Quarcoo, on the other hand, says that many African students are often disappointed by African American attitudes towards Africa. "Some Africans feel that African Americans don't really view Africa as it really is, they're trying to connect with a mythic motherland," he said. "When confronted with 'real Africans', some African Americans are less than welcoming." And because Africans tend to feel alienated from African Americans, they are sometimes accused of "not interacting enough in a meaningful way."

Quarcoo also feels that Africans should not be expected to share American conceptions of race. "At Harvard there are a lot of black students with roots outside the country where the notions of race are different." He said many of them come from predominantly black countries where people generally relate their identity to their tribes or nationalities. As co-president of HASA, which mainly comprises African students who were born in Africa or spent a portion of their lives on the continent, he has met many Africans who were not used to thinking in American racial terms when they arrived at Harvard.

"I am more Taita than I am Kenyan, and more Kenyan than I am black," said Mwashuma Nyatta, a sophomore from Kenya, referring to his tribal identity. He said until he came to the United States, "black" was not a way he normally identified himself. He is also reluctant to portray HASA as a "black" group because not all Harvard undergraduates from Africa are black. "Africans are not prepared for this notion of race as it exists here," said Quarcoo. "Economic and political struggles are more central in Africa, but here race is more central to the struggle." He feels that American society defines people too narrowly by race: in the United States, he said, "black" is an "all-encompassing" ethnic group.

Although different perspectives on race and identity are one of the main stumbling blocks confounding relations between Africans and African Americans on campus, Quarcoo is optimistic that black students from different parts of the world share enough to overcome their differences. He noted that many of the Africans in HASA came to the United States armed with

309

positive expectations of establishing close relationships with African Americans because of their own affinity for black American music, fashion, magazines, TV shows and movies, and said that many African arrivals do forge lasting friendships with American blacks.

Also, while most students agree that there are sometimes misunderstandings between the various groups, most would also agree that there should be some sense of unity between black students on campus.

Charles Peter Bright, a sophomore from Brooklyn who will be traveling to Senegal this summer, celebrates the diversity in Harvard's black community but feels that there should be more solidarity and cultural sharing. "One of the biggest things I find unacceptable is that there was not a lot of black outrage and protest on campus after the Amadou Diallo verdict," Bright said. He said he was especially surprised at the low turnout of students from Africa at rallies protesting the verdict.

HASA president-elect Ama Karikari, a New Yorker of Ghanaian origin, said all black students need to stress common goals that address the historical effects of racism and colonialism on all black people, and that understanding between the groups should be spearheaded by students who are informed about the cultural perspectives of all Africans in the diaspora. "Whether you're from the Caribbean and listen to reggae music every day, or if you're from Africa and eat fou fou every day, all black people have a lot in common," she said.

# Africans and African-Americans in Iowa City

Matthew Thomas
University of Iowa

Rebecca Lueth was the only member from the African Student Association to attend a rally protesting a racial insensitive cartoon published by the *Daily Iowan*. The cartoon commented on the acquittal of the young black men involved in the Reginald Denny beating in 1993, and tensions were high. Lueth hoped to address the hundred or so who gathered on the chilly October afternoon to add her support to the other angry voices of African Americans leading the protest.

Lueth endured the cold wind for hours with the others, but she was never given a chance to speak. A friend told her later that some of the African Americans at the rally felt she wasn't "black enough" to address the issue.

The incident reveals the tension which characterizes the relations between Africans and African Americans who come to Iowa City to study. The often-strained relations more than anything can be attributed to a pattern of cultural misunderstandings between the two groups.

Part of the problem is the assumption, often from both sides, that the two groups have more in common than they do. There are similarities, at least on the surface. Both groups share a common African heritage, both groups have parallel histories of oppression based on race, and both groups have to deal with many of the same negative stereotypes of African Americans prevalent in the U.S.

However, even their common experience living here in Iowa City is filtered through two very different cultures. Being African, and being American, have produced two perspectives of what it means to be a black woman or man in society which have little similarity.

Rebecca Lueth, 22, is from the East African country of Sudan which borders Egypt. She explained her perspective of the

311

incident at the rally: "No African is 'black enough' because the cultures are so different," said Lueth (pronounced lweth). Lueth has a unique cultural perspective because she moved to Ames from the Sudan when she was 16 years old. Growing up in small-town Iowa has given her a deeper understanding of America than most Africans, though Lueth identifies herself as African and not American.

Lueth said that being "black enough" is an American cultural term and has little to with race. She explained her outsider's view of what it means to her: "If you don't have a lot of black friends, or have too many white friends, or if you like Shakespeare or classical music, then you're not black enough," she said.

For Lueth, being "black enough" means how attuned an African American is to African American culture, or in other words, how much an individual accepts and embraces the larger African-American cultural identity.

She said that Africans don't grow up with the social pressures which make the issue of black identity a concern. Lueth said that these pressures trace back to the history of each group. The differences in their historical experiences of oppression to some extent produces a distinct perspective of today's society.

Akua Brathwaite is from the West African country of Ghana and a third-year law student and master's student in the African-American World Studies Program. She said that of the two historical experiences with oppression, colonization in Africa and slavery in the U.S., slavery was by far the most destructive of the two. "African Americans were uprooted and transported (from Africa) to America, where they were dehumanized in every single way. (White slave owners) tried systematically to make them shed their identity as Africans and as human beings," she said.

Brathwaite said she feels that the aftermath of slavery, and the only gradual acceptance of African Americans into a society of predominantly European descent, has left a greater residual anger among African Americans than colonization left among most Africans.

"As Africans, we can't get angry at the white man because the white man came and the white man left," Brathwaite said. She added that there is a sharp contrast between slavery and being ruled over by an unwanted government yet still retaining your citizenship, your family, your village, and your cultural identity as was the case on most of Africa, to some degree even in South Africa.

Drawing clear conclusions about individual's behavior today from history is impossible. However, history sets the stage for the current state of affairs, and Africans grow up in black societies, in contrast to African Americans, at least in terms of the country as a whole. In the U.S., being a person of color means that you are visibly different from the majority of the population, the majority of the images in the media, and different from the majority of those who hold positions of power.

Brathwaite relates a story which brought home to her this fundamental difference of perspective between Africans and African Americans. Several years ago, she was speaking to a class of African American sixth and seventh graders at a private school in New York State about life in Ghana. "When I told them about our president in Ghana, they asked me what color is your president. They nearly fell out of their chairs when I told them he was black," she said. "It wasn't part of their ideas. They could not conceive of a black man as president."

"Ghana is our country, and the decisions we make are ours," she said, speaking of her conviction that she is an integral part of Ghanaian society, in both its problems and its successes. She contrasted that conviction with her impression of many African Americans, who to this day do not feel that they are full members of American society. "It's different if you're made to feel you have to fight the whole system. That creates a sense of despair," she said. "In Africa, we don't have to deal with that. In every aspect of life, somebody just like you is in charge." She reflects for a moment. Her voice softens, emphasizing her words: "It's different. It's just very different."

For most Africans, having a black skin is nothing more than having a skin. It is the norm, neither positive nor negative. This is different for African Americans who are not Americans - they are African Americans or Black Americans. They are part of the minority, and a visible minority in a society conscious of racial differences.

African Americans grow up in a society where they are subjected to various negative stereotypes and racial prejudice based on the color of their skin. This fact puts solidarity between black people in the U.S. at a premium. Africans, on the other hand, because they haven't grown up with the same pressures, have a hard time understanding the need for connection between black people in America in the face of racial prejudice.

Lueth said that this is an important cultural difference between the two groups, because it often leads to a hyper-sensitivity, and at times mistrust, in the relations between the two groups. Because in Africa there are many tribes and ethnic groups which don't traditionally mix, or are even traditional enemies, it doesn't occur to Africans to try to bridge cultural gaps on the basis of race, she said. "Not all black people can get along. There's nearly a billion black Africans in the world, and to say that they have to get along because they are black is unrealistic. The concept just doesn't make sense to Africans."

Africans who come to Iowa City to study experience at least some of the negative stereotypes directed toward African Americans because they have the same skin color. Lueth said many Africans have experienced at least some racial prejudice since coming to Iowa City.

However, Africans tend to take incidents of racism directed at them less personally because they are visitors here, and their home is somewhere else, she said. "I don't feel so trapped by this society because I don't feel like this is my home," Lueth said. "I can go back to my country and speak a different language which (Americans) won't understand." "Besides," she added, "I know that this is not the only way it has to be."

# Village Square: Diary of a Nigerian Immigrant: Nigerian Life in the Diaspora : A Common Ground in African Heritage

## "Little Ethiopia Event Aims to Bring Black Americans and Immigrants Together"

Ann M. Simmons, *Los Angeles Times* Staff Writer

Growing up in Nigeria, Lillian Obiara and her peers idolized aspects of black America the vibrant culture, the dynamic music, and the movie and sports personalities they saw on TV. Some of Obiara's girlfriends dreamed that one day they might marry an African American.

But when Obiara finally came to the United States less than two months ago to pursue a nursing degree, she was dismayed by the lack of knowledge about Africa, the insulting comments about the way Africans live, and the hostility she encountered from some black Americans.

"Before I came, I thought that since they are black-skinned like us, they would be more open," said Obiara, 26 and a resident of Long Beach. "The reality here is very different. The whites are more receptive than the blacks."

Obiara's views are not uncommon among many of Southern California's 80,000-plus immigrants from sub-Saharan Africa the majority from Ethiopia, Nigeria and Ghana.

Relations Between African Immigrants and African Americans Pose A Paradox

Many African Americans feel an emotional and spiritual attachment to Africa. Some give their children African names Kwame, Kofi, Hakeem often employing elaborate African rituals. Weddings in which the bride and groom don ornate traditional attire, often a melange of costumes from across the continent, have grown in popularity.

Ethnic arts and crafts gathered from a growing number of festivals and fairs celebrating Africa's creative talent fill the homes of many African Americans, and trips to Africa by black Americans are becoming increasingly common.

Neighborhood Party

On Sunday, scores of Africans joined by some African Americans celebrated the first anniversary of the designation of one Los Angeles neighborhood a busy hub of businesses on a strip of Fairfax Avenue between Pico and Olympic boulevards as "Little Ethiopia."

As restaurants, shops and stalls sold traditional Ethiopian food, hawked T-shirts with the country's insignia and promoted trips to Africa, organizers said the celebration was designed to embrace black people from the diaspora as well as promote local businesses.

"We are trying to reach out to all African nations and to African Americans, anyone of African descent," said Anteneh Demelash, 24, a college student and one of the organizers.

Demelash, who emigrated from Addis Ababa, the Ethiopian capital, nine years ago, said young people were key to bridging the cultural divide between Africans and black Americans.

Lily Michael, 33, another event organizer and an Ethiopian immigrant whose husband is African American, agreed.

"My thing has not been to concentrate on ethnicity and nationality, but to concentrate on humanity," she said. "We are more similar than different."

Edith Gursel, an African American and a regular visitor to Little Ethiopia, dropped by the festivities on her way to a local Buddhist center.

"I always come here for lunch, once a week," said Gursel, 61, an artist and Valley resident. "These are my roots. I feel very comfortable here. It centers me. And I'd rather spend my money here, with my people."

And yet, even as black Americans such as Gursel embrace their African heritage, other American-born blacks are separated from African immigrants by a chasm widened by cultural differences and mutual misconceptions.

Many Africans believe that black Americans either romanticize the continent or snub Africans as unsophisticated.

Some African Americans, for their part, argue that many African immigrants do not make enough effort to integrate into black America and fail to appreciate how profoundly the legacy of slavery and the civil rights struggle has affected U.S.-born blacks.

"It goes back to misconceptions and, in large part, media images," said Ethiopian-born Azeb Tadesse, senior assistant director of the James S. Coleman African Studies Center at UCLA. "The way Africa is portrayed in the media and the way African Americans are portrayed feed into the stereotypes."

A clash of culture, language and class also plays a role, said Marcia Thomas, director of US for Africa, a grant-making foundation based in Los Angeles.

When immigrants from other parts of the world arrive in America, they can integrate into existing communities that share the same cultural perspective and typically speak the same language, she noted. Not so for Africans, who speak scores of different vernaculars and have distinct tribal affiliations, none of which American-born blacks can automatically identify with.

"Just because you look alike, you don't necessarily have the cultural context and understanding that relates to living in this country," said Thomas, 51.

Like many other immigrants, Africans typically come to the United States in search of education and jobs. Others are fleeing political instability or persecution in their home countries. Many are too caught up in the fight for everyday survival and for resources to support families back home to care about making an effort to get involved with black Americans.

Black Americans who visit Africa "are trying to get back home and connect with something," said James Burks, director of African Marketplace Inc., which serves as a showcase for black enterprise and creativity. "It is the land, it is the spirit, it is the ancestors, it is family, and the idea of being able to identify with Africa."

By contrast, he said, for African immigrants, "The majority that I've engaged are here to strengthen their own outlook for economic purposes. I don't think I have ever met an African who has told me that they are here to connect with African Americans."

Many Africans "have one foot here and one foot back home,"

said Muadi Mukenge, an immigrant from the Democratic Republic of Congo who works as program officer for Africa at the Pacific Institute for Women's Health, which is based in Koreatown. "There is less of a priority to organize with African Americans. People are concentrating on helping their families back home."

On arriving in the United States, many African immigrants have their first encounters with American racial prejudice. They face discrimination in housing and, like other immigrants, are not eligible for many of the social services for which U.S. citizens qualify.

Africans "come here and work two jobs, we don't get welfare," said Olawale Jimoh, vice president of the United African Federation. "We try hard to make ends meet." Jimoh, 49, moved from Nigeria 12 years ago and owns a security company and an agency that employs temporary health-care workers.

Being categorized by race stuns some Africans, who come from predominantly black societies where ethnic affiliations and class override color.

Many are humbled by what sociologists describe as a "downward assimilation." Like members of other immigrant groups, many Africans come to the United States as university graduates and professionals but find they must take jobs as cleaners, janitors or taxi drivers.

"All of a sudden, you find yourself down, down, down," said Yaw Adutwum, 39, a teacher at Manual Arts High School in Los Angeles who is a member of Ghana's Ashanti ethnic group, which comprises the country's royal elite. "It's a shocking experience."

Many Stereotypes

Mutual ignorance and stereotypes with which many Africans and African Americans regard each other can make the initial encounter worse.

"To them, you come from a place where people don't wear clothes, where you play with a monkey," said Adutwum, remembering encounters from his early years as a substitute teacher in Los Angeles' Crenshaw district.

At the same time, he said, many African immigrants, even

318

before they leave home, have adopted stereotypes of black Americans as being good only at sports and music and crime.

"You generally were not thinking that African Americans were the professional type," he said, recalling some of the media images he was exposed to in his home country.

From the images they see on television in Africa, Africans get a homogenous version of what our life is like," said Thomas, who has traveled widely on the continent as part of her work for US for Africa. "If I were to believe what I see on TV, I would believe that all black people do is stand on street corners, drive by and kill each other."

In an attempt to bridge the gap between the communities, several Southland residents and local groups are arranging social gatherings and trips to Africa and forging organizational and business partnerships. Those activities will become even more important as the number of African immigrants to Southern California continues to swell, the organizers said.

Members of Southern California's African business community are also making greater efforts to collaborate with black Americans. African hair salons, boutiques, restaurants and churches have sprung up throughout Southern California, with a high concentration in areas such as Crenshaw.

"Things are progressing slowly, but they are moving forward," said LaSandra Stratton of the Africa-U.S. Chamber of Commerce. "We have much to learn from each other."

MrsKenna
12-20-2003, 11:53 PM

Hey CXSM, this was an excellent article. I will share this one with my husband. This area in Los Angeles is only an hour away from me. My husband shops at the African stores in that Crenshaw district. I think we will all have to work together to break the stereotypes and try to understand each other's background, our lives, and where we all came from. I will provide more details on this by next week!

cxsm
01-04-2004, 04:59 AM

# NATIVE AFRICANS Vs AFRICAN AMERICANS:
## THE BAD-BLOOD, THE BATTLE AND THE BENEDICTION

Rudolph Okonkwo

TWO HUNDRED YEARS FROM NOW, A NEW GENERATION OF BLACK men and women will inhabit the earth. They will roam the streets of this world, from London to Lagos, from New York to Johannesburg, from Cairo to Rio de Janeiro. They will look back at this generation of ours and most likely proclaim us as those who lived in dark ages.

Among the things they would find baffling is how Whites who constitute only 13 percent of the world population control virtually all the continents of this earth. They will shudder at the reasons we the Black people of this age give for our inability to come together and reclaim our rightful place in the family of humanity.

They will look with shame at the Central African country of Zaire, a country ten times the size of Great Britain and five times that of France, with enough mineral resources to ground up to a third of the air power of the North Atlantic Treaty Organization (NATO), were it to decide not to export cobalt.

They will look at African Americans of today - arguably the most privileged group of Blacks - and wonder why in spite of living in the most powerful nation on earth they couldn't chart the path for the rest of the Black world.

They will weigh the excuses we give today against the fact that there are twice as many African Americans as there are Jews throughout the world. Yet, only a fraction of Jews, the American Jews, influence the United States policy towards the Middle East. If American Jews could find enough reasons to make America to give over two billion dollars in aid to Israel each year, African Americans could easily lay their hands on a million reasons why such favors should be extended to Africa, if they tried hard enough.

They will look at Nigeria, the so-called giant of Africa, and cry. A country that has one in every six blacks on earth, a country with enough crude oil reserve to dictate how much the price of a gallon of gas would cost anywhere in the world. But, the giant is there, flat on its stomach. Also, they will check the records Blacks hold across the world, the millions of untapped Black talents wasting away in several parts of the world, and wonder. The biggest question they will find very difficult to answer is why it was so hard. Did anybody really try?

I don't think we want the generations yet unborn to walk away asking, why couldn't our forefathers get along with their brothers around the world? Why did they keep to themselves while the rest of the world exploit the labor and the resources of Blacks? Why was it so difficult for them to understand each other?

When I was in Africa, I was bewildered by the enormous problems confronting Africa and I found no other viable solution but to look up to Africans in the Diaspora. Since I joined Africans in Diaspora I have come to appreciate more the degree of the problem facing Blacks around the globe. Irrespective of the fancy theory that the intellectual class proposes, there are visible cracks in the relationship between African Americans and native Africans, which is derailing very effort to establish political, economic, and cultural ties among all Black people. Misunderstanding and mistrust continue to thrive, despite wider exposure of people to other cultures and ways of life. A great proportion of the blame goes to the media that tend to perpetuate myths and unsubstantiated innuendoes.

Meanwhile, a frightening development is taking root. As African Americans embrace Islam, Kwaanza or any other concept associated with Africa, Africans in their romantic picture of the western world are letting themselves become Americanized. These contradictory trend and the shameful exploitation of the vast material and intellectual resources of Black people ought to be our concern. Instead, what we have is a myriad of characterizations promoted by some paranoids.

Some of these characterizations on both sides are insulting and unprintable. One thing is however common: both sides mistrust and misunderstand each other. In public there is a blatant denial of this disgusting dichotomy. So what shall we do about this? Talk, of course. Which was exactly what I did. I went out and walked to a cross section of Black people in an effort to find out why we are so divided. Here are some of the responses I got.

I asked an African (he pleaded anonymous) to describe the state of the relationship between Africans and African Americans. He answered, "There is no relationship. We have nothing in common with them except the color of our skin. Whatever we had in common was wiped out during slavery." When I confronted him with the fact that de-Africanization of Black America is moving at the same speed with the Americanization of native Africa he said, "They cannot be Africans in America. They should accept their American heritage and stick with it." When asked why some Africans feel so detached from their African American brothers and sisters, he gave an unprintable answer.

Just when I thought that the African in question, a computer science senior at Norfolk State University, has got a chronic misconception of African Americans, I met an African American who felt that anyone expecting anything good to come out of Africa is wasting his or her time. "We, the African Americans are the best Africa has to offer. What was left of Africa after slavery was the scum of the Black world. That is why two hundred years after the beginning of industrial revolution Africans are yet to feed themselves have remained wretched of the earth."

Kelly Willis, a Mass Communication major at Norfolk State University, who had met many Africans in his native state of New York, had a moderate view of the problem. He perceived the relationship between native Africans and African Americans to be good though he saw room for improvement. "I try not to look at the negative comments," he said. He however conceded that there are differences in attitude, which he attributed to the different political and economic experiences both sides have had. Africans, he observed, should learn from African Americans the tact needed when one is dealing with European Americans, "Only trust to a certain point."

In the same vein, Dominique Lancry, a Texan of Panamanian origin, decried the attitude of Africans whom she said carried themselves about like royalties and joined Whites to look down on African Americans. "I don't want them to judge us," she stated. "I want them to learn our heritage before they judge us." Hitting the same note, Thaddeus Freeman, a business major at N.S.U lamented," Everyone who comes to this country see the Black people as the people to do the work... They don't give us the respect we deserve." Mr. Freeman specially abhorred the attitude of some Africans whom, he alleged, had nicknamed African Americans "akata". In his opinion, we all should work together, "Unite Africa and take over the world."

Victoria Mckoy, a hair stylist refused to be drawn into any feud. "I try very hard not to judge people," she pleaded. "We are not different from Africans. Even if I experience a negative my attitude is to overcome it. I can't judge people. If I'm constantly talking about Africans, Jamaicans, Asians, what does that say about me?"

Such sentiments could not dissuade Dewitt Webster, a Norfolk based Public Health expert, who had traveled extensively in Africa and had lived in Nigeria for more than five years. He described the relationship between Africans and African Americans as "improving".

He blamed miscommunication for lack of understanding being experienced in some quarters. He noted that Africans who associate with only European Americans and let the biased media influence them, only experience one side of the American life and tend to pick up the attitude of European Americans about African Americans.

"African Americans," he said, "see Africans as arrogant but when I went to Africa I understood that it is about having self confidence. Having an understanding of who you are and where you come from - they are the key to having a strong personality."

He called for a more realistic look at Africa, noting that there is strength in our diversity. "We need to realize that in spite of how far away we may be, or how long ago we had left, there are so much of Africa that are part of us and vice versa."

Mr. Webster warned that Africans must be taught to hold on to their culture, while African Americans on their part should learn perseverance, respect for elders, and collaboration with Africans. "These are things we used to know," he lamented. African Americans, he noted, are the wealthiest blacks in the world and should join the rest of the world to explore the business opportunities in Africa. He advocated that African Americans should learn at least one African language, put in extra effort to understand the politics and economics of Africa so that they will take the lead in the area of transferring appropriate technology to

Africa.

Irrespective of what differences exist between African Americans and Africans, and how Blacks all over the world perceive each other, the destiny of all Black people are intertwined in their common African Heritage. There is truly only one way to go - either for all Black people to unite and regain their rightful place, or to remain disconnected and continue to be other peoples' pawns in this game of life.

cxsm
01-04-2004, 05:10 AM

Below is one of two available responses (by Nigerians) to the posting on Native Africans vs. African Americans:

I agree that African Americans have a place to play in the rejuvination of Africa, but what about the Africans (of direct parental hertiage)? I think we have a greater role to play than African Americans (descendants of slaves).

I just came back from a vacation in Ghana, and am currently living in the Republic of Benin for the Peace Corps. I visited Cape Coast, which houses some castles (i.e. Elimina and Cape Coast Castles) which served as forts to the slave trade. I found that it was emotionally overwhelming, but spiritually exuberating to see that we as a people can go through so much and keep on surviving.

I think that the conditions exemplified in Cape Coast should excuse some of the happenings in America on the part of African Americans because that system was never created for them to succeed, so it should be no surprise why they can't succeed in 'the greatest country on earth' (despite the fact that this greatest country was built with their sweat and tears and free labor).

The Africans have just as much apologizing to tell the African Americans as do the whites because it was a collaborative effort - it's to the Africans ignorance that we did not know what was up the white mans sleeves. Hence, an 'I'm sorry for selling you to those devils who ended up enslaving all of us anyways in some shape or form' is due first before any other talks. Then the problem gets even more intricate because there is the divide and

324

conquer rule that is still in effect, playing out in various tribalistic forms.

Now, I'm not saying to not take pride in your tribe - I am a very proud Igbo woman. The problem is drawing the line as to where pride becomes subject for conflict and as soon as AFRICANS are conscious that the way we have pride does cause conflict, there will be no progress for the black people of this earth.

History has told this story time and time again, and I suggest we play the history lesson but I hope you get the point I'm making.

The bottom line is that we if we are really talking of the progression of our race and our home (Africa) then we need to not speak abstractly or pseudo intellectually or creatively but realistically and strategically. The Japanese have a Four Hundred Year Plan, we're still collecting aide from USAID, SIDA, and the rest of foreign aide - I think it's time to wake up.

Sincerely,

Chioma M. Oruh
oruh@g...

cxsm
01-04-2004, 05:16 AM

Below is the second of two available responses (by Nigerians) to the posting on Native Africans vs. African Americans:

There's no question that African Americans should be expected to pull the rest of Africa by the boot straps, given the privilege of living in the greatest country on earth. To do this effectively, however, African Americans should find a way to empower themselves, first. They would need to go to school more, learn more skills, find a secure place in corporate and bureaucratic America, travel the world, make changes in their lifestyles, their values and consciousness.

My experience is that the younger generation of African Americans are ill-equipped, mentally, to deal with Africans in their midst, much less care about Africans in the motherland.

My experience is that African Americans, compared with Whites, are the first to tell me that I have an accent, that in fact I do not know the English language. African Americans are the least to be enthusiastic enough to ask me what part of Africa that I come from and to tell me that they have visited my country or planning a vacation to that part of the world. They are the least to be willing to take me home to know their houses and to be of help if I need one.

Of course, when I talk about African Americans here, I mean, largely, the less formally educated ones; and they are many. The more educated ones are better able to communicate with me and to be empathic. They are more friendly. They are more apt to discuss socio-economic and political issues involving Africa.

It is really a shame that Africans, both in Diaspora and in the motherland, can't yet find a common ground and a common cause that can bring them together to work for mutual benefit, in the interest of the black race. If we feel challenged enough by this article to take action, no matter how little, to advance the interests of Africa, humanity would be better for it.

Kelechi Eke <kceke@r...> wrote:
01-04-2004, 01:02 PM

The fact is that African-Americans like all other Americans in the United States are AMERICAN.

How many non-first generation Americans speak the language, eat the food, worship the religion or adopt the mannerisms of their ancestors? Very, very few.Therefore the only common ground between both groups is skin color and other physical attributes.

I see part of our psychological problems being rooted in the inability to let history and historical facts be so and move on. Why should I apologise to anyone because my race took part in the slave trade? Even if my great-grandfather was a direct participant, I'm not accountable for his sins! I don't even judge the people in the past too harshly, because I tend to see events within their historical context. Humans are on a constant learning   curve.

The events that have happened to us are not unique to us alone. Historical fact: the English, were once unlettered, slaves, Celts

326

were considered very barbaric and practiced human sacrifice. It is of course difficult to see this today in the modern U.K. History is full of many such instances.

I hope this might console those who are so psychologically wounded!

Common grounds should be between individuals. I must be quite strange, but I enjoy overall, a good relationship with African Americans. (as well as all people. My acquaintances cut across various strata of society. They ask questions, I offer opinions,explanations and answers. I don't get angry and beat anyone over the head about questions that may be considered ignorant or stereotypical. I answer questions based on my personal experience.

After all Africa- e big so. Yes, I see elephant before: for London zoo. (true). I tell stories, I make jokes (sometimes distasteful) and I pull legs too!!:) Even sef, me sef ask question too..(don't ask about what). I think we are getting too hung up on unimportant minutiae of life. I don't hear the French complaining about their body odor stereotype, the French maid thing, or their diet. I'm yet to hear a single Swede whine over the Swedish blonde thing.

There are more important issues people: Africans are still enslaving themselves, in Africa!!! Today!! By Africans, (Nigeria, West Africa), by Arabs, (Mauretania, Sudan). Why isn't anyone getting bent out of shape over this??

Is it embarrassing? Millions of African children are being born without provision for them to take part effectively in the modern world, culture and economy. We should be talking about EDUCATION, EDUCATION, EDUCATION for the African child. I'm sure we will find this will go a long way in healing our collectively injured psyche!!

amerbro
01-05-2004, 10:37 AM

cxsm
01-05-2004, 03:41 PM

Amebro,

Thanks for the link. It definitely offers a more enlightening view to those trying to understand the reasons why there are issues that need to be first understood in objective rather than emotional capacities to permit a true common ground between Africans and African-Americans.

One very important factor is in the misconceptions on both sides which was well described in his statements that -{{"Most People from Anglophone countries come to America well versed in the English language and Western culture, but speak with an accent, which is often foolishly equated with being backward or unable to speak English.

Some AFC come to the US with misgivings about whether the African-American community will accept them, and this gives them cause to feel ostracized when they enter the country. As a result they find solace in fellowship only with each other because they share a cultural identity and a commonality of interests.

Some African-Americans on the other hand may not be inclined to fellowship with AFC because they have been led to believe that the AFC have a superiority complex, and also because they do not share a common culture and a commonality of interests.

There are AFC as well as African-Americans, who do not subscribe to this line of thinking, but neither side is making any effort to reach out and so the misunderstanding ensues.

The misconceptions that are ingrained in 'some' Africans and African-Americans because of what they're already exposed to by media in their respective countries, I believe lead to the rough rather smooth alliances that result as each group is first exposed or introduced to the other.

I also believe that the environment in which each group is first exposed to the other plays a major role in influencing and affecting the individual's perceptions and experiences, which may further lead to an understanding or biases about the other group.

For instance an African who arrives in America and schools in a predominantly caucasian environment may or may not enjoy his first experience on exposure to African-Americans depending on how receptive they are based on their own enlightenment or biases, and these may result in the African's decision to either embrace or distance himself from other African Americans until and unless he gets other opportunities to have experiences that differ from that he was initially faced with.

Similarly, an African-American who meets an African from a country that is not war-torn, in which the African has simply come to further his education (without knowledge of the African's true disposition) may perceive him as privileged and thus consider him arrogant, rather than confident. After all, the only images of Africans he probably saw prior to meeting with an actual African may have been the media impressions showing naked starving Africans with kwashokor and flies looming over them. Nowadays with the prevailing negative media theme, the person might even assume that the African came to America with funds from stolen loot, hence his ability to afford a decent education, without knowledge of whether he might even be working 3 jobs to support his education.

On the other hand, if another uninformed African American's first encounter with an African is one emerging from a war torn country, he himself may feel superior to that African rather than relating to their historical similarities, and if this African works hard to excel and better his disposition and in fact does so, the African American may perceive him as one of those who come to take their jobs and encroach on the privileges they deem their ancestors and sweat worked for.

As we can all see that EDUCATION is the key to correcting these misconceptions and enlightening both groups as to the true disposition of the other. A major key in educating both sides I also begins with changing media miseducation, and if it takes both Africans and Afican Amrericans to obtain positions in newspapers, TV and radio stations to correct the misconceptions, then it has to be done.

A lot of people for instance are unaware that Tarzan was shot in a ranch in Santa Barbara California and thus believe the barbaric comparisons and innuendos portrayed about Africans in the series. No wonder some misled and miseducated people actually believe Africa is a jungle.

I can even remember my Mum telling me stories of how caucasian mates in her medical profession used to ask to see her tail in England, and you can imagine it was not only shocking to know that some humans could be very ignorant about Africans, but also extremely mean and racist.

To realize that in this present day, some people still possess the 3 aforementioned characteristics, which some Africans have experienced from people of all races, only proves that certain characteristics are so ingrained that only consistent education, and enlightenment can effectively begin to reverse the ensuing biases.

I also believe panel discussions and dialogues such as this will work towards educating and enlightening both groups, and hopefully lead to the point where each is more receptive of the other, thus enable them to overcome any residual longstanding psychological barriers (such as those resulting from causasian divide and conquer tactics that were implanted during days of colonization and slavery experienced by both groups).

Dialogues will also serve as a uniting effort to establish significant trust, where more African-Americans can begin to visit Africa to learn of and embrace their heritage; but also for them to begin to invest there not only for their own economic growth, but also to and aid in uplifting their fellow Africans.

Both groups should begin to seek economic growth and empowerment rather than remaining consumers on their individual continents. The media have discouraged African-Americans from visiting their land of heritage for too long, yet caucasians continually travel their for investment opportunities and even some have exploited in the process.

This effort to unite and for empowerment is also the purpose of the Black Heritage Festival events presently being held in some African countries to encourage Africa-Americans to visit.

cxsm
01-14-2004, 01:50 AM

ananzi2002@y....com writes:

In response to what has been said about African Americans, I would like to make a few positive points.

As for saying that those in the Diaspora are just slaves is a great misconception. Europeans were well aware of the skills that they needed to exploit to make America and other countries of the

Western Hemisphere great. One only has to look at the iron works made in the American South, those people were taken from Benin where they had great skill in iron.

People who were good with rice were taken for that reason. The young were taken because they could bear the brunt of the work. Females were taken to work and serve the sexual needs of their captors.

America was built on the backs of Africans who were from Africa. Slavery did not happen to Harry or Martin but Hassan, Jojo, Kwamena, and Babatunde. They went through a process that they did their best in. If you listen to the Gullah's of the Carolinas, you can still hear the ancients singing.

Long are the days when Kwame Nkrumah, Nnamdi Azikwe, and Babatunde Olatunji came to America. They walked the halls of Black Colleges, hung out with people to see who they really are and became involved in fraternities and social clubs. That rarely happens anymore.

As for myself, I have always wanted to be part of Africa no matter what any negative continental African said or cursed at me. I knew it was my heritage when heard the glimpses of Africa from words that my father's parents spoke to him as a child or the food my grandmother prepared. Because when I went to Senegal, Guinea and Ghana, I saw the same food there. A bit different only in a few of the ingredients. I have seen the same faces as I see here. The only difference is that they are there and we are here.

Oh, I went to Africa by myself and stayed there for three years. I lived in Senegal and Ghana. I seen the positive aspects of humanity and the deep dark hearts of my people. I have watched in Ghana where white people are still Gods where clerks will run to them forgetting their own brethren as customers. Sometimes these whites came from poor households but that did not matter but their color. I have watched how Lebanese and Indians rule the economic order and sex African women like nothing. I have seen the sons and daughters of slave dealers who still lie and cheat today. I have seen the atrocities of war with refugees. Also, many people do not know much about the Diaspora but what they see on TV or in the movies. Just like some folks here.

No, I did not go to Senegal with the Peace Corps or any program. I went there by myself. I ate at local and good

331

restaurants. I hung out at universities to have intellectual conversations with professors and students. I went to bars and bookstores outside of the tourist traps. I walked the streets of Ponty and strolled down Rawlings Park. I can really say that I did my best to experience my folks across the seas.

There is no one better than the other. We all did the best we can in our situation. Now, when is the time that each one of us teach and touch the heart of another. So we can stop being impoverished of the spirit and create a New Africa with a new heatbeat.

cxsm
01-14-2004, 01:55 AM

teazuqueen@a...

When I came from Liberia to the Midwestern United States, I immersed myself in the African-American culture without losing mine: joined a sorority, hung out with my sorors and did very well in school. I was ridiculed for not using slangs, speaking 'too properly' and making friends with Caucasians in a mostly-Caucasian college.

Undaunted, I remained in the African-American sorority and continued to embrace the new culture while hanging on to my own. I introduced my sorors to fine African cuisine, couture, writing, art and music. I ignored jokes about my food smelling 'funny,' knowing the jokes would not have been made had they only known what they were missing. In time they, too, learned to enjoy my culture.

Only you can determine your response to another person's actions. The new Africa mentioned above will come into existence when peoples of African ancestry fight mental slavery and corporate colonialism, not each other.

Gen Sani Abacha
01-14-2004, 01:47 PM

Folks,

332

The ff link is to an article where the author argues that native African US residents and their offspring/descendants will/should retain their own cultures, rather than assimilate into the African-American community:
http://www.nigerdeltacongress.com/articles/american_africans_an d_continenta.htm

Please read and provide your views later.

Regards

MrsKenna
01-14-2004, 05:21 PM

Gen Sani Abacha....your highness..this is MAIN DAWG. Anyway, I read that article and the writer seems to be a bit upset. As far as Black History Month being the shortest month....Black History does not need a month to define it. That is only a celebration. We should celebrate our heritage all year long not just for Martin Luther King or Black History Month. As far as the prominent Africans in History, Shaka Zulu, the Queen of Sheba and other great leaders are taught in the American schools. I guess it just depends on where you go to school. It was taught in my school but then again, most of my teachers from elementary through high school were strong black leaders in the education system and throughout their community. The only thing I would hate to see is the division that the article is trying to create.

Gen Sani Abacha
01-14-2004, 07:57 PM

I believe African expatriates are entitled to keep their mother tongues and culture and teach their children the same. Living in America doesn't mean they should stop being Zulu, Ashanti, Wolof etc. Generally black folks in the USA should be able to celebrate their common African ancestry without erasing individual culttural identities. Haitians can keep their Kweyol (French Creole), Jamaicans can keep Patois, native Africans their mother tongues and African-Americans Ebonics. I favour the Big-

Tent/Broad Church inclusive approach, rather than have one language/culture dominate, whereby other groups give up their own uniqueness.

Anyway sis, keep it coming.

Outtie.

MrsKenna
01-14-2004, 08:06 PM

Thanks your highness...by the way, be careful by the way you throw the word Ebonics around. Most black people don't speak like that. It's a stereotype...Wolof, Yoruba are languages not slang like Ebonics....sorry, this is a bit dear to the heart!
Anyway, I have no problem celebrating culture but then again, America has been said to be a "melting pot" where you cannot define what our real culture is as it is mixed! Just something I heard!

See ya! I am headed home!

amerbro
01-15-2004, 12:49 PM
.
MrsKenna
01-15-2004, 12:55 PM

Amerbro, I was hoping that you would elaborate on the issue at hand please...

Gen Sani Abacha
01-15-2004, 07:35 PM

Hiya Folks,

Amerbro good to have you back up in here. Sorry about your computer glitch. Perhaps Sola should open a computer problem solving forum to where members can post problems, and those in the know can give their own solutions. Now on to the matter at hand.

MrsK, you loveliness Mah MAIN D-A-Wizzle-Double Gizzle, I just view Ebonics/AAVE(African American Vernacular English as some linguists politely term it) as the AA equivalent of Jamaicans' Patois, Sierra Leone Krio, Nigerian Pidgin etc. No offense intended.

As per the USA being a melting pot, I ain't disputing that. What I keep insisting however, is that those Africans who want to retain their mother tongues and Ethno-cultural identities should. Native Africans know they are Black, but they also have specific cultural identities ie, Ashanti, Zulu, Wolof, Bangala, Buganda, Bakongo, Kikuyu etc. These cultural identities pre-date colonisation and should not be killed off on a whim. There is a saying in Nigeria "Unity in Diversity". There are too many black folks whose definition of unity is for everyone to speak one single language, in one dialect with the same accent. They seem to hate other blacks with a different language and culture to their own, and would like to make everyone conform to their own socio-cultural patterns. Anyone who doesn't conform is regarded as a "Traitor", "Anti-Black" etc. In my opinion, such people actually desire hegemony over the entire black race, they are no different to the Arabs and Europeans who came to colonize/enslave Africans.

Amerbro, as black folks, by all means we should defend our common interests, this doesn't mean we should conform to one single language and culture. Native Africans have around 2000 indigenous languages (not dialects), each with a unique culture and history of the people who speak it. Diasporic Africans also have several languages; Spanish for the Afrocubano, Portuguese for the AfroBrazileira, Gujurat for the Sidi ie Afro-descendants of Gujurat state India. Sindh for the African-Pakistani sidis of Sindh province in south-eastern Pakistan. We should be able to respect each other's cultural differences and idiosyncracies, while celebrating our common African origins. Unity does not have to mean Uniformity.        That is all I'm saying.

Regards

Bro, I have met some black folks over here in blighty who despise African culture and languages and go out of their way to ridicule Africans who speak their mother tongues or wear African clothes. These folks also ridicule African names deliberately mispronouncing them, as well as ridiculing African English accents. These peeps range from children to ELDERLY people, cutting across British raised Africans and Caribbeans raised in Britain and back home. I must stress that not all of them are like this, but for those who are, I ignore them. When such people now turn around and call for black people to stick together, they get angry when native Africans don't respond. They then turn around and call us naive.

Some of them have a "superiority complex" towards Africans, and don't like it when Africans aren't intimidated, or don't feel inferior. However, it saddens me to say, that some Africans actually feel inferior to these type of people, and try to conform to their opinions of what it means to be black.

On a personal level, I have no problems dealing with my Caribbean brethren, I just dismiss the silly/condescending ones.

As per adapting, this is standard procedure wherever on earth we may go. Even moving to a different neighbourhood or district of a city requires some level of adaption. The Americo-Liberians (descendants of African-Americans who returned to Liberia about 200 years ago) had to adapt to the local conditions, while retaining their own culture. They have kept their own dialect called "Merico" ( I don't know if it's a Gullah/Geechee style Creole dialect), and with English the official language, they weren't required to learn any of the indigenous Liberian languages. They took things too far however, by lording it over the indigenous folks. I'm sure you probably know a lot about their history by now.

Anyway bro, go easy on your "Liberian influence" and invite me to the wedding.

Yeah, and I'll look forward to you hitting me up with some collard greens, chitlings, apple pie and seeing as you've sojourned down south, throw in some good ole soul food.

Katchya

# CHILLY COEXISTENCE:
## Africans and African Americans in the Bronx

Oscar Johnson

It is easy for African immigrants who increasingly call the Bronx home to "just get along" with their American-born black neighbors. But it is a chilly coexistence - a fact both sides acknowledge from across a subtle yet vast cultural divide.

True, a certain kinship is noted. "We see them as the same," said the Rev. Michael Aggrey, 38, a visiting Catholic priest from Ghana who serves a growing congregation of Ghanaians in the West Bronx. "We used to have the same culture."

Indeed. The new immigrants and the descendents of those once imported by force share African origins. They both fit into America's "black" racial category, and often scrape by on low incomes.

But African immigrants differ from their black predecessors, not only culturally, but in experience and perspective. Those differences are rarely discussed but widely understood to be at the root of a great divide.

Like a dozen African immigrants and African Americans who in interviews were pressed about their lack of relationships, Aggrey evinced a diplomacy that eventually gave way to candor.

While some African Americans are "very nice," he said, "the difference is the way we have been raised. The few African Americans I have interacted with are embittered with the past."

Aggrey's candor soon revealed bewilderment. "Why are the African Americans so into sports?" he asked. "We can go higher. We can make education our priority. But if we are into basketball they (whites) can still be in control."

G. Ofori Anor, 50, a Ghanaian immigrant who moved to the Bronx 14 years ago, echoes Aggrey. Sober in spirit and conservatively casual in dress, he is the editor of Asante, a monthly newspaper. He said he renounced his first, or "Christian" name, but keeps the initial "G" in honor of his father who named him.

According to Anor, some aspects of African culture "embarrass" American blacks because the practices appear primitive to those used to more European standards. He said this embarrassment causes some black Americans to distance themselves from anything - or anyone - who is explicitly African.

"On our side," Anor said, "we don't understand the way it appears that African Americans treat one another: Black on black crime - especially the youth killing themselves.

Recalling a visit to a largely African-American housing project, he lamented "the propensity for African Americans to run down their own neighborhood in protest." Someone had urinated in the building elevator, he said. "If you are really mad at the white man why don't you pee in his elevator? He doesn't ride in this one - you do."

For those more aligned with the African-American experience, such as Jalani Ja Lion, a walnut-hued Rastafarian who claims Cherokee and West Indian lineage, there is another perception.

"Africans come here and they are under a lot of misconceptions that African Americans are losers" and don't take advantage of opportunities, said Ja Lion, who sells incense, scented oils and other sundries from a folding table near Jerome Avenue. "But not everything here is a bed of roses. As long as there's a cultural barrier it's going to breed ignorance."

In the last decade there has been ample opportunity for cultural barriers to arise among black people in the Bronx. More than 1,600 Ghanaians now immigrate annually to the city - a 380 percent increase since the early 1990s - according to the city Department of City Planning report released last year.

Immigration and Naturalization Service data shows that in 1996, about two-thirds of those Ghanaians visiting the United States (6,269), and nearly three-quarters of those naturalized (3,084), arrived in the city. Many have clustered in communities in Morris Heights, Highbridge and Tremont, making Ghana the No. 3 place of origin for immigrants to the Bronx, according to the report.

Meanwhile, city and community district data for the new millennium show that the borough's native-born black population - largely consisting of those traditionally called "black" and

"African American"- is leaving the South Bronx.

In the last decade, many have migrated north to Coop City. Some have left the Bronx altogether. Now, a full two thirds of the borough's "black" population is foreign-born.

Neither the immigrants nor the native-born seem to harbor any intentional ill will towards one another. But both speak of distinctions, assumptions and de facto segregation.

"I wouldn't say the relation is cold but I wouldn't say it's warm either," said Randolph Hinds, 38, president of the African American Association in Coop City, and adjunct professor of sociology at New Rochelle College. He said one reason relations are tepid is because many African Americans feel the immigrants "are so clannish that they're not going to let you in...It's almost like an arrogance and a put down."

But African Americans have their own misconceptions about Africans. Hinds said some Africans are seen as "stupid" because of their accents and Third World origins, or deemed "annoying" because African women in Harlem often solicit would-be customers to get their hair braided.

Hinds said he once tried to get the association, which formed in 1978 to meet the cultural, educational and social needs of Coop City's black population, to change its name to one that would be more inclusive of immigrants and native-born blacks alike.

Hinds, the youngest member of the group's board of directors, said the idea was voted down overwhelmingly by the older majority. "I'm one vote on a board," he said. The others simply "are not as progressive."

On another occasion, he said he attended a meeting for a Harlem-based rites-of-passage organization for black youths. When it was proposed that the program include a trip to an African country to mark the youths' transition to adulthood, the idea met with opposition. "Some said 'We're not welcomed over there,'" recalled Hinds. "' They treat us badly.'"

Negative images and impressions both of African Americans and developing African countries in mainstream media helps perpetuate the rift, according to Philippe Wamba, editor-in-chief of Africana.com, an online publication that covers a variety African and African-American topics. Wamba's father is from the Democratic Republic of Congo and his mother is from Michigan.

He spent much of his youth growing up in the native countries of both parents.

"The main thing is ignorance on both sides," said Wamba, who has also written a book and several articles on the relationship between Africans and African Americans. "If the people know anything at all (about each other) it is very little, and it is very skewed."

Newspaper editor Anor, who acknowledges that one reason so many Ghanaians come to the Bronx is because of the borough's black population, has similar thoughts.

"I think there is a flood of information from our experience of colonialism and that still keeps us from understanding," he said. "It still dogs our relationship."

Ghanaian immigrant Georgina Tackie, 38, who manages the African American Restaurant, which serves Ghanaian and American soul food, has been in the United States for 15 years. The fathers of the single mother's four children are African American.

Like other African immigrants, she notes the differences between the two groups but has stumbled across at least one trait from the other side of the divide she admires.

"Ghanaians like to work, pay your rent and stay out of trouble," Tackie said, echoing almost verbatim how nearly a half-dozen other Ghanaians distinguished themselves from African Americans. "We are not outspoken. That's one good thing about us. Where you have Ghanaians living you never have trouble."

Then, after a pause, she added: "The only thing that bothers me is this guy Amadou Diallo. It's the African Americans that have stood up but it should be us - he is one of ours. I felt so sad that we were not particularly involved."

Tackie's afterthought is a common one among African immigrants who have lived in the states for a while, according to Wamba. He said incidents such as the fatal police shooting of Diallo, an unarmed West African immigrant, cause many African newcomers to "consider going beyond our insular immigrant community."

According to Wamba: "It's an awakening to many Africans that, to many white people, they are indistinguishable from African Americans."

Similar histories of colonialism and slavery, or current experiences of discrimination in the United States and abroad can often serve as a bridge between the two groups' because racial inequality "seems to be a problem that all black people face," he said.

Hinds, the African American Association president, also finds something to learn from across the divide.

"It would be good to improve our relations between Africans and people here in America," he said. "We need to develop more of a world view, to not see ourselves so much as a minority.

"Because we have a breakdown in our history, I think it would help with our schizophrenic world view," Hinds said about the view of some black Americans that they are neither fully American nor African. "It could help with our social agony."

But Hinds said that only about 1 percent of his personal friends are African immigrants, despite the fact that he works with many of them. After some reflection, he adds: "My circle of friends could enlarge. It should.

"When I say it's only 1 percent, then I say: 'Maybe there's still a bit of work for me to do.'"

## Debate Highlights Black on Black Racism

posted: November 17, 2004

A debate sponsored by the African Students Association in Squires last night shed light on racism between Africans and African Americans.

Sam Healy
Staff Writer

Members of Virginia Tech's African and African American communities met to take part in the debate, "Black on Black: Why can't we all get along," last night at 7 p.m. in the Black Cultural Center in Squires. The debate was sponsored by the African Students Association.

"The purpose of this event is for everyone in the African and African American communities to realize that we are one culture and we're just going through different experiences," said Chike Akah, vice president of the ASA. "We need to work together as a university to achieve this."

The event started out by showing a clip from the movie "Coming to America" with Eddie Murphy, in which the ethnic stereotypes between the African and African American cultures were confronted.

Students were given the opportunity to share their perspectives of the relations between Africans and African Americans. Students discussed the common stereotypes that both African communities are forced to deal with in our culture.

"Before I came here, I thought that everyone was a gangster and into drugs," said Maame Boateng, programs officer for ASA and an African immigrant.

An African American student described how he felt offended when an African immigrant would put down his culture and always would talk about going back to Africa.

Boateng responded with a different view. "I don't feel I need to stay in the perfect world of America," she said. "I'd rather go

343

somewhere else and help that place become   perfect."

According to the discussion, many African immigrants come to the United States with better jobs. Some of these African Americans don't think it's fair for these immigrants to receive these jobs because they didn't work as hard or suffer as much.

But African immigrants are not the only ones facing hostility and jealously when coming to America, according to Dr. Ellington T. Graves, the assistant director of the Race and Social Policy Research Center.

"This is the same situation that many immigrants face, not just Africans, when coming to America," Graves said.

African immigrants shared some of their difficult experiences in adjusting into a new culture. Many of these immigrants were oblivious to some of the social stereotypes of what it is to be "black" when coming to America.

"Most of these immigrants would not realize that they would be played with or made fun of if they went on to join the chess team or something," said Dr. Anthony Kwame Harrison, an assistant professor of Sociology. "It would take them a couple of years to realize     this."

Kader Hassane, president of the ASA, discussed racism he dealt with when moving to America just four years ago. "The only racism I received when coming to Virginia Tech came from African Americans," he said.

"When you have your "brother" not embracing you because they've been here more decades, it hurts that much more," Akah said.

By participating in the open discussion, students were allowed to listen to and respect the other side's opinions and to embrace their ideas.

"We need to bring awareness and educate the community as a whole on issues pertaining to the African American and African cultures," Boateng said.

## The Challenges Facing Diaspora Africans Who Return To Africa

Published in a Liberian publication, *The Perspective*, Smyrna, Georgia, USA, July/September 1998

F. Wafula Okumu

Today there is a debate on whether African Americans can survive in Africa once they return to the Mother Continent. A question which is being asked is: If they returned to Africa, can they settle and make a difference, like the diasporic Jews have done for Israel?

Keith Richburg, in his book, *Out of America: A Black Man Confronts Africa*, profusely thanks God for bringing his "nameless ancestor . . . across the ocean in chains and leg irons" and for being American. He not only adamantly rejects his "African-ness" but forcefully disowns his relation to Africa: "I have been there, I have lived there and seen Africa in all its horror. I know that I am a stranger (t)here. I am an American, a black American, and I feel no connection to . . . (that) strange and violent place."

One wonders why some African Americans after reading, or hearing of, Richburg's excruciating and soul-wrenching experience will even dream of going to Africa. Richburg's unpleasant experience and subsequent renunciation of his African roots is not the first. Of course we are quite familiar with the realities most of our brothers and sisters had to face when they made a beeline to Africa in the sixties and seventies. Quite a sizable number made a retreat. Reading Maya Angelou's book *In the Heart of a Woman*, one can feel the deep resentment she brought back from her failed marriage to an African freedom fighter living in Cairo and Accra.

In the sixties, many African-Americans "returned" to Africa with high hopes of a new life in their ancestral homeland. Most of these returnees were active in the civil rights movement or escapees from the brutal police state that had targeted the movement for destruction. We know of the well publicized fugitive days of Eldridge Cleaver in Algeria and his subsequent return to the U.S. with deep resentment of Africa.

Another prominent civil right personality who went to Africa and spent quite a number of years was Bob Moses, the spiritual leader of the "Summer Freedom Rides" and the campaign to register voters in the South.

If the movement back to Africa in the 1960s by African-Americans can be called the third wave, the first and second waves having taken place in 1840s and 1930s respectively, we can call the nineties migration to Southern Africa a fourth wave. Since the liberation of South Africa and Namibia from the apartheid rule we have seen a migration of highly skilled African Americans to South Africa. These brothers and sisters have left for South Africa with hope of helping a newly independent black-ruled nation that is experiencing a massive brain drain (of white South Africans).

Despite leaving with enthusiasm bordering on missionary zeal, some have been disappointed by the chill reception from the South African blacks. Writing in the South African newspaper, *The Sunday Independent*, Charles T. Moses, a former adviser to Governor Mario Cuomo lamented that "Many of us have been lied to, misled and abused by our South African brothers and sisters, usually out of jealousy and ignorance."

Moses's article prompted Felicia Mabuza-Suttle, South Africa's Oprah Winfrey, to hold two one-hour programs on the tension between African Americans and black South Africans. The South African panel, which consisted of President Nelson Mandela's daughter, Makaziwe Mandela, openly accused African Americans of three things. First, the South Africans lambasted the African Americans who go to South Africa with an attitude of patronizing Africans.

They said these African Americans feel that they are doing South Africa a favor of rescuing it after the white brain drain. Secondly, the South Africans claimed, African Americans come to their country with a belief that they are owed something by black South Africans for leading the anti-apartheid movement in the United States. And third, they accused African Americans of socializing among themselves and being aloof from the black South Africans.

Many African Americans on reaching South Africa expect to

346

be embraced as brothers and sisters who have returned home. However, the hugs ends at the airport. After finding out that the only common thing they share is their skin color, pronounced differences emerges based on culture, language, lifestyle and expectations. For example, most of the African Americans have moved into the fanciest white neighborhoods where they live in palatial homes with maids and pools.

The emotional feeling that overwhelm African Americans when they land is sometimes misunderstood by black South African who do not understand how one can claim "oh, I'm home. I'm home" in a land where one has no family members. This misunderstanding is compounded by the fact that the new immigrants do not know anything about African cultures. Worse, many do not make an effort to be absorbed into African cultures. Worst of all, some want to be accepted and respected as they are-Americans.

Misconceptions, lack of understanding of each other, and hyped expectations have exacerbated the tensions between the two groups. While some South African blacks resent African Americans for hijacking the jobs that are created for them on the affirmative action basis, others suspect African Americans' commitment to the long-term interests of South Africa. The former think the latter are using their color similarities to gain acceptance so that they can act as local agents for American business interests. Indeed, 30 per cent of the African Americans in South Africa are representatives of American businesses.

With the escalation of tensions, some African Americans are cutting their stay short and hastily returning to America. It won't be long before we start reading or hearing more African tales like Richburg's.

But it will be disingenuous to assume that there are no African Americans who have returned to Africa, loved it, settled down, and made a huge difference. Listen to, and take to heart, the story of Pete O'Neal and his wife Charlotte Hill as told in the *Kansas Star* of February 20, 1993 and *The New York Times* of November 23, 1997:

"For more than a quarter of a century O'Neal has been living in the Tanzanian village of Imabaseni as a respected elder, loving

347

husband, doting father, a community activist, an exemplary farmer, a gourmet sausage maker, and owner of a safari business. According to the Kansas Star, O'Neal "has helped bring electricity, running water and tourists to his poor, remote village. He has taught his neighbors about electronics, carpentry and food preservation and has introduced them to art, poetry, music and dance."

But in order to understand who O'Neal is today and why he is one of the elders of the Wameru ethnic group one must go back to 1969 in Kansas City. Back then, O'Neal, as a member of the Black Panther Party, was a fire-brand revolutionary who carried out public protests against the racist white establishment while engaged in community activism and development.

But on Oct. 30, 1969, the 29-year-old O'Neal was arrested and charged for violating the Gun Control Act by taking a shotgun from Kansas to Missouri. One year later a jury found him guilty and sentenced him to four years in prison. However, it was apparent to many then that O'Neal was being convicted for his revolutionary beliefs and activities.

While out on bond awaiting his appeal to be heard, O'Neal and Hill escaped and surfaced in December 1972 in Algiers, where several revolutionary organizations and groups, including the Black Panthers, had bases. But his stay in Algiers was to be short-lived after the Algerian government became hostile and expelled him. From Algeria, O'Neal and his family headed to Tanzania where he has since settled and prospered. O'Neal is said to be the only former Black Panther still remaining in Africa.

Among their educational and cultural activities, O'Neal and Charlotte have built the "Malcolm X Theater, where they entertain visitors with documentaries about the civil rights movement; and the United African American Community Center, which enlists foreign students to build schools and clinics and sponsors training programs. The O'Neals also run an exchange program for troubled African American youths from Kansas City. While in Tanzania these teenage Americans learn the strength of the African family and African values of community and service.

Although still a fugitive from the U.S. laws, O'Neal has no intention of returning to the United States. He says if he were not in Africa he would be dead by now. He also acknowledges what became a reality; that his efforts as a Black Panther revolutionary would have failed. This sobering acknowledgment of the American reality is what endears Africa to the O'Neals to and makes them Africa's solid link to the Africans in the diaspora.

From O'Neal's experience in Imbassani, we can prescribe a number of things for those African Americans who really want to return to Africa without regretting their decision. One, they must prepare themselves culturally and emotionally. They must learn the African cultures and languages. They cannot assume that their skin color alone will endear them to their African brothers and sisters. Second, they should not expect to find another America in Africa without discrimination and oppression. Although they will find an Africa without racial prejudice it will be one with its own unique problems which they must be willing to help solve.

And, third, they should go to Africa with the intention of being Africanized. They cannot live an American lifestyle in Africa. They cannot demand special treatment for being Americans. They should be prepared to suffer alongside their African brothers and sisters. They should mingle, wiggle, and dissolve into Africa. This can easily be done by adopting one of the 1700 vibrant cultures and becoming bona fide members of the respective ethnic groups.

While reflecting on Pete O'Neal's enriching and fulfilling experience, they should also pay keen attention to the sagacious words of Charles T. Moses, who said: 'Where is the hope for us in America? We will never be in charge. We will always be 10 percent. We will always be fighting to keep some cop from shooting us in the back. But here it's worth the battle. You can win this here."

Yes, African Americans can survive in Africa if they want to. And yes, they can make a difference, like the diasporic Jews have made a difference in Israel, when they return to Africa. In fact, they should learn from diasporic Jews who have not only made a commitment to the survival of the Jewish state as a political, cultural and geographical entity but represent its interests wherever they are.

# Appendix II:

# Other Perspectives:
# African and African-American

## Race in America

Bridging a gap in understanding in Harlem: African immigrants, black teens discuss differences

By Petra Cahill
Reporter, MSNBC
Dec. 10, 2004

NEW YORK - Daba Diakhate talked about her life as an African immigrant in Harlem.

"They used to throw rocks at me, they used to throw sticks at me. They used to try to jump me," the 17-year-old said. "One time they tried to take my sneakers, but they realized they weren't name-brand, so they were like, 'Here, take your Payless sneakers,'" she said, to the jeers and laughter of her fellow students at the Umoja Media Project, a gathering of of black Americans and African and Caribbean immigrants.

For Diakhate and many other immigrants, the area around 116th Street in Harlem is a sanctuary, their little West Africa.

As vendors and customers stroll through the Malcolm Shabazz Market, greetings are more often exchanged in West African dialects than in English. Men wear traditional prayer robes, and women sport colorful fabrics cut in African styles that would be more familiar on the streets of Dakar than New York.

The shops and restaurants that line the street cater to a West African clientele. The Baobab Restaurant serves up hot thiebu djen - a traditional Senegalese meal of rice and fish stew - and the Harlem Phone Card and Communication shop sells inexpensive phone cards to call home.

But while 116th Street may offer a sense of comfortable familiarity, the rough streets are not too far away.

According to the participants in Umoja, the predominantly black American neighborhood has not always been welcoming to the wave of African immigrants, whose numbers have jumped from 42,000 in 1990 to 92,000 in 2000, according to the U.S. Census Bureau.

That is what the project seeks to address. Organizers want to resolve the tension, misunderstandings and misconceptions that have sometimes characterized the relationship between black Americans and the recent immigrants.

Umoja Media Project

It began after the attacks of Sept. 11, 2001, a time of increased tension between the traditional black American residents of Harlem and the recent African immigration population, many of whom are Muslim.

As part of the larger nonprofit agency known as the Harlem Children's Zone which offers an array of education and social service programs, the Umoja Media Project was given a grant to create a documentary film that explores the relationship between the two groups.

"Umoja" is a Swahili term for "unity," and the project now involves 16 students between the ages of 10 and 17 who meet twice a week after school at TRUCE, the youth development arm of the Harlem Children's Zone.
David Friedman / MSNBC.com
Tene Howard, TRUCE program coordinator, center, leads a gathering of the Umoja Media Project last month.

At the TRUCE center on 118th Street the children have access to numerous computers and state-of-the-art video-editing

351

technology to work on their documentary. The group is a mix of boys and girls who are the children of African and Caribbean immigrants born in this country and black American students.

When the group began, it discussed issues of of identity and stereotypes. Trying to work through labels like "African," "African-American," and "Black American" took hours of conversation. Eventually the group began to take their conversations about community, identity, and culture out on the streets of Harlem and began filming their documentary.

The children of recent African immigrants are often picked on at school because they are seen as different from their classmates. They are made fun of because they speak with a different accent, have darker skin, wear different clothes, and are told that Africans smell.

Nassou Camara, a 15-year-old 10th-grader whose parents hail from Senegal and the Gambia, told a story about what happened to her one day when she wore a necklace with a charm in the shape of the African continent around her neck. Another student said to her rhetorically, "You're not going to bring no disease here, right?"

Chika A. Onyeani, publisher and editor in chief of the *African Sun Times*, a weekly newspaper that caters to the African immigrant population in this country, said it was important to break down stereotypes.

"There is no doubt that there is always some kind of disconnect between the two groups - a lack of communication - but different organizations and the media need to try to bridge that gap," Onyeani said. "There will always be this angst, because there are just little crumbs that are left to us [the immigrant community] to fight for.

"But, there is more understanding and awareness now among teachers and parents. So, the stereotypes are not as commonplace as before," Onyeani said.

In-between world

Still, many of the students involved in the Umoja project are stuck in a weird in-between world in terms of their identity because their parents don't necessarily understand the harassment they

352

receive at school and are resistant to them becoming more like their American contemporaries.

A number of them said that when they returned to Africa with their parents, they were equally confused in terms of their identity.

Nassou Camara explained that when she and her twin, Amanata, returned to The Gambia and Senegal with their parents a few years ago, it only compounded the idea of feeling like she was stuck between two different worlds.

"I feel like when I'm in America, I'm too African; when I'm in Africa, I'm too American. So I just feel like I'm in the middle, but I'm African American, I know who I am."

*African Sun Times'* Onyeani, applauded the students' efforts to educate their American counterparts but also emphasized the importance that they know where they come from.

"You have to teach your children that they have to be responsible to their family back home - that if they send back even $50 it will help a lot of people," said Onyeani. "You can't just say that we have a nuclear family -- because, of course, in our culture you don't have 'brothers' or 'sisters'; we are all related."

Lessons learned

For Tene Howard, 25, the former program coordinator for the Umoja project who now heads up all of the youth programs for TRUCE, giving the young people a forum to speak about the difficult line they are treading is huge progress.

As the child of immigrants from Guyana,she can empathize with the struggles her students are going through and the organization has helped many of them negotiate that difficult terrain.

"I learned to have pride about where I come from. Not to be scared to say I'm African and to have a lot of confidence to tell people I'm African," said Amanata Camara. "I think Umoja had a big role and has made me more confident and it taught me things I didn't know before about my culture."

For Daba, the oldest sister of the Diakhate clan, Umoja has taught her to be "more calm" and not fight back when she is made fun of in school or some of her younger siblings are teased on the street.

The students are now working to complete their documentary. They have already begun showing it to different groups - they have shown it to a youth group associated with the local police precinct and violence prevention workshop for young third- and fourth-graders.

Their goal is to complete it and use it as a tool to bring their message of tolerance and understanding to a larger audience.

# African immigrants in Detroit

Thursday, May 29, 2003
David Guralnick / *The Detroit News*

Co-owner Kwasi Effah stocks goods at the K&K African Market in Detroit. More African immigrants in Detroit has meant more African-owned businesses.
(photo in *The Detroit News*)

## Africans find home in Detroit:
## Number has nearly doubled in past decade

By Oralandar Brand-Williams / *The Detroit News*
Charles V. Tines / *The Detroit News*

Larry Alebiosu came to the United States in 1982 from Lagos, Nigeria, to attend college. Now he owns a retail clothing business, Fashion International, in Southfield.
(photo in *The Detroit News*)

DETROIT -- In years past, when Kwaku Adwini-Poku wanted to make fufu, a staple of traditional African meals, it meant a trip to an Asian grocery store on the city's east side.

African immigrants such as Adwini-Poku, a 49-year-old Ghana native who has been in Detroit for more than 20 years, represented such a small group in Metro Detroit that the food products of their homeland were hard to find.

But that's changing. The number of African immigrants in Metro Detroit has nearly doubled in the past decade. According to U.S. census figures, 9,532 African immigrants now live in the Metro region. As a result, Metro Detroit has seen a surge in the number of African-owned businesses.

Businesses owned by African-born Metro Detroiters include 24-hour hair-braiding shops and supermarkets that carry imported traditional African food products, such as cassava roots and dried meats.

"There are more Africans settling on the northwest side," said

Adwini-Poku, an automotive engineer and secretary of the United African Community Organization.

"A decade ago, the population of Africans here was very small. Now that the population is bigger, there is a need to have more African stores, so people recognized that and are setting them up."

Historically, most African immigrants have been students or professionals who have sought careers in engineering and medical fields. But Adwini-Poku says many of the new immigrants are merchants and laborers who have come to Metro Detroit because of its job opportunities.

"They have found that there is a lot of employment here and they don't have to be professionals to do it," Adwini-Poku said. "The biggest challenge people face is the transportation. Many of the people who come here have never driven before."

Clothing retailer Larry Alebiosu came to the United States in 1982 from Lagos, Nigeria, to attend college. Five years later, he moved to Detroit to work for a cellular phone company.

He now owns a retail clothing business, Fashion International, on 10 Mile in Southfield.

Alebiosu says Metro Detroit is attractive to Africans because of the area's racial makeup.

"I blend in very well with the African-American community because we are black people," Alebiosu said. "It's easy to get along with people that are the same as you are. And you have a lot of African-Americans here who are interested in Africa."

Africans traditionally have been drawn to cities like New York, Houston and Atlanta. But now, they are moving to smaller cities and the Midwest.

"They are now very visible," said Jacob Olupona, a Nigerian, who is director of African-American and African studies at the University of California at Davis. "The numbers have doubled, if not quadrupled."

Civil wars in several African nations such as Sierra Leone, Liberia and Rwanda are driving many Africans to other parts of the world, Olupona said.

"In Kenya, there are a number of refugees waiting to come to the United States," he said.

Public relations executive Chinyere Ubamadu, 33, felt welcome in Metro Detroit, after living in Boston.

"The diverse environment ... and the attitudes seem to be more welcoming," said Ubamadu, who is a native of Nigeria and lives in Southfield. "Some might argue there is more a split in the culture and that there is discrimination in the area, but I witnessed racial discrimination in Boston and it's more blatant there ...like someone actually referring to me with the n-word."

But the influx of many African immigrants into Metro Detroit, as in other large American cities, hasn't translated into an immediate bonding between Africans and African-Americans.

In a recent study by the Lewis Mumford Center at the State University of New York at Albany, researchers found a growing cultural gap between American blacks and immigrants from Africa and the Caribbean.

"It's not that different than other immigrant groups from another country that bring different languages or cultures either through music, food or religion," said John Logan, a researcher for the center.

"It is really the same kind of question in the black community that you will find among Hispanics, where Central and South Americans are moving into areas that used to be Mexican or Puerto Rican. The same process took place on a larger scale 100 years ago, with respect to white immigrant groups like the Irish, Italians and Jews."

But African immigrants are forging relationships with African-Americans through several new programs and organizations, such as the United African Community Organization, a 1-year-old umbrella group that represents African immigrants.

Its president, Salewa Ola, said the relationship between Africans and American blacks needs to become stronger.

"We want to see how we can heal the wounds of the past," said Ola, a native of Nigeria. "We have more that brings us together than separates us."

On Saturday, the group is hosting a program at Detroit's Charles H. Wright Museum of African American History. It's aimed at bringing blacks and Africans together.

Ola and Adwini-Poku, the organization's secretary, hope the event spurs more interaction among African and American-born blacks. They also hope more African-Americans will be interested enough in African culture to travel to one of the continent's 54 countries.

"It's like the story of the lost son or daughter who comes home," Ola said. "When a black person goes to Africa, they are welcomed with open arms."

In January, an estimated 3,000 people turned out at the Wayne County Community College (WCCC) District's downtown campus to attend the Passport to Africa program, a cultural immersion program about Africa.

"Speakers taught people about the kinds of foods people eat and the country's exports and languages," said David Butty, WCCC's director of public affairs and a native of Liberia.

Butty said the program was so popular that it will become an annual event every January, preceding Black History Month.

"Africa has offered more to the world than we hear about," Butty said. "We hear more about the fighting and the famine. So people were happy that we were having something like this."

You can reach Oralandar Brand-Williams at (313) 222-2690 or bwilliams@detnews.com.

# OVERCOMING PERCEPTIONS:
## African Immigrants Seek Ties, Harmony with American Blacks

February 24, 2005

By Erin Chan
*Detroit Free Press* Staff Writer

Felix Asiedu, a co-owner of K&K African Market on Livernois in Detroit, rings up a customer's purchases Feb. 12. Saturday's a busy day as African immigrants come to shop for the comforts of home. Asiedu weighs plantains, which are cooked before they're eaten (photo in *Detroit Free Press*)

Onwuka Uchendu hears the questions over and over, from people of all skin tones, but it especially perplexes him when the people asking are black:

"Did you have shoes? Did you have a car? Do you have buildings?" they pester him about his life in Africa, as if he had just emerged from the bush.

Uchendu, 50, a Nigerian immigrant who lives in Southfield, often becomes so fatigued by ignorant questions, he no longer denies but embellishes.

"I say, 'Yes, we have cars, and we have traffic lights, and when they turn green, the cars go through, and when they turn red, the elephants go through,' " he said. "If they want to mock me and embarrass me, then I play the game."

It's misconceptions like these, say Uchendu and other African immigrants in metro Detroit, that divide some of them not only from other Americans but other African Americans.

"You can get discrimination from whites and blacks," said Kyrian Nwagwu, 46, an immigrant from Nigeria who became the first African-born councilman in Lathrup Village two years ago. "Some black Americans don't think we're like them or that we're truly black people."

African immigrants like Uchendu and Nwagwu said they realize such views are not held by all American-born blacks and that efforts are under way to increase understanding.

But rifts linger. For instance, Uchendu, president of the Old Bende Cultural Association, a group of metro Detroit residents who hail from the former Nigerian province of Bende, said he feels no link to Black History Month.

"February has no meaning," said Uchendu, a computer engineer on contract with General Motors Corp. "We don't feel a sense of connection."

The disconnect has become more evident as the population of sub-Saharan African-born immigrants more than tripled -- rising to 7,324 -- in southeast Michigan since 1990, according to the Lewis Mumford Center for Comparative Urban and Regional Research at the University at Albany in New York. The trend parallels the national increase in immigrants from sub-Saharan Africa, which nearly tripled in the 1990s to roughly 600,000.

There are attempts to reach across the cultural divide via educational programs and business partnerships, but reasons for why gaps and misperceptions emerge at all are about as diverse as the 53 countries of Africa.

"There's some contentiousness in the black community about black immigrants," said John Logan, a professor of urban sociology and race at Brown University in Rhode Island and coauthor of a 2003 report about black diversity in metropolitan areas. "On the one hand, 'Why aren't they more like us? Why don't they become part of our community? Why are they so separate?' On the other hand, there was a sense that we are all black Americans and we need to stand together.

"Both are sources of potential division but also reasons for unity."

Divisive backgrounds

Beyond divisions created by misplaced stereotypes, other fissures stem from differences in goals, geography, history and income.

Africans tend to emigrate, Logan said, because they have money or the hope of obtaining degrees and careers that lead to larger incomes and residency in wealthier neighborhoods. He found that African immigrant households nationally have a median income of $42,900 compared with $33,790 for U.S.-born blacks.

He also found that African immigrants tend to live in whiter neighborhoods. In southeast Michigan, according to data compiled by the Lewis Mumford Center, the population is about 45 percent white where African immigrants live but about 17 percent white where U.S.-born blacks reside.

Such differences give rise to stereotypes on both sides.

"Some African Americans born here feel we are too proud, and sometimes we think they're too lazy and not dedicated," Lafor Olabegi, 48, a Nigerian immigrant and entrepreneur from Eastpointe, said recently as he shopped for smoked fish at K & K African Market in northwest Detroit.

Another who senses the separation is Oria Jackson, 60, a Lathrup Village resident who traces her roots to her family's sharecropper days in the South.

"It's a feeling. It's the superiority that they present to the Afro American," she said, adding that she still has a good relationship with her neighbor, beautician and chiropractor, all of whom are originally from Africa. "I do feel that, and a lot of it is because of misconception and misunderstanding, mine and in a general sense."

Fleeting encounters between people help feed the stereotypes, said John White, a national spokesman for the National Association for the Advancement of Colored People.

Recognition needed

Creating more understanding requires the recognition of a significant difference in the histories of American-born blacks and African immigrants, said Steven Camarota, research director at the Center for Immigration Studies in Washington, D.C.

Separation by hundreds of years and the scar of slavery means American-born blacks may feel more removed from Africa and its immigrants, he said.

Christy Coleman, president of the Charles H. Wright Museum of African American History in Detroit, said both groups should remember they have a heritage of oppression based on African colonization and American slavery -- and their economic, social and political effects.

"The bottom line is that on the world's stage, the conditions of black and brown people are truly deplorable," she said. "That's a point of commonality with which to work."

Saying the museum can offer a place to build relationships, she pointed to programming this year with the theme "In the Spirit of Our Ancestors" and to such new, permanent exhibits as "And Still We Rise: Our Journey Through African American History and Culture." On Sunday, Brandi Hampton, 28, of Harper Woods studied a topographic map of Africa at the exhibit with her kids, ages 6 and 8. She said she knows few African immigrants but believes strongly in educating herself and her family about Africa.

"It's a part of our history, where we once came from, despite not being born there," she said.

Other educational efforts include the Wayne County Community College District's third annual Passport to Africa program, held last month, which highlighted the continent's countries. Organizer David Butty, a Liberian immigrant, said attendance has grown from about 1,500 people the first year to more than 2,300.

"My goal since coming to this country has been to help Americans to understand," Butty said. "People still think of Africa as one country."

Last year, the 10th Annual African World Expo, hosted in part by U.S. Rep. Carolyn Cheeks Kilpatrick, D-Detroit, brought people to Cobo Center for a five-day U.S.-Africa business summit to discuss trade and investment in sectors such as health care and manufacturing. This year's expo is scheduled for the second week of November at Cobo.

Other shifts in perspective lie with individuals like Uchendu who, despite having to field frustrating questions about his homeland, has begun to ponder whether immigrants like him should increase their involvement during Black History Month.

"Maybe there should be changes," he said. "Maybe it's time to blend with the black community here."

Contact Erin Chan at 248-351-3293 or chan@freepress.com.

## Akata: What It Means
## as a term used by some Africans
## to describe African Americans

From: "pamelakilgore" <pamelakilgore@
Mwananchi Yahoo discussion group
Date: Sun May 1, 2005  7:32 pm

Subject: Nigerians and African Americans: Akata and all that

What's the true meaning of akata? Is it really a Yoruba term? I have been told it means wild animal. Is that what some Nigerians mean when they call us, African Americans, akata?

I am not saying all Nigerians call us that. But I have heard it quite a few times as have other African Americans.

Can you please clarify this for us, we Africans in diaspora?

Pamela Kilgore

From: "George B.N. Ayittey" <ayittey@...>
Date: Mon May 2, 2005  6:44 am

Subject: Re: [Mwananchi] Nigerians and African Americans: Akata and all that          ayittey@...

Pamela,

Ghanaians also use the term "akata" and, if I am not mistaken, its use first arose among Ghanaians in the U.S. and then spread to other Africans in the diaspora.

It's use among the Ghanaians in the diaspora emerged from the

364

adulteration of the term "gotta" -- as in "I've got do this or that." The slang is "I gotta."

The term was the currency of African American singers, such as Wilson Pickett (Wicked Pickett) and Otis Redding, who were widely admired in Africa. Listen to Otis Redding's song, Try a Little Tenderness and you will hear "I gotta" more than 10 times in the song.

Naturally, when a local musician (Ghanaian) started to play or sing African American songs, the "I gotta" turned out sounding like "akata." Then people would say, he is trying to sound like the "akata" people (African Americans).

So, as far as I know, the term does not mean "wild animals." Rather, an alliteration of "I gotta."

George Ayittey,
Washington, DC

From: "George B.N. Ayittey" <ayittey@...>
Date: Mon May 2, 2005  7:53 pm

Pamela,

Although the term "obruni" or "Obroni" literally means a "white person," it is used rather loosely as a synonym for a "foreigner."

The traditional Twi vocabulary does not distinguish between a Briton, a French, a Chinese, a Russian, an Arab or an African American. They are all "abrofo" (plural). "Obroni" is the singular.

So, I don't think it is not a question of some Africans not considering you to be a part of them or insisting that you are no longer African, unless some Africans have told so.

My own view, and I could be wrong, is that there is much misunderstanding between black Americans and black Africans. There have been many black Americans who have returned from feeling very disappointed that they were not given the reception they anticipated. [I prefer the term "black Americans" when juxtaspositioning it against
black Africans in order to exclude Arab North Africa].

I think you will need to realize that TRIBALISM is still a very potent     force  in  Africa,  even  today.  Remember  that  over

800,000 Tutsis were slaughtered for no other reason that they were of a different tribe.

Also witness what is going on in Darfur, or even Tanzania, where a (presidential) candidate, Dr. Salim Amed Salim, is being disqualified because he is an Arab.

Therefore, gaining "acceptance" is a tricky thing in Africa if one does not belong someone's tribe or religion. I am not justifying it or saying that is the way it should be. I am only explaining why things are the way they are.

Hope this helps.

George Ayittey,
Washington, DC

pamelakilgore wrote:

Thank you very much for the clarification. I now feel better, much better. I thought it was an insult.

I have also heard of the term "obruni" used by some Ghanaians to describe African Americans. I have been told it means "white," and "foreigner" in the Twi language, and that it's mostly used to mean "white" to describe African Americans. We are NOT "white." It's sad that some Africans don't consider us to be a part of them and insist on saying we are no longer African.

Forums like Mwananchi should be used to clarify such issues which are important to the entire African world, including the diaspora, and to promote unity, not division among us.

Pamela

From: kayode familoni <kafamerry@...>
Date: Mon May 2, 2005  2:24 pm
Subject: AKATA'S AUTHENTIC CLARIFICATION

THE GHANIAN STORY ABOUT THE WORD "AKATA" FOR AFRICA AMERICANS IS NOT TRUE.

My late uncle, Chief  Frederick Jaiyeola Falodun was the creator of the word "akata " for African Americans,  during his student years at the University of Chicago, in the late 1940s-early 1950s.

Thanks

Kayode Balewa Familoni
U.S.A

From: "Dr. Valentine Ojo" <valojo@...>
Date: Tue May 3, 2005 10:06 pm
Subject: RE: Nigerians and African Americans: Akata and all that
    valojo@...
Send Email

Pamela:

 Professor Know All Ayittey is here talking through his hat, and
pontificating categorically on the genesis of a word he knows
nothing about.
    Truly, like you correctly surmised, "akata" is a Yoruba word,
meaning "jackal", and not a derivative or mispronunciation of "I
gotta". It is a rather pejorative word for African Americans which
probably came about as the behavior of African Americans - on
first contact with local Yoruba population - appeared "wild",
"untamed".
    It is also common in Yoruba to use the expression, "eranko",
a wild animal, as an insult when quarreling or in similar
situations, to describe someone who one considers not to be acting
right.
    Having said that, "akata" as used by some Yoruba speakers to
describe African Americans is only mildly pejorative really, just
like the word "oyinbo", white person, used for most non-African
foreigners, including sometimes for African Americans as well.
    Take my word for it, the usage and connotations of these
expressions - akata, eranko, oyinbo - are nowhere near the
acerbity of say the word "nigger" since it is more a humorous
descriptive epithet, than an actual putdown.
    Please feel free to confirm this with any competent speaker of
the Yoruba language, and I hope my explanation has been of
some help.

367

Val Ojo

From: msjoe21st@...
Date: Tue May 3, 2005  8:18 pm

Pam,

Kayode is being a perfect gentleman and I think other Africans do not want to be bothered with what they consider an consequential matter that may become acrimonoius.

But you sound sincere in knowing. Akata is a Nigerian (Yoruba) word commonly used by Africans to refer to African Americans. It is not a term of endearment, with a connotation to a wild animal - fox or something of that nature. However, the usage has lost its sting since we causally use it to refer to African Americans. Or maybe it depends on how and when used.

For example, when someone  heard Kwame Brown, the basketball player, he asked - is he Akata or African? because of the name Kwame. No offense is intended. You simply use it to differentiate between a Continental African and an African American. You can even say someone sounds like an Akata. That would mean a non African accent.

On the other hand, if someone tells an African woman. You behave just like an Akata. It means the woman is off, acting uncouth, uncultured.

Or comments like - she is even going out with an Akata man - meaning not decent enough. Or it is an Akata marriage - meaning a temporal arrangement for papers.

But I do not think you should be bothered because it is a stereotypical construct more relevant to the users and not to African Americans. Just like they use Tarzan movies to describe Africans. But my experience is that Continental Africans in the US are very proud and generally resist being referred to as African Americans.

MsJoe

Kayode,

Thank you very much for your response. I'm just getting more confused when I read two conflicting responses, yours and Ayittey's, and am still at a loss as to what "akata" means.

What's the definition of "akata"? Kayode, what did your uncle mean when he coined the term? Did he call black Americans - as we were called back then - "akata"? And what do Nigerians and other Africans mean when they call us, African Americans, "akata"? I have always been told that it's an insult to us.

You disagree, of course, with what Professor Ayyitey says. I need further clarification.

One African (from Tanzania) has written a book about that and other subjects on Africans and African Americans. A friend of mine who knows about the book referred me to a Nigerian web site where it's posted free and sent me the excerpt below on which I also seek clarification.

The work's title is "Relations Between Africans and African Americans." She said you can read the book at:
http://www.africananews.com
And here is the excerpt from the book she sent me:

"Almost invariably, whenever the Nigerians talked about African Americans, they would use the term "akata."

I didn't know what they meant by that and I never asked them. It didn't take me long to figure out that they were referring to American blacks. I did not detect any hostility towards them, or a condescending tone when they talked about these cousins of ours in the diaspora. They were always friendly and laughing, although I am not sure I interpreted correctly what the laughter meant most of the time back then.

It was not until years later that I found out what the term "akata" meant after I read an article in the *Detroit Free Press* by a Nigerian reporter, or someone with a Nigerian (Yoruba) name, who explained what it meant: a brutal wild animal or something like that. It is said to be a Yoruba term."

Please clarify.

Pamela Kilgore

From: "Dr. Valentine Ojo" <valojo@...>
Date: Tue May 3, 2005  11:19 pm

Pamela:

Ms Joe has given you concrete situational examples of how the word "akata" is used by the Yoruba and other Africans that have adopted this word to distinguish between Continental Africans and African American, and examples of its "negative" connotations as well.

I could not have done it any better.

Val Ojo


From: kayode familoni <kafamerry@...>
Date: Wed May 4, 2005  12:59 pm
NaijaPolitics
Subject: AFRICAN AMERICAN IS SIMPLY THAT KAYODE

Adaoma,

You are a stupid imbecile. And I want you to know that I am too big  and important and known to be lying over cyber space. Yes my uncle died of a stroke in November last year before I could see him to ask of his origin of the word "Akata" and yes he created the word , akata for African Americans in the early 1950s when he was a student at the univerisity of chicago, earning a masters degree and doing his preliminaries to have a Ph.D.

If he got  the word akata it from an animal or from other abusive words, I cannot say. Maybe when I see his bossom friend , Chief Olu Falae, he will be able to tell me more on this.

You must be a stupid and inconsiderate guy to think that I will come to cyber space to lie.

And I want you to know that I am not like that and I dont need to. My family and its extended lines is full of prominent and accomplished and rich people known to many Nigerians and foreigners.

Starting from my grand dad to my humble self:

Chief sk familoni, co founder action group and friend to awolowo and ajasin etc.

Chief ade akomolafe, former deputy governor of the western region and friend to awolowo and co.

Chief je babatola, former minister under awolowo and olu rotimi

Chief frederick falodun, former director of the census bureau and friend to falae and adetokunboh ademola

Chief richard falodun, friend to m.k.o abiola and a rich businessman residing in abeokuta

Dr niyi adebayo, former commisioner in old ondo state and chairman of the pilgrims board

Chief ade ojo, founder of elizade motors and nigerian billionaire

Colonel sk omojokun, former director of the nysc and member of the supreme military council of nigeria under obasanjo and buhari

Chief ayo ogunlade, former information minister and former economic development minister under late sani abacha.

Prof kayode familoni, co founder upn and chairman bida polytehcnic, prominent member of npn, etc.

Prof oshuntokun, a prof with many international awards

Chief oshuntokun of okeimesi, a frontline politician in the first republic

Oluwatoyin akomolafe, a nigerian billionaire in the oil industry

Adenike adamolekun, a founder of a prominent high school in ikeja, lagos

Kayode balewa familoni,my humble self who is rising .

Professor Williams, of the university of ileife

Chief mrs ade john, wife of chief ade john, former chairman of leventis etc.

Chief jm akinola, former clerk of the western house and gubernatorial candidate in ondo state as well permanent secretary under adeyinka adebayo.

If you have any training in you , will not becoming to cyber space to tell lies and accuse other of saying so.

If you want more tutelage, feel free to email me, at kafamerry@yahoo.com

Not everyone comes from the background of thugs and omo ajegunle etc, much as i like to work and advocate for the masses and down trodden in all societies.

thanks

kayode balewa familoni

adaoma_o <nwaakwukwo@yahoo.com> wrote:

KAYODE,

Whose attention are you trying to get?

For the record, AKATA means "Nigger" and Pamela should tell any African American that she comes in contact that asks... it is no complimentary term.

She was correct on the meaning. I liken it with the term "cockroach" which the Hutu's became comfortable calling the Tutsi.

To call another human by an inhuman name is to attempt to distance them from their humanity, for no good cause.

You are either lying about your Uncle having "created" the phrase or you lying about the that he died before you could get him to find out where "he got the term AKATA from".

I doubt you can fill her in, Kayode, when you have a warped idea of how African Americans live...

YOU WROTE:"MY MOTHER DID NOT GROW UP IN THE GHETTOES AND STREETS AND IS NOT A VAGABOND LIKE MOST OF THESE SO CALLED AFRICAN AMERICANS AND THEIR LEADERS."

MOST.

Please know that you don't know that you don't know.

Adaoma

Unfortunately, my uncle had died before I could get to him to find out where he got the term AKATA from.

However, my father explained that while my uncle , Chief Frederick Falodun was a student in the U.S.A , he was friends to many African American leaders of that era, but due to reasons still not clear, he noticed that they were stuborn and did not like Africans and Nigerians, mostly unprogressive and apathetic to some many things that should be important to them as a people.

He therefore felt that the Pan Africanist Movement was not something that could pursued seriously, for then you have enemies and Africans coming together to have an agenda that will be sabotaged under a so called black race agenda.

Well uncle later became the director and co chairman of the Nigerian population and census bureau and he headed and coordinated all the censuses that we have ever done in this country, till the present one that we are still using.

He was also Oluwo of the Reformed Ogboni fraternity under late Sir Adetokunboh Ademola and a chief of the Anglican church in Lagos and in Ilara Mokin in ondo state.

While he was mostly apolitical, and a bureaucrat, he was great friends and (or) related to people like late Justice Adetokunboh Ademola, Chief Olu Falae, Colonel S.k Omojokun, Alhaji Abudulaman Okene, Chief Fasanmi, General Adeyinka Adebayo, Chief Ade Ojo-founder of Elizade motors and Lady and Sir Mobolaji Bank Anthony among other Nigerian personalities.

He coined the Akata word from the stuborness of the African Americans and their unfaithful and self destructive attitudes, and something related to their desire not to seek proper education, when it was particularly needed and the ghetto lifestyle of most of their citizens, what they now call street life or all these hip- hop and rap shit and trash.

AKATA SIMPLY MEANS, THE AFRICAN AMERICANS IN THE U.S.A AND DECENDANTS OF SLAVES. THERE IS NO OTHER MEANING TO IT.

BY THE WAY I HAVE A NIGERIAN FATHER, PROF FAMILONI AND AN AFRICAN AMERICAN MOTHER, DR

PINKIE ANDREWS.

MY MOTHER DID NOT GROW UP IN THE GHETTOES AND STREETS AND IS NOT A VAGABOND LIKE MOST OF THESE SO CALLED AFRICAN AMERICANS AND THEIR LEADERS.

THANKS

KAYODE BALEWA FAMILONI

From: kayode familoni <kafamerry@...>
Date: Wed May 4, 2005 1:58 pm
Subject: "AKATA" MIGHT BE JUST LIKE THE" NGATI" WORD-Nwaakwukwo's mis education.

As I stated, my uncle started and created the term" AKATA TO BE USED TO CALL AND DESCRIBE AFRICAN AMERICANS IN THE EARLY 1950s."
If he created the word( or got it from some another word) I don't know.
After all, you igboes call Yorubas "ngbatis."
Ngati simply means; "when it occured" in Yoruba.
Someone, an Igboe with a biased mind, must have used and started this word to be used to call and describe " Yorubas" as a generality.
You need more and proper education

Thanks

kayode balewa familoni

nwaakwukwo <nwaakwukwo@yahoo.com> wrote:
NaijaPolitics

Kayode, I am repeating what you said. Either your uncle created the term or either he got it from somewhere. Both statements cannot be true. I did not read your mail past the first sentence. I responded to this issue, so this derogatory term will not be trivialized and people will stop using it. I did not wish to start a discussion with you. You are uniformed and would benefit from classes in African American history.

Adaoma

From: "George B.N. Ayittey" <ayittey@...>
Date: Wed May 4, 2005  7:25 pm
Subject: Re: [Mwananchi] RE: Nigerians and African Americans: Akata and all that          ayittey@...

Val,

You are a very strange character indeed.

First, you think all Ghanaians are Yoruba so when they use the term "akata" it is derived from a Yoruba word meaning "JACKAL."

Second, the downright supine HYPOCRISY of your response was nauseating.

In a paper you wrote and posted at this website:

"Culture, Identity and The Self:
Africanisms in The Americas," by Valentine Ojo,
http://www.theafrican.com/Magazine/Africanisms.html

You concluded:

"Nevertheless, let me state this clearly: The African-American is not--I repeat NOT--a direct descendant of the Greeks or of the Romans, nor of any of the European stocks for that matter. He, like his brothers and sisters on the continent of Africa and like the others in the Diaspora, is first and foremost, a person of African descent, whose African cultural mores and values, have, of necessity, been influenced and modified through contact to the cultures of Europe, especially to that of the strong Protestant variant to be found in North America.

He, nevertheless, shares this historical distinction with the Chinese, the Japanese, Koreans, Indians, Jews and Arabs, people whose cultures have also come under massive European influence. We may now ask: If these and other such people have not totally lost their identity and completely renounced their cultures in favor of those of the Europeans, why is it then that Americans of African origin must lose theirs and renounce their culture, and thereby deny themselves a sense of self?

Dr. Valentine Ojo
Center for African Studies
Lincoln University"

You argued that African Americans have not lost their cultural connection with Africa and must be proud of their cultural identity and self.

Now you are SLAPPING them with a culturally INFERIOR epithet -- "akata", which in Yoruba means "WILD ANIMALS." Then to add INSULT to injury, you tell African Americans that, by way of consolation, "akata" does not REALLY carry as much ascerbity or sting as "nigger." Some consolation.

I wonder what Oba, an African American who has adopted a Yoruba name, would think.

I am sure if Pat had said there is a Welsh term, "akytox" for African Americans which means "undesirables", you would have pounced on her like a WILD ANIMAL.

It is the same problem of intellectual astimatism. We can see with eagle-eyed clarity the injustices, slights and wrongs WHITE people heap on us. But we do not see the slights, the brutalities, and wrongs we heap upon ourselves. Pity.

George Ayittey,
Washington, DC

Pamela:

Professor Know All Ayittey is here talking through his hat, and pontificating categorically on the genesis of a word he knows nothing about.

Truly, like you correctly surmised, "akata" is a Yoruba word, meaning "jackal", and not a derivative or mispronunciation of "I gotta". It is a rather pejorative word for African Americans which probably came about as the behavior of African Americans - on first contact with local Yoruba population - appeared "wild", "untamed".

It is also common in Yoruba to use the expression, "eranko", a wild animal, as an insult when quarreling or in similar situations, to describe someone who one considers not to be acting right.

Having said that, "akata" as used by some Yoruba speakers to describe African Americans is only mildly pejorative really, just like the word "oyinbo", white person, used for most non-African foreigners, including sometimes for African Americans as well.

Take my word for it, the usage and connotations of these expressions - akata, eranko, oyinbo - are nowhere near the acerbity of say the word "nigger" since it is more a humorous descriptive epithet, than an actual putdown.

Please feel free to confirm this with any competent speaker of the Yoruba language, and I hope my explanation has been of some help.

Val Ojo


From: "Dr. Valentine Ojo" <valojo@...>
Date: Wed May 4, 2005  9:43 pm
Subject: RE: Nigerians and African Americans: Akata and all that
       valojo@...
Send Email

George:

Don't go bonkers on me on account of the word "akata".

Ask any Yoruba, we have so many expressions like that that are frequently tinged with humor. For example, the Yoruba who reside in Lagos, because they believe they are "more sophisticated" than those who reside inland, tend to call us (I reside inland, just like Dele for example), ara oke - meaning those from the 'mountains', read: from the backwoods.

It is slightly pejorative, but like I said always used with some humor. Even the expression, ajebota, meaning "those who eat butter", is a rather pejorative expression for the educated members of the upper middle, and upper societal strata, when it should actually be "positive".

But it is not. George, this is no place to give you a lecture on the dynamics of language change, and language evolution. You can take my word for it, or ignore it.

It is after all, a free world.

Take care!

Val Ojo

From: uko okpok <umaokpok@...>
Date: Wed May 4, 2005 10:20 pm
Subject: Re: [NaijaPoliticsForum] "AKATA" MIGHT BE JUST LIKE THE" NGATI" WORD-Nwaakwukwo's mis education.

Kayode:

The Ibibios have a traditional play known as AKATA. This masquerade appears only at night time, and on full moon.The masquerade usually is very talkative; so in Ibibio any person who indulges in excessive talking or verbosity is labeled "EKPRI AKATA" or AKATA period.

This is not the stereotypical AKATA that your uncle invented.

Ancestral guidance.

Uko Okpok

From: KolaT <kolathomas@...>
Date: Thu May 5, 2005 1:32 am

Subject: NGBATI is not emblematic of Yoruba People
    kolathomas@...

Gentle people:

The word NGABTI is not necessarily emblematic of Yoruba people. It is at best a "slang" of some sort, used by Lagosians who are not particularly versed in Yoruba Language - just like some

378

guys in Americans say "know what I mean".

It does not mean that "know what I mean" is another name for Americans. Not all Americans talk that way.

In the same manner, not all Yorubas talk "ngbati" - you really would not hear Yorubas from say Agege towards Abeokuta, Ibadan, Sagamu and all points Northwards talk "ngbati."

Unfortunately, Chukwuma Agwunobi in his contributions used this word most frequently as a derogatory reference to mean Yoruba people - just as some Yoruba Forumites responded to him in kind using "Nyanminrin" to refer to Igbo brethren.

But we really should be above these "unbecoming" epithets to are menat to put people down really. This Forum needs to rise above and be seen as a serious THINK TANK that policy
makers in Nigeria would always look up to, quote from, or to feel the pulse of Nigerians in the Diaspora.

Just a little point of observation.

KolaT

nwaakwukwo <nwaakwukwo@...> wrote:

Kayode,

I am repeating what you said. Either your uncle created the term or either he got it from somewhere. Both statements cannot be true.

I did not read your mail past the first sentence. I responded to this issue, so this derogatory term will not be trivialized and people will stop using it. I did not wish to start a discussion with you. You are uniformed and would benefit from classes in African American history.

Adaoma

From: kayode familoni <kafamerry@...>
Date: Wed May 4, 2005  2:10 pm

Subject: Re: STUPID MAN-NWAAKWUKWO. Kayode- please

379

stop it.

MY GRANDMOTHER, MY FATHER'S MOTHER, IS A FALODUN.

CHIEF MRS JULIANA EBUN FALODUN, THE SECOND CHILD OF LATE CHIEF FALODUN OF ILARA MOKIN, ONDO STATE, AND SENIOR SISTER TO THE LATE CHIEF FREDERICK FALODUN, COUSIN TO S.K OMOJOKUN AND ELIZADE AND CHIEF BAKARE AMONG OTHERS.

THANKS

KAYODE BALEWA FAMILONI

AdeAjayi@aol.com wrote:

Kayode,
Correction, Major-General Solomon Omojokun retired at that rank, not Colonel.
I also never knew you to be related to Major-General Omojokun and I should know. I know him to be related to the Faloduns.
Besides, Adaoma Nwaakwuo is a lady not a man. She may be sometimes disagreeable, but I do not think you should resort to calling her names. I think you should apologise.

Adesuyi

Posted: Tuesday May 17th, 2005 14:56

I am a black American and I have been in a relationship with a Cameroonian man for the past 3 years. Recently, one of his friends asked him if I was an akata. My boyfriend is anglophone, but his friend chose to ask the question in French (because I was standing there, and the poor guy assumed that I would not understand what he was saying).

Later, I asked my boyfriend what does "akata" mean. He told me that it is a term Africans use to refer to "African-Americans". That answer is not satisfactory for me, because otherwise his friend could have simply asked "Is your girlfriend an African American"...

So if anyone knows who or what "akata" is, could you please post it.

Thanks!

Shariff
Member

Posted: Tuesday May 17th, 2005 15:11 -

U don't wannna know. It's like the N word, insulting, derogatory and only used by tribalists. Sorry u had to go through that, from one born on the continent.

I wish your man had said a term SOME Africans use, but I'm sure that's what he meant. It's basically used by Nigerians and their Cameroonian and Benin neighbors, maybe some Ghanians.

Just another way to generalize about groups of people, basically tribalism, the very reason we're in this shyt of a situation in the first place. One.

Sweets_aka_B

Member

Location: London, United Kingdom
Lock onto the Village Radio

Posted: Tuesday May 17th, 2005 15:11

Ur boy frend was teling d truth about wot 'akata' means. 'Akata' is a word which is referred to western women.

Agape
Member

Posted: Tuesday May 17th, 2005 15:19 -

Sorry but you boyfriend is chatting shyt!!!!!! about it meaning 'African - American' it don't.

Akata is a term used to describe black people who are too westernised to put it kindly, it actually mean 'slave' a black person who don't know their roots.

Compare Ainsley Harriot (akata) to Nelson Mandela (non-akata).

A lot of african people (not all of them but those fresh off boat) think that British born black people are idiots and do not understand their talk.

Akata indeed!!!!!! trust me that is an insult.

lilac
Member

Posted: Tuesday May 17th, 2005 15:25

These are two very different responses:

Shariff - You say it's insulting, derogatory, etc.
Sweets - You say it's a term for western women. My bf didn't say western women, he said 'akata' is used to describe African-American people, which includes men and women - western women does not inlcude African-American men and it does

include white women.

To be honest, I don't get it, but I'll go with Shariff's response, otherwise why would the dude say it in French (assuming I didn't understand) if their's nothing wrong with the term?

Besides, why did the Nigerians, Ghanaians, or whoever make up a slang term for Americans anyway; Americans don't have a slang term for Africans - not that I know of. That's silly.

lilac
Member

Posted: Tuesday May 17th, 2005 15:30 -

So that's 2 for insult and 1 for western women...any others?

Shariff
Member

Posted: Tuesday May 17th, 2005 16:03

"Besides, why did the Nigerians, Ghanaians, or whoever make up a slang term for Americans anyway; Americans don't have a slang term for Africans - not that I know of. That's silly."

Lilac, true, Americans don't have a slang term for Africans. But they don't need one. For some, the very word "African" carries negative connotations and I've even heard some kids use it to insult or ridicule.

Both sides are guilty of generalizations about each other, as if they've never interacted on a personal, individual level with people from different cultures. U're right, it is silly. And sad.

chi
Member

Posted: Tuesday May 17th, 2005 16:22 -

Shariff wrote: "Besides, why did the Nigerians, Ghanaians, or whoever make up a slang term for Americans anyway; Americans don't have a slang term for Africans - not that I know of. That's

383

silly."

Lilac, true, Americans don't have a slang term for Africans. But they don't need one. For some, the very word "African" carries negative connotations and I've even heard some kids use it to insult or ridicule.

Both sides are guilty of generalizations about each other, as if they've never interacted on a personal, individual level with people from different cultures. U're right, it is silly. And sad.

I think the term for an African is a "boo-boo" or "bubu"....remember the film "coming to America"...............................................

Make sure you take the issue up with your man, you had better make sure he doesn't allow anyone to disrespect you in his presence again....ok.

I couldn't imagine if I was with a guy who was not African and his friend asked if I was a "bubu" and he didn't correct they guy within five seconds flat and make him apologize to me.........if not, somebody would be an instant ex...............................

Bele
Member


Posted: Tuesday May 17th, 2005 18:32 -

Akata is a Yoruba word literally translating as 'wild' or 'stubborn animal'. It does not mean 'cottonpicker', 'slave' or literally 'Black American' even though it refers to them.

I'm not justifying anyone referring to BA's as 'akatas' , it may be insulting inspite of the speaker's intentions, but my understanding is that Nigerians use the term 'akata' to decribe BA's casually the same way 'oyinbo' refers to White people and 'Jamo' to Jamaicans. I personally have never heard any Africans in my life ever use the word 'akata', I know of it just from frequenting websites.

" Americans don't have a slang term for Africans "

Spearchuckers. Monkeys/apes. Bootyscratchers. Bubus (WI's). Battycleaners ( WI's ).

384

Father_Time
Banned

Posted: Tuesday May 17th, 2005 21:19

It's a word that jealous and hateful tribalists use to "demean" the great American Black people.We laugh at those these people trying to "diss" us.God Bless America and God Bless the American Black people!

Father_Time

Posted: Tuesday May 17th, 2005 21:26 -

" Americans don't have a slang term for Africans "

The only problem with your terms is that American Blacks don't use these terms.Maybe that's what they say in Canada.

Masai05
Member

Location: South Of Da Border!, USA

Posted: Wednesday May 18th, 2005 09:30

Chi wrote:

I think the term for an African is a "boo-boo" or "bubu"....remember the film "coming to America".............................................

Make sure you take the issue up with your man, you had better make sure he doesn't allow anyone to disrespect you in his presence again....ok.
    I couldn't imagine if I was with a guy who was not African and his friend asked if I was a "bubu" and he didn't correct they guy within five seconds flat and make him apologize to me.........if

not, somebody would be an instant ex.............................

Menelik wrote:

" Americans don't have a slang term for Africans "

Spearchuckers. Monkeys/apes. Bootyscratchers. Bubus ( WI's ). Battycleaners ( WI's ).


Chi
This is the first time I have ever heard "Bubu" and I've been in 20 states and hundreds of Black Communities.

menelik
"Spearchuckers. Monkeys/apes. Bootyscratchers." These terms are what whites refered to Black People as throughout the centuries, I'm not sure what they call each other up in Canada but in the States Blacks are equal opportunity offenders. I've been called all of theses things so they are not exclusive to Africans young Blood!

Lilac
Akata is something that will carry different connotations for the speaker, some people will actually tell you it is not offensive because they feel you embodie all those negative traits but will still speak to you. I have a Friend who was born in Chicago, was raised in Nigeria and returned to the USA for College. When ever she returned home she was always called this. When I bring it up she shies away from the subject.
    I went to a college with a lot of West Africans that thought I was from these places or East African cause I spoke a little Swahili and the girls would seriously Dick Ride until they found out I was Black Amerikannn or Akata. If that didn't tell me something was wrong I don't know what will.

Peace!

Posted: Wednesday May 18th, 2005 13:58

menelik

"Spearchuckers. Monkeys/apes. Bootyscratchers." These terms are what whites refered to Black People as throughout the centuries, I'm not sure what they call each other up in Canada but in the States Blacks are equal opportunity offenders. I've been called all of theses things so they are not exclusive to Africans young Blood! "

And now some BA's use those terms to describe African people.

Father_Time

Posted: Wednesday May 18th, 2005 14:25 -

Where is your evidence other than what you heard on the internet?I have lived in America all my life and I have never heard these ugly terms to describe Africans especially "bubu".

Menelik
Member

Posted: Wednesday May 18th, 2005 14:29

Weren't you the one on BV calling Africans 'spearchuckers' and other deragatory terms? The internet is just another form of communication, whether someone calls me a spearchucker to my face, on the phone or by flying pidgeon. 'Bubu' is a West Indian term for Africans, if I'm not mistaken. I really wish you would get banned again.

eyelikebush
Member

Posted: Wednesday May 18th, 2005 21:55 -

AKATA MEANS SLAVE GIRL. you should slap any man you hear claling you that.

Baron_Samedi
Member

Posted: Wednesday May 18th, 2005 23:15

Dame:

I once beat a man senseless after he called me that, apparently he got disrespected by a Black female and felt he could rant and rave to me about Akata this, Akata that, then when I asked him what the hell that was he said slaves,lost Blacks. When I asked why he take it there if he felt this way and he got it twisted and started calling me this, put his hand in my face talking slave, akata and I beat him like a slave!

Stay away from those types Dame, don't waste your time on folks like that!

Blackpresident
Member

Posted: Thursday May 19th, 2005 04:40 -

Akata is an AFRICAN (Nigeria) word, yet African Americans are trying to give it their own meaning. African words can be translated literally to get their original  meaning BUT it's understanding their (modern) usage is how to truelly get the meaning of the word. In short Akata is used in the same way African American used the word 'Sell out." That's what is meant when the word is said - Selling out to African values. It's was a phrased used to highlight the loss of african roots to an individual (and hopefully inspire the return of one of our sons to some of the african values) Now it's simply seen and SOMETIMES used as an insult (as is the word 'sell out') IT IS NOW WHERE A PARELLEL TO THE WORD NI66A.

Our African brothers were stolen once - words like this exist so it won't happen to our african brothers again. - If you're a sell out then you deserve to be called Akata, if you're not then it shouldn't bother you, just set the ill-informed African brother straight. Hope this clears up a few grey arears.

388

Blackpresident

Posted: Thursday May 19th, 2005 08:47

Blackpresident wrote: "SELL OUT"

"Akata is an AFRICAN (Nigeria) word, yet African American's are trying to give it their own meaning. African words can be translated literally to get their original   meaning BUT it's understanding their (modern) usage is how to truelly get the meaning of the word. In short Akata is used in the same way African American used the word 'Sell out." That's what is meant when the word is said - Selling out to African values. It's was a phrased used to highlight the loss of african roots to an individual (and hopefully inspire the return of one of our sons to some of the african values) Now it's simply seen and SOMETIMES used as an insult (as is the word 'sell out') IT IS NOW WHERE A PARELLEL TO THE WORD NI66A.
Our African brothers were stolen once - words like this exist so it won't happen to our african brothers again. - If you're a sell out then you deserve to be called Akata, if you're not then it shouldn't bother you, just set the ill-informed African brother straight. Hope this clears up a few grey arears."

BP, that's a crock and u know it. How would u know someone was a sell out, simply based on what ethnic or cultural group they belong to? How can u encourage people to embrace their African roots by insulting them?
Keep it real, there's a cultural stigma attached to people whose ancestors were enslaved, that relegates them to inferior and almost subhuman status. This is widespread in West Africa, where cultural "superiority" seems to be based on who was enslaved and who did the enslaving.
Certain groups are called names meaning "slave people" and such, and in every country there are whispers and innuendoes about certain groups that were subjugated by other groups at one time or another.
That's the reason the American settlers in Liberia were never

accepted as Africans by some indigenous groups. They're still called "Americo-Liberians" 150 years later!

No one has the right to call a whole group of people anything dehumanizing, no matter what your intentions, or to decide who is more African than others. It's especially hypocritical when West African immigrants to the US are benefitting from the fruits of the "Akata"'s struggle.

I strongly doubt that Fela would call anybody Akata. It's tribalist, plain and simple.

Last edited on Thursday May 19th, 2005 09:00 by Shariff
Blackpresident
Member

Location: London To Las Gidi, United Kingdom

Posted: Thursday May 19th, 2005 09:26 -

Shariff wrote: Blackpresident wrote: "SELL OUT"

Akata is an AFRICAN (Nigeria) word, yet African American's are trying to give it their own meaning. African words can be translated literally to get their original  meaning BUT it's understanding their (modern) usage is how to truelly get the meaning of the word. In short Akata is used in the same way African American used the word 'Sell out." That's what is meant when the word is said - Selling out to African values. It's was a phrased used to highlight the loss of african roots to an individual (and hopefully inspire the return of one of our sons to some of the african values) Now it's simply seen and SOMETIMES used as an insult (as is the word 'sell out') IT IS NOW WHERE A PARELLEL TO THE WORD NI66A.

Our African brothers were stolen once - words like this exist so it won't happen to our african brothers again.  - If you're a sell out then you deserve to be called Akata, if you're not then it shouldn't bother you, just set the ill-informed African brother straight. Hope this clears up a few grey arears.

BP, that's a crock and u know it. How would u know someone was a sell out, simply based on what ethnic or cultural group they belong to?

Keep it real, there's a cultural stigma attached to people whose ancestors were enslaved, that relegates them to inferior and almost subhuman status. This is widespread in West Africa, where cultural "superiority" seems to be based on who was enslaved and who did the enslaving.

Certain groups are called names meaning "slave people" and such, and in every country there are whispers and innuendoes about certain groups that were subjugated by other groups at one time or another.

That's the reason the American settlers in Liberia were never accepted as Africans by some indigenous groups. They're still called "Americo-Liberians" 150 years later!

No one has the right to call a whole group of people anything dehumanizing, no matter what your intentions, or to decide who is more African than others. It's especially hypocritical when West African immigrants to the US are benefitting from the fruits of the "Akata"'s struggle.

I strongly doubt that Fela would call anybody Akata. It's tribalist, plain and simple.

Did you read my post at all!!! You have understood less than you think you have. The origins of the word are different from it's usage. GET IT!!!  IN IT's USAGE. Why is it soooo hard for you to comprehend that.. you can comprehend the various usage of the word "ni66a" can't you so why not 'Akata'.

example.. oyinbo is the word for a white man... it's ALSO a derogatory term when said with disdain. Mixed race people are sometime called oyinbo to poke fun at them which is less derogotory than it would be at a white man. Its too complex a translation to simply say it means one thing and one thing alone.

Ps. Fela wouldn't use akata...Nor would I.  However, Fela would say 'Set your minds Back to Africa.'

Posted: Thursday May 19th, 2005 10:31

Quote
Reply
BP wrote:

391

"Our African brothers were stolen once - words like this exist so it won't happen to our african brothers again. - If you're a sell out then you deserve to be called Akata, if you're not then it shouldn't bother you, just set the ill-informed African brother straight. Hope this clears up a few grey arears."

I'm big on semantics, just like GAY use to mean happy/blissfulness it now takes a negative connotation. I realize what you say and really understand but if someone was to call me this term to my face again I would kindly dispense of them, act out the new connotation of this word in a fashion that would cause them to cringe when they think about mouthing it again. It is really a shame when a few ignorant people take something meant to realign someone and negatively stigmatize it, it really is.

Location: London To Las Gidi, United Kingdom

Posted: Thursday May 19th, 2005 11:29 -

Baron_Samedi wrote: BP wrote:

"Our African brothers were stolen once - words like this exist so it won't happen to our african brothers again. - If you're a sell out then you deserve to be called Akata, if you're not then it shouldn't bother you, just set the ill-informed African brother straight. Hope this clears up a few grey arears.

I'm big on semantics, just like GAY use to mean happy/blissfulness it now takes a negative connotation. I realize what you say and really understand but if someone was to call me this term to my face again I would kindly dispense of them, act out the new connotation of this word in a fashion that would cause them to cringe when they think about mouthing it again. It is really a shame when a few ignorant people take something meant to realign someone and negatively stigmatize it, it really is.

@ baron...

True. Well, if Akata is used derogatory.. to mean "slave" or words to that effect, then i'd expect someone to get seriously 'shook' for it. Same as if an african gets called 'whatever it is we're called.' Frankly, It's just another instrument that keeps black Americas & black Africas apart -   It was worse between Jamaicans & Nigerians BUT now we're seeing each other more like brothers. Heres to black progress!!

CeeCee
Member

Posted: Thursday May 19th, 2005 12:18

Quote
Reply
lilac,

Like you I'm not African, but I dated a Nigerian. He told me that the word "Akata" means AA, but not in a good way.

Menelik
Member

Posted: Thursday May 19th, 2005 21:32 -

eyelikebush wrote: AKATA MEANS SLAVE GIRL. you should slap any man you hear claling you that.
    You fools in this thread don't listen to anything, Akata literally means 'wild or stubborn animal' in Yoruba, it is now used in reference to Black Americans. You fools can't turn it into whatever you want it to mean, like it was said.

Dame:

I once beat a man senseless after he called me that, apparently he got disrespected by a Black female and felt he could rant and rave to me about Akata this, Akata that, then when I asked him what the hell that was he said slaves,lost Blacks. When I asked why he take it there if he felt this way and he got it twisted and started calling me this, put his hand in my face talking slave, akata and I beat him like a slave!

Stay away from those types Dame, don't waste your time on folks like that!

I'd like to see you try that fake king kong shyt with me, I will feed you your genitals and wee wee on your head if I saw you harassing one of my African brothers. Even if you were in the right, I would still defend my own people just like you would your brother!

That's the reason the American settlers in Liberia were never accepted as Africans by some indigenous groups. They're still called "Americo-Liberians" 150 years later!

BULLSHYT! The Americo-Liberians fought wars with the indiginous African groups of that country ( and were backed up by the US government ). Liberia was a colony like any other, except dark skinned Americans were the colonialists. In 1929 an International Comission found Americo-Liberian government officials guilty of forced labour of indiginous Liberian people. The right to vote wasn't even extended to indiginous Liberian people until 1946! Let that idiot Father Time/PreEmptive_Strikes come in here and claim otherwise, these are the facts! It was never the intention of Americo-Liberians to assimilate into the indiginous Liberian population, they still considered themselves American ( hence Americo-Liberian ) they named the capital Monrovia after James Monroe, patterned Liberia's flag after the American flag, they considered the indiginous Liberian people to be inferior and in need of civilizing, just like any European colonialist. Even Marcus Garvey criticized the Liberian government and elite Americo-Liberian ruling class which is why they denied his request to settle his American/WI followers in Liberia. Maybe Americo Liberians viewed Liberia as a refuge from American racism but pan-Africanism certainly wasn't their idealogy.

http://memory.loc.gov/ammem/gmdhtml/libhtml/liberia.html

I strongly doubt that Fela would call anybody Akata. It's

tribalist, plain and simple.

Fela ( I love him, I just bought a compilation of his songs called Underground Spiritual Game and I like his son too, I plan on having a Fela collection ) was a staunch pan-Africanist and I'm sure most diasporan Blacks have never heard of him and if they did, could care less about his efforts to reach out to them.

Last edited on Thursday May 19th, 2005 21:35 by Menelik American_Exceptionalism

Posted: Thursday May 19th, 2005 22:40

Quote
Reply
eyelikebush wrote: AKATA MEANS SLAVE GIRL. you should slap any man you hear claling you that.

You fools in this thread don't listen to anything, Akata literally means 'wild or stubborn animal' in Yoruba, it is now used in reference to Black Americans. You fools can't turn it into whatever you want it to mean, like it was said.

So what? You shit eating pustules can call us American Black people what you will.

Dame:

I once beat a man senseless after he called me that, apparently he got disrespected by a Black female and felt he could rant and rave to me about Akata this, Akata that, then when I asked him what the hell that was he said slaves,lost Blacks. When I asked why he take it there if he felt this way and he got it twisted and started calling me this, put his hand in my face talking slave, akata and I beat him like a slave!

Stay away from those types Dame, don't waste your time on folks like that!

If I saw you harassing one of my African brothers. Even if you were in  the right, I would still defend my own people just like you would your brother!

That's the reason the American settlers in Liberia were never accepted as Africans by some indigenous groups. They're still called "Americo-Liberians" 150 years later!

The Americo-Liberians fought wars with the indiginous African groups of that country ( and were backed up by the US government ). Liberia was a colony like any other, except dark skinned Americans were the colonialists. In 1929 an International Comission found  Americo-Liberian government officials guilty of  forced labour of indiginous Liberian people. The right to vote wasn't even extended to indiginous Liberian people until 1946! Let that idiot Father Time/PreEmptive_Strikes come in here and claim otherwise, these are the facts! It was never the intention of Americo-Liberians to assimilate into the indiginous Liberian population, they still considered themselves American ( hence Americo-Liberian ) they named the capital Monrovia after James Monroe, patterned Liberia's flag after the American flag, they considered the indiginous Liberian people to be inferior and in need of civilizing, just like any European colonialist. Even Marcus Garvey criticized the Liberian government and elite Americo-Liberian ruling class which is why they denied his request to settle his American/WI followers in Liberia. Maybe Americo Liberians viewed Liberia as a refuge from American racism but pan-Africanism certainly wasn't their idealogy.

 Americo Liberians is the best thing Africa has ever had going for them...Too bad you screwed that up like everything else.

http://memory.loc.gov/ammem/gmdhtml/libhtml/liberia.html

I strongly doubt that Fela would call anybody Akata. It's tribalist, plain and simple.

Fela ( I love him, I just bought a compilation of his songs called Underground Spiritual Game and I like his son too, I plan on having a Fela collection ) was a staunch pan-Africanist and I'm sure most diasporan Blacks have never heard of him and if they did, could care less about his efforts to reach out to them.

Posted: Thursday May 19th, 2005 22:57 -

If someone wants to disrespect me they are going to feel the pain, African, West Indian, Englishmen or North American! If a Southern black disrespect an African Kat and he ruffed him up I'd sit, watch and cheer him cause wrong is wrong, Stupid. I beat the Shyt out of the Nigerian Kat who called me that and If I came to Canada and another unfortunate Black soul from Africa-West called me Akata, I'd beat the Shyt out of him and then take on your 19 yr old been in Canada for 16yrs, began school at 5 yrs old been in a twelve year cycle for 13 yrs in the 11th grade stupid Arse! You sound like an idiot, stay in a kids place! I frequent Montreal and Toronto yearly if you would like you and your dad can meet my on Lake Ontario during the Caribanna and I will beat your OCD Arse and slap your father around for raising such a stupid rotten KID, Free of Charge!

Au revior Merd!

Posted: Friday May 20th, 2005 10:07 -

I don't know nor care who these people are.I'm Black but if I was white then I don't see how I would jealous of "African unity" considering that Europe straight up conquered Africa while they (Euros) were often involved in dirty bloody wars amongst their own...Hypothetically speaking,even if Africans had "unity" in Africa back when they were selling folk to the white man they still would've got an asswhipping by the more advanced and technologically sophisticated Euros.."Unity" and other such great ideals are not the end all as there are far more important things like intelligence,competent leadership,long sighted national vision, and etc. that determine the course of a society besides just talking points like "unity"....

Baron_Samedi
Member

Location: Seattle, Washington USA

Posted: Wednesday June 1st, 2005 15:32

I'd never heard the term Akata until I dated a man from St.Vincent. Whenever we got into heated arguments about our cultures, he's fling that term at me. When I find out its meaning and connotation I was not pleased at all.

Baron_Samedi
Member

Posted: Thursday June 2nd, 2005 15:07 -

Baron_Samedi wrote: MamaZora:

How your man from the Caribbean gonna call you something that applies to him too. Sometimes it is meant as wild animal/fox, slave, etc. Last time I checked Whitey wasn't giving Joyrides across the Atlantic. In fact if you read Eric Williams "From Columbus to Castro" you get a better understanding of how ugly slave life was in the Caribbean, how bad miscegination is/was and how brutal Kats were treated. Some people are just silly, how you gonna disrespect someone you love?

My ex had alot of issues when it came to his heritage. He felt that West Indians were better than Africans and African-Americans alike. Needless to say we eventually broke up.

The Black Forum 2 - The Blacknet Village > Welcome to The Black Forum - The Blacknet Village > What is Black? What does Being Black mean to you? > Question: Who or What is Akata?

Tune into the
Black net
Community Village Radio

Welcome the Blacknet Village Community Radio

Or you may e-mail us:
Info@blacknet.co.uk      -      Webmaster@blacknet.co.uk      -
Sales@blacknet.co.uk - Promotions@blacknet.co.uk
or call us Tel: (+44) 0870 746 5000 - Fax: (+44) 020 8692 9755

**Nigerians in America Village Square:**
**www.nigeriansinamerica.com**

Danladi    07-07-2004 12:09 PM
Quote:
Originally Posted by TruTalk

With reference to the Akata term, akata is orginally on Partial Igbo extraction, if I am right...it means 'cotton picker' or as used in contemporary lingo, a descendant of cotton pickers..Emphasis not on the line of work itself, but on the class of people who get roped into it.

Quote:
Originally Posted by TruTalk
LOL! I wonder...if we took an internet poll, how many different definitions would we get for this word? Somehow, I get the idea that it has become one of those pervasive words that doesnt seem to carry the emotional weight it was supposed to....
    I think there is a bit of a flaw in your analysis. If Akata means "cotton picker" how come it is only used to refer to a woman?

Shikena!

TruTalk    07-07-2004 12:10 PM

It isn't used only for women...I have heard it commonly used as a derogatory term for both men and women

TruTalk    07-07-2004 12:15 PM
Better yet, refer to this site, scroll down to the seventh post, which is written by "Anonyme"...at least I am not delirious...You had me wondering myself for a hot minute. I have heard it used as such before...maybe wiht trans-cultural Nigerians with dual identities, the word is being tranformd to mean something else, as I said before: http://www.seneweb.com/discus/messa....html?995205953

Danladi      07-07-2004 12:24 PM
Quote:
Originally Posted by TruTalk

It isnt used only for women...I have heard it commonly used as a derogatory term for both men and women

I have always known Akata to be a Yoruba word, that is why I chose to speak to them. But if I am wrong ....

Shikena!

Waka-waka          07-12-2004 02:36 PM

If chinedu wants to marry ikechukwu, nothing concern me. When chinedu or ikechukwu carry dem yeyeness near me, then kata kata go burst!

Secondly, I have said this before, maybe there are black americans that are racist, who knows, all I can say is that there is no racist nigerian.

This dates back to the first white man to we saw in our village. You see, we had a serious draught at that time, but the medicine man said God would provide. We waited and waited and all of a sudden, this white man came walking into the village.....you can inagine the joy....we all had hopes in the word of the medicine man but none of us expected food to just walk into the village..

You see this is why we can not be racist. We love the white man....he tastes like chicken!

You are right. The original meaning of Akata (Sound: re-mi-mi) is Fox. Kolokolo (Sound: do-do-do-do) is Wolf.

All men have varying degrees of racism in them. For the good guys, this degree is negligible or infinitestimal. The extremists turn out in KKK, Nazism, etc.

panasharp 07-12-2004 03:53 PM
If Akata means Fox, does that make it right to call African-Americans fox?

Since Nigerians are very friendly, happy go luck people, warm and entertaining: How about I start calling Nigerians Black Monkey or Gorilla?

400

Danladi,

Your reasoning is warped. Akata is a derogatory word just like I am sure you will not like to be called Gorilla or black monkey.

Waka-waka        07-12-2004 04:14 PM
Danladi my friend,
you can call african americans fox, and even nigerians Gorilla's. Just make sure nobody is around you when you say this words otherwise you will use yah own nose to smell yah own nyash. Oloshi olori buruku, alangba olori kpukpa

Danladi    07-13-2004 09:21 AM
Quote:
Originally Posted by Waka-waka
Oloshi olori buruku, alangba olori kpukpa

Join Date: Feb 2004
Location: UK
Posts: 136
Quote:
Originally Posted by almondJOY

I didn't know that's what akata meant! no wonder my parents never say that. i first heard that word from my naija friends 2 years ago here @ college. wow, i learned something new!

Actually the word Akata is a yoruba word for a certain type of goat or donkey used for carrying heavy loads or working in the field all day and night, just like the slaves back then. That's where the connection came from.

It's a bad thing to say or call people. When I was in the States last year, my friends were using that word endlessly, and "Kokoye" for Spanish people, where did that come from?!

These words are derogatory, try not to use them girl. Stay blessed.

2nd Bass Jare

To my knowledge AKATA is a wild cat and The term was use to

address a group of certain Americans because of their wild behaviour by the early Nigerians who came over here for their education like you said it is derogatory KETEKETE i.e donkey is deferent from AKATA

mimi victor

**From Black People - Destee Community (USA)**
**www.desteecommunity.com**

02-21-2005, 02:16 PM
From panafrica:

I first became familar with the term "akata" upon hearing it in a movie (Sugar Hill) about 12 years ago. A Nigerian Drug Lord used it to refer to Wesley Snipes' character (a African American Drug Lord) in the movie.

I don't know if other Africans have similar terms for African Americans, or if this is unique to Nigerians. Either way it is an indication that much more work needs to be done to eliminate the tribalism and self-hated which is all too common within the black community!

panafrica

From khasm:

with people that are as proud as afrikans and afrikan-americans here...it is very easy to sow a seed of descent in between us...unfortunately...i also remember the term akata from sugar hill....smh

one love
khasm

02-22-2005, 01:54 PM
From pdiane:

This was a strong article, very revealing (the chapter on African attitudes toward African Americans posted here from Godfrey mwakikagile's book *Relations Between Africans and African Americans*).

I plan on moving to Senegal next year and I find this very informative. Some of my friends and family members feel I am being romantic about living in Senegal. I maybe, but someone has to make a way for my people in the diaspora, like that brother who building homes for diasporans in Ghana.

We have to learn to respect one another, we have to learn to love one another, the only way this can be done is by doing it.

I have learned the language, I don't act like I am better, I believe Senegal is mine no matter what some Senegalese may think about me. I happen to know my great grand father is Senegalese and as far as I am concerned it is my home too.

My husband is Senegalese and we have a very happy, realistic relationship. We have worked out our cultural issues and we have great respect for each others differences. He is learning about Africans in the diaspora and enjoys it. I am learning about west African culture as well.

We focus on the similiarities.

I think that Afrakans from the continent and from the diaspora have to work to make our relationships work. Focusing on the greater good, the future of our children, the future of our people.

Having a nationalistic spirit really helps, because it deals with history, it deals with what happened to all of us as people and what must be done to reverse our self-hate and destruction.

Last weekend, my African dance teacher give me and my sister a surprise birthday party. Needless to say, Afrakans from the continent and diaspora was there. One particular sister who was very standoffish in past encounters, from Senegal, was there. This time she and all of us danced, sang and ate together. She was very comfortable with us this time and we with her.

Someone has to break the ice.

pdiane

02-23-2005, 12:18 AM
Blackbird

Quote:
Originally Posted by panafrica
I first became familar with the term "akata" upon hearing it in a movie (Sugar Hill) about 12 years ago. A Nigerian Drug Lord used it to refer to Wesley Snipes' character (a African American

Drug Lord) in the movie. I don't know if other Africans have similar terms for African Americans, or if this is unique to Nigerians. Either way it is an indication that much more work needs to be done to eliminate the tribalism and self-hated which is all too common within the black community!

My wife is from Ghana and have overheard some of her Ghanaian folks refer to me and us as those "akata people." There is another Nigerian term, "eranko." It is sad that the fragmentation of our people cause to see each other as unrelated.

02-23-2005, 02:49 AM
panafrica

Originally Posted by Blackbird:

Quote:

"My wife is from Ghana and have overheard some of her Ghanaian folks refer to me and us as those "akata people." There is another Nigerian term, "eranko." It is sad that the fragmentation of our people cause to see each other as unrelated."

That is an understatement brother Blackbird. But if your wife, my wife, and sister Pdiane's husband are any indications not every African shares those views.

Posted by karmashines, March 8, 2005:

Well, I think relations between Africans and black Americans need a great deal of improvement. There are still many black Americans who subconsciously don't want to associate with African people because Africa = ugly, poor, uncivilized (a view adopted because of white cultural influence). These attitudes show up in their conscious behavior, as they make fun of Africans, whether showing disdain for their skin color, or their culture.

In fact, I have some personal experience in being confronted with some of these bigoted attitudes. I use to date an African guy, and boy did my parents make some ignorant comments. One of the most ignorant, (though this came years after the relationship ended), was when I went to take an HIV test, something that is pretty routine at the beginning of a pregnancy. My mother said she was glad my test turned out negative, because she was always afraid that my dating an African would cause me to get HIV.

Another stupid comment came from one of my friends and she was African herself! She had said, "Oh, he's cute for an African." Furious, I was like, "What do you mean cute for an African?" She said, "Because in America Africans are considered ugly."

So anyway, black Americans have got to do better in embracing ALL of their African heritage, (including Africa's tribal cultures), and their African brethren.

**From AfricanaAmerica.org - The African Diaspora, March 2005:**
www.africanamerica.org

Posted by sunnubian, March 13, 2005:

What is their equivalent name of the North Africans/Arabs that are enslaving, torturing, raping, and murdering Sudanese? What is their equivalent name of the Europeans ("peace keeper") who repeatedly come to their coutries and molest and rape their children and women? What is their equivalent name for Europeans that have enoculated nealry all of Africa with the AIDS virus? Sold regular evaporated mild on the African continent as infant formula for decades? What is their equivalent name for the American Whites and Europeans that brainwashed the entire world and African Americans to believe that all African were wild, cannelbalistic savages?

Also, just a reminder, ----it is all the wild brutal -"akata" - African Americans that made it possible for an African to ever get a visa or citizenship in this racist nation. It was the "akata" African Americans that fought died and went to prison and were lynched from trees in order to bring most of America's institutionalized racism to an end, at least enough or long enough that ANY Black Africans that are here now ever had a chance at coming to America, even as a domestic, let alone anything else (as well with ALL other people of color/black or brown on this planet that are here now). If you don't believe this, then please account for your lack in number before the civil rights movement, before affirmative action, before African Americans fought and died to give people of color some power and influence in this country? Where were all of you before then?

And by the way, it is still the "akata" -African Americans that keeps you from being harrassed and brutalized when you are here (particulary in certain parts of this country still).

Yea, the pot cannot call the kettle black. We are the same ultimately - in everyone else's eyes.

Posted by James Wesley Chester, March 14, 2005:

Quote:

"And by the way, it is still the 'akata' -African Americans that keeps you from being harrassed and brutalized when you are here (particulary in certain parts of this country still).
Yea, the pot cannot call the kettle black. We are the same ultimately - in everyone else's eyes.---sunnubian"

Thank you!!

I listen to this ever-growing cacophony of discord between African Americans and African nationals with a jaundiced eye.
Charges come from African nationals that they are not 'welcomed', or are otherwise disparaged.
Respect goes a long way, both when received and when given.
Ridicule pays little in dividends.
I get pissed off when someone who has been here 23 minutes begins to advise me on what to do to 'better myself.'
Particularly when that person is here because of my having 'bettered myself.'
In effect, I am the reason for his prosperity, and now he is going to instruct me!!
It does tend to piss one off.

Posted by zodo, March 14, 2005:

I would really like to read a book written by an African immigrant on their relationships with Latinos, Asians, Euro-Americans and any other ethnic group recently arrived to America but I'll guess I'll die from old age b4 that happens.
In their opinion AA's are the yard stick by which they measure failure. Many of them refute the impact of centuries of slavery and discrimination and a lot say that we shouldn't use the term "African-American" but use black-american. But my theory is that a lot of these misunderstandings lie with the recently arrived African immigrants as opposed to those who were born and raised here .

The irony is that many of them move into African-American neighborhoods living along side the very people (AA) they disparage. However I remain optimistic that this situation will hopefully iron itself out after a generation or decade or two.

Posted by folobatuyi (felix), April 29, 2005:

The African-American and African relations is indeed a tricky one at best. Being a Nigerian-American, it has been interesting to see people responses and facial expresssions when I respond to their respective questioning as to where I am from. I usually tell folks that I am an American born to Nigerian parents.

I love that the fact that I am an American and nothing is going to change about that. And then I procede to tell them that I went to Nigeria for the first time in 1985 at the age of 11 years. Yes, I was mad that Halloween Day in 1985 when I got on the plane to leave to Nigeria because I was scheduled to have a book club party at school that day for successfully reading a number of books and returning them on time while I was in the 4th grade. Anyway, to say the least, my experience in Nigeria during the 8 years I was there (1985-1993) was hellish. So, I don't miss it.

On coming back, my experience has been interesting as well. I get mixed signals from both the Nigerian community and the African-American community. In the Nigerian community, I am told that I do not act nor think like an true African or Nigerian because at the age of 31, I do not have a fancy car or big house or that I do not want to go back to Nigeria to live. Instead, I am told or at least in the past by some, that I have an obligation to assist others to get a green card and the reason why I am a doctor in training is because I am a Nigerian? BS....maybe because I simply love pathology and I do remember cracking open a few books or so along the way dating back to the age of 9 thanks to my mother.

So, in the Nigerian community, I am not really a Nigerian but really a fake African. Ok, I guess Jesus still loves me, so my bible tells me so. Despite the fact that I speak and read Yoruba fairly well with some exceptions, I have been told that I sound like an Hausa man when I speak Yoruba....hey, at least I tried.

On the other hand, the black community has been for the most part more accepting of my "flaws" if you. Yet, I do get the

409

occassional off-the-wall questions like, "did hyenas run wild while you were in Nigeria?" or "I would not help you to get a green card even if you asked me, becuase I know you Africans are always looking for someone to help you with that". These funny statements aside, the black community has been cool with me and vice versa.

In short, I think the problems stem from the lack of understanding of each other's viewpoint. On the part of Africans, one of the reasons for some misguided statements is the due largely to the misguided initial interactions they have with a few members of the black community if any at all. Most of them do not interact with people of such caliber as seen on this forum initially but instead on coming to America (very much like the movie), their first and, a lot of the times, only interaction with Black America are those within the hood. Not saying that the hood is filled with less intellectual folks, it is just that the hood does not provide a more complete representation of the wide range of talent that comprises the black community as a whole. Hence, some of them come to a faulty notion that blacks in America are all lazy etc. Unfortunately, the media does not help as well but as any wise person would know, the media is not the best source of information on minorities.

But like my parents, a good number of Africans just seem to think that blacks here are a cultureless, lazy and wild set of people stemming primarily from their interactions with a few set of people who may have these features and thereby extrapolating this to all black folks in the country. I think this applies to black folks over here as well with regards to their initial interaction with Africans along with their faulty preconcieved notions.

A sad thought and a self-limiting one at that....my philosophy is that the world is a bit bigger than Nigeria and I want to experience as much as I can.

Posted by DivineJoy, April 30, 2005:

My first experience with an African was bad. He was very hateful to me. He thought Black Americans hated Africans. After we talked, he realized the perception he had of Black Americans was wrong, or at least in my case. We became good friends.

I saw a Nigerian movie were one of the characters came to America to live for awhile. When he returned, he was thugged out. Rude and mean. The comment was "See, this is what happens when you go to America." Red Face

I heard a friend say, moving back to Africa would cause a Palestine/Israelite type conflict. Never thought of that, but he's probably right...

Posted by nayo, May 11, 2005:

'Akata', the hell..... I believe that the translation of that term means, 'wild animal', or 'beasts'. I 'visited' a Nigerian website, and saw that phrase bandied about. Is that what Africans call Black Americans. Pity.

Posted by folobatuyi, May 11, 2005:

Dear Nayo,

The sad truth is that the word "akata" is still used today...bad habits die hard. I am in no way supporting the use of this as I have been called that before.

Posted by Fagunwa, May 11, 2005:

I would never defend the use of the slur "akata" and I don't think I did in my post.

But I must say for the sake of historical correctness that the civil rights movement in this country was affected by the Liberation movements on the African continent too.

*Awon ti won segun ota, ko sohun ti yio fa iberu ota.*

Posted by folobatuyi (felix), May 11, 2005:

Dear Oshun,

My understanding of "akata" is wild animal...I was informed that it is a word derived from Yoruba or a dialect thereof meaning

411

a wild animal similiar to a fox. I could be wrong!

Posted by 4YAINFO, june 25, 2005:

African Americans and Africans have been spoon fed misinformation about one for decades which regurtitates as distrust and suspicion. It's rare when the media focuses on those of who try to bridge the info-gap. A particular program in Harlem, N.Y. where Sengalese and AA teens meet, discuss issues and share in teen oriented activities has proven to be highly successful but one would have to look far and wide to locate this program in the current media.

Posted by folobatuyi, June 27, 2005:

Quote originally posted by Sweetwuzzy:

"I think the best way to fix African and African American relations is for people to educate themselves. It's pretty sad that not many African americans don't know about africa's history and present. I think that Africans as well need to learn about African Americans history..........."

Now that would imply that these folks are even willingly to even consider that option..."educate themselves" ...geez, sweatwuzzy...that would imply work, effort, having an open mind....more work! Might win but a select few!
Personally, I am willingly to bet that more of African Americans (AA) would be more willing to take you up on that offer to educate themselves on African issue than Africans on AA related issues without a doubt in my mind. It always baffled me about that observation that to me it seemed that AAs were far more interested in learning about Africans and less likely to simply blow off the notion of learning about African culture as non-existent as some Africans I have come across who continue to just simply view AAs as cultureless..never understood it completely....I guess this is more reflective of our collective (albeit preprogrammed)self-hatred.

Posted by Fagunwa (Ile Ife, Nigeria), July 7, 2005:

Akata and I hate to even define the word, is a wild beast sort of. More an uncultured person so to speak, and is used for american born Africans by ignorant Nigerians.You should see Nollywood movies portraying African Americans (AA's),it's a shame and a scandle. I had to stop looking at them.

There had better be such a thing as Yoruba-americans or I and my children are folks without a designation! Can't have that in the USA. My brother is right about us although it pains me. My people need to get out more and deal with the African-american history and culture with more respect.Although this is changing it is very slow.

*Awon ti won segun ota, ko sohun ti yio fa iberu ota.*

Posted by zodo, July 7, 2005:

Folobatuyi I appreciate your opionions on this subject of AA's/A's and you're truly a minority of one. I've observed on certain websites how those who share your views are torn asunder by forumites.

The first time I heard the word "akata" it was explained in translation as "cotton-picker". When I became an observer in other web-forums the word was revealed as meaning "wild animal" and of course it gave fuel to my disappoinment. Still I believe that realtions between A and AA will improve within a generation or two.

Posted by Kisongo, July 16, 2005:

Sorry I am joining this debate so late..

I'm an African from Angola and I feel we have nothing in common (or a few things in common) with African-Americans and Black Carribeans. We don't think alike, we don't dress alike, we don't speak alike, we face different problems (when we Africans live on the continent). I can't relate to African-Americans as far as music, languages and lifestyles goes.

We need to recognize our cultural differences! We Africans can build a political unity with Black Americans and Caribbeans, but a CULTURAL one is not possible.. we ARE different!

Posted by sunnubian, July 17, 2005:

Oh, please, let me tell you what you have in common with African Americans and Carribeans ---DNA----anscestral tracing to Africa-----you are either new to America or you are one of those Africans who live in denial of obvious problems rooted in racism and bigotry facing people of African descent ALL over this world.
The racism that African Americans face in this country is because they are of African descent, just like you. And as far as cultural differences are concerned, so what! Every place on earth has cultural differences, whether they are the multitude of the cultural differences within Africa or between the west and the east, hell, within the US there are cultural differences from state to state and between north and south.

The point is, that all people of African descent all over this world are facing a multitude of problems that can all be traced back to racism, whether in the form of past slavery and jim crow in the America or colonization of the African continent(same difference as American slavery and jim crow, at least same effect)-----and the problems facing our entire race as a whole far out weighs and "cultural" differences.

Posted by folobatuyi, July 17, 2005:

Sunnubian,

I really and truly agree with your statement, but as I have always stated, such statements to most (not all) Africans will continue to fall on deaf ears....but I guess there is hope?

# Appendix III:

# Reparations for African Americans

THE issue of reparations for African Americans has pitted most blacks probably against most whites, and even most blacks against some blacks, even though it seems to be obvious why the descendants of former slaves are entitled to some kind of compensation for the unpaid labor of their ancestors.

African Americans are entitled to reparations for slavery on legal and moral grounds, although the legal argument may be weaker since slavery was a legal institution even if unjust and immoral. But after slavery was abolished, the freed slaves did not get what they were promised. African slaves, who helped lay the economic foundation of the United States and formed the backbone of the economy of the southern states which constituted the Confederacy, were never paid for their labor. They also were never compensated for the injustices they suffered.

After slavery ended, the freed slaves were each promised 40 acres of land and a mule. They never got anything. The government reneged on that promise. And even today, it still refuses to pay the descendants of those slaves what they are duly entitled to.

The argument that African Americans today are not entitled to reparations because those who may have been entitled to those reparations, their ancestors who were the former slaves, died a long time ago is not a valid one. Children are entitled to inheritance. They are entitled to the money that belongs to their parents, including money owed. They are also entitled to property that belongs to their parents.

Even money and property which belongs to grandparents and great-grandparents and other lineal ancestors is passed on to their grandchildren and great-grandchildren and others into the future. And so is the money and property owed to freed African slaves. African Americans today are entitled to all that. And it is more than just 40 acres of land and a mule, per person, in terms of monetary value; it exceeds all that numerous times when computed in terms of dollars and cents today.

And all whites, including the present generation and newly arrived white immigrants, have benefited from slavery and continue to reap benefits. Racial inequalities today are a legacy of slavery. All whites, including those who are sympathetic towards blacks and support racial equality, are beneficiaries of racial inequalities which the predominantly white society seems determined to perpetuate to maintain its privileged position over blacks and other non-whites.

Racial inequalities have made it possible for all whites to enjoy privileges and rights as a matter of right which blacks have never taken for granted like whites do. Whites are in an advantageous position at the expense of blacks because they constitute the dominant white society which deliberately denies blacks equal opportunities despite professions to the contrary.

And much of this, the paternalistic and racist attitudes of whites towards blacks and the hierarchical nature of the American society based on race as well as the stigmatized status of blacks, can be traced to the institution of slavery whose lingering effects are clearly evident even today, although this abominable institution was legally abolished more than 150 years ago following the Emancipation Proclamation.

Blacks in the United States are entitled to reparations as much as we in Africa are entitled to reparations from the European colonial powers who colonized and exploited us and who continue to exploit us even today. They also owe us reparations for enslaving millions of our people who were shipped to the Americas. The United States also owes us reparations for that. So do the Arabs who also enslaved us as much as Europeans did, and for an even much longer period.

The slave trade conducted by the Arabs in East Africa, especially in what is Tanzania today where I come from, went on

416

for more than 1,000 years, hundreds of years before the slave trade in West Africa by Europeans started. Europeans also shipped to the Americas, including the United States, a significant number of slaves from East Africa, especially from what is now Tanzania and Mozambique as the anti-slavery patrols intensified on the West African coast after the slave trade was declared illegal in the United States.

The United States, which is an extension of Europe hence a product and an integral part of the western European nations which colonized and exploited Africa, wouldn't be what it is today as the richest and most powerful country in the world had it not been for the labor extracted from African slaves. And it is doubtful, perhaps even highly unlikely, that America would have survived as a nation without the labor of African slaves. And like its mother countries of western Europe, especially Britain, the United States also colonized Africa.

It did not have colonies on African soil in the legal sense, but it shipped millions of Africans to America and colonized and exploited them on its own territory, creating a colony within its own borders, with whites constituting the mother country and African slaves a colonial entity.

Therefore the United States owes Africa reparations as much as it does the children of Africa, African Americans today who are the descendants of millions of Africans who were taken to America in chains to work as slaves.

And the image of America in the eyes of many Africans - by no means all - especially the politically conscious ones who constitute a significant number, is largely determined by the way the predominantly white society treats its black citizens, African Americans, more than anybody else.

And the refusal, or unwillingness, by the United States to pay reparations to African Americans, as well as the persistence of racism - overt and covert - especially against blacks in this citadel of democracy are some of the issues which shape African perceptions of America, as much as support for the diabolical regime of apartheid in South Africa by the United States government and other white interest groups determined the way many Africans perceived America. And those perceptions of this "promised land" have not always been positive among Africans at home and abroad many of whom support reparations for African Americans.

Some of the biggest opponents of reparations for African Americans are conservatives, including black American conservatives many of whom don't even want to be called African American; they are black Americans, or just Americans, they say. As Larry Elder once said, the term African American is "silly terminology" coined by Jesse Jackson and his colleagues in the black civil rights establishment.

One of the most outspoken opponents is David Horowitz, a white radical who worked with the Black Panthers in the sixties. When I was a student at Wayne State University in Detroit in the early and mid-seventies, and relatively new in the United States having coming from Tanzania, David Horowitz was one of the most well-known white radicals in the country, together with Tom Hayden and others.

He later became one of the most vociferous and uncompromising champions and spokesmen of conservative causes including opposition to reparations and affirmative action, both intended to help black people (as well as white women more than anybody else, including blacks, in the case of affirmative action), the very same people he claimed to have cared about so much during his radical years in the sixties when he worked with the members of the Black Panther Party including its leaders such as Eldridge Cleaver.

Not long before he died, Cleaver had some harsh words for Horowitz in an interview with Henry Louis Gates Jr., chairman of the American Studies Center at Harvard University, broadcast on PBS television.

Reproduced here in its entirety is a response to David Horowitz by two African American professors:

## Ten Reasons: A Response to David Horowitz by Robert Chrisman and Ernest Allen, Jr.

David Horowitz's article, "Ten Reasons Why Reparations for Slavery is a Bad Idea and Racist Too," recently achieved circulation in a handful of college newspapers throughout the United States as a paid advertisement sponsored by the Center for

418

the Study of Popular Culture. While Horowitz's article pretends to address the issues of reparations, it is not about reparations at all. It is, rather, a well-heeled, coordinated attack on Black Americans which is calculated to elicit division and strife.

Horowitz reportedly attempted to place his article in some 50 student newspapers at universities and colleges across the country, and was successful in purchasing space in such newspapers at Brown, Duke, Arizona, UC Berkeley, UC Davis, University of Chicago, and University of Wisconsin, paying an average of $700 per paper.

His campaign has succeeded in fomenting outrage, dissension, and grief wherever it has appeared.

Unfortunately, both its supporters and its foes too often have categorized the issue as one centering on "free speech." The sale and purchase of advertising space is not a matter of free speech, however, but involves an exchange of commodities. Professor Lewis Gordon of Brown University put it very well, saying that "what concerned me was that the ad was both hate speech and a solicitation for financial support to develop antiblack ad space. I was concerned that it would embolden white supremacists and antiblack racists."

At a March 15 panel held at UC Berkeley, Horowitz also conceded that his paid advertisement did not constitute a free speech issue.

As one examines the text of Horowitz's article, it becomes apparent that it is not a reasoned essay addressed to the topic of reparations: it is, rather, a racist polemic against African Americans and Africans that is neither responsible nor informed, relying heavily upon sophistry and a Hitlerian "Big Lie" technique.

To our knowledge, only one of Horowitz's ten "reasons" has been challenged by a black scholar as to source, accuracy, and validity. It is our intention here to briefly rebut his slanders in order to pave the way for an honest and forthright debate on reparations.

In these efforts we focus not just on slavery, but also the legacy of slavery which continues to inform institutional as well as individual behavior in the U.S. to this day. Although we recognize that white America still owes a debt to the descendants of slaves, in addressing Horowitz's distortions of history we do not act as advocates for a specific form of reparations.

## 1. There Is No Single Group Clearly Responsible For The Crime Of Slavery

Horowitz's first argument, relativist in structure, can only lead to two conclusions: 1) societies are not responsible for their actions and 2) since "everyone" was responsible for slavery, no one was responsible. While diverse groups on different continents certainly participated in the trade, the principal responsibility for internationalization of that trade and the institutionalization of slavery in the so-called New World rests with European and American individuals and institutions.

The transatlantic slave trade began with the importation of African slaves into Hispaniola by Spain in the early 1500s. Nationals of France, England, Portugal, and the Netherlands, supported by their respective governments and powerful religious institutions, quickly entered the trade and extracted their pieces of silver as well. By conservative estimates, 14 million enslaved Africans survived the horror of the Middle Passage for the purpose of producing wealth for Europeans and Euro-Americans in the New World.

While there is some evidence of blacks owning slaves for profit purposes--most notably the creole caste in Louisiana--the numbers were small. As historian James Oakes noted, "By 1830 there were some 3,775 free black slaveholders across the South. . . . The evidence is overwhelming that the vast majority of black slaveholders were free men who purchased members of their families or who acted out of benevolence." (Oakes, 47-48).

## 2. There Is No Single Group That Benefited Exclusively From Slavery

Horowitz's second point, which is also a relativist one, seeks to dismiss the argument that white Americans benefited as a group from slavery, contending that the material benefits of slavery could not accrue in an exclusive way to a single group. But such sophistry evades the basic issue: who benefited primarily from

420

slavery?

Those who were responsible for the institutionalized enslavement of people of African descent also received the primary benefits from such actions. New England slave traders, merchants, bankers, and insurance companies all profited from the slave trade, which required a wide variety of commodities ranging from sails, chandlery, foodstuffs, and guns, to cloth goods and other items for trading purposes.

Both prior to and after the American Revolution, slaveholding was a principal path for white upward mobility in the South. The white native-born as well as immigrant groups such as Germans, Scots-Irish, and the like participated. In 1860, cotton was the country's largest single export. As Eric Williams and C.L.R. James have demonstrated, the free labor provided by slavery was central to the growth of industry in western Europe and the United States; simultaneously, as Walter Rodney has argued, slavery depressed and destabilized the economies of African states.

Slaveholders benefited primarily from the institution, of course, and generally in proportion to the number of slaves which they held. But the sharing of the proceeds of slave exploitation spilled across class lines within white communities as well. As historian John Hope Franklin recently affirmed in a rebuttal to Horowitz's claims:

"All whites and no slaves benefited from American slavery. All blacks had no rights that they could claim as their own. All whites, including the vast majority who had no slaves, were not only encouraged but authorized to exercise dominion over all slaves, thereby adding strength to the system of control.

If David Horowitz had read James D. DeBow's "The Interest in Slavery of the Southern Non-slaveholder," he would not have blundered into the fantasy of claiming that no single group benefited from slavery. Planters did, of course. New York merchants did, of course.

Even poor whites benefited from the legal advantage they enjoyed over all blacks as well as from the psychological advantage of having a group beneath them."

The context of the African-American argument for reparations is confined to the practice and consequences of slavery within the United States, from the colonial period on through final abolition and the aftermath, circa 1619-1865. Contrary to Horowitz's assertion, there is no record of institutionalized white enslavement in colonial America.

Horowitz is confusing the indenture of white labor, which usually lasted seven years or so during the early colonial period, with enslavement. African slavery was expanded, in fact, to replace the inefficient and unenforceable white indenture system. (Smith).

Seeking to claim that African Americans, too, have benefited from slavery, Horowitz points to the relative prosperity of African Americans in comparison to their counterparts on the African continent.

However, his argument that, "the GNP of black America makes the African-American community the 10th most prosperous "nation" in the world is based upon a false analogy. GNP is defined as "the total market value of all the goods and services produced by a nation during a specified period." Black Americans are not a nation and have no GNP. Horowitz confuses disposable income and "consumer power" with the generation of wealth.

### 3. Only A Tiny Minority Of White Americans Ever Owned Slaves, And Others Gave Their Lives To Free Them

Most white union troops were drafted into the union army in a war which the federal government initially defined as a "war to preserve the union." In large part because they feared that freed slaves would flee the South and "take their jobs" while they themselves were engaged in warfare with Confederate troops, recently drafted white conscripts in New York City and elsewhere rioted during the summer of 1863, taking a heavy toll on black civilian life and property.

Too many instances can be cited where white northern troops plundered the personal property of slaves, appropriating their bedding, chickens, pigs, and foodstuffs as they swept through the South. On the other hand, it is certainly true that there also existed principled white commanders and troops who were committed abolitionists.

However, Horowitz's focus on what he mistakenly considers to be the overriding, benevolent aim of white union troops in the Civil War obscures the role that blacks themselves played in their own liberation. African Americans were initially forbidden by the Union to fight in the Civil War, and black leaders such as Frederick Douglass and Martin Delany demanded the right to fight for their freedom.

When racist doctrine finally conceded to military necessity, blacks were recruited into the Union Army in 1862 at approximately half the pay of white soldiers--a situation which was partially rectified by an act of Congress in mid-1864. Some 170,000 blacks served in the Civil War, representing nearly one third of the free black population.

By 1860, four million blacks in the U.S. were enslaved; some 500,000 were nominally free. Because of slavery, racist laws, and racist policies, blacks were denied the chance to compete for the opportunities and resources of America that were available to native whites and immigrants: labor opportunities, free enterprise, and land.

The promise of "forty acres and a mule" to former slaves was effectively nullified by the actions of President Andrew Johnson. And because the best land offered by the Homestead Act of 1862 and its subsequent revisions quickly fell under the sway of white homesteaders and speculators, most former slaves were unable to take advantage of its provisions.

## 4. Most Living Americans Have No Connection (Direct Or Indirect) To Slavery

As Joseph Anderson, member of the National Council of African American Men, observed, "the arguments for reparations aren't made on the basis of whether every white person directly gained from slavery. The arguments are made on the basis that slavery was institutionalized and protected by law in the United States. As the government is an entity that survives generations, its debts and obligations survive the lifespan of any particular individuals. . . . Governments make restitution to victims as a group or class." (San Francisco Chronicle, March 26, 2001, p.

A21).

Most Americans today were not alive during World War II. Yet reparations to Japanese Americans for their internment in concentration camps during the war was paid out of current government sources contributed to by contemporary Americans. Passage of time does not negate the responsibility of government in crimes against humanity.

Similarly, German corporations are not the "same" corporations that supported the Holocaust; their personnel and policies today belong to generations removed from their earlier criminal behavior. Yet, these corporations are being successfully sued by Jews for their past actions. In the same vein, the U.S. government is not the same government as it was in the pre-civil war era, yet its debts and obligations from the past are no less relevant today.

## 5. The Historical Precedents Used To Justify The Reparations Clain Do Not Apply, And The Claim Itself Is Based On Race Not Injury

As noted in our response to "Reason 4," the historical precedents for the reparations claims of African Americans are fully consistent with restitution accorded other historical groups for atrocities committed against them. Second, the injury in question--that of slavery--was inflicted upon a people designated as a race. The descendants of that people--still socially constructed as a race today--continue to suffer the institutional legacies of slavery some one hundred thirty-five years after its demise.

To attempt to separate the issue of so-called race from that of injury in this instance is pure sophistry. For example, the criminal (in)justice system today largely continues to operate as it did under slavery--for the protection of white citizens against black "outsiders."

Although no longer inscribed in law, this very attitude is implicit to processes of law enforcement, prosecution, and incarceration, guiding the behavior of police, prosecutors, judges, juries, wardens, and parole boards. Hence, African Americans continue to experience higher rates of incarceration than do whites

424

charged with similar crimes, endure longer sentences for the same classes of crimes perpetrated by whites, and, compared to white inmates, receive far less consideration by parole boards when being considered for release.

Slavery was an institution sanctioned by the highest laws of the land with a degree of support from the Constitution itself. The institution of slavery established the idea and the practice that American democracy was "for whites only." There are many white Americans whose actions (or lack thereof) reveal such sentiments today--witness the response of the media and the general populace to the blatant disfranchisement of African Americans in Florida during the last presidential election.

Would such complacency exist if African Americans were considered "real citizens"? And despite the dramatic successes of the Civil Rights movement of the 1950s and 60s, the majority of black Americans do not enjoy the same rights as white Americans in the economic sphere. (We continue this argument in the following section).

**6. The Reparations Argument Is Based On The Unfounded Claim That All African-American Descendants of Slaves Suffer From The Economic Consequences Of Slavery And Discrimination**

Most blacks suffered and continue to suffer the economic consequences of slavery and its aftermath. As of 1998, median white family income in the U.S. was $49,023; median black family income was $29,404, just 60% of white income. (2001 New York Times Almanac, p. 319) Further, the costs of living within the United States far exceed those of African nations. The present poverty level for an American family of four is $17,029. Twenty-three and three-fifths percent (23.6%) of all black families live below the poverty level.

When one examines net financial worth, which reflects, in part, the wealth handed down within families from generation to generation, the figures appear much starker.

Recently, sociologists Melvin L. Oliver and Thomas M. Shapiro found that just a little over a decade ago, the net financial worth of white American families with zero or negative net financial worth stood at around 25%; that of Hispanic households at 54%; and that of black American households at almost 61%. (Oliver & Shapiro, p. 87).

The inability to accrue net financial worth is also directly related to hiring practices in which black Americans are "last hired" when the economy experiences an upturn, and "first fired" when it falls on hard    times.

And as historian John Hope Franklin remarked on the legacy of slavery for black education: "laws enacted by states forbade the teaching of blacks any means of acquiring knowledge-including the alphabet-which is the legacy of disadvantage of educational privatization and discrimination experienced by African Americans in 2001."

Horowitz's comparison of African Americans with Jamaicans is a false analogy, ignoring the different historical contexts of the two populations. The British government ended slavery in Jamaica and its other West Indian territories in 1836, paying West Indian slaveholders $20,000,000 pounds ($100,000,000 U.S. dollars) to free the slaves, and leaving the black Jamaicans, who comprised 90% of that island's population, relatively free. Though still facing racist obstacles, Jamaicans come to the U.S. as voluntary immigrants, with greater opportunity to weigh, choose, and develop their options.

**7. The Reparation Claim Is One More Attempt To Turn African Americans Into Victims. It Sends A Damaging Message To The African-American Community**

What is a victim? Black people have certainly been victimized, but acknowledgment of that fact is not a case of "playing the victim" but of seeking justice. There is no validity to Horowitz's comparison between black Americans and victims of oppressive regimes who have voluntary immigrated to these shores. Further, many members of those populations, such as Chileans and Salvadorans, direct their energies for redress toward the governments of their own oppressive nations--which is precisely what black Americans are doing.

Horowitz's racism is expressed in his contemptuous characterization of reparations as "an extravagant new handout that is only necessary because some blacks can't seem to locate the ladder of opportunity within reach of others, many of whom are less privileged than themselves."

What Horowitz fails to acknowledge is that racism continues as an ideology and a material force within the U.S., providing blacks with no ladder that reaches the top. The damage lies in the systematic treatment of black people in the U.S., not their claims against those who initiated this damage and their spiritual descendants who continue its perpetuation.

## 8. Reparations To African Americans Have Already Been Paid

The nearest the U.S. government came to full and permanent restitution of African Americans was the spontaneous redistribution of land brought about by General William Sherman's Field Order 15 in January, 1865, which empowered Union commanders to make land grants and give other material assistance to newly liberated blacks.

But that order was rescinded by President Andrew Johnson later in the year. Efforts by Representative Thaddeus Stevens and other radical Republicans to provide the proverbial "40 acres and a mule" which would have carved up huge plantations of the defeated Confederacy into modest land grants for blacks and poor whites never got out of the House of Representatives. The debt has not been paid.

"Welfare benefits and racial preferences" are not reparations. The welfare system was set in place in the 1930s to alleviate the poverty of the Great Depression, and more whites than blacks received welfare. So-called "racial preferences" come not from benevolence but from lawsuits by blacks against white businesses, government agencies, and municipalities which practice racial discrimination.

## 9. What About The Debt Blacks Owe to America?

Horowitz's assertion that "in the thousand years of slavery's existence, there never was an anti-slavery movement until white Anglo-Saxon Christians created one," only demonstrates his ignorance concerning the formidable efforts of blacks to free themselves.

Led by black Toussaint L'Ouverture, the Haitian revolution of 1793 overthrew the French slave system, created the first black republic in the world, and intensified the activities of black and white anti-slavery movements in the U.S.

Slave insurrections and conspiracies such as those of Gabriel (1800), Denmark Vesey (1822), and Nat Turner (1831) were potent sources of black resistance; black abolitionists such as Harriet Tubman, Frederick Douglass, Richard Allen, Sojourner Truth, Martin Delany, David Walker, and Henry Highland Garnet waged an incessant struggle against slavery through agencies such as the press, notably Douglass's North Star and its variants, which ran from 1847 to 1863 (blacks, moreover, constituted some 75 % of the subscribers to William Lloyd Garrison's Liberator newspaper in its first four years); the Underground Railroad, the Negro Convention Movement, local, state, and national anti-slavery societies, and the slave narrative.

Black Americans were in no ways the passive recipients of freedom from anyone, whether viewed from the perspective of black participation in the abolitionist movement, the flight of slaves from plantations and farms during the Civil War, or the enlistment of black troops in the Union army.

The idea of black debt to U.S. society is a rehash of the Christian missionary argument of the 17th and 18th centuries: because Africans were considered heathens, it was therefore legitimate to enslave them and drag them in chains to a Christian nation. Following their partial conversion, their moral and material lot were improved, for which black folk should be eternally grateful.

Slave ideologues John Calhoun and George Fitzhugh updated this idea in the 19th century, arguing that blacks were better off under slavery than whites in the North who received wages, due to the paternalism and benevolence of the plantation system which assured perpetual employment, shelter, and board. Please excuse the analogy, but if someone chops off your fingers and then hands them back to you, should you be "grateful" for having received your mangled fingers, or enraged that they were chopped off in the first place?

**10. The Reparations Claim Is A Separatist Idea That Sets African Americans Against The Nation That Gave Them Freedom**

Again, Horowitz reverses matters. Blacks are already separated from white America in fundamental matters such as income, family wealth, housing, legal treatment, education, and political representation. Andrew Hacker, for example, has argued the case persuasively in his book *Two Nations*.

To ignore such divisions, and then charge those who raise valid claims against society with promoting divisiveness, offers a classic example of "blaming the victim." And we have already refuted the spurious point that African Americans were the passive recipients of benevolent white individuals or institutions which "gave" them freedom.

Too many Americans tend to view history as "something that happened in the past," something that is "over and done," and thus has no bearing upon the present. Especially in the case of slavery, nothing could be further from the truth. As historian John Hope Franklin noted in his response to Horowitz:

"Most living Americans do have a connection with slavery. They have inherited the preferential advantage, if they are white, or the loathsome disadvantage, if they are black; and those positions are virtually as alive today as they were in the 19th century.

The pattern of housing, the discrimination in employment, the resistance to equal opportunity in education, the racial profiling, the inequities in the administration of justice, the low expectation of blacks in the discharge of duties assigned to them, the widespread belief that blacks have physical prowess but little intellectual capacities and the widespread opposition to affirmative action, as if that had not been enjoyed by whites for three centuries, all indicate that the vestiges of slavery are still with us.

And as long as there are pro-slavery protagonists among us, hiding behind such absurdities as "we are all in this together" or "it hurts me as much as it hurts you" or "slavery benefited you as much as it benefited me," we will suffer from the inability to confront the tragic legacies of slavery and deal with them in a forthright and constructive manner.

Most important, we must never fall victim to some scheme designed to create a controversy among potential allies in order to divide them and, at the same time, exploit them for its own special purpose."

Ernest Allen, Jr. is Professor of Afro-American Studies at the University of Massachusetts, Amherst; Robert Chrisman is Editor-in-Chief and Publisher, *The Black Scholar* (April 2, 2001).

# Appendix IV:

# African Immigrants in the United States

## African Immigrant Culture in Metropolitan Washington, D.C.: Building and Bridging Communities

### Diana Baird N'Diaye

In Somalia, Rukia Hussein grew up surrounded by the bounteous expression of *buraanbur*, a tradition of women's sung poetry and dance.

In the 1960s, she was a leader with her husband in the Somali struggle for independence. She served as a diplomat during the transition to Somali independence.

Mrs. Hussein is recognized by fellow Somalis as a fine poet. When the war in her country tore apart the rich fabric of cultural and social life at home, she found herself living in the Washington, D.C., area for an indefinite period.

Here she uses her intimate knowledge and talents in *buraanbur* and other expressive arts to do the delicate work of repairing torn relations between Somalis from different families, drawing people together across clan lines. As Somali community scholar Abdirahman Dahir observes, "*Buraanbur* brings harmony to the community; it brings participation of women from all the clans."

Rukia Hussein and other Somali women in Northern Virginia

and Washington, D.C., share the task of organizing occasions that ease the pain of adjusting to a new environment, restore relations, and construct community identity.

Through their efforts, Somali women's poetry, once restricted to women's circles, has become a source of pride, enjoyment, and solidarity for all Somali immigrants.

Across the metropolitan Washington region, African immigrants actively redefine their ideas of tradition and community by creating institutions and events that draw on expressive African forms.

African-born area residents establish language and culture schools where their American-born children learn the social and artistic skills of their ancestral homes. Family and friends come together to celebrate births, weddings, and other rites of passage. African immigrant entrepreneurs employ their knowledge of personal adornment and of the social needs of their home communities to serve fellow immigrants and other Washingtonians.

As did the collaborative research project that led to the 1997 Festival of American Folklife program African Immigrant Folklife, this essay explores several cultural dimensions: the use made of knowledge, skills, values, and expressive forms brought from home to construct new communities and identities; and the new tradition that grows from encounters with groups in the African Diaspora and in American society as a whole that contributes to the rich cultural landscape of the United States.

The Washington, D.C., region has one of the largest and most diverse populations in the United States of immigrants born on the African continent, some 60,000 people.

According to Bereket Selassie, "The majority have come from the Horn of Africa, more than 30,000 Ethiopians, Eritreans, and Somalis combined, with the largest numbers from Ethiopia and Eritrea. The next largest group, 10,000 to 15,000, are from Nigeria. Substantial numbers from Ghana, Sierra Leone, Senegal, Cameroon, and dozens of other African countries add to the mix of African cultures" (Selassie 1996).

They are students, workers, self-employed business people, and their families. Selassie notes that a large number of African immigrants in Washington have come as political refugees.

The nation's capital also is home to African diplomats and professionals serving in embassies, international and nongovernmental organizations, and at academic institutions.

The years from 1965 to the present can be considered the third and fourth waves of African immigration. The first was involuntary, of course, the result of violent sequestrations in Africa between the 17th and the 19th centuries. The next wave of immigration from Africa was approximately 150 years ago from Cape Verde and was driven by severe conditions of drought on these islands off the West African coast.

Prior to 1965, most Africans tended to emigrate to the European metropoles which had colonized their lands. In 1965, however, new immigration legislation was enacted in the United States which eliminated the system of national quotas for the Western hemisphere and replaced it with an overall limit of 120,000 immigrants.

In 1986 amnesty laws enabled many long-term African residents to regularize their status. But now in 1997, debates recalling those of the 1920s dispute the value or threat of immigration. Proposed immigration legislation is increasingly restrictive.

Neighbors, clients, patrons, and co-congregants of African newcomers living in the Washington area often include African Americans - the descendants of those who were brought unwillingly from Africa centuries ago, some of whose families migrated from the lower South during the 1930s and 1940s and others who came via the Caribbean and South America.

Some long-term local residents and their organizations have welcomed Africans of the new diaspora to their churches and community organizations. Other area residents have been slow to embrace newcomers to neighborhoods they see as their own. Many African immigrants, like their counterparts from the Caribbean, encounter the dilemma of being projected in the media as model minorities while paradoxically facing challenges arising from anti-immigrant sentiment and resurgent racism.

Culture shock or disillusion, concern over the possible loss of culture, and the desire to communicate their community traditions to a wider public often go hand in hand. Women particularly note the need for children to learn the traditions of their parents' homeland as part of a good upbringing.

Nomvula Cook, born in Lesotho, came to the United States with her African-American husband:

In 1981 I arrive in the United States. Little do I know that this becomes a turning point in my life. I meet new people, and I make new friends. It doesn't take me long to realize that I am now swimming in the belly of a new culture. The question is, do I swim or do I sink?

I begin to feel the burden of being expected to think and rationalize like an American.... The fear of losing my culture and tradition in a foreign country continues to stay with me....

I begin to feel a tremendous guilt of raising my children in a culture that has no room to accommodate my cultural identity. At this point ... maybe this fear begins to motivate me to be actively involved in collecting, preserving the cultural music and art of Basotho people.


African newcomers to the United States describe a development of consciousness of themselves as members of an ethnic group, of a larger national community, of Africa as a whole, and ultimately of a larger African world that includes African-American and Caribbean peoples. They perform these evolving identities through participation in various cultural activities.

For many African newcomers to the United States, their sojourn is temporary; they plan to return to their countries at a later date. Others have decided to live permanently in the United States by becoming American citizens. This decision is not taken lightly and without sacrifice.

Yusef Ford, associate director of the Ethiopian Community Center, notes that in becoming an American citizen - a move that he hesitated to make for two decades in the United States - he was obliged to forfeit rights to his father's inheritance in Ethiopia.

A few Africans are able to move between residences on the African and North American continents. Following a Caribbean pattern, some African countries are beginning to permit continued citizenship to emigrants and are even establishing ministries of emigrant affairs. Whether Africans are permanent residents, citizens, or temporary sojourners, they often have the responsibility of sending support to families at home.

As the continental Africans living in the nation's capital region have increased in number, they have stamped their presence on the ethnic map and cultural calendar of the area. Africans present cultural programs, conferences, and forums about their communities. Akwa Ibom, for example, an organization composed of members from Nigeria's Cross Rivers State, presents dance and masquerade traditions representing the Efik, Anang, and Ibibio ethnic groups of that region.

Some organizations like the Ghanaian group Fantse-Kuo and the Sudanese Association organize by country, region, or ethnic group. Other groups present traditional culture from a pan-African perspective.

Using traditional skills and knowledge, African-born entrepreneurs develop services for immigrants and the community at large: Nigerian-run Oyingbo International Market in Hyattsville, Maryland, is an example, as are tailors, dressmakers, couturiers, textile shops, and hair-braiding salons.

Immigrants run weekend schools and camps to nurture cultural identity and transmit traditions to their children. African journalists, talk-show hosts, and disk jockeys feature news, interviews, music, and discussions of interest to the African immigrant community.

Events such as the annual Ethiopian soccer tournament, institutions such as the AME Methodist Church African Liberation Ministry, and "friends" and "sister cities" organizations bring together different communities in the Washington area. Community institutions sometimes use traditional forms of social organization like tontines - revolving credit and savings societies - other kinds of investment groups, and town associations, to get things done.

Some organizations retain close links to embassies, and their programs often center around events in the home country. But many others exist outside the sphere of official contact with their former lands.

As communities become more established and populous, organizations become more like those of other American ethnic groups. Community scholar Gorgui N'Diaye notes that twenty years ago, children born to Senegalese parents in the United States were usually sent home to be educated, with the expectation that the entire family would eventually return.

At that time, they felt no need for cultural training outside the family. As more Senegalese and their Gambian neighbors have begun to raise their children here, Senegambians have begun to explore organized cultural activities for their young growing up in America.

African immigrants bring to America ideas of ethnic and region-based organizations that were devised when Africans first migrated from rural towns to urban centers in Africa.

These patterns of organization continue in the United States. In the greater Washington metropolitan area, the Nwannedinamba Social Club of Nigeria, the Asante Kotoko Association, and the Ethiopian Business Association are among the many organizations that revitalize traditional norms, values, and civic unity (Olumba 1995).

Political, social, and cultural bridges are gradually being built between continental African and Caribbean communities, who share similar experiences of immigration, accommodation, and ongoing transnational interests. They recognize an identity based on shared African ancestry and the experience of racial discrimination. This growing consciousness is shared with established African-American communities.

These relationships have led Washington's Mayor Marion Barry to appoint a Commission of African and Caribbean Community Affairs, which is composed of equal numbers of continental African and Caribbean Americans.

African-American organizations have formed "sister city" relationships with cities in Africa and the Caribbean. These organizations develop exchange visits between African and American children and adults, sponsor cultural activities, and raise funds for civic gifts - ambulances, computers, etc. The organizations work closely with African and Caribbean immigrant organizations from their "adopted" regions.

As African expatriates become immigrants, and as immigrants become citizens, they use aspects of traditional culture to maintain connections with their roots, affirm their identity, maintain positive self-images for their children, express their links to other African world people, and assert their unique contribution to their land of adoption.

There is a need for greater understanding of the cultures and experiences of continental Africans living in the United States.

Perhaps a continuing annual event, like Brooklyn's West Indian Day carnival parade or the Latino festival in the District of Columbia, will be invented to mobilize and define African immigrants publicly as a single community.

Most importantly, there is a need for connection and collaboration between Africans in America and African Americans, between Washington's immigrants and its long-established populations.

*Issues of immigrant culture, community, and identity touch close to home for Diana Baird N'Diaye, who directed the African Immigrant Folklife Study Project and co-curates the 1997 Festival program.*

*She was born to immigrants from Guyana and Barbados and is married to African-born co-researcher Gorgui N'Diaye. Diana's doctoral dissertation is an ethnographic study of the African Immigrant Folklife research and presentation project.*

Source:
*1997 Festival of American Folklife Program Book*, Washington, D.C.

# Suggested Works

Philippe E. Wamba, *Kinship*: *A Family's Journey in Africa and America* (New York: Plume Books, 2000).

Jacob Drachler, editor, *Black Homeland/Black Diaspora*: *Cross-Currents of African Relationships* (New York: Kennikat Press, 1975).

Ernest Dunbar, editor, *The Black Expatriates*: *A Study of American Negroes in Exile* (New York: Dutton, 1968).

Kevin Gaines, "African American Expatriates in Ghana and the Black Radical Tradition," Souls (Fall 1999).

Ernesto "Che" Guevara, *The African Dream*: *The Diaries of the Revolutionary War in the Congo* (New York: Grove Press, 1999).

Joseph Harris, editor, *Global Dimensions of the African Diaspora* (Washington D.C.: Howard University Press, 1993).

David Jenkins, *Black Zion*: *Africa, Imagined and Real, as Seen by Today's Blacks* (New York: Harcourt Brace Jovanovich, 1975).

Robert Johnson, *Why Blacks Left America for Africa: Interviews with Repatriates 1971 - 1999* (Connecticut: Praeger, 1999).

Rupert C. Lewis, *Walter Rodney's Intellectual and Political Thought* (Detroit: Wayne State University Press, 1998).

Bernard Magubane, *The Ties That Bind*: *African-American Consciousness of Africa* (New Jersey: Africa World Press, 1987).

James Hunter Meriwether, *Proudly We Can Be Africans*: *Black Americans and Africa, 1935 - 1961* (Chapel Hill: University of North Carolina Press, 2002).

Brenda Gayle Plummer, *Rising Wind*: *Black Americans and U.S. Foreign Affairs, 1935 - 1960* (Chapel Hill: The University of

North Carolina Press, 1996).

William L. Van De Burg, *New Day in Babylon*: *The Black Power Movement and American Culture, 1965 - 1975* (Chicago: University of Chicago Press, 1992).

Penny Von Eschen, *Race Against Empire*: *Black Americans and Ati-Colonialism, 1937 - 1957* (Ithaca, New York: Cornell University Press, 1998).

Ronald Walters, *Pan-Africanism in the African Diaspora*: *An Analysis of Modern Afrocentric Political Movements* (Detroit, Michigan: Wayne State University Press, 1993).

Keith B. Richburg, *Out of America*: *A Black Man Confronts Africa* ( New York: Basic Books, 1998).

George B.N. Ayittey, *Africa in Chaos* (New York: St. Martin's Press, 1998).

# About the Author

GODFREY MWAKIKAGILE comes from Tanzania, East Africa. He has lived with African Americans in the United States for more than 30 years.

When he was still in Tanzania working as a news reporter, he corresponded with a number of African Americans who were living in the United States and discussed the same subject he has addressed in this book, relations between Africans and African Americans, as well as other other issues in a Pan-African context.